International Crimes, Peace, and Human Rights: The Role of the International Criminal Court

Edited by
Dinah Shelton

Transnational Publishers, Inc.
Ardsley, New York

Published and distributed by *Transnational Publishers, Inc.*
Ardsley Park
Science and Technology Center
410 Saw Mill River Road
Ardsley, NY 10502

Phone: 914–693–5100
Fax: 914–693–4430
E-mail: info@transnationalpubs.com
Web: www.transnationalpubs.com

Library of Congress Cataloging-in-Publication Data

International crimes, peace, and human rights : the role of the International
Criminal Court / Dinah Shelton, editor and contributor.
    p. cm.
  ISBN 1–57105–138–4
   1. International Criminal Court. 2. International criminal courts. 3.
Criminal justice, Administration of. 4. International offenses. I. Shelton, Dinah.

KZ6310 .I576 2000
341.7'7—dc21

                                00–044348

Manufactured in the United States of America

CONTENTS

**Part III: International Public Policy and the ICC:
Accountability, Deterrence, and Redress**

Part IV: Problems of Jurisdiction and Effectiveness

CONTRIBUTORS

Kelly Dawn Askin (B.S., J.D., Ph.D. in law) is Legal Coordinator of the War Crimes Research Office, Washington College of Law, American University. Her doctoral thesis "War Crimes Against Women: Prosecution in International War Crimes Tribunal" was published by Kluwer in 1998. She was a visiting scholar at the Center for Civil and Human Rights, Notre Dame Law School, from 1995–1999, during which time she organized, co-edited, and authored chapters in the three-volume treatise *Women and International Human Rights Law*, published by Transnational Publishers. She participated as an NGO delegate to the Rome Diplomatic Conference to Establish an International Criminal Court, on behalf of Notre Dame Law School.

Roger S. Clark is a graduate of Victoria University of Wellington, New Zealand (B.A., LL.D.) and received an LL.M. and J.S.D. from Columbia University. He is the Board of Governors Professor at Rutgers University School of Law, Camden, New Jersey. He served as a member of the U.N. Commission on Crime Prevention and Control and is a trustee of the International League for Human Rights.

Sandra Coliver is the Senior Rule of Law Adviser of the International Foundation for Election Systems. She worked in Bosnia (1996–98) as a UN human rights expert tasked with training the international police, Legal Counsel to the Election Appeals Sub-Commission of the Organization for Security and Cooperation in Europe (OSCE), and Legal Advisor to the International Crisis Group, an independent advocacy think-tank chaired by former US Senator George Mitchell. Previously she served as Law Program Director of Article 19, the International Centre Against Censorship, headquartered in London. She practiced law for several years, taught courses on international law, human rights, and international women's rights at several law schools, and chaired the International Committee of the US Board of Amnesty International.

Clarence J. Dias is the President of the International Center for Law in Development. He holds doctoral degrees in law from Bombay University and Cornell University and has taught at Boston College of Law and the Department of Law of the University of Bombay. He has practiced law and published extensively on issues of law, development and human rights. He has been a consultant to various United Nations organs and agencies, including the Human Rights Center and UNDP and has worked extensively on issues of human rights in the Asia-Pacific region.

Benjamin Ferencz graduated from Harvard Law School in 1943. During the Second World War he served in the European Theater, where he became part of the newly-created War Crimes Branch of the Army and was involved in investigating Nazi crimes and apprehending the individuals responsible for them. After a short return to private practice, he became the Chief Prosecutor for the United States at the age of twenty-seven in the biggest murder trial in history, the case of twenty-two defendants who were charged with murdering over a million people. He published one of the first books on an international criminal court in 1980.

Gustavo Gallón has been Director of the Colombian Commission of Jurists since its creation in 1988. Before and during his tenure on the Commission of Jurists he taught state theory and constitutional law at several Colombian universities. He is also a member of the board of the Center for Justice and International Law (Washington) and the International Service for Human Rights (Geneva), and a member of the International Commission of Jurists (Geneva) and the Andean Commission of Jurists (Lima). He has served as an independent expert on special Colombian government commissions for peace (1991) and the reform of the military criminal code (1995). His recent publications include *Retos del siglo XXI para los derechos humanos en Colombia* (Ideele-Diakonia, 1996) and *Colombia, derechos humanos y derecho humanitario* (edited volume, CCJ, 1997). He is the recipient of the 1989 Human Rights Watch and the 1997 Lawyers Committee for Human Rights awards for international human rights monitors. In August 1999 he was appointed Special Representative of the UN Commission of Human Rights for Equatorial Guinea.

Thordis Ingadottir graduated as "Cand. Juris" from the University of Iceland, Reykjavik, and holds an LL.M. in International Legal Studies from the New York University School of Law, where she studied with the support of a J. William Fulbright Scholarship. As an attorney, a legal counselor for NGOs and legal scholar, Ms. Ingadottir has worked on various legal issues including conflicts of law and the international legislative process. She currently manages PICT's website (News section).

Alinikisa Mafwenga is a Tanzanian magistrate. He was educated at the University of Dar-es-Salaam, and then at the University of Wales where he obtained a Masters degree in criminology and criminal justice. In 1996 he was appointed private secretary to the Minister for Justice and Constitutional Affairs of Tanzania. Later that year he became a legal assistant to the International Criminal Tribunal for Rwanda and in October 1998 was sent on mission to The Hague as a legal assistant to the Appeals Chamber of the ICTR. The views expressed in his contribution are his own and do not necessarily reflect the official views of the ICTR or the United Nations.

Fiona McKay is Legal Officer at REDRESS, a London-based human rights organization which seeks to promote the right of torture survivors to reparation. One of her major projects at REDRESS has been lobbying for the rights of victims in the International Criminal Court. Ms. McKay is a solicitor and has an LL.M.

in international law and human rights. Prior to working at REDRESS, she worked with Palestinian human rights organizations in the Occupied Territories and within Israel.

Garth Meintjes, a South African lawyer, is the associate director of the Center for Civil and Human Rights at Notre Dame Law School. He has received degrees in law from the University of Stellenbosch, the University of Cape Town, and the University of Notre Dame, and has taught constitutional law at the University of the Western Cape. He serves as director of the LL.M. Program in international human rights law and teaches graduate seminars on the Accountability for Gross Violations of Human Rights, and Human Rights Practice. He is responsible for the Center's internship programs. He wishes to acknowledge the assistance of Michelle Mack in the preparation of his contribution to this volume.

Juan E. Méndez is the Director of the Center for Civil and Human Rights, Notre Dame Law School. He was formerly Executive Director of the Inter-American Institute on Human Rights, San José, Costa Rica (1996–99), and General Counsel, Human Rights Watch, New York, 1994–96.

Madeline Morris is Professor of Law, Duke University, where she teaches international criminal law and criminal justice and is Faculty Co-Director of the Duke/Geneva Institute in Transnational Law. She is a graduate of Yale Law School. Professor Morris commenced her legal career with a clerkship for Judge John Minor Wisdom of the United States Court of Appeals for the Fifth Circuit. Professor Morris served as Advisor on Justice to the President of Rwanda, 1995–97. She was Co-convenor, in 1996–97, of the Inter-African Cooperation on Truth and Justice program, and served in 1997 as Consultant and Adjunct Faculty Member of the U.S. Naval Justice School. She is a Member of the Board of Advisors of the Center on Law, Ethics and National Security, Duke University.

Naomi Roht-Arriaza is a professor of law at the University of California, Hastings College of Law, San Francisco. Professor Roht-Arriaza teaches in the areas of domestic and international human rights law, international environmental law and torts. She is the author of *State Responsibility to Investigate and Prosecute Grave Human Rights Violations in International Law*, 78 CAL. L. REV. 451 (1990) and editor of *Impunity and Human Rights in International Law and Practice* (1995).

William A. Schabas is director of the Irish Centre for Human Rights at the National University of Ireland, Galway, where he also holds the professorship in human rights law. He was previously professor of human rights law and criminal law and chair of the Département des sciences juridiques of the Université du Québec à Montréal and he has been a visiting or adjunct professor at universities throughout the world. He is a member of the Québec Bar, and was a member of the Québec Human Rights Tribunal from 1996 to 2000. He is the author of twelve books and more than seventy-five articles dealing in whole or in part with international human rights law. He has participated in international human rights missions on behalf of non-governmental organizations. He has also worked as a consultant to the Ministry of Justice of Rwanda and the United States Agency for International Development. He was a delegate of the International Centre for Criminal Law Reform and Criminal Justice Policy to the 1998 United Nations Diplomatic Conference of Plenipotentiaries on the Establishment of an International Criminal Court, Rome.

David Scheffer was appointed in 1993 Senior Advisor and Counsel to then Ambassador Albright. His tasks have focused primarily on war crimes issues and peace-keeping policies. Until 1997 he was an Adjunct Professor of International Law at Georgetown University Law Center. He has lectured and written extensively on international affairs and law while serving in various capacities at numerous academic and policy-making institutions. He has been Senior Associate in International and National Security Law at the Carnegie Endowment for International Peace; Senior Consultant to the Committee on Foreign Affairs in the U.S. Congress, House of Representatives; International Affairs Fellow at the Council on Foreign Relations, Adjunct Professor at Columbia University, and Research Associate at Harvard University Center for International Affairs. He received degrees from Harvard College and Oxford University.

Dinah L. Shelton is professor of international law at the Center for Civil and Human Rights, Notre Dame Law School, and a graduate of the University of California, Berkeley (B.A. 1967, J.D. 1970). She is a member of the executive councils of the Marangopoulos Foundation for Human Rights, Redress International, the International Institute of Human Rights, and Environnement sans frontière. She is co-author of *Protecting Human Rights in the Americas* (with T. Buergenthal; winner of the 1982 book prize of the Inter-American Bar Association), *International Environmental Law, and European Environmental Law* (with A. Kiss). She is an editor of the *Yearbook of International Environmental Law*, and has also authored numerous articles and studies. Her current work includes *Remedies for Human Rights Violations* (Oxford University Press, 1999) and studies on compliance with non-binding international norms and global governance. She has been a consultant to international governmental and non-governmental organizations on the subjects of international environmental law and international human rights law.

Patrick Zahnd is Deputy Head of the Delegation of the International Committee of the Red Cross to the United Nations. He has served as both a legal and political adviser, as well as in management of operations, at ICRC headquarters and in the field. He has worked mostly in Africa, and also in the Middle East and Central America. Prior to joining the ICRC, Mr. Zahnd was assistant professor at the University of Dijon, France.

INTRODUCTION

Dinah L. Shelton

The Statute of the International Criminal Court, adopted in Rome on July 17, 1998, may be considered as among the most significant developments in international law of the twentieth century. Appropriately, the Statute came into being during the year that marked the fiftieth anniversary of two other landmarks, the Universal Declaration of Human Rights[1] and the Convention on the Prevention and Punishment of the Crime of Genocide.[2] The earlier documents, together with the human rights provisions of the United Nations Charter and the 1949 Geneva Conventions,[3] brought fully into the international arena concern over the treatment of individuals during war and peace. The agreements gave conventional force to the condemnation resulting from the trials in Nuremberg and Tokyo, where crimes against peace, crimes against humanity[4] and war crimes were prosecuted and punished by the international community on the basis of customary and prior conventional law.

Despite the trials, international crimes have continued to be committed in many of the hundreds of armed conflicts of the past fifty years. Some estimates count 250 armed conflicts since World War II with casualties numbering upwards of 170 million people.[5] In most cases there has been little accountability for the

---

[1] Adopted Dec. 10, 1948, G.A. Res. 217A, U.N. GAOR, 3d Sess., pt. 1, Resolutions, at 71, U.N. Doc. A/810 (1948).

[2] Dec. 9, 1948, 78 U.N.T.S. 277 (*entered into force* Jan. 12, 1951) (*entered into force with respect to the United States* Nov. 25, 1989), *reprinted in* 28 I.L.M. 763 (1989).

[3] Geneva Convention for the Amelioration of the Condition of the Wounded and Sick in Armed Forces in the Field (Geneva I), Aug. 12, 1949, 6 U.S.T. 3114, 75 U.N.T.S. 31; Geneva Convention for the Amelioration of the Condition of Wounded, Sick and Shipwrecked Members of Armed Forces at Sea (Geneva II), Aug. 12, 1949, 6 U.S.T. 3217, 75 U.N.T.S. 85; Geneva Convention Relative to the Treatment of Prisoners of War (Geneva III), Aug. 12, 1949, 6 U.S.T. 3316, 75 U.N.T.S. 135; Geneva Convention Relative to the Protection of Civilian Persons in Time of War (Geneva IV), Aug. 12, 1949, 6 U.S.T. 3516, 75 U.N.T.S. 287.

[4] The Charter of the International Military Tribunal, Aug. 8, 1945, 59 Stat. 1544, 82 U.N.T.S. 279, art. 6(c) defined crimes against humanity as: murder, extermination, enslavement, deportation, and other inhumane acts committed against any civilian populations, before or during the war; or persecutions on political, racial or religious grounds in execution of or in connection with any crime within the jurisdiction of the Tribunal, whether or not in violation of the domestic law of the country where perpetrated. *See also* Charter of the International Military Tribunal for the Far East, Jan. 19, 1946, T.I.A.S. No. 1589, at 3, art. 5(e).

[5] *See* Jennifer L. Balint, *An Empirical Study of Conflict, Conflict Victimization and Legal Redress*, 14 NOUVELLES ÉTUDES PÉNALES 101 (C.C. Joyner & M. Cherif Bassiouni eds., 1998).

crimes committed, despite the fact that nearly all states have incorporated prohibitions on war crimes into their national law. Prosecutions for war crimes are rare.[6] In 1993, the U.N. Security Council for the first time took action to make effective the norms of international criminal law, by adopting the Statute of the International Criminal Tribunal for the former Yugoslavia (ICTY).[7] A year later, it created the International Criminal Tribunal for Rwanda (ICTR).[8]

The Rome Statute builds on these precedents. Although the treaty may not enter into force for some years, the decision to create the ICC reflects the judgment of the international community as a whole that impunity for war crimes, crimes against humanity, and genocide is no longer acceptable. The Statute has been hailed by its proponents as an important avenue for holding accountable those who commit violations of international criminal law. Some human rights activists and academics, on the other hand, while recognizing the important changes in international law signaled by the adoption of the ICC Statute, nonetheless question the emphasis being given the establishment of the Court, in the light of the resources the Court will require and the fact that key states, including the United States, refused to sign the Statute.

On March 19 and 20, 1999, the Center for Civil and Human Rights of Notre Dame Law School and the Joan B. Kroc Institute for International Peace Studies, Notre Dame University, convened experts to discuss the question of whether the proposed permanent international criminal court will make a difference for peace and human rights. By bringing together proponents and critics of the Court, the sponsors created a forum for dialogue about the prospects for an effective international court that will contribute to the goals of justice and peace in the international community. The exchanges of ideas at the conference can be found in the contributions to this volume.

The creation of an international criminal court is not a new idea. In the aftermath of the Second World War, the International Criminal Tribunal at Nuremberg and the International Military Tribunal for the Far East were established to try major German and Japanese war criminals. Later, as noted above, atrocities committed in the Former Yugoslavia and Rwanda prompted the United Nations Security Council to establish two *ad hoc* international criminal jurisdictions. The

---

[6] *See* cases cited by M. Cherif Bassiouni, *Strengthening the Norms of International Humanitarian Law to Combat Impunity*, in THE FUTURE OF INTERNATIONAL HUMAN RIGHTS (Burns H. Weston & Stephen P. Marks, eds. 1999) 245, 277–79.

[7] Statute of the International Tribunal (for the Prosecution of Persons Responsible for Serious Violations of Humanitarian Law Committed in the Territory of the Former Yugoslavia), May 25, 1993, S.C. Res. 827, U.N. SCOR, 48th Sess., 3217th mtg., U.N. Doc. S/RES/827 (1993), *reprinted in* 32 I.L.M. 1159 (1993).

[8] Resolution 955 (1994) Establishing the International Tribunal for Rwanda, Nov. 8, 1994, S.C. Res. 955, U.N. SCOR, 49th Sess., 3453 mtg., U.N. Doc. S/RES/955 (1994), *reprinted in* 33 I.L.M. 1598 (1994).

Statute of the International Criminal Court significantly differs from the predecessor tribunals. First, it is a permanent international tribunal. Second, it has global jurisdiction. Third, for the first time victims of crimes and their families can access the Court and claim reparation for the wrongs suffered.

Part I of the book analyses the precedent courts and the lessons they provide for the assessment of the possible role of the ICC in resolving international conflicts and restoring justice. First, Benjamin Ferencz draws upon his experience as a prosecutor at Nuremberg to reflect upon the importance of an international criminal tribunal. Next, Judge Alinikisa Mafwenga describes the role of the ICTR in promoting reconciliation in Rwanda, while Sandra Coliver considers the ICTY and its role the peace process in Bosnia.

The essays in Part I lead naturally to the question of how developing international criminal law interacts with and perhaps influences, or is influenced by, related areas of international law, in particular international human rights law and international humanitarian law. The contributors in Part II address these issues. Clarence Dias proposes further development in the field of international criminal law by suggesting the addition of a number of international human rights crimes. Patrick Zahnd of the International Committee of the Red Cross describes how the ICC should further international humanitarian law. Professor Kelly Dawn Askin looks at the issue of women's international human rights and how issues of concern to women are addressed in the ICC Statute. Part II ends with a discussion by Professor Juan Méndez of the possible convergence of, and new relationships between, international human rights law, international humanitarian law and international criminal law and procedure.

The aim of international criminal justice is essentially to deter crime and help restore international peace and security by punishing those responsible for international crimes committed during armed conflicts. The impartial trial and punishment of criminals is itself a vindication of the rule of law. Part III begins with a discussion of deterrence and punishment in the Statute of the ICC. Professor Naomi Roht-Arriaza and Professor Garth Meintjes address the issue of amnesties. Professor Gustavo Gallón then considers the problem of deterrence and Professor William Schabas details the content and drafting history of the penalty provisions in the ICC Statute.

The third part of the book also considers the role of the ICC in affording reparations to victims of international crimes. The idea that individuals are entitled to have international judicial fora decide upon and award reparations is not new. The European Court of Human Rights and the Inter-American Court of Human Rights have, for decades, been awarding victims reparations. As contributions in this book show, the individual's right to reparation is a fundamental human right that is expressly guaranteed by global and regional human rights instruments and applied by international and national courts. The questions raised by the inclusion of victim reparations in the ICC Statute are discussed in contributions by Professor Dinah Shelton and by Fiona McKay, attorney with Redress International. In addition to including a provision on reparations (Article 75), the ICC Statute provides another means for victims of crimes to receive redress. Article 79 of the Rome Statute provides for the establishment of a Trust Fund for "the benefit of victims of crimes within the jurisdiction of the Court, and of the families of such victims." The Trust Fund is dealt with by Thordis Ingadottir.

A final set of issues concerns ICC jurisdiction and the potential effectiveness of the proposed court. The decision of the drafters of the ICC Statute to found jurisdiction on a principle of complementarity raises a number of problems that are discussed by Professor Madeline Morris. This issue and others of concern to the United States are debated by U.S. Ambassador David Scheffer and Professor Roger Clark. One of the questions they address in particular is the extent to which the ICC can or should extend its jurisdiction to nationals of non-party states. This problem is also treated extensively in the final contribution to the volume, by Professor Madeline Morris.

As many of the contributions indicate, the gestation of the Rome Statute was long and complex.[9] The possibility of a permanent international criminal court was raised in the aftermath of the trials at Nuremberg and Tokyo in order to ensure that international crimes did not go unpunished and to avoid a repeat of the ad hoc establishment of a forum for prosecution and punishment. First, in 1947, the General Assembly mandated the predecessor of the International Law Commission (ILC) to formulate principles of international law recognized in the Charter of the Nuremberg Tribunal and in the judgment of the Tribunal and to prepare a draft code of offences against the peace and security of mankind.[10] The ILC began this work two years later and it continues today.[11] The ILC also began work on a draft statute for the establishment of an international criminal court, appointing two different rapporteurs within a short time. The General Assembly established a Special Committee in 1950, composed of the representatives of seventeen states, for the purpose of drafting a convention for the establishment of an international criminal court. The Committee finished its work in 1951[12] and pre-

---

[9] For a more detailed history of the twentieth century efforts to establish an international criminal court, *see* M. Cherif Bassiouni, *Establishing an International Criminal Court: Historical Survey*, 149 MIL. L. REV. 49–63 (1995) and M. Cherif Bassiouni, *From Versailles to Rwanda in Seventy-Five Years: The Need to Establish a Permanent International Criminal Court*, 10 HARV. HUM. RTS. J. 11–62 (1997).

[10] G.A. Res. 174, U.N. GAOR, 2d Sess., U.N. Doc. A/519 (1947).

[11] Articles for the Draft Code of Crimes Against the Peace and Security of Mankind were adopted by the ILC at its 48th session. *See* Draft Code of Crimes Against the Peace and Security of Mankind: Titles and Articles on the Draft Code, adopted by the International Law Commission at its Forty-Eighth Session, U.N. GAOR, 51st Sess., U.N. Doc. A/CN.4L.532 (1996) rev'd by U.N. Doc. A/CN.4L.532/Corr.1 and U.N. Doc. A/CN.4L.532/Corr.3.

[12] *See* Report of the Preparatory Committee for the Establishment of an International Criminal Court, U.N. Doc. A/51/22.

sented a revised text in 1953.[13] In both instances, the draft statutes were tabled for political and legal reasons.

The issue lay dormant within the United Nations until 1989, when Trinidad and Tobago, during a special session of the General Assembly on the problem of drug trafficking, proposed the creation of an International Criminal Court to aid in fighting the narcotics problem. The General Assembly requested that the ILC prepare a report on the issue.[14] The ILC reported back in 1990 and extended its discussion beyond the issue of narcotics crimes. The General Assembly approved the approach and in Resolution 46/54 (1991) asked the Commission to consider the question of an international criminal jurisdiction, including proposals for the establishment of an international criminal court or other international criminal trial mechanism, and to provide guidance to the General Assembly on the matter.[15]

As a result of the General Assembly mandate, the ILC established a Working Group on an International Criminal Court which set forth the parameters of a draft statute.[16] The General Assembly endorsed the conclusions of the Working Group and the ILC and in Resolution 47/33 of November 25, 1992, requested that the International Law Commission (ILC) undertake the elaboration of a draft statute for a permanent International Criminal Court.[17] When the draft was produced,[18] the General Assembly, in Resolution 49/53 of December 9, 1994, established an Ad Hoc Committee to review the major substantive and administrative issues arising out of the draft statute.

The Ad Hoc Committee met for two sessions in 1995 and produced a report that led to the creation of a Preparatory Committee in 1996. The mandate of the PrepCom was to prepare a consolidated text based on the draft statute prepared by the ILC taking into account the report of the ad hoc Committee and written comments by states and relevant organizations. The 1996 PrepCom was unable to produce a consolidated text, instead compiling various proposals into a report.[19] The mandate of the PrepCom was extended for a further two years. Further meetings led

---

[13] Draft Statute for an International Criminal Court, Aug. 31, 1951, 7 GAOR Supp. 11, U.N. Doc. A/21/36 (1952).

[14] G.A. Res. 43/164 (1988) and 44/39 (1989).

[15] G.A. Res. 46/54 (1991), U.N. GAOR, 46th Sess., Supp. No. 49, at 286, U.N. Doc. A/46/49 (1991).

[16] Report of the International Law Commission on the Work of Its Forty-Fourth Session, U.N. GAOR, 47th Sess., Supp. No. 10, U.N. Doc. A/47/10 (1992) and Report of the Working Group on the question of an international criminal jurisdiction, Annex to *id.*, at 143.

[17] G.A. Res. 47/33, U.N. GAOR, 47th Sess., Supp. No. 49, at 287, U.N. Doc. A/47/49 (1992).

[18] *See* Report of the International Law Commission on the Work of Its Forty-Sixth Session, U.N. GAOR, 49th Sess., Supp. No. 10, U.N. Doc. A/49/10.

[19] *See* Report of the Preparatory Committee on the Establishment of an International Criminal Court, U.N. GAOR 51st Sess., Supp. No. 22, U.N. Doc. A/51/22, Vols. I and II.

to the Diplomatic Conference convened in Rome in 1998. At the Conference, 160 states, seventeen inter-governmental organizations, fourteen specialized agencies of the United Nations and representatives of 250 accredited non-governmental organizations participated in the final drafting of the Statute.

As the Rome Conference demonstrates, the United Nations did not act to create a criminal court in a closed series of meetings. A worldwide campaign of civil society, including organizations and survivors of systematic abuse advocated creation of a permanent court. In 1994, more than 800 non-governmental organizations formed a Coalition for an International Criminal Court, participating in discussions and meetings of the U.N. Sixth (Legal) Committee, the Ad Hoc Committee, the PrepCom and the Diplomatic Conference. The name of another group, "No Peace without Justice"—a committee of parliamentarians, mayors and citizens—vividly expresses one of the major justifications for the creation of an international criminal court. The non-governmental groups mobilized political support and worked to advance the principles of accountability and redress for victims.

The participation of states, inter-governmental groups and non-governmental organizations indicates the range of interests to be served by an International Criminal Court. The eventual Court's purposes and functions concern not only the achievement of justice, including redress, accountability, punishment, and revelation of the truth, but also deterrence, reconciliation, and the restoration and maintenance of peace. The variety of concerns and interests, sometimes compatible but sometimes divergent, resulted in a lengthy and complex Statute, many details of which remain to be worked out by the States Parties in collaboration with civil society. It is an enormous mandate and gives rise to equally large expectations. Once it is established, the Court will have to extend maximum efforts to live up to the dreams of its creators.

PART I
PRECEDENTS AND
THEIR LESSONS

CHAPTER 1

THE EXPERIENCE OF NUREMBERG

Benjamin Ferencz

A. INTRODUCTION

At the age of twenty-seven, I became the chief prosecutor of the biggest murder trial in history. Ever since that time, I have been trying to create a more
humane world. The question to be considered is whether the Permanent
International Criminal Court will make a difference in this regard; will it contribute to peace and human rights? A simple yes or no would not advance matters
very far. The truth is, I do not know the answer, and the best alternative for me
is to recount events of the last sixty years and attempt to draw lessons from them.
My personal stories relate to the topics and the questions with which we must
contend. Will a permanent international criminal court make a difference in connection with conflict, with wars, with human rights, with justice for the victims?
And if so, how? What has been learned in all these years?

The first stage of the process of creating a more humane world is, of course,
to stop the killings. The second stage is to try to apprehend the persons responsible for such crimes and bring them to justice. Justice is related to peace. The
next step, which is often omitted, is to do something to rehabilitate the victims.
The victims are often forgotten, as people pay attention to the crimes and the
criminals, ignoring the survivors. The next question is how to prevent such events
from happening again. That, of course, is the most important of all. In each of
these areas the question that must be asked about any action is whether it does
any good. The experience of Nuremberg suggests that international criminal
responsibility has a positive role to play.

B. STOPPING THE KILLING

During the Second World War, I was a member of the US army—and I won
the war single-handed. Before that, I was in law school, where I was a very poor
student. My grades were fine, but I had no money. Since I had developed the
habit of eating when I was an infant, I needed to earn food or money, so I became
the research assistant for Harvard professor Sheldon Glueck, an outstanding
American criminologist. The war was under way and reports of atrocities were
already arriving. Professor Glueck decided to do a book on war crimes and I did
the research. By the time I graduated from law school, I was an authority, having
read everything in the Harvard Law Library on war crimes.

The army immediately recognized my talents and I became a private in the artillery. I jumped into the war at Normandy Beach. The Germans heard I was coming and began to retreat with me running after them. I chased them through the Maginot Line, the Siegfried Line, and across the Rhine, through the Battle of the Bulge, Bastogne, and other places. Somehow, I was not killed, for which the army rewarded me with five battle stars. I thought it was the end of my army career, but we began to receive reports of atrocities, such as the murder by German people on the ground of allied fliers who had been shot down. The fliers were killed because they were perceived to be war criminals who had bombed the population of Germany, sometimes killing children.

C. INVESTIGATING THE CRIMES

I have been asked how I investigated these crimes. We had a very simple procedure. It was a one-man operation where I went out in a jeep with a pistol and a carbine in the back of the car. When I entered a town where crimes had been committed, I would look for a person in authority, such as a police chief, although most of them had run away. I would line up all the people who had been in the area and put them against a wall. They were told to sit down and write exactly what happened and they were told that any one who lied would be shot. This was the "pre-Miranda" rule - and it was a violation of international law and human rights as we know it today, but that is how it happened. Sometimes twenty-five people would write the details of what they had seen. Ten of them would say they were not there and had not seen or heard anything, while fifteen of them would have a consistent story of what had happened. I would then write a report, attaching the twenty-five statements indicating who was killed, by whom, and under what circumstances. An arrest order was issued to seize the accused and bring him in to stand trial. Occasionally, I had to dig up the bodies. It had to be done by hand to prove how the victim died. It was a pretty grisly business.

Eventually, we came to the concentration camps, although we didn't know the term "concentration camp" at the time. All we knew was that groups of people had been in camps and were starving and beaten and they were getting out on the roads. Our troops were approaching and reports were being relayed to us in the war crimes section. A tank division would go into a camp and I would join the troops. After we entered the camp, I would ask to meet the colonel in charge. I said I was there on orders of General Patton and I wanted immediately to secure the office where records and all camp documents were kept. Nobody was to enter or leave the site without my permission. I seized all the documents, including the registers of the people who had been killed in the camp. The records actually never used the word "killed" but had euphemisms such as "shot while trying to escape," "died of diphtheria," or "malaria." I would seize the books and find out who had been in charge of that camp. After that I would return to headquarters, type the report, and recommend that the military find and arrest the criminals.

D. CONDUCTING THE TRIALS

I personally nailed up the first sign in the Dachau Concentration Camp saying "U.S. Army War Crimes Trials, Dachau." We brought in some of the accused people and we put them before military commissions. They were tried on the basis of documentary evidence and witnesses—some of whom we later tried as well—and they were either convicted or acquitted. The trials were very quick. The defense counsel were American military personnel and the judges were American military personnel. From a legal point of view it was problematic, but there was a rough sense of justice. No innocent people were tried.

The next stage was Nuremberg. While the Dachau trials were still in progress, I went home to America, never wanting to return to Germany again. Very soon after my honorable discharge, however, I received a telegram from the Pentagon inviting me to come to Washington. The military asked if I would go back and assist with the prosecution of war criminals. They offered me the rank of colonel to do what I had been doing as a sergeant. Eventually, I agreed to go back as a civilian.

Justice Robert Jackson, on leave from the U.S. Supreme Court, was the Chief American Prosecutor in the Nuremberg trial in which German Field Marshal Herman Goering was the Chief Defendant, and other Nazi leaders were on trial. That case was already in process and twelve other trials followed. Chief Counsel was Telford Taylor. The first of the twelve subsequent trials was called the "medical case" and was brought against doctors who had participated in and directed medical experiments on innocent victims. The problem remains very current today. At that time, there were no precedents whatsoever for the trials. We were simply trying to establish a rough kind of justice. In the proceedings, everyone was very, very cautious to follow the strictest standards of fairness to the defendants. The judges were all trained legal people. The prosecutors were all experienced, trained lawyers and the defendants were defended by attorneys of their choice, former Nazi lawyers.

I was the chief prosecutor for what was known as the *Einsatzgruppen* case. It concerned extermination squads that came in behind the German troops and murdered all men, women and children simply because they were Jews or Gypsies, or because they were considered to be potential threats to the German Reich. Very conveniently, they wrote detailed reports of their work. One report boasted: "On September 29, 1941, units of Einsatzgruppe A in the vicinity of Kiev, within the first forty-eight hours succeeded in killing 33,771 Jews." That later became famous as the massacre at Babi Yar. We had never heard of Babi Yar, the district where the mass graves were uncovered. It is still amazing that one small SS unit, assisted by local militia, could murder 15,000 people a day.

I knew the identities of the murdered because their names were on the reports. To go to trial we needed two things: we needed conclusive evidence and we needed the defendant. If you have one without the other, you have nothing. So when one of our staff people in Berlin came upon the series of reports in loose-leaf folders, recounting how many people these special units had murdered in all these different towns, I seized the folders and went to Nuremberg where I spoke to General Telford Taylor and asked that the case be prosecuted. He said he had no additional staff and the trial program was already set. I objected that these cold-blooded murderers should not escape and showed him all the proof, the doc-umentation. He asked if I could handle the case and I said I could. Thus, I became the Chief Prosecutor in the biggest murder case in the history of the world. It was my first case.

We tried only twenty-two defendants, despite the fact that there were 3,000 men who for two years did nothing else but murder people because of their race, ethnicity, and their religion. We had only twenty-two seats in the dock, so we chose only a sampling of the highest ranking defendants available at the time. Some of those responsible escaped and showed up years later. We aimed to do jus-tice knowing we could not do perfect justice.

The prosecution rested its case after three days. The trial lasted about six or eight months, the time needed to rebut the denials and alibis presented by the accused. I submitted all the documentation I had acquired. The accused, of course, denied the charges. They said the documents were fake and created alibis in an attempt to show they were not present. On the basis of their own reports and after very short, intense questioning, the truth became clear. In the end, I secured con-victions of all the accused. There were thirteen death sentences and long prison sentences for the others.

As the Chief Prosecutor, I faced the problem of deciding what to ask the court for in sentencing those convicted. I had to make a recommendation and everybody expected me to demand the death penalty. I did not do so, however, knowing that no punishment could ever balance the lives of twenty-two mass murderers against the million people murdered. It was impossible. In my mind, the only utility of any significance that could come from the trial would result from asking the Tribunal, which I did, to affirm, by their judgment and under international penal law, the right of all human beings to live in peace and dignity regardless of their race or creed. I felt that if such a principle could be firmly established in law, then maybe it would lead to a more peaceful world. I was for-tunate in having a very good judge, a devout Catholic, Michael Musmanno of Pennsylvania, who confirmed my view of the law, even though we differed on sentencing.

E.   REPARATIONS AND REHABILITATION OF VICTIMS

What do you do after you've stopped the killing and you've brought to jus-tice some of those who were responsible for the crimes? You have to do some-thing for the survivors, for the victims. Very little has been written on this topic.

I moved from being a one-man prosecutor to setting up a program for Nazi victims, about which practically nothing is known.

The Military Government law provided for the restitution of property taken from Nazi victims. Successor organizations, representing leading charities, were authorized to recover heirless and unclaimed assets for the benefit of survivors. Most legal and practical problems encountered in recovering homes, businesses, communal, cultural and other properties in West Germany were resolved during the twenty-five-year-period from 1947 to 1972.

In 1951 we negotiated a treaty between West Germany (the East Germans would not participate) and the state of Israel and a consortium of leading Jewish organizations outside Israel, to which I was counsel. The reparations treaty which was signed in 1952 provided a list of injuries for which compensation would be paid, such as false arrest, incarceration in concentration camps, damage to health, and loss of economic opportunity. The legal framework, although inadequate, became the basis of the German Federal Indemnification Law. Nazi victims of all denominations could file claims and millions were filed, because each inmate survivor had many separate claims. These claims, which had to be substantiated, were adjudicated in a judicial system throughout the German courts. Claims were filed with a special agency, appeals were heard by another court, and cases could go the Supreme Court or even the Constitutional court.

The legal aid society set up to help the victims in the name of Jewish charities became the biggest legal aid society in the world. There were 250 German lawyers employed and my staff exceeded 1200 people, most of whom were themselves survivors of persecution. Offices were opened in nineteen countries and every major city in Germany. Claims flooded in and were dealt with, and compensation to the victims was paid. The total amount of reparations paid to Nazi survivors throughout the world, according to official statements of the German government, exceeded DM 100 *billion*. (Fluctuating exchange rates over the years make a precise dollar equivalent difficult to ascertain.) That program is still continuing and it has its ramifications in all of the current claims against German companies and Swiss banks. Rehabilitation programs will continue as long as Nazi victims remain alive.

F. PREVENTION AND DETERRENCE

The last and the main topic is how to prevent these crimes from happening again. There's a very simple answer to that. You prevent war. That may seem idealistic, because there have been wars since man has recorded history, but it can be done. It requires an international criminal court and much more, because the world is a very complicated place. It requires an improved United Nations. It requires disarmament; there can be no peaceful world when everyone can buy America's weapons to kill each other. It requires another system of sanctioning, whether it be economic sanctions or other sanctions. It requires social justice;

peace cannot exist in a country of inequality where people are starving. All of the environment and the population problems must be resolved in some way before there will be tranquillity or peace—the final step in all of this.

G. THE ROLE OF THE INTERNATIONAL CRIMINAL COURT: LESSON FROM NUREMBERG

The International Criminal Court, now being organized at the United Nations, will make a difference in achieving a more peaceful and just world. The Nuremberg trials made a difference. They made a difference in conflict resolution and prevention. Let me give a single example. Do you think that there's any danger today of Germany going to war against France, or France going to war against Germany? The answer to that, obviously, is no, of course not. When World War II was over, America did what Cicero had recommended: "to have peace you must make your enemy your friend." The European Community, leaving the Balkans aside for the moment, has developed as an organization of states with its own Parliament, its own laws, its own military force. So while there are no perfect solutions, there is progress.

Did the Nuremberg trials lead to better respect for human rights? Of course. The evidence is overwhelming. A former Polish lawyer, Raphael Lemkin, came to Nuremberg to push for a new concept. The Nazis killed fifty or so members of his family because they were Jews. He called it a crime against the people and said that it should have a special name—genocide. He wrote a book which helped, along with the trials, to worldwide acceptance of the 1948 Convention against Genocide. As a consequence, some mass killers have recently been convicted of the crime of genocide in Rwanda.

Also as a result of the trials and the evidence brought out during them, René Cassin, a lawyer from Paris who fled with General De Gaulle, wrote the first draft of the Universal Declaration of Human Rights. It states that all people in the world have certain fundamental rights. For his work, Cassin was awarded the Nobel Peace Prize. He and Eleanor Roosevelt promoted the Declaration and today everybody knows about human rights.

The things described here did not exist before. When the Nuremberg Charter called crimes against humanity and aggressive war criminal acts, this was an innovation. It was not a pure invention, but the concept had not fully evolved in law. The law took a step forward at Nuremberg. As Justice Jackson said, the time had come to hold people responsible for aggressive war, which the Tribunal said is "the supreme international crime."

Although people have condemned the trials as imposing *ex post facto* punishment, that is nonsense. The *ex post facto* principle is a principle of justice: that no one should be accused of an illegal act when the act was not known to be illegal at the time it was done. Who didn't know that it was illegal to murder a million innocent people, including hundreds of thousands of women and children, helpless people, because of their color, their race, or their religion? Who didn't know that such conduct was illegal? It was not *ex post facto*, but was putting into positive international law fundamental principles of humanity and of morality, and national law, and making them legally binding through international law. What was done in the International Military Tribunal and reinforced in the twelve subsequent trials is the basis for the current efforts to build a permanent International Criminal Court and other institutions to hold individuals responsible for their criminal acts.

The evidence of the evolution can be seen in the Pinochet case. For the first time a dictator and former head of state, accused of committing crimes in his own country against his own people, was held prisoner in England for possible extradition to Spain to stand trial for crimes committed against Spanish nationals. The ultimate outcome of the case is less important than the principle established. Other dictators now know that they could find themselves under indictment and subject to trial for human rights abuses. The establishment of the International Tribunal is the next step.

The proposed Court as stipulated in the Rome Statute is not perfect. (It was approved by the overwhelming majority of states on July 17, 1998, with only seven votes against it—including the US.) Babies are not born full-grown. First, they crawl, they cry, they mess up, they throw up, and they need help. You must pick them up and help them go on. Eventually, with care and nurturing they grow and become useful citizens. Will the International Criminal Court become an effective court? I do not know the answer to that, but I do know that I have waited fifty years for it to come into existence. It was a very exciting day in Rome when 120 nations declared that an International Criminal Tribunal "is hereby established." Sixty ratifications are required for it to become operational and there are a lot of complications, but Pope John Paul II summed it up well when he said we have to think in terms of the human family. We are all human beings living on one small planet, and we've got to learn to share the results of this planet in a rational and humane way, so that everyone can live in peace and dignity.

Peace can be achieved and it can be done fairly simply. There will be difficulties along the way and it will not be cheap, quick, or easy, because we live in a very dangerous world. The capacity of man to kill human beings is enormous and is growing every day despite all of the safeguards. Ask yourself what kind of world you want and if you are prepared to do something to create it. It takes more than one generation to bring about change in such fundamental things as notions of sovereignty, rigid nationalism, and ethnicity. These ideas, that must change to meet contemporary needs, come from deeply ingrained feelings and are ideas still held by many people of good will and intelligence. If each person makes an effort, however, it is possible to build on the lessons of Nuremberg. It is important never to give up and never to lose hope. If one project doesn't work, try again. If that doesn't work, try harder. If everyone does that, there will be a more peaceful and humane world.

CHAPTER 2

THE CONTRIBUTION OF THE INTERNATIONAL CRIMINAL TRIBUNAL FOR RWANDA TO RECONCILIATION IN RWANDA

Alinikisa Mafwenga

A. INTRODUCTION

Until relatively recently, crime was largely a national issue mainly confined within the borders of each national state. Because crime was localized, courts exercised jurisdiction over crimes committed within their territory, although in some instances they were prepared to try their nationals for crimes committed abroad. The idea of an International Criminal Court to try those that had waged war or pursued national policies in defiance of civilized standards surfaced only briefly after World War II with the Nuremberg and Tokyo trials. The situation has now fundamentally changed, but the historical context is necessary to understand how the contribution, achievements and experience of the International Criminal Tribunal for Rwanda (ICTR) can be used for the benefit of a permanent International Criminal Court.

B. THE MANDATE OF THE ICTR

The United Nations Security Council established the International Criminal Tribunal for Rwanda by Resolution 955 of 1994. The Council acted under Chapter VII of the United Nations Charter which empowers it to make decisions, binding upon states, in the interest of maintenance of international peace and security. The earlier International Criminal Tribunal for Yugoslavia was established during the conflict in Bosnia to punish the perpetrators of atrocities that were still being committed, in the belief that prosecution and punishment would halt violations of international humanitarian law. In contrast, the ICTR was established at the end of a bitter year of genocide in the conviction that this would contribute to the process of reconciliation among the people of the country.

The perceived importance of the role of the ICTR in bringing peace and reconciliation in Rwanda is apparent in the language of the resolution that created the Tribunal. Although the preamble to any legal instrument is not formally part of the law, it reflects the spirit of the legal instrument and the intention of the drafters. In the case of the ICTR, the Security Council expressed its concern and determination to put an end to genocide and crimes against humanity by bringing perpetrators of such crimes to justice, being "convinced that, in the particular circumstances of Rwanda, the prosecution of persons responsible for serious violations of international humanitarian law would enable this aim to be achieved and would contribute to the process of national reconciliation and to the restoration and maintenance of peace. . . ."[1] Ultimately, the success of the ICTR will be considered a success of the United Nations and the global community as a whole.

Reconciliation and healing through the judicial process in Rwanda very much depend on the success of the ICTR in delivering speedy justice to the Rwandan community. This in turn depends on the financial and moral support the ICTR receives from the international community, because the conclusion of any criminal proceedings very much depends on the availability of evidence and witnesses who are able to testify. The ICTR under the authority of the Registrar has introduced a comprehensive scheme for the protection of witnesses and victims of crime in Rwanda. Without means to enable victims to travel to the seat of the Tribunal to testify, the reconciliation process in Rwanda would be a distant dream.

In view of the importance of this program to the success of the Tribunal, the legal provision giving authority to the Registrar to introduce such a program is reproduced below.

Rule 34

A.   There shall be set up under the authority of the Registrar, a victim and witness support unit consisting of qualified staff to:

  i.   Recommend the adoption of protective measures for victims and witnesses in accordance with Article 21 of the Statute;
  ii.   Ensure that they receive relevant support, including physical and psychological rehabilitation, especially counseling in cases of rape and sexual assaults; and
  iii.   Develop short and long-term plans for the protection of witnesses who have testified before the Tribunal and who fear a threat to their life, property or family.

. . . A gender sensitive approach to victims and witnesses protective and support measures should be adopted and due considerations given, in the appointment of staff within this unit, to the employment of qualified women.

---

[1]   Preamble to the ICTR Statute, Resolution 955, S/RES/955, Nov. 8, 1994.

The ICTR has committed itself to promoting reconciliation and the healing process in Rwanda by seeing to it that witnesses and victims who come to testify are well protected. The success of the program is reflected in the number of cases that have been concluded and that are ongoing. These prosecutions are essential to the achievement of peace and reconciliation in Rwanda.

C. ICTR ACHIEVEMENTS IN PROMOTING PEACE AND RECONCILIATION IN RWANDA

The ICTR contribution in the ongoing reconciliation and healing process in Rwanda can only be assessed by looking at the number of witnesses who have been enabled to travel to Arusha to testify and the number and importance of cases so far decided. Despite the insecure environment in the countries of residence of some of the witnesses, the Witness and Victims Support Section of the ICTR has facilitated the travel of more that 150 prosecution and defense witnesses to Arusha from more than a dozen countries of Africa, Europe, and America. Some twenty witnesses thought to be particularly at risk have been relocated. The Section also has discharged the difficult task of maintaining the anonymity of witnesses during and after their testimony. This has encouraged other witnesses to travel to Arusha and to participate more willingly in the search for justice and reconciliation in Rwanda.

The question of what is and what is not justice is difficult to answer and it is perhaps better to raise questions rather than to attempt to answer the question. First, it must be asked what is international justice? The fact that the ICTR is manned and funded by members of the international community is clear testimony to the fact that the world is determined to take collective and corrective measures under the United Nations to achieve the common goal of achieving international justice. Justice before a court of law means justice as seen in the eyes of the law, without entering into a discussion of whether court decisions according to law always represent moral justice. According to Blacks Law Dictionary,[2] justice is defined simply as "proper administration of laws."

By that definition, the apartheid court that sentenced Nelson Mandela to life imprisonment did justice according to law. The question is, was the law itself just? Just cause is "a cause outside legal cause, which must be based on reasonable grounds, and there must be a fair and honest cause of reason, regulated by good faith."[3] Within the framework of the definition, was the African National Congress pursuing a just cause through its armed struggle in pursuit of equality among South Africans of all races? As it is evident now, the aim was not to replace a white for a black apartheid regime. The lesson from South Africa is that oppressive regimes cannot resist forces of progressive change. They in fact act as catalysts and sow seeds of civil unrest.

---

[2] BLACK'S LAW DICTIONARY 864 (6th ed.) .

[3] *Id.* at 863.

The goal of justice for victims raises several other questions. Does it mean justice for direct victims of the international crimes so committed? What about deceased victims? Does international justice to the victims only mean facilitating their travel to and security before and after going to court? Is justice done to the victims if a case concludes with a conviction? Is an acquittal a failure of justice in the eyes of the victims?

In fact, the concept of international justice means understanding that the international community as a whole is the victim of genocide and crimes against humanity. All humanity suffers indirectly from such crimes. From this point of view, justice to the international community can only be done by ensuring that justice is done to the accused and the victims. In recognition of this fact, the ICTR statute gives equal protection to witnesses who come to testify for the defense and those who are there for the prosecution. The ICTR legal aid scheme aims to achieve justice for both victims and defendants, knowing well that the only way to promote reconciliation in Rwanda is to have trials that are fair and just to both parties.

It must be borne in mind that most of the accused persons facing charges before the ICTR have been high-ranking officials of the previous government. Unfair trials of such accused, who are mainly the Hutu who comprise 80 percent of the Rwandan population, would not bring peace and reconciliation in Rwanda, but instead would sow seeds of revenge. Promoting reconciliation in Rwanda requires doing justice to both parties. The ICTR was willing to spend more than US $500,000 to provide legal services to one defendant in order to see to it that justice was done to the accused, with a view of promoting reconciliation in Rwanda through justice.[4]

D.   WHO SHOULD COMPENSATE THE VICTIMS?

Sometimes, individuals commit international crimes in their private capacity. At other times they act as agents of the state in pursuance of policies of the state. In both situations, the individual incurs responsibility and may be prosecuted for the crime. In recent years, it has been suggested that the state itself also may be criminally liable, but this is still very controversial. No doubt, state officials commit crimes that are of international concern acting within or outside their authority. It is one thing to hold them individually culpable and another thing to hold the state itself "criminally responsible." Finding a state guilty of criminal liability amounts to finding its people as a whole criminally liable, even those who may have been victims or innocent bystanders. In the case of Rwanda, it is not possible to punish the previous government because it is no longer in power. Many Rwandan played no part in committing the crimes or even condoning them; witness the many moderate Hutus who were killed in Rwanda during the genocide.

---

[4]   The Prosecutor v. Akayesu, ICTR–96–4–T. By Oct. 26, 1998, the ICTR spent US$575,600 on defense services for Mr. Akayesu (ICTR Press Release ICTR/INF–9–004, Oct. 26, 1998).

The trend today is to require the state to make reparation for wrongful acts, but to refrain from holding it subject to criminal punishment. In Rwanda, the context of the conflict was mainly based on ethnicity. The ICTR as a neutral organ has played and continues to play a very important role in the reconciliation process. Trial of all those responsible, including the leaders in Rwanda, could be undermined by allegations of partiality.

An international criminal court like ICTR is free from the constraints of national policies and prejudices. The Rwandan community sees the ICTR as doing justice to both parties, thus promoting peace and reconciliation in Rwanda. In order to achieve reconciliation in Rwanda, justice must not only be done, but it must be seen to be done by an impartial Tribunal. The role of the ICTR in this direction need not be emphasized as, despite their good work, the Nuremberg and Tokyo Tribunals are still haunted by the fact that they were victor's tribunals trying the defeated and thus viewed as lacking legitimacy.

E.   LEARNING FROM HISTORY

A sustainable ICC cannot avoid learning from history. The experience of the Nuremberg Tribunal and the ICTY and later ICTR Tribunals is at the disposal of ICC. The ICC has to look at global history in order to fortify itself for the important task ahead. World history is full of misunderstandings among nations. War as a necessity is still lawful. If the ICTR contributes to promoting international justice for victims and reconciliation in Rwanda, it is in fact the achievement of the global community in this direction.

In the historical context, the world owes a lot to, and can learn from, the reconciliation process in South Africa and similar processes other parts of the world. The South African experience teaches that victims of crime are in the forefront in promoting reconciliation. Having spent more than twenty years in prison, President Mandela, with the support of the entire population of South Africa, black and white, is engaged in promoting peace and reconciliation among white and black South Africans. Earlier, President Mandela spoke "in mitigation" to the judges who convicted him of crimes under the apartheid regime. Instead of mitigating for a lenient sentence, he told the judges that for the crime of which he was convicted, fighting for equality among all South Africans, life imprisonment was a lenient sentence because he was willing to die for that cause. Today Nelson Mandela has proved that he is not willing to exact revenge.

The lesson that the ICC can learn is that victims of crimes may need only an apology and knowledge of the truth, not necessarily monetary compensation. The ongoing good relations between former colonial masters and the colonized, e.g., the commonwealth countries, reinforces the point. Colonialism, which continued even after the Universal Declaration of Human Rights (UDHR) was adopted, is incompatible with human rights principles, even if it is not legally speaking a crime. Some of the nations that were in the forefront in signing the Universal

Declaration of Human Rights did not grant independence to their colonies immediately thereafter and, in fact, resisted the struggle for freedom, equality and justice. Today, there is reconciliation.

Justice is the key to human development. There can be no development without peace and no genuine peace can co-exist with injustice. A world committed to promoting peace has to promote justice. Oppressed peoples will always rise against their oppressors, leading to civil or international wars. Genocide and crimes against humanity are massive crimes in which a population has to be mobilized to systematically kill people. Justice thus requires not only justice before a court of law after the fact, but preventive social justice.

F. ICTR DECISIONS PROMOTING RECONCILIATION AND HEALING IN RWANDA

The most difficult task for a permanent International Criminal Court will be to define crimes that will fall under its jurisdiction. History shows that nations have been jealous about surrendering their jurisdiction over criminal matters affecting their citizens; the saga of the Libyan Lockerbie suspects is indicative. In this regard, the ICTR experience is helpful. The ICTR has established the precedent that killing innocent civilians is not a political issue or political offense. It has become clear that perpetrators of crime cannot hide from the hands of the international community. This is so because the ICTR became the first Tribunal to track down, arrest and try a former Prime Minister of a country.[5] The message has reached all politicians in the world, making the ICTR decisions a deterrent to future perpetrators of crime. As such, they promote peace and reconciliation not only in Rwanda, but the global community as a whole.

It must be assumed that the ICTR judgment in the case involving the former prime minister has contributed greatly to the reconciliation in Rwanda, much more than the trials of all those who committed crimes acting under superior orders. The message from the ICTR is that heads of states and government policy makers are not immune and cannot avoid responsibility for their conduct by wrapping themselves in the blanket of state sovereignty, secure that no international mechanism can call them to account. The message clearly announces that there will be no more genocide and crimes against humanity without punishment.[6]

It also must be recalled that, for the first time in the history of international humanitarian law, the ICTR tried and convicted someone accused of rape as a crime against humanity.[7] The world did not witness any trial involving rape during the Nuremberg and Tokyo proceedings. The *Akayesu* decision on rape will promote peace in Rwanda because rape victims and their relatives will get psychological satisfaction that justice has been done.

---

[5] The Prosecutor v. Kambanda, ICTR–97–23–S (Sept. 4, 1998).

[6] The *Pinochet* case sent a similar message to political leaders.

[7] The Prosecutor v. Akayesu, *supra* note 4.

The achievement of the ICTR in promoting peace and reconciliation in Rwanda should be assessed within the framework of its mandate, by the degree to which the prosecution of cases achieves the Security Council's stated goals of deterrence, justice and peace—halting future and redressing past violations of international humanitarian law and breaking the circle of ethnic violence and retribution in the region.

G. CONCLUSIONS

The future of the ICC in achieving the goal of reconciliation through prosecution and punishment of perpetrators will very much depend on the desire of the international community to utilize the services of the ICC. This may involve the international community in reviewing the concept of granting unconditional amnesty to those who committed politically-motivated crimes. Such amnesties are sometimes announced by the state without the approval of the population (including the victims), thus alienating the very force necessary for achieving reconciliation and lasting peace. In some instances, unrestricted pardon is the result of self-amnesty that outgoing leaders unilaterally award themselves before a democratic transition proceeds. In some cases impunity is the result of the negotiation between the old and the new leaders without the consent of the majority of the population. The South African Truth Commission is different. It is a product of the South African people themselves, hoping that a truth-telling operation, including full disclosure of all human rights abuses, can ensure that the facts are not forgotten but remain alive in the memory for the benefit of peace and reconciliation. It does not preclude all prosecutions nor deny reparations.

The ICTR has made a great contribution to the healing and reconciliation process in Rwanda. It has helped the families of the victims and survivors through its decisions, sending the message that the world recognizes their pain and trauma. The international community still needs to contemplate a sustainable program for the ICTR—and in future the ICC—for the economic and psychological rehabilitation of the victims. This may include monetary compensation, psychological treatment, and religious and academic education for survivors and indigent members of the deceased family. Religion can be very important in giving moral strength to victims to forgive those who have wronged them and society. Religion promises eternal life in heaven to the victims who forgive. Other rehabilitation projects may include home building and re-establishment of lost businesses for survivors. National communities will need to address the ongoing debate about post-war or post-abuse justice. It is not possible to prosecute leaders of a previous regime without giving them the necessary legal support; if the trials are not seen to be fair and just and the question of victims is not addressed the new regime will be put at risk. To restore the moral order that has broken down, justice must be done to the accused and the victims. Telling the truth about the past before a Tribunal or a Commission undermines the seeds of revenge. The cases concluded before the ICTR have served that purpose.

CHAPTER 3

THE CONTRIBUTION OF THE INTERNATIONAL CRIMINAL TRIBUNAL FOR THE FORMER YUGOSLAVIA TO RECONCILIATION IN BOSNIA AND HERZEGOVINA

Sandra Coliver

A. INTRODUCTION

The International Criminal Tribunal for the Former Yugoslavia ("ICTY" or "Tribunal") was established in May 1993 by U.N. Security Council Resolution 827. The Tribunal's "sole purpose" was to prosecute "persons responsible for serious violations of international humanitarian law committed in the former Yugoslavia between January 1, 1991, and a date to be determined by the Security Council" and thereby to "contribute to the restoration and maintenance of peace."[1] In contrast with the 1994 resolution establishing the International Criminal Tribunal for Rwanda,[2] the resolution establishing the ICTY does not explicitly declare national reconciliation to be one of its intended purposes. Nevertheless, reconciliation is widely considered, even by the Tribunal's judges and prosecutors, to be an important objective, albeit an implicit one.

By 1999, the ICTY was indeed contributing to the process in Bosnia and Herzegovina ("Bosnia") of what is often called reconciliation. However, conversations with families of those missing and killed during the conflict reveal that they rejected the term "reconciliation" as a goal of international organizations to the extent that the term included forgiveness. One family member said that the international community should not ask, and should not expect, them ever to forgive those who had killed their loved ones and expelled them from their homes.

---

[1] S.C. Res. 827 (1993), adopted May 25, 1993, operative para. 2 and preambular para. 6.

[2] The U.N. Security Council, in the preamble to the Rwanda Tribunal's statute, declared its conviction that "the prosecution of persons responsible for serious violations of international humanitarian law" would put an end to such crimes in Rwanda and would also "contribute to the process of national reconciliation and to the restoration and maintenance of peace." S.C. Res. 955 (1994), S/RES/955 (1994), adopted Nov. 8, 1994.

He nonetheless hoped that the Tribunal would bring a measure of justice, take power away from the war criminals, and help people understand what had happened in their country. Within the last year, the Tribunal has begun to make progress towards all three of those goals in Bosnia.

B. THE TRIBUNAL'S RECORD DURING ITS FIRST FIVE YEARS (1993–1998)

By the end of 1997, two years after the signing of the Dayton Peace Agreement and the introduction of 60,000 NATO-led troops in Bosnia, the Tribunal was somewhat more than a paper tiger. Seventy-seven alleged war criminals had been indicted (three Bosniaks,[3] eighteen Bosnian Croats, fifty-two Bosnian Serbs, three Serbians, and one Croatian Serb), of whom twenty were in detention at the Hague. More than 200 victims had had the chance to tell their stories in court and two men had been convicted (neither with substantial command authority). One court room was fully functional, and two more were planned. The Tribunal had adopted its rules of procedure and had made critical clarifications on a number of issues, including its jurisdiction, the nature of the armed conflict, the power of the court *vis à vis* sovereign states, war crimes committed under duress, and the legality of arrests by international organizations.

Nevertheless, the Tribunal was far from a success. Its potential impact was eviscerated by the failure to arrest those accused of having organized the genocide against the Bosniaks and other crimes against humanity,[4] and most Bosnians understood very little about the basis of the Tribunal's legitimacy, what it was trying to do, or how it was conducting its work.

Most Croats and Serbs viewed the Tribunal as utterly biased against their communities, and as more than willing to turn a blind eye to atrocities committed by Bosniaks. Most Croats and Serbs believed that too many of "their people" had been pilloried and that too few others had been indicted or arrested for crimes committed against their communities. Croats complained, with justification, that no Serbs had been indicted for the 1991 attack on Dubrovnik or the 1992 offensive against Croats in Bosnia, including the destruction of Mostar. Nor had any Bosniaks been indicted for the expulsion of Croats from parts of Central Bosnia.[5]

---

[3] "Bosniak" is the term used to refer to the ethnicity of Bosnian Muslims. Throughout this chapter, "Croat" and "Serb" are used to refer to ethnic communities within Bosnia. "Croatian" is used to refer to citizens of Croatia, and "Serbian" to citizens of Serbia.

[4] The Dayton Peace Agreement entrusted primary responsibility for arresting those indicted by the Tribunal to the parties to the Agreement.

[5] While the last point is true, no compelling evidence has surfaced of war crimes committed by Bosniaks, other than the three already arrested and prosecuted. The Bosniak leader most widely condemned by the Croats is Dzerad Mlaco, Mayor of Bugogno since 1993. He was widely accused in the Croat media of responsibility for the disappearance (and presumed murder) in 1993 of twenty-one Croats in an area under his control.

Many Serbs felt that the Serbs had been demonized, and many even believed that only Serbs had been indicted, or at least that no one had been indicted for atrocities committed against Serbs. Many considered Alija Izetbegovic a war criminal who should be indicted and viewed his holding of the Presidency as an insult inflicted by the West, all the more rankling in light of the enforced exclusion of Radovan Karadzic, war-time leader of the Bosnian Serbs, from official politics.

Moreover, large portions of the Serb and Croat communities rejected the very legitimacy of the Tribunal. It was one thing for the NATO-led troops to be occupying their territory, but the Tribunal was supposed to be an institution of justice. They viewed the war as a civil war, and considered the Tribunal to be wholly without just foundation.

For their part, large segments of the Bosniak community were disappointed by the Tribunal. They remained skeptical that the architects of the genocide, especially Karadzic and Ratko Mladic, head of the Bosnian Serb Army during the war, would ever be brought to justice. While more than half of all Bosnians had been displaced during the war, the displacement was particularly bitter for Bosniaks, most of whom wanted to return to their pre-war homes and to live in a multi-ethnic country, and some 600,000 of whom had been forced to flee the region altogether.[6] Most Bosniaks were convinced that ultimately the West would sanction the partition of the country and thereby hand victory to the ethnic cleansers. Viewed in such light, the Tribunal struck many Bosniaks as a cynical gesture to salve the guilty conscience of the West, by going after rogue sadists, horrific as their crimes unquestionably were, while allowing the political leaders to remain in power and consolidate the ethnic cleansing. Many thoughtful Bosniaks expressed the view that prosecuting individual killers while granting impunity to the political leaders and top generals was more damaging to the pursuit of justice than no punishment at all.

For Bosniaks, the injustice lay first and foremost in the failure to arrest Karadzic and Mladic, and was compounded by the failure even to indict certain notorious leaders. Sarajevans, in particular, could not comprehend the failure to indict General Galic, the commander of the Serbian Army Corp that had laid siege to Sarajevo for three and one-half years, killing 11,000 civilians. For those Bosniaks who had lived pre-war in areas that became part of the illegal para-state of Herzeg-Bosna (dissolved *de jure* but not *de facto* in 1994), there was the added insult that none of the political leaders of the para-state had even been indicted. The only Croats indicted until 1999 were those responsible for the ethnic cleansing of Central Bosnia.

---

6 In contrast, Serbs and Croats who fled the country during the war went to either neighboring Serbia or Croatia. Those who fled to areas within Bosnia controlled by their ethnic groups were exhorted by their ultra-nationalist leaders to remain. Some were even terrorized into leaving their homes following the final transfer of territories at the end of the war, including 70,000 Serbs who left Bosniak-controlled Sarajevo for Republika Srpska in February 1996.

Disillusionment (primarily among Bosniaks) and feelings of bias (among Serbs and Croats) grew during 1998. International troops arrested two "big fish" in mid-1997 and killed a third when he resisted arrest,[7] but no major war-time leaders were arrested during the following seventeen months.[8] Although thirty-three people had been detained at the Hague by the end of 1998,[9] only the two mentioned, who were indicted for genocide, could be considered "big fish" and in June and August 1998, both of them died in detention: one (Slavko Dokmanovic) due to suicide, and the other (Milan Kovacevic), due to heart attack. Serb leaders blamed the deaths on poor prison conditions and lengthy pre-trial detention. The Serb media trumpeted these charges, leading to widespread condemnation of the Tribunal within the Serb community. The deaths were viewed as cheating justice for quite a different reason within the Bosniak community. The Tribunal decided that the deaths deprived it of jurisdiction, and therefore declined to render verdicts, even in the case of Dokmanovic, who committed suicide on the eve of the verdict's announcement in his case. These would have been the first cases completed on charges of genocide.

A further flashpoint of Serb criticism was October 1998 acquittal of Zejnil Delalić, the Bosniak commander of the Čelebići prison camp where Serbs had been brutalized and murdered. The Tribunal concluded that the evidence did not clearly establish that he had actual knowledge of the murders and other atrocities committed in his camp. Three sub-commanders were convicted, with the harshest punishments meted out for the crimes for which they bore individual, rather than superior, responsibility.

---

[7] Slavko Dokmanovic, a Croatian Serb and former Mayor of Vukovar, was arrested in June 1997, pursuant to the first sealed indictment, by members of the U.N. Transitional Authority for Eastern Slavonia. He was indicted for his leadership role in the massacre of 261 hospital patients, mostly Croats. Milan Kovacevic was arrested by British troops on July 10, 1997. Head of the Prijedor hospital, he was was charged, along with Simo Drljaca, with genocide for their leadership roles in the organization and management of concentration camps in the Prijedor area. Drljaca, Prijedor's Police Chief and Head of the Crisis Staff that controlled Prijedor during the war, was shot by British soldiers, also on July 10, while resisting arrest.

[8] Although Goran Jelisić, arrested Jan. 22, 1998, was indicted for genocide and accused of crimes of horrific brutality, he was (and remains) a gravely mentally disturbed young man who was not a major leader. He pled guilty to thirty-one counts of crimes against humanity and violations of the laws or customs of war; the genocide charge was dismissed for lack of evidence. On Dec. 14, 1999, he was sentenced to forty years' imprisonment.

[9] The information about arrests and detention is drawn from bulletins issued by the Tribunal, and supplemented by information from the Institute for War and Peace Reporting and the Coalition for International Justice. Of the thirty-three who had been detained by the end of 1998, eight were no longer in detention: two had died, one had been transferred to a foreign prison following conviction, one was found not guilty and released, one was released after serving his two and one-half year sentence, and three were released after charges were dropped.

Most Bosnians, to the extent they were aware of these developments, learned of them from their nationalist leaders and the media they controlled. Many concluded that commanders were likely to escape punishment, so long as they personally did not commit atrocities; and that the West, starting with NATO, did not have the will to arrest the major war-time leaders.

The disillusionment among Bosnians with the Tribunal and perceptions of its bias thus arose from several sources: the actual record of the Tribunal, the NATO-led troops, western politicians, and the distortions of the nationalist media. In 1996, the control of the nationalist parties over information, as well as the security and livelihood of their communities, was so strong that it is unlikely that any amount of information from the international community could have made a significant impression. By 1998 the situation was shifting, with the growth of indigenous, independent media. At least some of the negative impressions might have been countered with accurate information.

Even well-read, pluralistic, politically-interested Bosnians of all ethnic communities lacked basic information. At a meeting in November 1998 with Tribunal representatives, Sarajevan civil society leaders made clear that they, and their communities, lacked information about the Tribunal and its procedures, as well as about the evidence it was amassing of what had taken place in Bosnia. Only one had watched more than one of a series of hour-long programs on the Tribunal produced and broadcast by the EU-funded Open Broadcast Network. The general view was that the programs focused on details rather than on fundamental information and issues. The Sarajevans wanted to know the basics. How many people were under indictment, how many were in detention and for what crimes? One journalist, who was fluent in English and thus had access to foreign as well as Bosnian media, thought that there must be 300 people in detention; others did not correct him. What crimes were Croats accused of? Serbs? Bosniaks? What evidence supported the indictments for these crimes? What was the process for deciding whom to investigate and indict? What are the legal requirements of genocide, and the difference, if any, between genocide and ethnic cleansing? And, most basic of all, what was the basis of the Tribunal's legitimacy? One of Bosnia's leading law professors urged that any public information campaign needed to begin with extensive discussion of the Tribunal's position on whether the war had been a war of aggression or a civil war. Most Serbs believed that the war was a civil war within the former Yugoslavia that started when non-Serb republics initiated discrimination, including threats of violence and expulsion, against Serb communities within their midst. They believed, moreover, that an international Tribunal could not have legitimacy over purely internal matters. Many Bosnians believed that, even if atrocities against non-combatants had been committed, they could and should not be punished by an international court if there was substantial provocation.

C. GROWING IMPACT OF THE TRIBUNAL: DECEMBER 1998 TO THE PRESENT

1. Increasing Arrests and Indictments

December 1998 marked the start of a more robust international approach to indicting and arresting the major war-time leaders. Nine persons were arrested within a period of fourteen months, at least four of whom were major figures with substantial command responsibility.[10] General Radislav Krstic, the commander at Srebrenica with authority directly below that of Mladic, was arrested on December 2, 1998. He was charged with command responsibility for, as well as direct participation in, the atrocities committed there. General Momir Talic, Chief-of-Staff of the Bosnian Serb Army since 1998 and war-time commander of the First Krajina Corps, was arrested on August 25, 1999, by Austrian police en route to an OSCE meeting. He and Radoslav Brdjanin (arrested on July 6th) were charged with genocide and other crimes against humanity, including the forced expulsion of 100,000 non-Serbs from the Serb-controlled Autonomous Region of Krajina. The arrest of Brdjanin, a member of Republika Srpska's Parliament and former head of Banja Luka's Crisis Staff, is particularly significant given his status as a civilian leader who masterminded the ethnic cleansing in his region and derived personal gain from his crimes. Pensioned RS Army General Stanislav Galic, the Commander of the Corps that laid siege to, and terrorized the population of Sarajevo for three and a half years, was arrested on December 20 for crimes against humanity.

Two of the nine arrests were made by French and German troops in the French-controlled sector. The French had made only one prior arrest, despite the fact that more than twenty indictees, including Karadzic, are widely believed to reside in the sector they control. Given that the French must approve of, or make, the arrests in their sector, their new resolve is an important step towards the arrest of Karadzic.

Moreover, in March, Louise Arbour, the Tribunal's then-prosecutor, made public the previously sealed arrest warrant against Zeljko "Arkan" Raznjatovic, a Serbian warlord notorious for his brutality, and leader of the paramilitary Tigers. His failure to be publicly indicted had led many non-Serbs to question the Tribunal's investigative capacity. Arbour unsealed the warrant, issued in September 1997, following reports of his involvement in the ethnic cleansing of Albanians from Kosovo, in the hope that disclosure that he was under indictment would discourage others from following his lead. In fact, the disclosure does not seem to have had that effect.

---

[10] The other five were by no means insignificant. All of them had committed numerous atrocities and some exercised at least low-level command responsibility. Dragan Kolundžija and Damir Dosen, both shift commanders at the Keraterm prison camp, were charged with crimes against humanity. Zoran Vukovic and Radomir Kovac were charged with torturing and raping Muslim women, among other atrocities, in Foca. Mitar Vasiljevic was charged, as a member of the White Eagles, with killing more than 100 non-Serbs in the Visegrad area.

The indictments of Slobodan Milosevic and four members of his inner cabinet, made public on May 27, were viewed within Bosnia as extremely significant, even though the indictments are limited to crimes committed in Kosovo. The indictments ensure that representatives of the international community will make no more deals with Milosevic, as they did during the Croatian and Bosnian wars.

On August 9, 1999, Croatia's government succumbed to the Tribunal's demands to transfer to the Tribunal Vinko "Stela" Martinovic, the second most notorious paramilitary, mafia leader in Herceg-Bosna. Charged with crimes against humanity in connection with the expulsion by force and terror of Bosniaks from the Mostar and surrounding areas, and the torture of Bosniaks detained at the Heliodrom center, he is the first indictee from the Bosnian Croat heartland to be brought to the Hague. The Zagreb authorities, however, continued to refuse to transfer his co-indictee, the most wanted paramilitary leader, Mladen "Tuta" Natelic, on health grounds, even though Croatia's Supreme Court ruled in October that no legal impediments to his transfer remained. Tuta is assumed to have evidence that would implicate top Croatian and Bosnian Croat hard-line leaders.

The increasing deaths of paramilitary leaders, during arrests or murders, contributed to a sense among their victims of at least a rough justice, and among their cohorts, of growing apprehension that they might be safer in the Hague than on the streets.[11]

2. Increasing Media Discussion of War Crimes

Complementing the increased arrest of major war-time leaders has been the increased coverage of the crimes with which they are charged. The most dramatic change in coverage has taken place in Republika Srspka, where such coverage had been most lacking and where it is most needed if Bosnia is to remain one country. According to the Institute for War and Peace Reporting, a widely respected reporting service, on September 8, 1999, *Nezavisne Novine*, Republika Srpska's best-selling daily newspaper, "published the first detailed account of mass crimes committed by Serbs against Bosnian Muslims to appear in Republika Srpska and asked why no one has been brought to account."[12] The article referred to the August 1992 massacre of more than 200 men who had survived the Omarska camp outside Prijedor only to be transported to the Koricani cliffs, where they were forced to their deaths. The massacre was the subject of a prosecution at The

---

[11] Slobodan Miljkovic, Deputy Commander of the Gray Wolves, a Bosnian Serb para-military group, was killed in a gun battle in Serbia on Aug. 8, 1998. He had been charged with crimes against humanity, including mass murder. Dragan Gagovic, the former police chief of Foca, was shot while resisting arrest by SFOR troops (the NATO-led Stabilization Force) on Jan. 8, 1999. Arkan was gunned down in Belgrade in mid-January 2000, in order, according to widely-circulating rumors, to keep him from testifying against Milosevic.

[12] Jadranka Slatina, "Bosnian Serb Daily Breaks Taboos," in *Balkan Crisis Reports*, Sept. 10, 1999, published by the Institute for War and Peace Reporting, London.

Hague, and *Nezavisne Novine* also published the testimony of a surviving witness. Following publication of the story, Republika Srpska's public prosecutor reopened a criminal investigation that had been closed seven years earlier. Zeljko Kopanja, the paper's editor-in-chief, received death threats and, on October 22, lost both his legs in a car explosion. Many prominent Serbs condemned the attack. Kopanja, who has continued his war crimes coverage, claims that "Bosnian Serbs are slowly waking up to the reality of what took place during the Bosnian war and that an ever increasing number wish to see individuals tried for war crimes so as to lift the burden of collective guilt." The statements of Milorad Dodik, Republika Srpska's Prime Minister, welcoming the August arrest of General Talic is further evidence of the increasing acceptance among Bosnian Serbs of the Tribunal's legitimacy.

Other papers in Republika Srpska, published in Banja Luka and Bijeljina, have also carried stories of the Tribunal's arrests and charges. The stories are a marked change from earlier accounts portraying most indictees as national martyrs. Despite progress, the martyr image likely still prevails; as of late 1999, the RS government continued to pay 500 German Marks per month to the families of Serbs imprisoned in The Hague.

3.   Increasing Impact

The above developments have contributed to three processes of reconciliation in Bosnia. First, the indictments, and the fear of indictments, have undeniably contributed to the neutralization of some of the leading ethnic cleansers.[13] The shooting of Simo Drljaca by British troops in July 1997, and the arrest of his top cohort, Kovacevic, provide the clearest instances of neutralization. The impact was of two kinds: first, Drljaca and Kovacevic were unequivocally removed from power (unlike mere indictment without arrest); and second, the willingness of British troops to go after Drljaca, the most powerful and best armed person in their sector under public indictment, led to the exodus of most of the indictees then living in the sector, according to reliable reports. As a result, the atmosphere in the Prijedor region dramatically improved, although it has not returned to "normal." The non-Serbs who fled have not returned, as they have not returned to any part of Republika Srpska other than Brcko, which is under an exceptional international mandate. But Prijedor no longer has the feel of a place run by thugs, and serious steps, including numerous assessment visits by displaced persons, are being taken to enable return of pre-war residents. Radovan Karadzic, the war-time leader of Republiska Srpska, was sidelined within his own party, in part as a result of the indictment against him, which forced his withdrawal from official politics. However, there can be little doubt that a more significant cause of his marginal-

---

[13] I use the term "ethnic cleanser" rather than "war criminal" because "war criminal" has a legal meaning as well as a meaning in common parlance, and no one may be called a "war criminal" in the legal sense until trial and conviction.

ization was the 1997 action by NATO-led troops against the paramilitary police and smuggling operations that formed his main power base.

Some prominent political leaders who were involved in ethnic cleansing but have *not* been publicly indicted have become more "moderate," probably at least in part due to the hope that their "born-again" embrace of a unified Bosnia will spare them from indictment. The best example is Bosnia's current foreign minister, Jadranko Prlic. He was one of the top leaders of the illegal state of Herceg-Bosna. It is likely that he signed key orders, including those setting up detention camps. He is considered a master opportunist, and by 1994 was already making statements in support of a unified Bosnia, while nonetheless retaining his position as Vice-President of the HDZ, the Bosnian Croat hard-line nationalist party. He is viewed by his Bosniak "colleagues" in government, as well as by impartial observers, as playing a critical role in Bosnia's future. The threat of indictment very likely has moderated his politics. The specter of an indictment likely also influenced the shift towards moderate nationalism of Biljana Plavsic, widely believed to share responsibility for the ethnic cleansing of Bijeljina and Vukovar. By 1996, she had refashioned herself as a moderate, and became a favorite of the West during her two years as President of Republika Srpska (September 1996 through September 1998). Following the arrest of General Talic in August 1999, "many prominent war-time Serb leaders . . . decided to keep a low profile," according to the Institute for War and Peace Reporting.[14]

A second "reconciliation" process to which the Tribunal has contributed, directly related to the neutralization of some war criminals, is the return of persons who fled in terror from their homes. For instance, the arrest of six persons indicted for the 1992 massacre of residents of the village of Ahmici, and the conviction of five of them in January 2000, has reduced the influence of the remaining ethnic separatists; since the arrests, hundreds of Bosniaks have returned to the area. The neutralization of war criminals may not be the primary reason for return, but it is certainly a necessary condition. For most displaced persons whose homes are now in territory controlled by a different ethnic group, the primary condition for return is security, and removal of the ethnic cleansers is clearly an important security requirement. The chief factor in most cases, however, is the commitment of the NATO-led troops in the area: where they are prepared to intervene to support "minority returns," people are indeed returning. Other important conditions for sustained return include adequate housing, even if not to the prewar home; for working people, the prospect of reasonable work; and for people with children, access to adequate education and basic health care.

A third reconciliation process, for which the Tribunal undeniably deserves primary credit, is the compilation of a copious record of what took place and why, which in turn has begun to promote greater understanding of what happened and acceptance by increasing, though still small, numbers of people of the guilt of

---

[14] Slatina, *supra* note 12.

individuals belonging to their own ethnic communities. The prediction of Judge Antonio Cassese, made in 1997 at the end of his four years as the Tribunal's first President, that the Tribunal would help "to prevent historical amnesia and impede revisionists from denying what happened," is beginning to be realized.

D.   LESSONS TO BE DRAWN FROM THE IMPACT OF THE ICTY IN BOSNIA

1.   The Need to Indict and Arrest the Leaders

The clearest lesson to emerge from the experience of the ICTY is the need to indict and arrest the people with criminal responsibility at the highest political and military levels. This lesson appears also to be borne out by the experience of the International Criminal Tribunal for Rwanda.[15]

Key to the ICTY's impact in Bosnia has been the arrest of major war-time leaders. These arrests have increased respect for the Tribunal and have tended to subdue many other war-time leaders who now fear indictment. The arrests have begun to counter the concerns of victim populations that the Tribunal was merely a paper tiger intended to salve the guilt of the West. Moreover, the arrests of those who continued to wield power in the interests of ethnic separation have helped improve the security situation in a few areas, enabling the return of displaced persons. All of the top leaders under indictment must be arrested, even if they no longer exert influence, if a basic record of the primary events under scrutiny is to be complete.

The importance of arresting the major war-time leaders does not mean that indictments should not be issued by an international criminal court in the absence of the political will and capacity to make such arrests. To the contrary, the ICTY's experience demonstrates that the political will and means to make arrests may develop over time as other options prove ineffective, or as the risk of casualties during arrest drops to an acceptable level, or when a new administration takes office in a troop-deploying country.[16]

2.   The Need for Public Outreach

The second lesson to be drawn from the experience of the ICTY is the importance of public outreach if the International Criminal Court (ICC) is to help enable those affected by the crimes to understand what happened in their country. The capacity to undertake public outreach should be funded from the Court's inception, or, at least, from the initiation of each new set of prosecutions. Information from the start is necessary to counter perceptions of the Court's bias and illegitimacy, which are bound to be fanned by the media controlled by or supportive of those persons who are targets of investigation.

---

[15]   *See* Alinikisa Mafwenga, *supra* Chapter 2.

[16]   For instance, when Tony Blair became head of Britain's government, he and his Foreign Minister Robin Cook launched a dramatic change in Britain's policy towards making arrests.

Information is also needed to help establish realistic expectations. Regrettably and inevitably, the work of the ICC will be slow. It will be even slower if the will or means to arrest indicted persons is lacking. Information cannot affect the pace of arrests, but it can, at least, counter the view among victim populations that a slow pace of arrests reflects the court's ineffectiveness, lack of resolve and/or very legitimacy.

Information must be tailored to and for the populations and needs for which it is intended. The information must be in local languages. At least initially it must address basic issues, including the Court's legitimacy. The international media and non-governmental organizations can contribute to public understanding of an international court, but they cannot fully address issues of legitimacy. The international court itself must have a public outreach capacity and strategy. Local journalists must be brought to the court's seat to see how it operates, to cover its proceedings, and to interview its leading figures and staff. The Court's chief judge/s and prosecutor/s must travel to the country to speak at public forums and, in particular, to journalists and local legal professionals—judges, prosecutors, law professors, lawyers, law students—who can then accurately portray the court to their communities. Conversations with Bosnians suggest that spokespersons and deputy prosecutors could usefully supplement the visits of judges and the prosecutor, but that several visits of the chief judge and prosecutor are needed to establish the Court's credibility. The ICTY finally launched a public outreach program in October 1999. By June 2000, the program should have three regional coordinators operating out of Banja Luka, Zagreb and Pristina as well as staff in the Hague. Delays in the program's launch were due to lack of funds: the current budget calls for US$1 to 2 million per year to be drawn from a trust fund outside the main ICTY budget.[17]

3. The Need to Encourage Other Efforts to Promote Justice, Security, and Reconciliation

Those involved in establishing the ICC, and those who work for it, should recognize its limits. Clearly, it will not be able to prosecute all those who come within its jurisdiction, even if it addresses only exceptional crimes in terms of scale or brutality; it will not even be able to prosecute all those responsible for planning and orchestrating the crimes.

What it can do is develop a strategy for prosecuting representative crimes, and explain that strategy to the affected populations. To the extent possible, it

---

[17] The basic aims of the program will be to dismantle barriers preventing the free flow of accurate information about the Tribunal and to demystify its work; ensure that printed Tribunal materials—press releases, judgments, summaries, updates—are available in local languages at relevant libraries, law schools and public offices in the region; establish partnerships and regional networks with Tribunal counterparts in the region, including prosecutors and defense counsel; and support the launch of a new Tribunal regional television program.

should also support other efforts to hold individuals accountable and discover and publicize the truth of what happened. Of course, such other efforts could undermine the Court and the interests of justice and they should be encouraged only to the extent that they do neither, but where initiatives could promote justice or understanding, the Court, and other international organizations, should do what they can to help. In the long run this will benefit the Court, by relieving it of some of the expectations that it will not be able to satisfy.

The ICTY has not supported other efforts to the extent feasible. In particular, it has not exercised the authority granted it to supervise domestic prosecutions, in large part because of the understandable decision not to devote precious resources to what were viewed as secondary tasks. Pursuant to an agreement reached in February 1996, popularly dubbed "the Rules of the Road," the former warring factions agreed not to arrest persons on suspicion of war crimes until the Tribunal had reviewed files of the charges against them. Although the Tribunal was not a party to the agreement, it did agree to the increased responsibility, brokered by the Office of the High Representative, to the extent consistent with available resources. It took the Tribunal nearly three years to establish a systematic process for reviewing the files, by which time there was a backlog of some 300 to 400 files.[18] This backlog caused substantial delays in local prosecutions.[19] While many Bosnian courts are not sufficiently independent to conduct fair war crimes trials, in some regions courts have demonstrated independence. The court in the city of Tuzla, for instance, dismissed war crimes charges against two persons on the grounds of insufficient evidence. The approach envisioned by the Rules of the Road and the Tribunal's Statute was that the Tribunal would authorize domestic prosecutions where sufficient evidence was presented, and then would exercise its authority to intervene if and when international standards were violated. The Tribunal has declined to exercise its authority to intervene even where violations appeared blatant. Both delay and failure to intervene are understandable given the Tribunal's limited resources. It may be hoped that adequate resources will be allocated to the ICC to enable it to support procedures established to supervise domestic prosecutions.

Efforts should also be made to devise procedures by which the ICC may share information with responsible authorities concerning the criminal culpability of police, members of the armed forces, and public officials, even in the absence of sufficient evidence for an indictment. Of course, such sharing of infor-

---

[18] The Tribunal finally devoted resources, in early 1999, to hire two lawyers to review the Rules of the Road files. Until that time, it had made available up to five language assistants to work with volunteer lawyers, each of whom spent several months at the Hague and were supplied by the Coalition for International Justice and the American Bar Association's Central and Eastern Europe Law Initiative.

[19] The backlog also resulted in routine breaches of the Rules of the Road, whereby parties arrested persons before their files had been reviewed, but delayed pursuing prosecutions, so that suspects remained in pre-trial detention for unnecessary periods.

mation should only be considered where a responsible procedure exists for the vetting of these sectors, and where a procedure can be devised that safeguards the rights of the suspects. Discussions to this end have been under way in Bosnia between the Tribunal, the U.N. (responsible for the vetting of the Bosnian police), and the Office of the High Representative.

A vexing question concerns the compatibility between prosecutions and a truth commission that aims to examine roughly the same time period and events. The ICTY's prosecutor has objected to efforts to establish a truth commission on the grounds that the commission, as proposed, could undermine ICTY's prosecutions, or be used by nationalist authorities as a "soft option" and an excuse not to cooperate with the ICTY. Although these arguments undeniably have merit, it is clear that the ICTY will never address all of the information gaps about what happened, even during the period of its jurisdiction beginning in 1991.[20] One Bosnian civil society leader who opposes establishment of a truth commission until conclusion of the trials of the major indictees, identifies at least two huge gaps in information that will be left when the Tribunal finishes its work:

1. What were the developments pre-1991 that led to the wars of Yugoslavia's dissolution?

2. *Why* were particular crimes committed?

The Bosnian who poses these questions fully realizes their irrelevance to the work of the Tribunal, but believes that Bosnians will need answers to these questions if they are to understand and accept the Tribunal's findings.

---

[20] For instance, its decision not to pursue investigations or publish information about persons who have died means that several persons of major responsibility will escape the Tribunal's scrutiny, including those most responsible for the illegal para-state of Herceg Bosna (Franjo Tudjman, former Croatian Defense Minister Susak, and Herceg-Bosna war-time President Mate Boban), Simo Drljaca, Slavko Dokmanovic and Arkan.

PART II
A MERGER OF INTERNATIONAL CRIMINAL LAW, HUMANITARIAN LAW, AND HUMAN RIGHTS LAW?

CHAPTER 4

TOWARD INTERNATIONAL HUMAN RIGHTS CRIMES: AN ASIAN PERSPECTIVE ON HUMAN RIGHTS AND INTERNATIONAL CRIMINAL LAW

Clarence J. Dias

The renowned Czech author, Milan Kundera, reminds us that "the struggle of man over power is the struggle of memory over forgetting." Two memories are recalled herein. The first relates to the fact that the preparatory process leading up to the U.N. World Conference on Human Rights (Vienna, 1993) involved repeated calls for an International Criminal Court (ICC). The plea was explicitly reiterated in the Vienna Declaration and Programme of Action (VDPA) adopted by consensus at the Vienna World Conference. Vienna clearly provided new impetus for the creation of an international criminal court, after debate over instituting such a tribunal seemed to have reached a stalemate during several long years of discussions within the International Law Commission. In the tortuous process of negotiations that culminated in the Rome Treaty, the role of the Vienna Conference might have been submerged amidst discussions on numerous and complex issues of criminal law that needed resolution. It is important and pertinent, however, to recall the link between the protection of human rights and the ICC. The second memory is based in the Asia-Pacific region, the only region in the world yet to create a regional human rights system.

A. THE ASIA-PACIFIC REGION AND THE VIENNA WORLD CONFERENCE ON HUMAN RIGHTS

In preparation for the Vienna World Conference on Human Rights, some 240 representatives of more than 110 non-governmental organizations from some twenty-six countries across Asia and the Pacific came together in Bangkok from March 23 to 25, 1993. They produced the Bangkok NGO Declaration on Human Rights, a document that calls for effective relief and remedies for victims of human rights violations and for full accountability from all violators of human rights. It is worth recalling the words of the NGO statement issued in Bangkok on April 2, 1993: "It must be said and said again, that the NGOs of the Asia-Pacific region are united as never before. The threshold has been crossed and we will *not* allow further erosion of human rights. We will not rest until existing rights are not just words but become a reality for all peoples of Asia and the Pacific." Key to achieving such an objective are the criminalization, under international law, of human rights violations and the unwavering enforcement of such criminalization through an effective permanent international penal court.

During the Bangkok Conference, diverse NGOs worked on issues relating to women, children, minorities, indigenous peoples, workers, the disabled, and other groups, and focused on a range of concerns including torture, arbitrary detention, involuntary disappearances, militarization and war, impoverishment, exploitation, sexual and other forms of slavery, expulsion, marginalization, and discrimination. The participants united around a common agenda:

- identifying and defining human rights crimes,
- eliminating all forms and practices of impunity,
- ensuring prompt and effective relief, redress and remedies for victims of human rights violations and denials, and
- holding all perpetrators of human rights violations fully accountable and criminally liable for their acts or omissions.

The Bangkok NGO Conference singled out political arrest and detention and the criminalization of political prisoners, torture in any form whatsoever, and involuntary disappearances as areas around which human rights crimes need to be defined and enforced. On the question of impunity, the Conference stressed that international standards clearly require all states to:

1. undertake proper investigations into human rights violations if the full truth is to emerge;
2. ensure that all those responsible for human rights violations are brought to justice by prosecution of the public officials responsible and by ensuring action against immunity or exemption from punishment;
3. ensure that all alleged perpetrators are brought to trial and that such trials conclude with a clear verdict of guilt or innocence; and
4. ensure against "the systematic imposition of penalties that bear little relationship to the seriousness of the offenses" and fail to deter further human rights violations.

The Bangkok NGO Conference called for the creation of "adequate international machinery to which individuals whose rights are violated could turn for protection" and, in particular, for the establishment of an international penal court to try cases of gross violations of human rights. Among its list for "Action by the United Nations," the Bangkok NGO Conference specifically called for establishing a Permanent International Court on Human Rights with compulsory jurisdiction over all cases of human rights violations, and for a Permanent International Criminal Court, to which individuals have direct access, that would provide both criminal sanctions and civil remedies in cases of war crimes, crimes against peace and crimes against humanity, including gender-specific abuses in international and internal armed conflicts.

Immediately after the Bangkok NGO Conference, the ministers and other representatives of Asian states met at Bangkok from March 29 to April 2, 1993, and produced their own intergovernmental Bangkok Declaration. Responding to that Declaration, the NGOs issued a statement of particular relevance to the present topic. The NGO Response questioned: "We could not help but note that specific references to torture, freedom of expression and the lack of rule of law have been deleted in the final draft. We are left to ask *why*?" In addition, the Response commented: "The fear of governments in our region to account for the continued violation of human rights is evident in their attempt to give primacy to national human rights mechanisms—mechanisms which we know too well they will direct and control themselves. This is *not* accountability and offers little hope of appropriate remedies." The Asia-Pacific NGOs pursued this issue at the Vienna NGO Forum on All Human Rights for All, where some three thousand delegates from 1529 registered NGOs adopted a Report of the Forum which stressed that a permanent, independent and impartial International Criminal Court should be established to prosecute gross violations of human rights and humanitarian law, including genocide, arbitrary killings, disappearances, torture, apartheid, war crimes, and other grave breaches of the Geneva Conventions. The Report recommended that non-governmental organizations have an input into this work.

The VDPA reaffirmed this call and, five years later, the Rome Conference adopted the treaty creating the ICC. The process of negotiations leading to the treaty was a difficult one. Human rights were not forgotten in the process but often were *sub silentio*. Even with the success of Rome, there are formidable tasks and challenges ahead for the human rights movement in Asia and the Pacific. It may still be premature to press for the central concerns that are involved, but the time will come, and there is no reason to stifle the processes of thinking, strategizing, and forging solidarities around such concerns.

B. FROM CRIMES AGAINST HUMANITY TO INTERNATIONAL HUMAN RIGHTS CRIMES

The concept of crimes against international law, for which violators bear an individual criminal responsibility, is well-established. Since the time of Grotius, the development of customary international law has included consideration of certain conduct as a violation of the law of nations and therefore a universal crime. Piracy on the high seas was perhaps the first and still classic example of this category of universal crime whose perpetrators are considered the enemies of mankind. International law permits any state to define and prescribe punishment for offenses deemed to be international crimes. It also permits any state to apply its laws to prosecute and punish such offenses, even in cases where the state has no links of territory with the offense and no links of nationality with either the offender or the victim. This is a most important development in international law. It ensures that the perpetrator of an international crime will have no place to hide but may be brought to justice anywhere in the world where found, free from political and procedural wrangling over extradition.

The process of defining international crimes received a great impetus at the end of World War II with the decision of the allied victors to create an international military tribunal for the trial of war criminals. The London Agreement of August 8, 1945, between the United States, U.S.S.R., Great Britain, and France created the International Military Tribunal in a Charter that provided for the composition and basic procedures of the Tribunal. Article 6 of the Charter defined the crimes within the jurisdiction of the Tribunal as:

a. *Crimes against peace:* Namely, planning, preparation, initiation or waging a war of aggression, or a war in violation of international treaties, agreements or assurances, or participation in a common plan or conspiracy for the accomplishment of any of the foregoing.

b. *War crimes:* Namely, violations of the laws or customs of war. Such violations shall include, but not be limited to, murder, ill-treatment or deportation for slave labor or for any other purpose of civilian populations of or in occupied territory, murder or ill-treatment of prisoners of war or persons on the seas, killing of hostages, plunder of public or private property, wanton destruction of cities, towns or villages, or devastation not justified by military necessity.

c. *Crimes against humanity:* Namely, murder, extermination, enslavement, deportation, and other inhumane acts committed against any civilian population, before or during the war, or persecutions on political, racial or religious grounds in execution of or in connection with any crime within the jurisdiction of the Tribunal, whether or not in violation of the domestic law of the country where perpetrated.

International law scholars criticized the Charter for retroactively defining crimes, especially in the category of crimes against humanity. A few eminent jurists, notably Chief Justice Harlan Fiske Stone of the U.S. Supreme Court, denounced the Nuremberg trials based on the Charter as an attempt to justify the application of the power of the victor to the vanquished, "dressed up with a false facade of legality" and as a "high-grade lynching party."[1]

Whatever the state of the law in 1945, the Charter was subsequently adhered to by nineteen other states and in December 1946 the United Nations General

[1] MASON, ALPHEUS THOMAS, HARLAN FISKE STONE: PILLAR OF THE LAW 715 (1956).

Assembly unanimously adopted a resolution affirming the principles of law recognized by the Charter of the Nuremberg Tribunal and the judgment of the Tribunal.[2] Since 1946, the process of defining international crimes has proceeded under customary law and under treaties that have criminalized such matters as the unlawful seizure of aircraft, the taking of hostages, genocide and traffic in persons for prostitution. Draft articles on state responsibility, prepared in the context of the International Law Commission, add that an international crime may result from "a serious breach on a widespread scale of an international obligation of essential importance for safeguarding the human being, such as those prohibiting slavery, genocide and apartheid." In addition, the International Law Commission has drafted a Code of Offenses against the Peace and Security of Mankind which it transmitted to governments for comments and observations.[3] Part II of the Code identifies twelve specific crimes against peace and security: aggression (Article 15); threat of aggression (Article 16); intervention (Article 17); colonial domination and other forms of alien domination (Article 18); genocide (Article 19); apartheid (Article 20); systematic or mass violations of human rights (Article 21); exceptionally serious war crimes (Article 22); the recruitment, use, financing, and training of mercenaries (Article 23); international terrorism (Article 24); illicit traffic in narcotic drugs (Article 25); and wilful and serious damage to the environment (Article 26).

Many of the above revisions remain controversial and consensus among governments is unlikely to be reached in the foreseeable future. Moreover, since the Draft Articles are limited in their coverage to crimes that threaten the peace and security of mankind, Article 21 of the Draft covers only systematic or mass violations of human rights and not violations that are less widespread. Hence, much work remains to define international human rights crimes, especially when not linked to war crimes or threats to the peace and security of mankind. The negotiations in Rome were sufficiently complex and delicate that a compromise was struck regarding the definition of the crimes over which the ICC would exercise jurisdiction. The Statute provides for jurisdiction over genocide, war crimes, crimes against humanity and aggression. The crimes against humanity are listed and defined to include: murder, extermination, enslavement, deportation or forcible transfer of populations, imprisonment, torture, rape, sexual slavery, enforced prostitution, forced pregnancy and enforced sterilization, persecution, enforced disappearances, apartheid, and other inhumane acts. Both state and non-state actors are within the reach of the Court's jurisdiction insofar as these crimes are concerned, but, in order to gain acceptance, a compromise was reached to raise the threshold through requiring that the act be in "furtherance of a state or organizational policy" (Article (2)(a)). The threshold for investigation was low-

---

[2] Affirmation of the Principles of International Law Recognized by the Charter of the Nuremberg Tribunal, G.A. Res. 95, 1st Sess., Supp., Oct. 23–Dec. 15, 1946, at 188, U.N. Doc. A/236 (1946).

[3] Draft Articles on the Draft Code of Crimes Against the Peace and Security of Mankind, U.N. Doc. A/46/405 (1991), 30 I.L.M. 1584 (1991).

ered, however, by requiring that the acts under investigation have been committed on a "widespread *or* systematic" scale, rather than a widespread *and* systematic scale. Thus either a pattern (systematic) or quantitative (widespread) element will suffice to commence an investigation.

The ICC Statute's inclusion of war crimes and aggression is significant because human rights violations inevitably accompany such crimes, but it should be recalled that the human rights community during the Vienna World Conference called for an International Criminal Court and not just an International War Crimes Court. Similarly, the inclusion of genocide in the Statute is welcome, although the continued requirement of specific intent in the definition of the crime may need reconsideration in the light of fifty years of experience.

In sum, significant progress was made at Rome towards the definition of international human rights crimes, but clearly much work lies ahead. In this respect, it is worth recalling paragraph 30 of the first section of the VDPA, which provides a list of potential international human rights crimes. They are torture and cruel, inhuman and degrading treatment or punishment; summary and arbitrary executions; disappearances; arbitrary detentions; all forms of racism, racial discrimination and apartheid; foreign occupation and colonial domination; xenophobia; poverty; hunger and other denials of economic, social and cultural rights; religious intolerance; terrorism; discrimination against women, and the lack of the rule of law.

C. THE PROBLEM OF COMPLEMENTARITY IN ASIA

The ICC Statute unequivocally adopts the principle of complementarity as a central and essential element. This means that while the jurisdiction of the ICC, within the limits imposed by the Statute, is inherent, such jurisdiction is neither primary nor exclusive. The ICC is not replacing prosecution by national courts nor arrogating to itself the right to try all cases where the core crimes are implicated. As a result of the principle of complementarity, the ICC can step in only where and when national trial procedures are either unavailable or ineffective. Regardless of the type of crime involved, the ICC must determine before proceeding that national prosecution is unavailable or inadequate.

The regime of complementarity is meant to protect national sovereignty while ensuring that criminals are prosecuted. If a State Party does not want ICC investigation, in principle such Party must undertake an effective investigation itself. In the Asian context, however, the principle of complementarity may well degenerate into a glaring loophole and wide-open escape clause. It is unrealistic to expect many Asian governments to rush ratify the ICC Statute. Indeed, aside from the U.S., the strongest resistance in Rome came from the Asian states. It is thus crucial for Asian NGOs to appreciate the vital need to campaign strongly for the development and strengthening of national criminal justice systems.

Such a campaign has a legislative component and an institutional component. Legislatively, Asian governments must fully incorporate into national law the definitions of international human rights crimes adopted prior to, during, and after the Rome Conference. The reluctance of Asian governments to ratify the Rome treaty should not extend to accepting the internationally-negotiated definition of crimes against humanity. No Asian government, and indeed no government worldwide, can expect to retain its credibility or its legitimacy if it claims a sovereign right to perpetrate or condone crimes against humanity. The claim to decline international jurisdiction for reasons of sovereignty is unmasked as sheer hypocrisy if it is accompanied by a refusal to accept and exercise national jurisdiction. Hence, a cardinal national legislative task is to incorporate fully definitions of international (universal) crimes into national law. An important related task is to review and repeal national legislation granting immunity from liability or process and to prohibit totally any policies, laws or practices of impunity.

An important institutional agenda must accompany and complement the legislative agenda outlined. It is essential to develop and strengthen national investigative, prosecutorial and judicial mechanisms and institutions. Failure to do so will make mockery of national laws and constitute an open invitation to lawlessness.

At the international level much remains to be done, but Rome provided a foundation upon which to build. At the national level, especially in the countries of Asia, NGOs and activists need to work creatively to convert the gains of Rome into national advances that can guarantee not only truth and justice but human security, dignity and well-being.

CHAPTER 5

HOW THE INTERNATIONAL CRIMINAL COURT SHOULD HELP IMPLEMENT INTERNATIONAL HUMANITARIAN LAW

Patrick Zahnd

The Martens Clause, which is the bottom line and the essence of international humanitarian law (IHL), was codified a century ago during the first Peace Conference of 1899.[1] Its centennial and the celebration in 1999 of the fiftieth anniversary of the four Geneva Conventions[2] was an opportunity to listen to the voices of the victims of war speak about the importance of these laws, of limits in war, and the echoes of conflict, expressing the dictates of the public conscience.

The International Criminal Court (ICC) is being established in order to address one of the most serious problems of armed conflicts, namely, the fact that too many atrocities are committed during such conflicts. Such atrocities create hatred and disruption in society, exacerbating the effects of the conflicts themselves and sowing the seeds for further confrontation in later generations. The ideal, of course, would be to avoid armed conflict altogether. Since that has so far not proved possible, there must be serious and effective efforts to implement the absolute limitations that are part of all civilizations and that have been codified and universally accepted by all states as the laws of humanity, the *jus in bello.*

---

[1] The Martens Clause was included in the Preamble to the second Convention during the Hague Peace Conference of 1899. It reads: "The inhabitants and the belligerents remain under the protection and the rule of the principles of the law of nations, as they result from the usages established among civilized peoples, from the laws of humanity, and from the dictates of public conscience." Convention (II) Respecting the Laws and Customs of War on Land, July 29, 1899, T.S. No. 403, 32 Stat. 1803.

[2] Geneva Convention for the Amelioration of the Condition of the Wounded and Sick in Armed Forces in the Field (Geneva Convention I), Aug. 12, 1949, 75 U.N.T.S. 31; 6 U.S.T.S. 3114, 4 Bevans 853; Geneva Convention for the Amelioration of the Condition of the Wounded, Sick and Shipwrecked Members of Armed Forces at Sea (Geneva Convention II), Aug. 12, 1949, 75 U.N.T.S. 85; 6 U.S.T.S. 3217; Geneva Convention Relative to the Treatment of Prisoners of War (Geneva Convention III), Aug. 12, 1949, 75 U.N.T.S. 135; 6 U.S.T.S. 3316; Geneva Convention Relative to the Protection of Civilian Persons in Time of War (Geneva Convention IV), Aug. 12, 1949, 75 U.N.T.S. 287; 6 U.S.T.S. 3516.

Unfortunately, the law of armed conflict is not taken sufficiently seriously. One goal should be to make its respect a matter of disciplined behavior and automatic reaction. Instead, sometimes it is not taught at all and in other instances it is insufficiently integrated into military doctrine and practice or it is referred to in a way that is not conducive to its genuine incorporation in military training. Another reason for the lack of serious attention is the fact that violations of this law often are not punished. A law that is neither properly taught nor properly enforced loses credibility. The purpose of the ICC is to restore this credibility, not only with the military, but also with the civilian society from which the military stems and receives support, and from which so many combatants are enlisted.

The concept that a state can punish war criminals even if they are not its own nationals, and even if the crime occurred in another territory, is a long-standing one. In fact, the first trial of this sort took place in the fifteenth century,[3] and states continue to exercise this right. Most notable, of course, are the Nuremberg and Tokyo trials and the recent international tribunals created for the former Yugoslavia and for Rwanda. There have also been many national trials of war criminals. The Geneva Conventions of 1949, to which virtually all states of the world are party, reinforces this universal jurisdiction by making it a duty for states to identify, prosecute, and punish all persons, whatever their nationality, who have committed particularly serious war crimes ("grave breaches"). The list of grave breaches has been extended in Protocol I of 1977 Additional to the Geneva Conventions, to which over 150 states are party.[4]

If all the States Party to the Geneva Conventions properly carried out their duty, there would be few of the problems being faced today during armed conflicts. Unfortunately, too many states have not adopted the necessary national legislation, and even those that have done so all too often have not applied the law. Some improvement has occurred as a result of efforts of the Advisory Services on international humanitarian law (IHL) that were created in 1996 by the International Committee of the Red Cross (ICRC), following a recommendation to this effect by States Party to the Geneva Conventions. A growing and important number of states are now in the process of adopting national legislation allowing for the prosecution of foreign nationals who are suspected of war crimes. The examples of Belgium and Spain and the initiatives taking place in Central America may be cited. The ICRC thus has supported the idea that the ICC should be complementary to national systems, an approach adopted in the ICC Statute.

---

[3] In 1474 Peter von Hagenbach was tried and condemned before a court composed of twenty-seven judges of the Holy Roman Empire for crimes committed by his troops against civilians. Paul A. Marquardt, *The Constitutionality of an International Criminal Court*, 33 COLUM. J. TRANSNAT'L L. 73, 76–77 (1995).

[4] Protocol Additional (No. I) to the Geneva Conventions of Aug. 12, 1949, and Relating to the Protection of Victims of International Armed Conflicts (Protocol I) of June 8, 1977, 1977 U.N.J.Y.B. 95, arts. 11 and 85(3).

It thus remains first and foremost the duty of states to punish violations of IHL; the ICC will only hear a case if it is clear that the state having jurisdiction is unable or obviously unwilling to bring the suspect to trial.

For the ICRC, deterrence is the main purpose of enacting criminal sanctions for violations of IHL, that is, the hope that criminalization will improve compliance with the rules and thereby reduce the number of victims of such violations. It is anticipated that states will make a greater effort to teach and integrate the law effectively within state institutions and civil society, and will prosecute and punish the perpetrators of any IHL violations. Additional motivation to do so should come from the ability of the ICC to exercise complementary jurisdiction and step in if the state fails to act. New motivation for individuals to comply should stem from their awareness that the law is taken seriously and there is a real likelihood of prosecution and punishment should the law be violated.

In this regard, it is extremely important that the law be seen to apply to all persons equally. There must be no sense of immunity stemming from an accused's assumption that the state will provide protection against prosecution. By definition, IHL lays down international standards: no individual and no nation can be above the law, for such an approach would totally undermine the foundation that deems certain behavior in war always unacceptable, irrespective of who started the conflict and why.

It is a very positive sign that the ICC Statute establishes the Court's jurisdiction over crimes committed in both international and non-international armed conflicts. The range of crimes to be included in non-international armed conflicts was the subject of much debate because some states remain uncomfortable with the idea that international law regulates what is done by a state in its own territory. A compromise was reached, however, which gives important recognition to the notion that a violation of just one of the many rules in internal armed conflict amounts to an international crime. The list is not complete—in particular and regrettably, neither the use of prohibited weapons is included, nor the intentional starvation of civilians, although these are prohibited under customary law rules. It is gratifying, however, that there was no undue difficulty in listing the use of children under fifteen as combatants in internal armed conflict and sexual violence, as well as the more classic list of rules relating to the protection of persons in the power of the enemy and basic rules relating to the conduct of hostilities.

The list of crimes for international armed conflict is more complete, apart from the rather obvious and politically-motivated exclusion of certain weapons of mass destruction. Even here, the Statute provides for the possibility of adding to the list of prohibited weapons, provided that such prohibition is clearly generally recognized.

The most unfortunate part of the Statute is Article 124, which gives ratifying states the possibility of preventing the Court from having jurisdiction over their war crimes for a period of seven years. This provision was probably included so that states could feel more confident that they would have sufficient time to properly train their military. The ICRC regrets this setback and hopes that states will make an effort not to use this provision.

A positive aspect of the Statute is the power it gives the Prosecutor to initiate investigations and indict persons if there is sufficient evidence. The power is quite severely circumscribed by procedure to ensure that the prosecutor cannot come to any quick or arbitrary decision. Nonetheless, giving the right to bring cases to a body other than states holds great hope that this issue will become depoliticized. One of the great problems with IHL previously, and one that created considerable cynicism, has been the fact that decisions to prosecute have been selective and based on criteria that are not related to objective rules of international law. The ICC procedure should ensure greater objectivity and therefore foster a greater sense of justice.

For its part, the ICRC has actively supported the creation of the ICC and intends to encourage wide ratification of the Statute. In so doing, it hopes to help create awareness of how the Court should work, as provided for in its long and somewhat complicated Statute. Unfortunately, a lot of incorrect information has been circulated that has raised unfounded fears. In this regard, it is important to point out that the Statute will not have retroactive effect, so states will be given the chance to start afresh. The ICRC's Advisory Service on IHL, through its delegations around the world, will cooperate with states in order to help introduce the necessary modifications in law and practice that will be needed to enable ratification and correct implementation of the Statute.

CHAPTER 6

WOMEN'S ISSUES IN INTERNATIONAL CRIMINAL LAW: RECENT DEVELOPMENTS AND THE POTENTIAL CONTRIBUTION OF THE ICC

Kelly Dawn Askin

A. INTRODUCTION

International criminal law has made greater progress on women's issues since 1993 than during any other time in recorded history. Assessing the current status of women's issues in this field necessitates a review of the treatment of gender and sex based crimes in the International Criminal Tribunals for the former Yugoslavia (ICTY) and Rwanda (ICTR).[1] Following this, pertinent provisions of the ICC Statute[2] are described and discussed.

The Yugoslavian and Rwandan Tribunals, established by the United Nations Security Council in 1993 and 1994 under the mandate of Chapter VII of the U.N. Charter, have jurisdiction to prosecute certain serious violations of international humanitarian law committed in the territories of the former Yugoslavia and in Rwanda. The Tribunals, which are subsidiary organs of the U.N. Security Council,

---

[1] International Tribunal for the Prosecution of Persons Responsible for Serious Violations of International Humanitarian Law Committed in the Territory of the Former Yugoslavia Since 1991, U.N. Doc. S/25704, Annex (1993), *reprinted in* 32 I.L.M. 1192 (1993) [hereinafter Yugoslavian Statute or ICTY Statute]; International Criminal Tribunal for the Prosecution of Persons Responsible for Genocide and Other Serious Violations of International Humanitarian Law Committed in the Territory of Rwanda and Rwandan Citizens Responsible for Genocide and Other Such Violations Committed in the Territory of Neighboring states, Between 1 January 1994 and 31 December 1994, S.C. Res. 955, Annex, U.N. SCOR, 49th Sess., Res. & Dec., at 15, U.N. Doc. S/INF/50 Annex (1994), *reprinted in* 33 I.L.M. 1602 (1994) [hereinafter Rwandan Statute or ICTR Statute].

[2] United Nations Diplomatic Conference of Plenipotentiaries on the Establishment of an International Criminal Court, Rome Statute of the International Criminal Court, July 17, 1998, U.N. Doc. A/CONF.183/9, *reprinted in* 37 I.L.M. 999 (1998) [hereinafter ICC Statute].

are historic for many reasons, including the participation and influence of women in them and the Tribunals' prosecution and redress of gender and sex based crimes.

Traditionally, waging war, proscribing the conduct of war, and prosecuting violations of the laws of war, have been considered man's business, despite the reality that women frequently suffer enormous casualties during periods of armed conflict and women increasingly participate in conflicts as combatants. Recently, some of the misguided perceptions that have led to excluding women from the purview of humanitarian law have begun to change, in turn bringing about an evolution in law. As a prime example, the International Criminal Tribunals are composed of three separate organs: the Registry, the Judges Chambers, and the Office of the Prosecutor. All three of these organs have been headed by a woman, sometimes concurrently.[3] Judges Florence Mumba and Patricia Wald are the two females of the fourteen judges who sit on the Yugoslavian Tribunal. On the Rwandan Tribunal, President Navanethem Pillay is the sole female out of nine judges. Thus, in the two Tribunals, only three of the twenty-three judges are women. Of course, there were no women judges and no high level female prosecutors participating in the Nuremberg and Tokyo Trials, so three female judges, while an inadequate number, nevertheless constitutes progress, and their presence has made a remarkable difference in the jurisprudence coming out of the Tribunals, including, but not limited to, the jurisprudence concerning gender or sex based crimes.

The presence of women in decision-making positions provides invaluable contributions to law, society, and the legitimacy as well as the functioning of the Tribunals. Significantly, each of the twenty-three judges, regardless of their sex, have a mandate to fairly and impartially adjudicate the crimes being prosecuted, regardless of the sex of the victim or perpetrator, and irrespective of the gendered or sexualized nature of the crime(s). The presence of both sexes incorporates a wider range of knowledge, experience, and perspective into all aspects of the Tribunal's work than would occur if the panel of judges were limited to men only. It is also crucial to incorporate women's participation and experience throughout the Tribunal, including as investigators and translators. It should be noted that gender, racial, and geographic equity are notably absent in professional level positions and higher. Within the ICTY in particular, white men from Western countries dominate the high level positions.

---

[3] Judge Gabrielle Kirk McDonald (U.S.) was the President of the ICTY from 1997–1999; Judge Florence Mumba (Zambia) was elected Vice-President of the ICTY in 1999; Judge Louise Arbour (Canada) was the Chief Prosecutor of both Tribunals from 1996–1999, until replaced by Carla Del Ponte (Switzerland) in 1999; Dorothee de Sampayo Garrido-Nijgh (Netherlands) has served as the Registrar of the ICTY since 1995. Thus, for some two years between 1997–1999, all three organs of the ICTY were headed by a woman. Judge Navanethem Pillay was elected to the Presidency of the ICTR in 1999.

In the past few years, extraordinary progress in defining and prosecuting gender and sex based crimes has been achieved in the Yugoslavian and Rwandan Tribunals,[4] and the ICC Statute takes even further strides in identifying and potentially redressing crimes committed exclusively or disproportionately against women and girls.

B. JUDGMENTS OF THE ICTY AND ICTR

Over half of the public indictments in the ICTY have brought charges for sex crimes; the ICTR has shown far less effort to include charges of various forms of sexual violence in its indictments, even though reports suggest that its commission is just as prevalent.[5] When the charges are included in the original or amended indictments, prosecution of the gender or sex based crimes has proved to be extremely successful.

The sole Article of the Yugoslavian Statute that explicitly mentions sex crimes is Article 5(g) which designates rape as a crime against humanity. In the Rwandan Statute, Article 3(g) includes rape as a crime against humanity, while Article 4(e) enunciates rape and enforced prostitution as a violation of Common Article 3 and Additional Protocol II. It is significant that the Office of the Prosecutor (OTP) has moved beyond the explicit language of these provisions to find other bases on which to prosecute sex crimes. The OTP has charged, and the judges have accepted by confirming the indictments, various forms of sexual violence as grave breaches, violations of the laws or customs of war, genocide, crimes against humanity, and violations of Common Article 3 and Additional Protocol II.[6]

Despite the prosecutions, the fact remains that the language of most humanitarian law instruments is deficient when it comes to addressing women's issues and crimes committed on the basis of sex or gender.[7] Long established or specifically identifiable crimes thus must be prosecuted under language that inappro-

---

[4] For a review of the historical treatment of women in wartime, *see* SUSAN BROWN-MILLER, AGAINST OUR WILL (1975); Patricia Viseur Sellers, *Rape and Sexual Assault as Violations of International Humanitarian Law, in* SUBSTANTIVE AND PROCEDURAL ASPECTS OF INTERNATIONAL CRIMINAL LAW (Gabrielle Kirk McDonald & Olivia Swaak-Goldman eds., forthcoming 2000); KELLY DAWN ASKIN, WAR CRIMES AGAINST WOMEN: PROSECUTION IN INTERNATIONAL WAR CRIMES TRIBUNALS (1997).

[5] *See* Tribunal web sites at: <www.un.org/icty; www.ictr.org>. For a review of the indictments in each Tribunal which bring charges of sexual violence, *see* Kelly D. Askin, *Sexual Violence in Decisions and Indictments of the Yugoslav and Rwandan Tribunals: Current Status,* 93 AM. J. INT'L L. 97 (1999).

[6] For extensive treatment of women's issues in the Tribunals, *see* Sellers, *Rape and Sexual Assault as Violations of International Humanitarian Law, supra* note 4.

[7] The Hague Regulations provide, as regards to sexual violence: "Family honour and rights . . . must be respected." Convention Respecting the Laws and Customs of War on Land (Second Hague IV), of Oct. 18, 1907, 36 Stat. 2277, T.S. No. 539, at art. XLVI. The Fourth Geneva

priately characterizes certain crimes and perpetuates harmful stereotypes of the victims.[8] In the Yugoslavian Tribunal, for example, the OTP often indicts sex crimes as violations of the laws or customs of war under the language of Common Article 3, and charges rape crimes as "outrages upon personal dignity, in particular humiliating and degrading treatment." This mischaracterization of sexual violence as a violation of the victim's dignity or honor stigmatizes the victim by inferring that she is somehow dishonored, defiled, or shamed by the sexual violence committed against her. In addition, the language fails to identify the sexual nature of the crime committed and neglects to treat rape crimes as crimes of violence instead of crimes of moral integrity. As described below, this is an area where the ICC Statute has made enormous progress in both expansively enumerating and more appropriately characterizing various forms of gender or sex based crimes.

The two Tribunals have issued judgments after full trials on the merits[9] in three cases to be discussed here, specifically the Čelebići and Furundžija Judgments of the Yugoslavian Tribunal and the Akayesu Judgment of the Rwandan Tribunal. The Tadić Judgment also addressed sexual violence and Tadić was successfully prosecuted for crimes involving cruel treatment and inhumane acts that included sexual violence against men,[10] but the other three judgments develop the women's issues more substantively.

1. Čelebići Judgment

In *Čelebići,* the first trial in the ICTY to address command responsibility, the four accused were charged with crimes allegedly committed by them personally

---

Convention provides: "Women shall be protected especially against any attack on their honour, in particular against rape, enforced prostitution, or any form of indecent assault." Geneva Convention (IV) Relative to the Protection of Civilian Persons in Time of War, Aug. 12, 1949, 75 U.N.T.S. 287, 6 U.T.S. 3316, TIAS No. 3364, at art. 27.

[8]   *See, e.g.*, Kelly D. Askin, *Women and International Humanitarian Law, in* WOMEN AND INTERNATIONAL HUMAN RIGHTS LAW (Kelly Askin & Dorean Koenig eds., Vol. 1, 1999); Kelly D. Askin, *Crimes Within the Jurisdiction of the International Criminal Court*, 10 CRIM. L. FORUM 33 (1999).

[9]   In the ICTY: Prosecutor v. Tadić, Opinion and Judgment, IT–94–1–T, May 7, 1997 [hereinafter Tadić Judgment]; Prosecutor v. Delalić et al., Judgement, IT–96–21–T, Nov. 16, 1998 [hereinafter Čelebići Judgment]; Prosecutor v. Furundžija, Judgment, IT–95–17/1–T, Dec. 10, 1998 [hereinafter Furundžija Judgment]. In the ICTR: Prosecutor v. Akayesu, Judgment, ICTR–96–4–T, Sept. 2, 1998 [hereinafter Akayesu Judgment].

[10]   For an enriching article which reviews the Trial Chamber judgment in *Tadić* in regards to its jurisprudence on women's issues, *see* Patricia Viseur-Sellers, *Emerging Jurisprudence of Sexual Violence under International Law, in* CONTEMPORARY INTERNATIONAL LAW ISSUES: NEW FORMS, NEW APPLICATIONS (Proceedings of the Fourth Hague Joint Conference, 1998). For other recommended Articles which deal extensively with the jurisdictional aspects of *Tadić, see* W. J. Fenrick, *International Humanitarian Law and Criminal Trials*, 7 TRANSNAT'L L. & CONTEMP. PROBS. 23 (1997); Theodor Meron, *The Continuing Role of Custom in the Formation of International Humanitarian Law*, 90 AM. J. INT'L L. 238 (1996).

or by persons under their authority, with two of these convicted of crimes that included various forms of sexual violence. One of the accused, Hazim Delić, was charged with torture as a grave breach and a violation of the laws or customs of war, for an *actus reus* of forcible sexual penetration.[11] The Judgment made specific reference to rape as torture[12] and Delić was found guilty of torture by means of rape.[13] The Trial Chamber noted that, in addition to other purposes behind the rape, the sexualized violence suffered by the victims was inflicted because they were female and "this represents a form of discrimination which constitutes a prohibited purpose for the offence of torture."[14]

Additionally, one of the accused was found guilty of grave breaches for wilfully causing great suffering when persons under his authority tied a burning fuse cord around the genitals of a victim. He was also convicted of inhuman treatment for command responsibility of subordinates who forced two brothers publicly to perform fellatio on each other. Significantly, the Trial Chamber noted that the forced fellatio "could constitute rape for which liability could have been found if pleaded in the appropriate manner."[15] Thus if the indictment had charged the fellatio as rape instead of as inhuman treatment, he would have been convicted of the more precise crime. The suggested characterization of the crime appropriately amends the traditional notion of rape as exclusively entailing male/female sexual intercourse by force or without consent. Indictments and jurisprudence increasingly recognize that oral and anal sex may constitute rape and that males can be raped. Indeed, five of the Yugoslavian Indictments have brought charges for various forms of sexual violence committed against men.[16]

The primary defect of the Čelebići Judgment was the use of concurrent sentencing rather than a mixture of concurrent and consecutive sentencing.[17]

---

[11] *See* Prosecutor v. Delalić et al., "Čelebići," Indictment, IT–96–21, Mar. 21, 1996, at Counts 18 and 19.

[12] Čelebići Judgment, *supra* note 9, at paras. 475–496.

[13] *Id.* at para. 943.

[14] *Id.* at paras. 941, 963.

[15] *Id.* at para. 1066.

[16] However, the sexual violence against men as charged in the ICTY indictments are generally not the same form of violence as sex crimes against women. When women are raped or subjected to other forms of sexual violence, the accused is typically the physical perpetrator (or a superior to the physical perpetrator or an aider and abettor.) In contrast, male rape has generally entailed forcing two detainees to have oral sex, and the sexual violence has tended to be along the lines of kicking, burning, biting, or otherwise injuring the genitals or testicles. There have not been any indictments for a male being subjected to anal or oral sex physically perpetrated by an accused or his subordinate. *See* discussion of Tadić, Čelebići, Jelisić and Cesic, Sikirica, and Simić Indictments, in Askin, *Sexual Violence in Decisions and Indictments, supra* note 5.

[17] For instance, when the accused is found guilty of the same act under different theories of liability or which protect different interests (arts. 7(1) and 7(3) in the ICTY Statute, arts. 6(1)

Concurrent sentencing means that the convicted person merely serves the longest sentence imposed. The inadequacies of this sentencing are demonstrated by the sentences imposed on Delić and Mucić. Delić was noted to derive particular pleasure from torturing and mistreating detainees and he showed no remorse. He was characterized as a "sadistic individual" who displayed a total disregard for life and dignity. He personally killed detainees and raped several women. For his conduct, Delić received guilty verdicts on fourteen Counts carrying seven to twenty-year prison terms, totaling 188 years.[18] Due to the concurrent sentencing,[19] however, he received a twenty year sentence for the wilful killing of several victims; his subsequent convictions for murder, torture, rape, and other crimes carried no additional prison time because the remaining sentences were essentially subsumed within the first sentence. The Čelebići camp commander, Mucić, received eleven separate seven year sentences for a wide variety of heinous crimes. Instead of seventy-seven years of imprisonment, he must serve seven years, less of course the time already served in detention prior to and during trial. His ten subsequent convictions and corresponding seven year sentences impose no additional jail time. Seven years total imprisonment is inappropriately lenient for a person found to be responsible for the murder, torture, and gross mistreatment of persons detained in Čelebići camp. A mixture of concurrent and consecutive sentencing would result in a more palatable and equitable sentence that is commensurate with the crimes committed.

2.   Akayesu Judgment

The *Akayesu* Judgment was delivered by the Rwandan Tribunal on September 2, 1998. This Judgment may well be the most important decision rendered thus far in the history of women's jurisprudence.[20] First, it is the seminal

---

and 6(3) in the ICTR Statute; or, e.g., as grave breaches and violations of the laws or customs of war), then concurrent sentencing is appropriate. When the accused is convicted of a wholly separate crime (murder of A, rape of B, and plunder of village C), then consecutive sentencing is not only appropriate, but preferable.

[18]   Čelebići Judgment, *supra* note 9, at pp. 443–446.

[19]   The concurrent sentencing policy adopted by the Tribunals seems primarily based on Prosecutor v. Tadić, Decision on the Defence Motion on the Form of the Indictment, IT–94–1–T, Nov. 14, 1995, in which Trial Chamber II stated: "[P]enalty cannot be made to depend upon whether offences arising from the same conduct are alleged cumulatively or in the alternative. What is to be punished by penalty is proven criminal conduct and that will not depend upon technicalities of pleading." (Para. 17). In sentencing, the *Tadić* Trial Chamber imposed concurrent sentencing for each cumulative charge (with crimes against humanity convictions receiving a sentence of one year longer than convictions for violations of the laws or customs of war.) *See* Prosecutor v. Tadić, Sentencing Judgment, IT–94–1–T, 14 July 1997. The *Akayesu* Trial Chamber expounded upon this, holding: "[I]t is acceptable to convict the accused of two offences in relation to the same set of facts in the following circumstances: (1) where the offences have different elements; or (2) where the provisions creating the offences protect different interests; or (3) where it is necessary to record a conviction for both offences in order fully to describe what the accused did." Akayesu Judgment, *supra* note 9, at para. 468.

[20]   For a more extensive treatment of gender issues by the ICTR, *see* Kelly Dawn Askin, *The*

case in which an accused has been found guilty of genocide for crimes which expressly included sexualized violence; indeed the language in the decision explicitly recognizes that "sexual violence was an integral part of the process of destruction" of the genocidal regime.[21] Second, it is the first time that an accused has been found guilty of rape as a crime against humanity.[22] Third, it is the first time that rape and sexual violence have been defined in international law and the definition takes into account the coercive nature of wartime sexual violence and the various forms this violence can take. This decision will undoubtedly play a vital role in the development of gender jurisprudence in international adjudicative bodies and one may hope it will serve to increase international awareness of the devastating impact gender or sex based crimes have on the victim, the victim's family, associated group(s), the local community, and society as a whole.

Akayesu, mayor of a local commune, was found guilty of numerous crimes, including responsibility under Article 6(1) for various forms of sexual violence committed by Hutu men against Tutsi women in the Taba commune. While it was not alleged that Akayesu physically perpetrated rape crimes, the Trial Chamber found that Akayesu either ordered, instigated, or aided and abetted the rapes and other forms of sexual violence.[23] The Trial Chamber defined rape as:

> a physical invasion of a sexual nature, committed on a person under circumstances which are coercive. . . . [S]exual violence, which includes rape, [is] any act of a sexual nature which is committed on a person under circumstances which are coercive. Sexual violence is not limited to physical invasion of the human body and may include acts which do not involve penetration or even physical contact.[24]

Forced public nudity was cited in the Judgment as constituting sexual violence and successfully prosecuted as an "inhumane act."[25]

While it is easy on the one hand to be positive about the *Akayesu* decision and its unusual gender-sensitivity, there is concern on the other hand about certain language used in the decision,[26] about some findings that appear to lack legal

---

International Criminal Tribunal for Rwanda and Its Treatment of Crimes Against Women, in INTERNATIONAL HUMANITARIAN LAW: ORIGINS, CHALLENGES & PROSPECTS (John Carey & R. John Pritchard eds., 2000).

[21] Akayesu Judgment, *supra* note 9, at para. 731.

[22] *Id.* at p. 294 ("Count 13: Guilty of Crime against Humanity (Rape)").

[23] *Id.* at paras. 692–694.

[24] *Id.* at para. 688; *see also* para. 598.

[25] *Id.* at paras. 692–693.

[26] For instance the Trial Chamber, in discussing the law relating to Common Article 3 and Additional Protocol II, states that "the crimes must not be committed by the perpetrator for

support or a basis in reasoned analysis,[27] and about essentially attributing combatant status to civilian leaders for responsibility under Common Article 3,[28] an attribution contrary to post-World War II jurisprudence.[29] These issues are, however, beyond the scope of the present study.

---

purely personal motives." *Id.* at para. 636. Rape crimes are regularly committed for personal motives, although many times personal motives are mixed with other motives, but the intent is difficult to establish. *See* testimony recounted in the Akayesu Judgment in which two boys raped two girls "'because they didn't know how it was done.'" *Id.* at para. 431. Intent to commit the crime which has a sufficient nexus to the armed conflict should be sufficient, regardless of personal motive.

[27] For instance, the Trial Chamber included grave breach language within the elements of crimes against humanity, without providing any legal support or reasoning. *Id.* at para. 578 (crimes against humanity contain "four essential elements, namely: (i) the act must be inhumane in nature and character, causing great suffering, or serious injury to body or to mental or physical health"). It later assimilated into the crimes against humanity "civilian population" the categories of persons protected by Common Article 3, an attribution which is progressive, but which nevertheless is provided without any sort of legal analysis or reasoning. *Id.* at para. 582 and n. 146 ("Members of the civilian population are people who are not taking any active part in the hostilities, including members of the armed forces who laid down their arms and those persons placed *hors de combat* by sickness, wounds, detention or any other cause.")

[28] Akayesu was found not guilty of Common Article 3 crimes because the Trial Chamber determined, it seems to me arbitrarily, unnecessarily, and incorrectly, that to hold non-military leaders responsible for violations of the laws or customs of war the accused must be acting both under color of state authority and must also be acting in furtherance of the war effort. *Id.* at paras. 640–643 ("Akayesu would incur individual criminal responsibility for his acts if it were proved that by virtue of his authority he directly engaged in the conduct of hostilities. Hence, the Prosecutor will have to . . . prove that Akayesu . . . was legitimately mandated and expected, as a public official or agent or person otherwise holding public authority or *de facto* representing the Government, to support or fulfil the war efforts.") *Id.* at para. 640.

[29] *See, e.g.,* LAW REPORTS OF TRIALS OF WAR CRIMINALS, Trial of Washio Awochi, Case No. 76 (1946), Vol. XIII, at 122 (Japanese hotel-keeper forced women into prostitution during the war for financial profit); *Flick Case*, Case No. 48 (1947), Vol. IX, at 17–18 (officials of private industrial enterprises convicted of crimes including enslavement and deportation for financial gain); *Hadamar Trial*, Case No. 4 (1945), Vol. I, at 51–54 (civilian staff members of sanitorium complicit in killing patients simply because it was an institutional policy); *Krupp Case* (1948), Vol. X, at 150 (private persons profiting from war through illicit means convicted of war crimes); *Essen Lynching Case*, Case No. 8 (1945),Vol. I, at 89 (civilians attacked and killed captured British airmen who were paraded through town); *Belsen Trial*, Case No. 10 (1945),Vol. II, at 105–106 (camp personnel, including camp inmates given minor authority, mistreated others in camp); *Zyklon B Case*, Case No. 9 (1946), Vol. I, at 93 (industrialists convicted of knowingly supplying poisonous gas to concentration camp for profit, even though knew it was to murder inmates). Thus, there is a plethora of post World War II caselaw in which civilians, without acting under any state authority or to further the war effort, were convicted of war crimes for personal gain or motive, such as financial profit. While no previous international war crimes trial has prosecuted these crimes under Common Article 3, there is no reason or supporting authority to assign a higher standard than that normally attributed to war crimes. There is certainly no reason to assign Common Article 3 crimes a higher threshold than crimes against humanity or genocide. Even if the standard articulated in Akayesu is correct, the evidence supports that Akayesu satisfied that standard. It is puzzling that Akayesu could be found guilty of genocide, a specific intent crime, and crimes against humanity, and yet to be found to have not

3. Furundžija Judgment

The Furundžija Judgment was rendered by the Yugoslavian Tribunal on December 10, 1998. When the Tribunals were established, the historical culture of impunity surrounding sex crimes made it imperative to establish the precedent that rape or other forms of sexual violence against one victim are serious violations of international humanitarian law, that the perpetrator need not commit additional crimes before being held accountable, and the victim does not have to be brutally killed before the crime is deemed worthy of prosecution. There needed to be at least one trial in which an accused would be tried exclusively for sexual violence against a single victim, even though the resources of the Tribunal are limited and it is difficult to justify prosecution of an accused for crimes against one individual (regardless of whether it is a single murder, rape, or other atrocity). The *Furundžija* case, while an excerpted and redacted version of a larger indictment containing a broader scope of crimes, was essentially about the multiple rapes of one woman by a single physical perpetrator during one day of the Yugoslavian conflict.[30] The accused was not the alleged physical perpetrator, an important point to emphasize: he was present during at least part of the rape and he could have prevented the rape but failed to do so. Moreover, his presence, acts or omissions, and words were found to have encouraged and facilitated the rape, so he was found guilty of criminal responsibility for the rape, as a co-perpetrator of torture and as an aider and abettor of outrages upon personal dignity including rape, both being violations of the laws or customs of war.

In the judgment, the Trial Chamber stipulated that the "objective elements" of rape consist of:

   i. the sexual penetration, however slight:
      a of the vagina or anus of the victim by the penis of the perpetrator or any other object used by the perpetrator; or
      b. of the mouth of the victim by the penis of the perpetrator;
   ii. by coercion or force or threat of force against the victim or a third person.[31]

Similar to the definition advanced by the ICTR in *Akayesu*, the ICTY's articulation of the "elements" of rape in *Furundžija* emphasize some form of coercive penetration.

---

acted to "support or fulfil the war effort." For a more detailed discussion, *see* Askin, *The International Criminal Tribunal for Rwanda, supra* note 20.

[30] *See* Prosecutor v. Furundžija, Indictment (Amended-Redacted), IT–95–17/1–PT, June 2, 1998, in which Counts 1–14 and 15–25 against additional accused are redacted. For a more extensive treatment of the significance of this case in regards to gender jurisprudence, *see* Kelly D. Ashkin [sic], *The International War Crimes Trial of Anto Furundžija: Major Progress Toward Ending the Cycle of Impunity for Rape Crimes*, 12 LEIDEN J. INT'L L. (1999).

[31] Furundžija Judgment, *supra* note 9, at para. 185.

The trial, which lasted a total of eleven trial days and was the shortest trial held to date in either Tribunal, appropriately confirms that a single instance of sexual violence committed with a nexus to an armed conflict warrants prosecution as a war crime. This case perhaps can deter what is likely the most common form of wartime rape: random, isolated rape, crimes sometimes committed simply because the atmosphere of war, its hatred and violence and the breakdown of law and order, creates the opportunity. It also can serve as persuasive authority for courts martial, state courts, and regional courts in the prosecution of such.

While the judgment was reformative, there were issues of concern throughout the trial process.[32] Indeed, one of the last issues that arose in the case stemmed from proceedings against Augusto Pinochet in the British House of Lords. Recall that in the initial appeal, the House of Lords reversed an order of a Law Lords Panel which would have permitted extradition of Augusto Pinochet to Spain to stand trial for crimes against humanity. The failure of Lord Hoffmann to disclose his associations with Amnesty International, an organization that played an active role in seeking Pinochet's extradition, was found to have tainted the proceedings.[33] In *Furundžija*, the defense sought to overturn the Judgment on an allegedly similar basis, by having the Presiding Judge, Florence Mumba, disqualified for failing to disclose that she had previously served as a member of the U.N.'s Commission on the Status of Women.[34]

The defense motion accurately noted that while a member of the CSW during 1992 to 1995, the Commission issued a resolution condemning the sexual violence committed during the Yugoslavian conflict, urged the prosecution to seek justice for these victims, advocated a broad definition of wartime rape, and helped prepare the Beijing Platform of Action which condemned various forms of sexual violence. The defense asserted, in effect, that Judge Mumba used her position as a judge of the

---

[32] There were several troubling aspects to the trial and pre-trial proceedings, problems raised by human rights lawyers. The Center for Civil and Human Rights of Notre Dame Law School filed an *amicus* brief with the Tribunal in response to some of the issues. *See* Prosecutor v. Anto Furundžija, Amicus Curiae Brief on Protective Measures for Victims or Witnesses of Sexual Violence and Other Traumatic Events, Submitted on behalf of the Center for Civil and Human Rights, Notre Dame Law School, Nov. 6, 1998. A group of lawyers from other human rights groups, feminist organizations and law schools filed another *amicus* brief on some of the same, as well as other, issues. *See* Amicus Curiae Brief Respecting the Decision and Order of the Tribunal of July 16, 1998 Requesting that the Tribunal Reconsider Its Decision Having Regard for the Rights of Witness "A" to Equality, Privacy and Security of the Person, and to Representation by Counsel, Nov. 4, 1998.

[33] *See* Clare Dyer, *Pinochet ruling set aside by Lords*, THE GUARDIAN (London), 18 Dec. 1998, at 7.

[34] *See* Prosecutor v. Furundžija, Defendant's Post-Trial Application to the Bureau of the Tribunal for the Disqualification of Presiding Judge Mumba, Motion to Vacate Conviction and Sentence, and Motion for a New Trial, Furundžija, IT–95–17/1–A, Feb. 3, 1999. Incredibly, the Application then cites Judge Mumba's official and public biography with the ICTY as evidence that she sat as a member of CSW. *Id.* at n. 19.

ICTY to promote a common feminist agenda to the unfair detriment of Furundžija. The defense also strongly suggested that there was collusion between Mumba and prosecuting attorney Patricia Sellers, the legal advisor for gender based crimes in both Tribunals, and several members of the second *amicus* brief filed in the case. These organizations had either participated in CSW meetings or the Beijing Conference. In addition, several attorneys for the *amicus* attended feminist or international law conferences along with Sellers and/or Mumba, and they purportedly shared a common agenda to promote the philosophies of the Commission on the Status of Women and women's rights in general. The defense clearly insinuated that women judges, particularly women who have attempted to redress human rights violations against women, cannot be impartial because they are predisposed to promote a feminist agenda, and therefore they should be recused from adjudicating any cases involving crimes against women. Obviously, a similar argument can be made against judges specializing in other areas of the law or who have written or spoken advocating particular legal or philosophical positions. The issue is a serious one in international criminal procedure. It demands consideration of where to draw the line between personal interest and impartiality, when a judge must withdraw, and when disqualification should occur. Extensive analysis and debate is required as a result of *In re Pinochet*. In the ICTY, such analysis did not occur, because the Bureau rejected the defense motion on a technicality and thus it did not reject the motion on the merits.[35] As noted *infra*, the ICC Statute specifically included language to ensure women's participation as judges on the Court, and emphasized the need to include judges with expertise in cases involving violence against women. Thus, in contrast to implications that may be derived from *Furundžija*, this explicit inclusion represents an affirmation by the international community that experts in cases involving gender or sex based crimes would make an important contribution to the Court.

In summary, the jurisprudence flowing from the ICTY and ICTR has enriched and developed case law on gender and sex based crimes, most notably by recognizing *inter alia*, that:

- sexual violence may be committed with genocidal intent and as part of the process of genocidal destruction
- widespread or systematic rape crimes may constitute a crime against humanity

---

[35] Prosecutor v. Anto Furundžija, In the Bureau, Decision on Post-Trial Application by Anto Furundžija to the Bureau of the Tribunal for the Disqualification of Presiding Judge Mumba, Motion to Vacate Conviction and Sentence, and Motion for a New Trial, IT–95–17/1–T, 11 Mar. 1999. Essentially, the application was rejected for being outside the temporal jusidiction provided in the Rules, based on the fact that Rule 15(B) of the Rules of Procedure and Evidence only provide for disqualification up until the time of Judgment. It is regrettable that the Bureau's rejection was not on the merits. It is also important to note that because the decision was unanimous, disqualification of one judge would not have changed the outcome of the decision. Recall that this Pinochet decision by the House of Lords was a 3–2 decision, and thus the disqualification of Lord Hoffmann made the decision 2–2.

- a victim may be tortured by means of rape
- the rape of one person constitutes a serious violation of international humanitarian law
- not only the physical perpetrator but also anyone who orders, aids, abets, or otherwise facilitates a rape crime may be held accountable
- forcible nudity constitutes sexual violence and is a serious crime
- forcible or coercive oral, anal, or vaginal penetration constitutes rape
- men may be victims of sexual violence
- rape crimes may be committed as a form of discrimination
- women may be subjected to persecution on the basis of their sex
- the definition and elements of rape must necessarily be broad enough to cover the factual realities
- any form of captivity vitiates consent; and
- failing to adequately investigate, document, and prosecute these crimes is contrary to the interests of justice.

The judgments discussed above reflect a more sophisticated understanding of the devastating impact these crimes have on victims, associated groups, and society at large. The Tribunals have established that, depending on the circumstances of each case, various forms of gender or sex based crimes may be legitimately indicted and prosecuted, *inter alia*, as grave breaches, as serious violations of the laws or customs of war, including violations of Common Article 3 and the Additional Protocols, as crimes against humanity, and as genocide.

B. THE INTERNATIONAL CRIMINAL COURT AND WOMEN'S ISSUES

The Statute for the International Criminal Court adopted in Rome grants the Court jurisdiction over genocide, war crimes, crimes against humanity, and eventually, aggression.[36] The Statute, while clearly imperfect, nevertheless explicitly and implicitly allows prosecution of a broad range of gender based or sex based crimes, incorporates language guaranteeing certain protections to victims of these crimes, and mandates the inclusion of women in the different organs of the Court.[37]

The International Criminal Court's jurisdiction over these crimes will potentially have an enormous impact upon crimes committed exclusively or disproportionately against women and girls. In general, the ICC Statute is wonderfully progressive with regard to women's issues and gender or sex based crimes, but in

---

[36] ICC Statute, *supra* note 2, at art. 5. *See also* Kelly D. Askin, *Crimes Within the Jurisdiction of the International Criminal Court*, 10 CRIM. L. FORUM 33 (1999).

[37] Much of the information in the following section was modified from text contained in Dorean M. Koenig & Kelly D. Askin, *International Criminal Law and the International Criminal Court Statute: Crimes Against Women, in* WOMEN AND INTERNATIONAL HUMAN RIGHTS LAW (Kelly D. Askin & Dorean M. Koenig eds., Vol. 2, 2000).

some provisions the language or omission is inappropriately restrictive and reflective of patriarchal mores.

The language of Article 6 on genocide is taken directly from the Genocide Convention and thus does not specifically include reference to gender or sex based crimes,[38] but the jurisprudence flowing from the ICTR and ICTY Tribunals can serve to guide prosecution of such crimes.

In Article 7, crimes against humanity include certain crimes that have never before been specifically enumerated in an international humanitarian law instrument or an international criminal law treaty. Specifically, it allows for prosecution of "rape, sexual slavery, enforced prostitution, forced pregnancy, enforced sterilization, or any other form of sexual violence of comparable gravity," when these crimes are committed as part of a widespread or systematic attack against a civilian population.[39] The only one of these crimes defined in the Statute is forced pregnancy, which is said to mean "the unlawful confinement, of a woman forcibly made pregnant, with the intent of affecting the ethnic composition of any population or carrying out other grave violations of international law. This definition shall not in any way be interpreted as affecting national laws relating to pregnancy."[40] The crime of forced pregnancy was the subject of very heated and aggressive debate throughout the diplomatic conference in Rome, especially between members of the Women's Caucus and the Holy See. It was viewed suspiciously by the Holy See and conservative countries as a feminist attempt to get abortion on the international agenda. For most women activists, inclusion of the crime was instead about recognizing that forced impregnation and forced maternity—raping a woman until she becomes pregnant and detaining her until past the point of abortion so that she will carry the child of the rapist[41] to term—were additional crimes to rape, and deserved separate prosecution and punishment. In other words, in addition to being raped, being made pregnant is a separate crime, comprising at least one additional crime.[42]

Rape and enforced prostitution are widely recognized as international crimes and their prohibitions have been included in language in international treaties, such as the Fourth Geneva Convention and Additional Protocols. The other enu-

---

[38] It has only been recently that women have achieved participation in international bodies or venues, so the failure of the Genocide Convention to incorporate women's issues in 1948 is scarcely surprising.

[39] ICC Statute, *supra* note 2, at art. 7, para. 1(g).

[40] *Id.* at art. 7, para. 2(f).

[41] Usually a person of a different ethnicity and from a culture, society, or religion in which the ethnicity of the father is deemed to determine the ethnicity of the child.

[42] For a discussion of inclusion of forced pregnancy within the terms of the Statute, and the exclusion of terms such as (en)forced impregnation, (en)forced maternity, and (en)forced abortion, *see* Koenig & Askin, *International Criminal Law and the International Criminal Court Statute, supra* note 37.

merated crimes—sexual slavery, forced pregnancy, and enforced sterilization—
have not been explicitly criminalized in a prior international instrument. The difference is between enforced prostitution, sexual slavery, and the crime of
enslavement when the enslavement involves sexual services,[43] is unclear and will
need to be determined by the PrepComs.[44] There is also a rapidly increasing body
of case law and decisions by regional bodies that recognize that rape may constitute torture.[45] There will certainly be some overlap. With emerging jurisprudence in the Yugoslavian and Rwandan Tribunals that recognizes various forms
of sexual violence as constituting "wilfully causing great suffering," "cruel treatment," "inhumane acts," etc., crimes which are also included within the jurisdiction of the ICC, it will be important to satisfactorily distinguish the elements
of the crimes. Broad, vague, or catch-all phrases should only be used to prosecute crimes when it is impossible to satisfy the elements of the specifically enumerated crimes that more accurately reflect the acts and identify the crimes
committed.

Paragraph (g) also allows prosecution of "any other form of sexual violence
of comparable gravity." The language is not ideal because it implies that some
sexual violence is not particularly serious, but it does appropriately ensure that
the list is illustrative, and not exhaustive.[46] It also is troublesome in that it allows
dispute as to whether an offense such as enforced abortion is incorporated within
"sexual violence."

Also under crimes against humanity, paragraph (h) includes "gender" as a
prosecutable form of persecution. Recognition is long overdue that persons are
regularly persecuted either exclusively because of their gender, because gender
(or sex) is one of a number of isolated factors, or because gender is intersected or
intertwined with another factor.[47] Often, gender is intricately linked to other fac-

---

[43] Indeed, in Prosecutor v. Dragoljub Kunarac, Amended Indictment, IT–96–23–I, Aug. 19,
1998 (amended Foča Indictment), the accused is charged with enslavement for enslaving women
for sexual services. This is likely due to the fact that "enslavement" is a specifically enumerated
crime in the ICTY Statute, while sexual slavery and enforced prostitution are not specifically
enumerated in the Statute.

[44] I have previously enunciated somewhat different usage by the Special Rapporteur on
Violence Against Women and as reflected in international instruments, in Askin, *Crimes Within
the Jurisdiction of the International Criminal Court, supra* note 9.

[45] *See, e.g.,* Čelebići Judgment, *supra* note 9, at paras. 475–496, 936–965; Akayesu
Judgment, *id.,* at para. 597; Furundžija Judgment, *id.,* at paras. 163–164, and cases cited therein.

[46] ICC Statute, *supra* note 2, at art. 7, para. 1(g). This residual language could be used to
prosecute crimes which are not explicitly listed, such as (en)forced maternity, (en)forced abortion, forced marriage, and sexual mutilation.

[47] For instance, sometimes women are raped solely because of their sex (any female will
do); sometimes they are raped because of a number of factors, including because of their gender; sometimes they are raped precisely because they are women of a particular, for instance,
race, religion, or ethnicity (even though they are women, they would not have been raped if they

tors, such as race, ethnicity, nationality, religion, or social status. Unfortunately, the Statute defines gender as referring "to the two sexes, male and female, within the context of society." Under U.N. usage, "sex" is used to refer to biological differences, and "gender" is used to refer to socially constructed differences, taking into account factors such as power imbalances, socioeconomic factors, and cultural stereotypes.[48] The statutory definition represents a strange and unsatisfactory compromise reached between progressive states supporting women's rights and conservative states which often deny women's rights. There has been grave concern expressed by women's groups that this definition, or quasi-definition, of gender could be used by certain societies to undermine the human rights of women. They fear that the definition, particularly the language of "within the context of society," could be used to invoke religious, cultural, or social mores to deny rights to women. Nonetheless, because Article 21 of the Statute (applicable law) very specifically stipulates that the law applied by the Court must be consistent with internationally recognized human rights norms and be without any adverse distinction, this superficial demarcation of gender cannot provide protection to any who persecute or commit atrocities against women because of their gender.

Another crime specifically included as prosecutable as a crime against humanity is enslavement, defined as "the exercise of any or all of the powers attaching to the right of ownership over a person and includes the exercise of such power in the course of trafficking in persons, in particular women and children."[49] Thus, the definition of slavery contained in the Slavery Convention was adopted,[50] and, as an illustrative example of a crime which could be prosecuted as enslavement, trafficking in women and children is cited.

Article 8 concerns war crimes committed in international and non-international armed conflicts. The enumeration of grave breaches mirrors the language found in the grave breach provisions of the Geneva Conventions, but it is important to note that paragraph 2(b)(xxii), concerning international armed conflict,

---

were not a member of this particular group; if they were a man of the offending race, religion, or ethnicity, they would not have been raped, such as targeting for sexual violence Bosnian Muslim women during the Yugoslavian conflict (Bosnian Muslim men and Serbian women would not have been raped.))

   [48]   *See* U.N. Doc. E/EN.4/1997/40, Report of the Secretary-General, Integrating the Human Rights of Women Throughout the United Nations System, Dec. 20, 1996, at 10 (acknowledging "the distinction between the biological and social differences of men and women" and then elaborating upon differences in the terms "sex" and "gender").

   [49]   ICC Statute, *supra* note 2, at art. 7, para. 2(c).

   [50]   Slavery Convention (Sept. 25, 1926) 212 U.N.T.S. 17; 60 L.N.T.S. 253 *as amended by* Protocol amending the Slavery Convention signed at Geneva on Sept. 25, 1926 (Oct. 23, 1953), G.A. Res. 794 (VIII), at art.1, defining slavery as "the status or condition of a person over whom any or all of the powers attaching to the right of ownership are exercised."

includes "committing rape, sexual slavery, enforced prostitution, forced pregnancy . . . , enforced sterilization, or any other form of sexual violence also constituting a grave breach of the Geneva Conventions." This quite clearly indicates
that each of the aforementioned crimes constitute a grave breach, at least when
committed in an international armed conflict. Regarding internal armed conflicts,
the language in paragraph 2(e)(vi) allows for prosecution of "rape, sexual slavery, enforced prostitution, forced pregnancy, . . . enforced sterilization, and any
other form of sexual violence also constituting a serious violation of Article 3
common to the four Geneva Conventions." Again, the assumption is that these
crimes are already subsumed within Common Article 3, an attribution consistent
with Additional Protocol II to the 1949 Geneva Conventions.[51] It is additionally
significant that sexual violence was intentionally and rightfully separated from
the language of Common Article 3, paragraphs 2(b)(xxi) and 2(c)(ii), that refers
to committing outrages upon personal dignity, in particular humiliating and
degrading treatment.[52] As mentioned previously, it is important to delink sexual
violence with language concerning violations of honor or dignity.

Other Articles of the ICC Statute also will have a major impact on women
and crimes committed predominately against them. Concerning the inclusion of
women within the composition of Chambers, Article 36 of the ICC Statute, the
provision concerning the qualification of judges, requires that there be "fair representation of female and male judges"[53] How many of the eighteen judges need
to be female to constitute "fair representation" will undoubtedly be contentious.
Paragraph 8 also provides that judges with legal expertise on specific issues,
including but not limited to violence against women or children, should be
sought. This appropriately recognizes that expertise in a particular area is positive, a contribution to be valued. Explicit inclusion of the provision implies that
there is no presumption of bias or predisposition of experts to rule a certain way.
Significantly, it recognizes the moral and intellectual integrity of judges as impartial and independent triers of fact and finders of law.

In Article 54, the Prosecutor is mandated to take into account the nature of the
crimes alleged, and to be particularly sensitive to victims and witnesses when the
crime involves "sexual violence, gender violence or violence against children."[54]

---

[51] Protocol [II] Additional to the Geneva Conventions of 1949, and Relating to the
Protection of Victims of Non-International Armed Conflicts, 1125 U.N.T.S. 609 (1977), at art.
4(2)(e).

[52] Common Article 3 language which is, incidentally, included in art. 8, para. 2(b)(xxi) of
the ICC Statute as serious violations of the laws or customs of war applicable in *international*
armed conflicts. This appropriately recognizes the customary international law stature of
Common Article 3, making it applicable to international or internal armed conflicts. *See especially* Prosecutor v. Tadić, Decision on the Defense Motion for Interlocutory Appeal on
Jurisdiction, IT–94–1–AR72, Oct. 2, 1995, at para. 98.

[53] ICC Statute, *supra* note 2, at art. 36, para. 8.

[54] *Id.* at art. 54, para. 1(B).

Article 68 further requires the Court to take special measures necessary to protect the dignity and privacy of victims of sex crimes.[55] Notably, Article 43 places a Victims and Witnesses Unit in the Registry, and requires that the Unit "shall include staff with expertise in trauma, including trauma related to crimes of sexual violence." Clearly, the international community has collectively recognized that sexual violence constitutes a threat to the peace, security, and well-being of the world and considers it one of the most serious international crimes.[56]

The Rules of Procedure and Evidence and the elements of crimes drafted during the Preparatory Commissions (PrepComs)[57] will help determine whether the Statute and the Court can in fact provide any real remedy through prosecuting gender and sex based crimes or whether impunity will likely result when such crimes are committed. History has repeatedly demonstrated that women and girls are regularly singled out for sex crimes that are committed against them with a vengeance. Society cannot be complicit or complacent in ignoring these crimes, nor silent when positioned to redress them. Although the culture of impunity for these crimes is finally being ameliorated, it is important to be vigilant in ensuring that past, current, and future victims of sexualized violence are not ignored.

---

[55] *Id.* at art. 68, paras. 1, 2.

[56] The Preamble of the ICC Statute, *supra* note 2, recognizes that the crimes listed therein "threaten the peace, security and well-being of the world" and Article 1 affords jurisdiction to the Court exclusively over "the most serious crimes of international concern." Inclusion of various forms of sexual violence acknowledges the devastating impact these crimes have on the victims and the world community at large.

[57] The Final Act of the United Nations Diplomatic Conference of Plenipotentiaries on the Establishment of an International Criminal Court, U.N. Doc. A/CONF.183/10 (1998), Annex I, Resolution adopted by the United Nations Diplomatic Conference of Plenipotentiaries on the Establishment of an International Criminal Court, established a Preparatory Commission for the ICC to work on (para. 5) Rules of Procedure and Evidence and Elements of Crimes, among other things. Paragraph 6 provides that the draft texts of the Rules of Procedure and Evidence and of the Elements of Crimes are to be finalized by June 30, 2000.

CHAPTER 7

INTERNATIONAL HUMAN RIGHTS LAW, INTERNATIONAL HUMANITARIAN LAW, AND INTERNATIONAL CRIMINAL LAW AND PROCEDURE: NEW RELATIONSHIPS

Juan E. Méndez

From the perspective of those who seek to use and improve the protections available to victims of human rights abuses, the last few years have witnessed encouraging normative and practical developments. These innovations result from the fact that practitioners of human rights law increasingly have directed their attention to *protection* mechanisms. Although *standard-setting* activity has by no means ceased on the international scene, there has been a growing realization of the need to develop effective implementation if the lofty standards of human rights are to be more than mere aspirations.

Protection mechanisms are present in some of the most important international human rights treaties, and in certain regions of the world these mechanisms have become sophisticated and enjoy acceptable levels of effectiveness. But the reality of egregious human rights violations, especially those that are massive and systematic, and the pervasive impunity enjoyed by perpetrators, have led to impatience with the limitations of existing mechanisms. To be sure, those mechanisms must continue to be developed, especially through their assiduous and creative use by victims and practitioners, but in the best of cases international petition procedures can result only in a sanction imposed on a state. Frequently, the conclusion is in essence a declaratory judgment. Where damages are awarded, they are usually imposed on the taxpayers of the state. In many cases, a successor democratic government must carry the burden respecting violations committed by a predecessor regime. In the meantime, the actual perpetrators, including previously all-powerful leaders, remain free and may even be an obstacle to the victims' obtaining redress.

For these reasons, a nominal sanction on the state can only offer partial help in preventing the recurrence of massive abuses. Families of the disappeared or murdered, victims of torture, and innocent civilians subjected to war crimes have a right to see justice done. Moreover, prevention of future occurrences is not the only justification for redress. It is important to break the cycle of impunity for these crimes, and impunity reigns in a very personal and visible way when the architects and executors of murderous policies benefit from non-prosecution, be it *de jure* (via amnesties and pseudo-amnesties) or *de facto* (via countless mechanisms by which the powerful impose their will over the law and institutions).

It follows that the struggle against impunity must seek to establish credible and legitimate criminal prosecutions for mass atrocities if the norm prohibiting them is to be effective. Since the 1980s, many domestic human rights organizations have resorted to the national criminal law and courts, not so much to continue to defend those previously and wrongly accused for political reasons, but also to prosecute and punish the guilty. From the start, however, it has been clear that this struggle cannot take place merely on the national stage. In varying degrees, transitional regimes have proven incapable or unwilling to live up to this tremendous responsibility. The efforts increasingly have shifted to the international community.

International organs to supervise implementation of human rights treaties produced landmark precedents delineating the international obligations of the state in the face of massive and deliberate patterns of gross human rights violations.[1] When it came to war crimes, however, there was no effort whatsoever to do justice, especially if the war crimes and the underlying conflict were ongoing. Thus, the question of whether the state was unwilling or, instead, was incapable of living up to its obligations was immaterial. At the same time, international humanitarian law had clear norms regarding the international community's right and obligation to punish if the state or force primarily responsible did not act. In the 1990s, the international community was confronted with the reality of savage conflicts and the obligation to prevent war crimes from going unpunished.[2]

---

[1] Question of Impunity of Perpetrators of Violations of Human Rights (Civil and Political): Final Report Prepared by Mr. L. Joinet, pursuant to Sub-Commission Resolution 1995/35, U.N. ESCOR, Comm'n on Hum. Rts. 48th Sess., Provisional Agenda Item 10, U.N. Doc. E/CN. 4/Sub.2/1996/18 (1996). *See also* Diane F. Orentlicher, *Settling Accounts: The Duty to Prosecute Human Rights Violations of a Prior Regime*, 100 YALE L.J. 2537 (1991); Diane F. Orentlicher, *Addressing Gross Human Rights Abuses: Punishment and Victim Compensation, in* HUMAN RIGHTS: AN AGENDA FOR THE NEXT CENTURY (L. Henkin & J.L. Hargrove eds.,1994); NAOMI ROHT-ARRIAZA, ED., IMPUNITY AND HUMAN RIGHTS IN INTERNATIONAL LAW AND PRACTICE (1995).

[2] The four Geneva Conventions establish the notion of "grave breaches"and an obligation to prosecute them. *See* arts. 50, 50, 130 and 147 respectively, and arts. 11, 85 and 86 of Protocol I. The impetus to act on these atrocities has resulted in an important normative development: the practical obliteration of the distinction, in this regard, between international and non-international conflict (until the 1990s, it was understood that the obligation to punish grave breaches applied only in international wars). *See* T. Meron, *International Criminalization of Internal*

The practicality of establishing international courts and merging different legal traditions in acceptable consensus over what constitutes a fair trial has made it necessary for human rights practitioners to learn about international humanitarian law and about international criminal law and procedure. The result is an important degree of convergence between three distinct bodies of law, as well as cooperation between specialists who are challenged by completely new needs and unprecedented legal developments. International criminal law certainly involves more than a comparative law exercise that yields new norms acceptable to different legal traditions. It also concerns the opportunities to obtain personal jurisdiction over known criminals found abroad.

Jurisdictional questions present the chance to test local norms designed, in many countries, to give effect to the principle of universal jurisdiction. In this sense, traditional criminal law and procedure, heretofore strictly limited to the territorial principle, is giving way to a limited extra-territoriality for a defined category of egregious crimes. Without such evolution, human rights cases may require the application of extradition treaties and law, a matter fraught with technical complexities that never previously had much to do with human rights enforcement.

A. THE CONVERGENCE OF HUMAN RIGHTS AND HUMANITARIAN LAW

The convergence of international human rights law (IHRL) and international humanitarian law (IHL), from the perspective of their respective application by practitioners, is not entirely a new development. International human rights organizations were preoccupied, in the 1960s and 1970s, with the release of political prisoners, preventing torture in detention, stamping out censorship, and similar problems associated with repressive dictatorships. For these problems, the corpus of international human rights law was sufficient. By the 1980s, however, many of the more pressing human rights problems were associated with armed conflict, particularly civil wars and wars of national liberation raging in many countries. The previously mentioned patterns of repression were certainly there in these countries as well, but more significant were outrages against the personal dignity of captured combatants, murder of unarmed adversaries, violations of the neutrality of medical personnel and other protected persons, and attacks against civilians. In most cases, both parties to the conflict engaged in such conduct.

To the extent that IHRL directs itself solely to governments responsible for its implementation, this corpus was not as useful in the context of armed conflict, because to be effective similar standards had to apply to all culpable parties. IHL, insofar as it was applicable to non-international conflicts, provided a common rational basis to judge behavior independent of the justice of the cause pursued

---

Atrocities, 89 AM. J. INT'L L. 554 (1995). *See also* Prosecutor v. Dusko Tadić, Decision on Jurisdiction, ICT for the former Yugoslavia, App. Chamber (IT–94–1–AR72), *reprinted in* 35 I.L.M. 32 (1996).

by force of arms. And, by their explicit terms, these norms applied to government forces as well as to non-state actors.[3] Although there were objections to this approach, based on a certain orthodoxy of human rights advocacy, over the years IHL proved a very effective tool, and rigorous standards applied to on-the-ground research contributed to enhancing the credibility of human rights organizations.

IHL and IHRL are two of the three corpuses of international law dedicated to the protection of the human person. The third is refugee law, originated mostly in the 1951 Convention on the Status of Refugees and its 1967 Additional Protocol.[4] Although each body of law has given rise to specialized organizations, all three are now widely used by non-governmental and inter-governmental organizations dedicated to the promotion and protection of rights. This broadening of the normative basis for advocacy has the benefit of more precise and specific obligations solemnly assumed by states, and of flexibility, allowing adaptation to changing circumstances and varying situations. Obviously, this results in a concomitant broadening of the mandate of human rights organizations, even as we had always assumed that a narrow mandate was key to their credibility and success. Inasmuch as there is a common thread to all three bodies of law, namely the international protection of the human person in different circumstances, this broader mandate does not in general result in dilution of the movement's strength and effectiveness.

When the problems of impunity for the most serious offenses against human dignity began to loom large on the horizon of advocacy organizations, the "marriage" between IHRL and IHL proved essential. IHL contributed the notion of "grave breaches" (even though applicable at first only to international conflicts) and the clear obligation to punish them.[5] This was a first, but major, building block towards the construction of a theory of obligation to prosecute. It served the movement well in opposing blanket amnesty laws that crystallized impunity.[6] In fact, domestic courts in some countries where impunity is an issue have begun to limit the effect of amnesty laws by reference to international obligations assumed by states when they ratify the Geneva Conventions.[7] The struggle against impunity is by no means over, but this aspect of the convergence of IHL and IHRL has resulted in some clear progress: blanket amnesties are now universally

---

[3] Common Article 3 to the four Geneva Conventions of Aug. 12, 1949, Protocol II to the Geneva Conventions of Dec. 12, 1977.

[4] CANÇADO TRINDADE, ANTONIO A., LAS TRES VERTIENTES DE LA PROTECCION INTERNACIONAL DE LOS DERECHOS HUMANOS (IIDH, San José, 1995).

[5] SASSOLI, M. AND BOVIER, A.A., HOW DOES LAW PROTECT IN WAR? 241–252 (ICRC, Geneva, 1999).

[6] For complete analysis of the normative basis for these emerging principles, *see supra* note 1.

[7] Prosecutor v. Roma Mena, App. Court of Santiago (Chile), Case *Lumi Videla*, No. 13597–94, Sept. 26, 1994.

condemned as in violation of ethical, political and legal obligations of state and society. The most recent amnesty law in Latin America, passed in Guatemala in December 1996 as a step in the implementation of the peace accords, is the first law whose text limits the scope of the benefit of non-prosecution. Tracking the international law standard, it establishes that genocide, war crimes and crimes against humanity are not included in the amnesty.

B. CRITICS OF CONVERGENCE

Many authors have commented on the convergence of IHL and IHRL. Among those describing or encouraging the development are John Dugard and Daniel O'Donnell, in a special issue of the *International Review of the Red Cross* dedicated to the Fiftieth Anniversary of the Geneva Conventions. Dugard, in fact, emphasizes the connection of the two bodies of law via punishment of offenders, a decisive step in the direction of accountability. O'Donnell chronicles the extensive citation of IHL by special rapporteurs and United Nations bodies charged primarily with human rights monitoring or promotion.[8]

Not every commentator is comfortable, however, with the degree of convergence currently seen between IHL and IHRL. Professor William Schabas has commented to the author that IHRL seems to be giving way to IHL in this convergence. Prof. Schabas mentioned the Advisory Opinion of the International Court of Justice on the threat and use of nuclear weapons, which can be read as applying only IHRL standards and discarding human rights norms as the basis of its decision.[9] An even more serious objection is sometimes raised by front line defenders of human rights in countries with ongoing armed conflicts. According to them, governments and the high command of the armed forces are quick to proclaim that they will abide by IHL. At first blush, this appears as a welcome development, because few armies ever recognize that their fight against insurgent forces is subject to regulation, but the thrust of the declarations is to *deny or replace* human rights norms—including those applying in emergencies—with lower IHL standards. These lofty declarations make it possible, for example, to use ruses, ambushes, and shoot-to-kill rules of engagement even for law enforcement, actions that clearly violate human rights standards. In other words, the declaration of a state of armed conflict is presented as presumptive justification of actions that are otherwise not justified.

The effect of applying IHL to the detriment of human rights would be not only wrong but in bad faith. During a conflict, IHL applies to combat situations,

---

[8] John Dugard, *Bridging the Gap Between Human Rights and Humanitarian Law: The Punishment of Offenders*, 324 INTERNATIONAL REVIEW OF THE RED CROSS 445–453; Daniel O'Donnell, *Trends in the Application of International Humanitarian Law by United Nations Human Rights Mechanisms, id.* at 481–503.

[9] Legality of the Threat or Use of Nuclear Weapons, Advisory Opinion of July 8, 1996, I.C.J. Rep. 1996.

but it does not by any means replace the norms guiding law enforcement operations, even against identified insurgents in the process of being detained. Due process standards and rules regarding use of force are those that apply in peacetime, at least until the subject by his or her resistance turns the action into combat. In other words, a state of civil war gives rise to the application of either Common Article 3 or Protocol II, depending on the intensity and level of the conflict and other conditions, but the standards contained therein are in force contemporaneously and coexisting with human rights norms, both international and domestic. There will be some gray areas where both apply, but a good faith interpretation points to the need to apply norms that are most protective of human rights whenever possible. The language of the ICJ advisory opinion on nuclear weapons is deplorable and the basis of decision could have been better, but it does not appear to be signaling a dangerous trend towards giving prevalence to one set of norms over the other. The many ways other bodies have used both systems of law[10] seems more to indicate that neither system takes precedence over the other.

C. THE ROLE OF INTERNATIONAL CRIMINAL LAW

International criminal law is the newcomer in this convergence, at least in relative terms. Until very recently, practitioners of human rights did not need to dwell much on the intricate technicalities of extradition law and other forms of international cooperation in law enforcement. In many ways, criminal law specialists have now become interested in human rights protection and accountability. Technically there is not much difference between bringing a member of organized crime to justice and doing the same with one who commits or committed crimes in abuse of state power. Specialists have found, however, that the political, diplomatic and ethical complications of prosecuting state crimes requires innovations. In any event, the human rights movement is definitely benefitting from this cross-fertilization with a different but related discipline.

One large contribution that international criminal law and procedure are making is an enhanced appreciation for the nuances of due process. There cannot be shortcuts to justice, however imperative the need to bring state criminals and war criminals to justice. Any lessening of fair trial standards would only diminish the moral high ground human rights practitioners must always occupy. This means learning to be scrupulous about due process guarantees for accused who never bothered with such niceties when they repressed others.

Progressive-minded criminal law specialists are joining the human rights movement from this perspective and strengthening it, especially in the area of due process. At the same time, the process of convergence is not without difficulty. Criminal law practitioners are sometimes uncomfortable with some aspects of

---

[10] *See* examples given by O'Donnell, *supra* note 8, and the ICTY decision in the *Tadić* case, *supra* note 2.

recent developments, even if ethically they share in the values of human rights. For example, the foundation of criminal law has always been the territoriality principle, because the power to punish is linked in the most direct way with the attributes of sovereignty. Jurisdictional schemes to extend subject matter and even *in personam* jurisdiction to countries other than the one where the crimes were committed are viewed with skepticism if not disapproval. In addition, some arguments supporting international criminalization of human rights violations are reminiscent of the "victims' rights" arguments made in some domestic jurisdictions to justify repressive and anti-due process policies.[11] Finally, progressive criminal law specialists are uncomfortable with the decisive thrust towards effective punishment involved in efforts to produce truth and justice internationally. They alert us to the unsavory and undemocratic uses of criminal law, critiquing the rush to "warehouse" defendants, and arguing for decriminalization of certain behaviors. Yet when it comes to human rights crimes, it is hard to argue for leniency and rehabilitation without falling into the trap of false reconciliation that only masks the problem of impunity.

In the end, however, these are growing pains of an otherwise very profitable partnership. Progressive criminal law jurists are not only on the side of accountability for crimes committed in abuse of authority; they are also adding considerable expertise and vision to a more sophisticated analysis of the problems involved in doing justice.

D. THE *PINOCHET* CASE

The October 1998 arrest of General Augusto Pinochet in Great Britain has given new meaning and urgency to the convergence of three legal disciplines, and has been a proving ground for many novel features of human rights work. The progress made in only a few months is astounding, based solely on the legal and policy developments created by the Pinochet case. For decades "universal jurisdiction" was largely a theoretical possibility. Jurists proclaimed that certain violations of human rights were so severe and so shocking to the conscience of humanity that they could and should be punished by any and all civilized nations of the world.[12] Dutifully, government representatives in international fora professed to uphold the notion of universal jurisdiction. In reality, however, domestic parliaments rarely enacted legislation to make universal jurisdiction effective, and domestic courts dismissed most such criminal claims, except in regard to the prosecution of former Nazi war criminals. The arrest warrant issued by Spanish judge Baltazar Garzon, and its serious treatment by British authorities changed

---

[11] For example, when politicians manipulate the process to remove prosecutors considered "soft" on the death penalty. *See* Rachel L. Swarns, *Governor Removes Bronx Prosecutor from Murder Case*, N.Y. TIMES, Mar. 22, 1996, p. A–1.

[12] RESTATEMENT (THIRD) OF THE FOREIGN RELATIONS LAW OF THE U.S., § 702, comment b (1987).

all that. The decisions in the *Pinochet* case of the Law Lords,[13] of the British trial magistrates and High Court, and of the Home Secretary will generate lively discussions and advocacy initiatives for years to come. Even if there is disagreement about some aspects of the judicial decisions, they are undoubtedly thoughtful and thought-provoking; they are bound to have an influence in future policy debates in a variety of settings where accountability is at issue. At the very least, they constitute recognition of the viability of the principle of universal jurisdiction, and of its applicability even to the most politically sensitive matters. In a way, accountability comes of age when it is treated in a serious way in conjunction with weighty matters like diplomatic relations among three democratic states.

In addition to conferring legitimacy on universal jurisdiction, the *Pinochet* case established far-reaching precedents on more technical legal matters, especially respecting the treatment of head of state immunity. According to the Law Lords, a former head of state is not immune from prosecution abroad if the offenses alleged are serious enough to constitute genocide, war crimes or crimes against humanity.

The government of Chile (seconded on this point by most Latin American governments) took a strong position against extra-territoriality of criminal law even for these crimes. In so doing, and in pursuing Pinochet's return to Chile, it was forced into a corner and expressed positions that, paradoxically, help the human rights cause in other ways. The first advance stemmed from the fact that the Latin American governments had previously voted in *en bloc* in favor of the International Criminal Court, and their votes helped make possible the Rome Statute in July 1998. Since the Rome Statute is in essence a step in the direction of accountability *and* of universal jurisdiction for these crimes, Chile and other Latin democracies hastened to add that they *favor* universal jurisdiction only insofar as it is bestowed upon an international criminal court, but they are *against* it if exercised by the courts of another independent nation, no matter how democratic its regime or how independent and impartial its judiciary.

The view presented may boost the chances for ratification of the Statute of Rome, but it is a fatally flawed argument. The ICC is not and was never intended to become the *sole* means of making effective universal jurisdiction. On the contrary, many of its provisions are premised on the fact that in some cases there will be competing claims to jurisdiction over the same acts or over the same defendants. An ICC and the domestic courts of other nations will always be complementary; indeed, the state where the events occurred will always have primary responsibility for prosecution. When the courts of that state are unable or unwilling to prosecute, an ICC will take only some of the potential cases; others will have to be tried by other countries exercising their duty to extradite or prosecute (*aut dedere aut judicare*). That is exactly what is happening with the precursors

---

[13] House of Lords, Regina v. Bartle, *Ex Parte* Pinochet and Regina v. Evans, *Ex Parte* Pinochet, Mar. 24, 1999, *reprinted in* 38 I.L.M. 581 (1999).

of the envisioned ICC. Defendants accused of the Rwandan genocide are being tried by the International Criminal Tribunal for Rwanda (ICTR) set up by the U.N. Security Council, by domestic courts in Rwanda, and by third-party countries like Belgium, that have jurisdictional statutes permitting such prosecution.

E. THE INTERNATIONAL CRIMINAL COURT

Even more than the *Pinochet* case, the greatest impulse towards convergence of IHL, IHRL and international criminal law and procedure (ICL) comes from the project to create an International Criminal Court. When such a court comes into being after the required number of ratifications, the impulse will only grow as the court applies the law, giving it shape and content through specific cases. An organ vested with authority to apply standards and norms to real life situations promotes not only stability but also progress in international law, by filling in the necessarily vague standards with meaning drawn from actual cases. Clearly, the greatest advances in IHRL have come from authoritative applications of treaties by their organs; if those organs are of a judicial nature, the progress made is always greater. The ICC will have an additional advantage: it will be charged with providing authoritative interpretation of norms drawn from all three corpuses of law.

Indeed, the Rome Statute is, by itself, a great achievement in the process of convergence. The careful building of consensus and the broad participation of the best legal minds of virtually every country in the world have resulted in a text that is exemplary in many ways. In the first place, regarding substantive criminal norms, it is an accurate reflection of the present state of development of ICL regarding the definitions of genocide, war crimes and crimes against humanity. Even if the so-called "elements of the crime" remain to be worked out at the Preparatory Committee meetings, the Diplomatic Conference went to great lengths in defining the details of the offenses. To that extent, the resulting text can rightfully be quoted as declarative of the present state of the law as understood by a great majority of nations. Secondly, procedural norms also reflect the present state of the law of due process and the precise meaning of fair trial guarantees as they apply to criminal prosecutions. IHL norms incorporated in the Rome Statute to provide accurate definitions of war crimes are also accurate declarations of the consensus reached by humanity *vis-à-vis* the customs and uses of war.

This is not to say that the Rome Statute is merely a good summary of existing law. That would have been useful in and of itself, because the Statute concerns three converging bodies of law that needed to be harmonized and drafted into a coherent whole. Indeed, the frame of mind of the drafters seems to have been, for the most part, the need to develop a consensus, and therefore, declare the law as it is rather than to legislate anew. Nevertheless, there are some important additions, notably in the application of all of these principles to the perspective of women. On the other hand, nothing that is new in the Rome Statute sounds a discordant note, nor does it create insurmountable problems for ratification. In sum, the Rome Statute is a great achievement on two grounds: first, it describes very accurately and in clear terms the present state of the law in three converging bodies; second, it shows the way towards future development in appropriate new areas in which new norms are being constructed without radical ruptures with the current practice of nations.

As mentioned earlier, international law advances best through the decisions of authoritative bodies of a judicial nature. For that to be true, however, a special kind of judicial body is needed: one that is truly independent, impartial, effective and fair. In the international realm, an independent body is one that is shielded from interference in the appointment process and in functioning from the pressures of political or diplomatic bodies or from the states that give rise to it. To be impartial, an independent body has to show that, in applying standards, it is guided only by the letter of the law and by universal principles of justice. An effective body is one whose decisions are obeyed and, when compliance by states or individuals is not voluntary, has political organs ready and willing to put their weight behind the judicial body's orders. Finally, a judicial organ is fair if its processes are governed by clear procedural norms that are applied in good faith to each aspect of each case. It is well known that all of these aspects were open to discussion during the debates preceding the Rome Diplomatic Conference, and even during the final five weeks of deliberation. The fact that most norms that are decisive to the independence, impartiality, effectiveness and fairness of the ICC were retained is, of course, cause for celebration.

PART III
INTERNATIONAL PUBLIC POLICY AND THE ICC: ACCOUNTABILITY, DETERRENCE, AND REDRESS

CHAPTER 8

AMNESTY AND THE INTERNATIONAL CRIMINAL COURT

Naomi Roht-Arriaza

Domestic amnesties, often put in place at the end of civil conflict or to protect those who have committed atrocities, are not directly addressed in the Rome Statute of the International Criminal Court (ICC). Nonetheless, the issue goes to the heart of the aims and purposes of the ICC. This essay briefly sketches the existing international law on amnesties,[1] discusses how the Statute potentially deals with the issue, and applies these possibilities to some examples.

A. WHAT DOES INTERNATIONAL LAW SAY ABOUT AMNESTIES?

The easiest answer is that of treaty law: there can be no amnesty where a treaty requires prosecution. The 1948 Genocide Convention,[2] for instance, requires prosecution of both public officials and private citizens. The substantive provisions of the Genocide Convention have been widely recognized as embodying customary law. The definition of genocide given in the Convention is reproduced as Article 6 of the ICC Statute.

Grave breaches of the 1949 Geneva Conventions[3] are now listed as well in Article 8(a) of the Statute. Those provisions require states to prosecute violators,

---

[1] This brief summary omits most of the details and subtleties on the subject of amnesties. For fuller accounts, see NAOMI ROHT-ARRIAZA, ED., IMPUNITY AND HUMAN RIGHTS IN INTER-NATIONAL LAW AND PRACTICE (1995); Diane Orentlicher, *Settling Accounts: The Duty to Prosecute Human Rights Violations of a Prior Regime*, 100 YALE L.J. 2569 (1991).

[2] Convention on the Prevention and Punishment of the Crime of Genocide, Dec. 9, 1948, 78 U.N.T.S. 277, *reprinted in* 28 I.L.M. 763 (1989) and 3 INTERNATIONAL LAW AND WORLD ORDER: BASIC DOCUMENTS III.J.1 (Burns H. Weston, ed., 5 vols., 1994–).

[3] Convention for the Amelioration of the Condition of the Wounded and Sick in Armed Forces in the Field, Aug. 12, 1949, 75 U.N.T.S. 31; 6 U.S.T.S. 3114, 4 Bevans 853 (Convention No. I); Convention for the Amelioration of the Condition of the Wounded, Sick and Shipwrecked Members of Armed Forces at Sea, Aug. 12, 1949, 75 U.N.T.S. 85; 6 U.S.T.S. 3217 (Convention No. II); Convention Relative to the Treatment of Prisoners of War, Aug. 12, 1949, 75 U.N.T.S. 135; 6 U.S.T.S. 3316 (Convention No. III); Convention Relative to the Protection of Civilian Persons in Time of War, Aug. 12, 1949, 75 U.N.T.S. 287; 6 U.S.T.S. 3516.

or extradite them to a state that will. Grave breaches include wilful killing, torture or inhuman treatment, and others, but only in the context of an international armed conflict. Other parts of Article 8—other violations of the laws and customs of war in 8(b), or war crimes in internal armed conflicts (Article 8(c) and (e))—have no corresponding preexisting treaty obligation.

The Torture Convention[4] requires prosecution or extradition as well. There is no specific Article in the ICC Statute on torture, but it can be a constituent offense of any of the three core crimes if the specific requirements of those crimes are satisfied. In addition, general and regional human rights treaties, through the obligations they contain to ensure rights, to provide a remedy, and to a fair trial, have been interpreted by the respective treaty monitoring bodies as requiring prosecution, even where truth commissions or disciplinary bodies have considered the situation.

The most ambiguous case is that of crimes against humanity, defined in Article 7 of the ICC Statute. No pre-existing convention defines the crime, although the Nuremberg precedent[5] would imply that non-prosecution would be inconsistent with the demand for prosecution at Nuremberg. So too would subsequent U.N. resolutions and declarations and some judicial, diplomatic and legislative practice.[6] Commentators agree there is permissive jurisdiction to prosecute, but some take the position that state practice doesn't support an obligation to prosecute crimes against humanity as customary law.

So, as an initial matter, there is an almost but not quite complete overlap of the core crimes within ICC's jurisdiction with those crimes that require investigation and prosecution under existing international law. Of course, the fact that existing law says that *states* have an obligation to prosecute does not *per se* mean that the ICC has the same obligation. However, if the purpose of the Court is to provide a forum for prosecutions, then a Court decision not to prosecute in a situation where states have an obligation to go forward would be problematic.

---

[4] Convention Against Torture and Other Cruel, Inhuman or Degrading Treatment or Punishment, Dec. 10, 1984, G.A. Res. 39/46 (Annex), U.N. GAOR, 39th Sess., Supp. No. 51, at 197, U.N. Doc. A/RES/39/51 (1985), *reprinted in* 23 I.L.M. 1027 (1984) *and* 3 Weston III.K.2, *supra* note 2.

[5] Art. 6(c) of the 1945 London Charter provided for the prosecution of those who committed crimes against humanity. Agreement by the Government of the United Kingdom of Great Britain and Northern Ireland, the Government of the United States of America, the Provisional Government of the French Republic, and the Government of the Union of the Soviet Socialist Republics for the Prosecution and Punishment of the Major War Criminals of the European Axis and the Charter of the International Military Tribunal, Aug. 8, 1945, 59 Stat. 1544, 1546, 82 U.N.T.S. 279, 3 Bevans 1238, *reprinted in* 2 Weston II.E.1, *supra* note 2.

[6] *See* Orentlicher, *supra* note 1, at 2590–2592.

B. THE COURT AND AMNESTIES: FUNDAMENTAL AMBIGUITY

Given this background, it is notable that the ICC Statute does not deal with the question of amnesty. During one of the preparatory meetings, the U.S. delegation put out an informal "nonpaper" suggesting that the Court should take domestic amnesties into account when deciding whether or not to exercise jurisdiction. Other countries responded with expressions of fear that domestic amnesties could and would be abused by dictators and war criminals trying to avoid justice, and so would eviscerate the Court. Nonetheless, ambiguities and leeway in the Statute make it possible to take such amnesties into account in certain circumstances.

These ambiguities stem from a fundamental ambiguity in the Court project itself. If the Court exists because the core crimes, by their grievous nature, are international crimes that therefore must be punished by the international community, then the international community's interest is independent of the needs or vagaries of domestic political processes. A domestic amnesty serves to preclude domestic but not international prosecutions; it should have no bearing on the decision to prosecute by the ICC. If, on the other hand, the complementarity provisions of the Statute are emphasized, then the Court exists to provide supplementary venue only when the domestic venues break down, and in that case if amnesty does not represent a breakdown but a reasoned decision, perhaps it should be respected.

1. Complementarity

Amnesty could be dealt with, first, through application of the complementarity provisions. A state or accused (or the Court on its own motion) may argue that a case is inadmissible under Article 17 because a state that has jurisdiction is investigating or prosecuting or has investigated and decided not to prosecute. For example, a state that couples an amnesty with a truth commission, such as South Africa, might argue that "investigation" doesn't equal criminal investigation. However, a case is admissible where the state "is unwilling or unable genuinely to carry out the investigation or prosecution." Unwillingness may be shown where there is an "unjustified delay" or proceedings are "not conducted independently or impartially, and in a manner inconsistent with an intent to bring the person concerned to justice." This clearly suggests that criminal justice is the goal of investigation.

One of the hallmarks of unwillingness is that the "proceedings were undertaken or decision made for the purpose of shielding the person concerned from criminal responsibility for crimes within the jurisdiction of the Court." Amnesties generally by definition shield certain individuals from criminal responsibility, so this provision seems to apply. The affected state could argue an amnesty was not enacted for the *purpose* of shielding, but that shielding is merely a by-product of a decision taken for the *purpose* of national reconciliation. The Inter-American

Commission on Human Rights has found in considering a number of Latin American amnesties (including Chile and El Salvador) that the national reconciliation context is not enough to validate the amnesties,[7] but it is unclear how the ICC would rule on the issue.

A similar argument might be raised under Article 20, which precludes trial by the ICC for any person who has been tried by another court. Again, there is an exception for trials that were "for the purpose of shielding the person concerned from criminal responsibility" or "conducted in a manner which was inconsistent with an intent to bring the person concerned to justice." Thus, for instance, if an accused has been the subject of a judicial investigation which was closed through application of an amnesty law (as has happened in the Southern Cone states of Latin America), the individuals could argue that they have already been "tried." They likely would confront the prohibition on proceedings that are inconsistent with an intent to bring the person concerned to justice. Thus the principle *ne bis in idem* would not preclude ICC jurisdiction.

2. Security Council Deferral

Second, the Security Council could delay prosecution for renewable twelve month periods by adopting a resolution under Chapter VII of the U.N. Charter.[8] Thus, for example, if the Council wished to encourage a party to a conflict to participate in peace negotiations, it could reassure the individual through a resolution. It is not inconceivable that this route would have been chosen had the ICC been in existence during the conflict in the former Yugoslavia, and Yugoslav President Slobodan Milosovic been indicted by an ICC Prosecutor. Chapter VII requires the Security Council to determine the existence of a threat to the peace, a breach of the peace or an act of aggression in order to act.[9] This requirement has been broadly construed in recent years and would not be problematic. More problematic is the requirement that Security Council action be consistent with the purposes and principles of the U.N., including promoting respect for human rights.[10] Thus, if preexisting law as described above requires prosecution, it is not clear the Security Council can override that law through resolutions aimed at the ICC. The Court should be able to determine its own jurisdiction in that case. Moreover, there would be a political cost to the Security Council in detailing its reasons for invoking its right to deferral.

---

[7] *See* Douglass Cassel, *Lessons from the Americas: Guidelines for International Response to Amnesties for Atrocities*, 59 LAW & CONTEMP. PROBS. 205 (1996).

[8] "Actions with Respect to Threats to the Peace, Breaches of the Peace, and Acts of Aggression," U.N. CHARTER, Ch. VII, June 16, 1945, U.S.T. 993, 59 Stat. 1031.

[9] *Id.*, art. 39.

[10] *Id.*, art. 24(2).

3. Prosecutorial Discretion

The third, and most likely, avenue for dealing with amnesty involves a decision by the prosecutor to exercise discretion not to go forward even in cases that fall within the Court's jurisdiction. Thus, the prosecutor may seek a ruling from the Court regarding admissibility, putting the onus of a politically-charged decision on the validity of an amnesty on the Court. If she does so, victims may submit observations to the Court to ensure that not only states' views of the purpose and scope of an amnesty are heard.

More important, under Article 53, even if a case is otherwise admissible, the prosecutor may decline to investigate if, "taking into account the gravity of the crime and the interests of victims, there are nonetheless substantial reasons to believe that an investigation would not serve the interests of justice." After investigation, the prosecutor may decline to prosecute where prosecution is "not in the interests of justice, taking into account all the circumstances, including the gravity of the crime, the interests of victims and the age or infirmity of the alleged perpetrator, and his or her role in the alleged crime." The pre-trial chamber may decide to review the prosecutor's decision. Thus, the prosecutor, and, if it chooses, the Court, may evaluate the balance of benefits and costs of recognizing an amnesty under a wide-ranging set of criteria.

This is the most likely scenario if one assumes the ICC's existence in a case like that of South Africa. There, crimes within the ICC's jurisdiction were almost certainly committed; yet the international community has largely supported South Africa's attempt to establish the truth, and some measure of justice, through a combination of truth commission, reparations and an amnesty-for-confession scheme. Although many, including survivors' representatives, would likely disagree as to whether or not this scheme is permissible under international law, prosecuting the F.W. de Klerks of the world might not be the best use of an ICC Prosecutor's resources. The Prosecutor would not be forced to go forward; however, she would have to explain the decision not to go forward to the pre-trial chamber by weighing the factors listed above. It is interesting to note that while the alleged perpetrator's "role in the alleged crime" is listed among the factors to be considered, the person's role in peace negotiations or in bringing a period of strife to an end is not listed.

There is a fourth and final way to deal with the amnesty issue, but it depends on interpreting domestic amnesty provisions rather than the ICC statute. A number of domestic courts have interpreted their country's amnesty to apply only to the extent it is compatible with the state's international legal obligations, including those under human rights and humanitarian law treaties. The Court could read a domestic amnesty in light of the state's international commitments, find that it cannot preclude prosecution of the crimes at issue, and authorize an investigation and subsequent prosecution. This would put the onus on the state to start its own *bona fide* investigatory process, which would be subject to the Article 17 tests described above. If it did not, the amnesty would not impede ICC jurisdiction. But this would require the Court to interpret not its own Statute, but general international law—a much more risky proposition and one a new institution would rightly be wary of undertaking.

CHAPTER 9
DOMESTIC AMNESTIES AND INTERNATIONAL ACCOUNTABILITY

Garth Meintjes

The international community increasingly views domestic amnesties[1] as instruments of impunity and not of justice.[2] This trend stems in part from the tireless efforts of human rights groups to find ways of using international mechanisms to do justice where domestic efforts have failed.[3] In a significant victory, supporters of international accountability successfully discouraged any consideration of including direct legal recognition of domestic amnesties within the Rome Statute of the International Criminal Court (ICC).[4] This is fortunate, because such a negotiated provision might have served only to legitimize impunity. However, as result, we must now rely on indirect indicators to answer the question of what are the national and international legal effects of domestic amnesties.

---

[1] Throughout this discussion the term domestic amnesty refers to a national or municipal law which has the effect of negating accountability for serious violations of human rights. The term domestic is also applied to the national or municipal legal system when distinguishing between the domestic and international frameworks of accountability. However, for the sake of convenience, the term national is maintained to distinguish between national and international laws.

[2] *See* Question of the Impunity of Perpetrators of Human Rights Violations (Civil and Political): Revised Final Report Prepared by Mr. Joinet Pursuant to Subcommission Decision 1996/119, U.N. Subcommission on Prevention of Discrimination and Protection of Minorities, 49th Sess., U.N. Doc. E/CN.4/Sub.2/1997/20/Rev.1 (1997) para. 3. *See generally* Douglas Cassel, *Accountability for International Crime and Serious Violations of Fundamental Rights: Lessons from the Americas: Guidelines for the International Response to Amnesties for Atrocities*, 59 LAW & CONTEMP. PROBS. 197 (1996).

[3] *See* General Comment No. 20 (44), art. 7, U.N. Doc. CCPR/C21/REV.I/Add.3, para. 15 (Apr. 1992). *See also* Inter-Am. C.H.R. Rep. No. 24/92 (Argentina), OEA/ser. L/V/II. 82, doc. 24 (Oct. 2, 1992); Inter-Am. C.H.R. Rep. No. 29/92 (Uruguay), OEA/ser. L/V/II. 82, doc. 25 (Oct. 2, 1992); Inter-Am. C.H.R. Report on the Situation of Human Rights in El Salvador, OEA/ser. L/V/II. 85, doc. 28 (Feb. 11, 1994); and Inter-Am. C.H.R. Rep. No. 36/96 (Chile), OEA/ser. L/V/II. 95, doc. 25 (Oct. 15, 1996).

[4] During one of the preparatory meetings before the Rome Conference the United States circulated an informal "non-paper" on the question of whether the ICC should take domestic amnesties into account when deciding whether to exercise its jurisdiction. A copy of the paper can be found at: <gopher://gopher.igc.apc.org:70/00/orgs/iccnatldocs/prepcom4/amnesty.us> (visited on Feb. 14, 2000).

According to Naomi Roht-Arriaza "the easiest answer is that of treaty law: there can be no amnesty where a treaty requires prosecution."[5] Elsewhere, Aryeh Neier, when speaking of successor governments, claims that "amnesties are invalid when they conflict with international treaties that obligate states to prosecute and punish."[6] While both these statements are essentially correct in their description of the international effects of an amnesty law, they are open to significant misinterpretation. In fact there can be valid domestic amnesties which conflict with international law, even in cases where treaties require prosecution. Accountability can be enhanced by recognizing the complexity of the legal framework.[7] The following is only a preliminary exploration, and aims to complement the likewise preliminary essay by Naomi Roht-Arriaza.[8]

A. AMNESTIES IN THE INTERNATIONAL FRAMEWORK OF ACCOUNTABILITY

It is useful at the outset to bear in mind that the international legal framework of accountability is the result of at least two converging proscriptive processes aimed at curbing organized violence and repression. Generally speaking, human rights law evolved as a set of internationally guaranteed rights which individuals can invoke against their own governments or its agents. When these rights are violated or neglected, it is usually the state and not some individual or group that is held responsible. Humanitarian law, by comparison, creates international obligations for both individuals and states. Admittedly, both areas of law have much in common and, given the trend in organized violence away from international wars towards domestic or internal armed conflicts, it is becoming increasingly difficult to distinguish between the effects of each proscriptive process.

One consequence of this normative evolution is that acts of violence may in certain circumstances give rise to multiple legal consequences or liabilities within both the domestic and international legal frameworks of accountability. Thus, for example, when members of a state's armed forces commit acts of torture or disappearances during an internal armed conflict, the multiple potential legal consequences include:

---

[5] *See supra* Chapter 8.

[6] ARYEH NEIER, WAR CRIMES 1998, 98.

[7] *See generally,* Juan E. Méndez, *Accountability for the Past,* 19 HUM. RTS. Q. 255 (1997). According to his careful exposition of the current requirements of international law, there are at least four distinct obligations which transitional states face:
1. they must investigate and seek to establish the truth about their repressive past;
2. they must prosecute those implicated in gross violations;
3. they must pay to compensation to the victims or their relatives; and
4. they must redress past violations by adopting such reforms as are needed to ensure that these violations are not repeated.

[8] *See also* IMPUNITY AND HUMAN RIGHTS IN INTERNATIONAL LAW (Naomi Roth-Arriaza ed., 1995).

1. individual criminal liability at the domestic, international,[9] and foreign domestic levels;[10]
2. individual civil liability at the domestic or foreign domestic levels[11] (and potentially at the ICC level[12]);
3. state liability at the domestic and foreign domestic levels;[13]
4. state responsibility for injury towards aliens and others (at the international and foreign domestic levels);[14] and
5. a state obligation to prosecute (or extradite) the individual perpetrators.[15]

The point of highlighting these multiple potential legal consequences is that each may be affected differently by the adoption of a domestic amnesty. For the sake of clarity, therefore, it is useful to bear in mind first, that acts may be sub-

---

[9] *See* Agreement for the Prosecution and Punishment of the Major War Criminals of the European Axis Powers and Charter of the International Military Tribunal, Aug. 8, 1945, 59 Stat. 1544, 82 U.N.T.S. 279; International Military Tribunal to Prosecute the Major War Criminals of the Far East, Jan. 19, 1946, T.I.A.S. No. 1589, 4 Bevans 20; Statute of the International Tribunal for the Prosecution of Persons Responsible for Serious Violations of International Humanitarian Law Committed in the Territory of the Former Yugoslavia since 1991, U.N. Doc. S/25704, Annex (1993), *reprinted in* 32 I.L.M. 1192 (1993); Statute of the International Tribunal for the Prosecution of Persons Responsible for Genocide and Other Serious Violations of International Humanitarian Law Committed in the Territory of Rwanda, S.C. Res. 955, U.N. SCOR, 49th Sess., Res. & Dec., U.N. Doc. S/INF/50 (1994), *reprinted in* 33 I.L.M. 1602 (1994); and Rome Statute of the International Criminal Court, U.N. Doc. A/CONF.183/9 (July 17, 1998), *reprinted in* 37 I.L.M. 999 (1998), available in Documents (visited Oct. 22, 1999) <http://www.un.org/icc>.

[10] The term foreign domestic courts is used here to refer to the courts of states other than the one in which the crime was committed. Prosecutions in such cases may be based on either universal or extraterritorial jurisdiction (based on nationality of the victim). *See generally* Convention Against Torture and Other Cruel, Inhuman or Degrading Treatment or Punishment, G.A. Res. 39/46, U.N. GAOR, 39th Sess., U.N. Doc. E/CN.4/1984/72 (1984), art. 5 [hereinafter Torture Convention] (requiring state parties to assume jurisdiction over torture committed anywhere): and R v. Bow Street Metropolitan Stipendiary Magistrate; *Ex Parte* Pinochet Ugarte, 2 All E.R. 97, 165 (H.L 1999) (ruling that Pinochet can be extradited to Spain to stand trial for torture committed in Chile).

[11] *See* Filartiga v. Pena-Irala, 630 F.2d 876 (2d Cir. N.Y.), June 30, 1980 (No. 79–6090, 191) (the first U.S. case to hold that the family of a torture victim may rely on the Alien Tort Claims Act to bring suit against a defendant who comes within the jurisdiction of U.S. courts).

[12] *See* Rome Statute, *supra* note 9, art. 75 (providing for the possibility of reparations to victims).

[13] *See* Siderman de Blake v. Republic of Argentina, 965 F.2d 699, 60 U.S.L.W. 2771 (9th Cir. Cal. May 22, 1992) (No. 85–5773) (plaintiff successfully overcame Argentina's defense claim of sovereign immunity).

[14] *See generally* IAN BROWNLIE, PRINCIPLES OF PUBLIC INTERNATIONAL LAW Chs. XX and XXIII (4th ed. 1990).

[15] *See generally* Diane F. Orentlicher, *Settling Accounts: The Duty to Prosecute Human Rights Violations of a Prior Regime*, 100 YALE L.J. 2537 (1991).

stantively criminalized or prohibited by both national and international laws, and second that multiple jurisdictions may be competent to deal with any alleged transgressions. Further, it is also useful to distinguish between individual liability on the one hand and state obligations, responsibility and liability on the other. For present purposes, however, it is only necessary to refer to the distinction between state obligations and individual liability or accountability under international law.

B. HOW DO DOMESTIC AMNESTIES AFFECT THE ACCOUNTABILITY CREATED BY INTERNATIONAL LAW?

As noted earlier, some human rights scholars argue that there can be no amnesty where a treaty requires prosecution or that amnesties which violate international law are invalid. Such statements neglect some of the nuances in the evolution of the international framework of accountability. In fact, the effects of a domestic amnesty may vary in accordance with the area of international law which it implicates. For example, while it is true that individual liability before the ICC will not be affected by an amnesty which violates a state's duty to prosecute, the same is true even of an amnesty which does not violate such a duty. This is not because international law directly invalidates domestic amnesties, but rather because states cannot use domestic legislation to bar international criminal liability. Similarly, a domestic amnesty which seeks to negate the criminality of an act that has been previously criminalized under both national and international law may be *valid* with regard to the former while simply being *ineffective* with regard to the latter. This is certainly possible in all states which follow a "dualist" approach to international law.[16]

From the ICC's perspective this theoretical distinction between whether a domestic amnesty is *invalid* or *ineffective* in terms of its effect upon the Court's own jurisdiction may seem like little more than a semantic debate. It certainly appears so when one considers the impact of a domestic amnesty that both violates a state's international duty to prosecute and conflicts with an international criminal prohibition. However, the usefulness of understanding this distinction becomes apparent in the case of a domestic amnesty that does not violate a state's international duty to prosecute but does conflict with an international criminal prohibition. In such a case, the ICC would be correct in concluding that notwithstanding its domestic validity and compliance with international law, an amnesty purporting to excuse individual culpability for an internationally defined crime is simply ineffective. Of course, this does not mean that the ICC or international prosecutor will necessarily always decide to prosecute in such cases, but only than they will not be legally barred from doing so.

---

[16] In states which follow a "monist" approach to international law it may be appropriate to term a domestic amnesty which violates international law invalid.

It appears, for example, that the international community has provisionally accepted South Africa's efforts to deal with its past as a good faith attempt to comply with its international obligations.[17] This implies that it acted legitimately when it established a truth and reconciliation process in which many individuals received amnesties in exchange for full disclosures about politically motivated crimes. Nevertheless, it is conceivable that a foreign prosecutor could legitimately decide, notwithstanding the domestic amnesties, to bring charges against persons accused of international crimes which are subject to universal jurisdiction.

The basis for the suggested distinction lies in the nature of the international laws dealing with peace and security. On the one hand, international treaties such as the Genocide[18] and Geneva Conventions[19] seek to deal with the problem of organized violence and war by directly criminalizing the prohibited conduct under the proscriptive authority of the international community. In cases where acts are directly criminalized by the international community a domestic amnesty will always be ineffective in negating international culpability. Thus, regardless of whether or not the amnesty may be valid under national law, it will have no effect upon the criminality of such acts—even within the state's own territory. Accordingly, it is more appropriate to use the term ineffective instead of invalid when referring to a domestic amnesty which conflicts with an international criminal prohibition.

On the other hand, regional and international laws such as the various human rights conventions seek to avoid the dangers of organized violence and repression by requiring states to act in accordance with international standards. Specialized treaties such as the Torture Convention[20] go even further by requiring states to use their own proscriptive authority to criminalize specific acts. Together these various treaties create obligations which potentially may be violated by the adoption

---

[17] *See* John Dugard, *Reconciliation and Justice: The South African Experience*, 8 TRANSNAT'L L. & CONTEMP. PROBS. 277, 301 (Fall 1998) (noting that the international community has given its full support to the South African truth and reconciliation process).

[18] *See* Convention on the Prevention and Punishment of the Crime of Genocide, G.A. Res. 260 A (III), art. I (Dec. 9, 1948) (entry into force Jan. 12, 1951).

[19] *See generally* Geneva Convention for the Amelioration of the Condition of the Wounded and Sick in Armed Forces in the Field, Aug. 12, 1949, 6 U.S.T. 3114, 75 U.N.T.S. 31; Geneva Convention for the Amelioration of the Condition of Wounded, Sick and Shipwrecked Members of Armed Forces at Sea, Aug. 12, 1949, 6 U.S.T. 3217, 75 U.N.T.S. 85; Geneva Convention Relative to the Treatment of Prisoners of War, Aug. 12, 1949, 6 U.S.T. 3316, 75 U.N.T.S. 135; Geneva Convention Relative to the Protection of Civilian Persons in Time of War, Aug. 12, 1949, 6 U.S.T. 3516, 75 U.N.T.S. 287; Protocol Additional to the Geneva Conventions of Aug. 12, 1949 and Relating to the Protection of Victims of International Armed Conflicts, June 8, 1977, 1125 U.N.T.S. 3; Protocol Additional to the Geneva Conventions of Aug. 12, 1949 and Relating to the Protection of Victims of Non-International Armed Conflicts, June 8, 1977, 1125 U.N.T.S. 609.

[20] *See* Torture Convention, *supra* note 10, art. 4.

of a domestic amnesty. However, it would be wrong to describe such an amnesty as being automatically invalidated by international law. For while it is true that there may be cases in which domestic amnesties are invalid, a closer examination of such cases reveals that their validity or invalidity is determined by national and not international law.

The first circumstance in which a domestic amnesty may be termed invalid is when the national law has been adopted in a procedurally illegitimate manner. This would be the case, for example, where a powerful political elite or military junta has adopted a self-amnesty prior to the establishment or reestablishment of democratic governance. Such self-amnesties are invalid, not because the national law has been trumped by an overriding international law, but because they do not comply with the national rules of recognition which international law supports.

The second instance in which a domestic amnesty may be termed invalid is when the national law of a state incorporates international law in a manner which places international norms above rather than on par with ordinary legislation. Although this is not yet the practice of most states, it may be done, for example, by giving international law the same status as a constitutional bill of rights. Yet even in these cases, it is the constitutional framework of the state that renders the domestic amnesty invalid and not international law.

With these theoretical clarifications in mind, it is easier to understand the role played by the international community in helping states to deal with the past without compromising the future.

C. HOW DOES INTERNATIONAL LAW SERVE TO PROMOTE PEACE AND ACCOUNTABILITY?

Some peacemakers or transitional governments have argued that there is sometimes an inevitable choice between peace and justice.[21] In other words, they claim that it is sometimes necessary to forgo accountability for past abuses in order to avoid the threat of renewed conflict or repression. Although many of these claims are unfounded or exaggerated, some divided societies may in fact face such painful choices.

In determining how the international community can best deal with such cases, it is useful to recall the multiple legal consequences which may be triggered by acts of organized violence and repression. Since some of these consequences are designed to have an impact on the way a domestic government may use its powers, it may be reasonable in some cases to recognize the temporary inability of such governments to comply with their obligations. Obviously, it is not in the interests of the international community to force a fledgling democracy to com-

---

[21] *See* NEIER, *supra* note 6, at 97 (where he refers to precisely such an argument by Uruguay's President Julio Sanguinetti).

mit political suicide. However, it must also be noted that these are continuing obligations and that the expectations of the international community will likely become more and more demanding as the new government's situation improves.

Nevertheless, state obligations are only one side of the accountability framework. On the other side is individual accountability under international law. Today, thanks to the increased recognition being accorded to the principle of universal jurisdiction, to the precedent of the establishment of two *ad hoc* tribunals, and to the growing prospects for a future ICC, the latter part of the accountability framework is not dependent upon a subject state's willingness or ability to provide justice. As a result, while the international community still favors local enforcement of accountability, it is no longer necessary to compromise this aspect of accountability in order to make peace or consolidate democracy.

Distinguishing between state obligations and individual accountability also allows for a better differentiation between what the international community expects of states and what it expects of individuals. For example, most international judgements to date about the legitimacy of amnesties have been made in the context of state obligations under regional or international human rights law and not in the context of individual criminal prosecutions. In the case of the former, it is obviously reasonable to take into account a broad range of social and political considerations, and to give some deference to the democratically supported policies and decisions of a transitional government. Thus, a judgement about whether Rwanda has complied with its international obligations in terms of its past might appropriately consider the vast magnitude of the genocide and its impact on the country's judicial infrastructure.

Although informative, it would be wrong to confuse such considerations with those that may be relevant in determining whether to hold individuals accountable under international law. In the case of individual criminal or civil liability, the issue, arguably, should be focused much more narrowly on factors which reflect on the individual's culpability or blameworthiness. To do otherwise would be to politicize the pursuit of international justice and compromise the independence of the ICC or a foreign court. This recognition explains the rationale behind the Rome Statute's allowance for prosecutorial discretion, and its restriction of the ability of the Security Council to bar prosecutions.

The role of the international community in peacemaking and conflict resolution is thus more nuanced than simply deciding whether or not amnesties should be granted. Instead, it supports the efforts of domestic peacemakers, on the one hand, by requiring states to do the best they can in remedying past human rights abuses and, on the other hand, by no longer giving them the sole discretion of deciding whether or not individuals should be held accountable for such abuses.

D. CONCLUSION

The proposition that a domestic amnesty may be valid even when it conflicts with an international obligation to prosecute, serves to separate the issue of individual criminal accountability under international law from the question of whether a state has fulfilled its international obligations. The purpose of doing this is to make it clear that judgments about the one should not be confused with judgments about the other. In particular, the criteria by which the international community decides whether a state has fulfilled its international obligations should not be transposed onto determinations about whether the ICC or a foreign prosecutor ought to pay deference to a domestic amnesty.

This preliminary exploration also points to the need for a deeper reflection on the political philosophy underlying the establishment of the international framework of accountability and its mechanisms. Such a reflection could usefully draw on the idea of the social contract as a basis for both the domestic and international frameworks of accountability, encompassing the notion of two interlocking social contracts. At the national level, Rawls' well known theory of justice would provide an adequate theoretical explanation of the agreements that underlie most democratic transitions.[22]

At the international level the key issue is whether the participants in the social contract are states or individuals.[23] While traditional state practice on treaty making can be adequately explained by a theory of justice based upon states as the members of the social contract, it is not clear that this is sufficient to explain all aspects of the international framework of accountability. For example, such a theory would not adequately explain the vitally important role played by thousands of NGOs in the negotiations before and during the Rome Conference. To account for these actors, it is probably necessary to develop a theory of justice which makes some room for the participation of individuals or their representatives in the formulation of the social contract.

One benefit of a theory of justice that views individuals as being among the contractees of the international social contract is that it answers the problem raised by Madeline Morris in this collection about the impact of the ICC on the

---

[22] JOHN RAWLS, A THEORY OF JUSTICE (1971).

[23] Rawls has in his more recent writings attempted to develop a more international theory of justice. Unfortunately, his most recent book, THE LAW OF PEOPLES (1999), does not achieve a satisfactory explanation of international justice. In it he describes an international "original position" in which only the representatives of "peoples" and not individuals are allowed to participate. Presumably this is done to avoid the criticism of being biased in favor of western individualism by making room for communitarianism. However, the trouble with this approach is that much of the modern world is no longer composed of "peoples." Instead, individuals are forming bonds and communities which transcend such traditional constituencies. The same is equally true of nation states. As a result, individuals now often belong to multiple groups through which they express their expectations about fairness and accountability.

interests of non-party states. Under such a theory, the Rome agreement would be seen as the product of negotiations that took into account the interests of most states together with collective interests of individuals (as expressed by NGOs), while rejecting some of the claims put forward by one or more states which were based on a narrow construction of the latter states' domestic interests. To have done otherwise would have severely prejudiced the collective interest of many individuals who are unfortunate enough to live in states where the domestic social contract does not adequately protected their interests.

This reflection on the events at Rome should not be seen as a claim that treaties are now based on the collective interests of individuals rather than on the interests of states. At the end of the day it is still states which sign the treaties. However, in describing the process through which the agreement was reached, it is probably more accurate to see Rome as a healthy combination of both sets of interests. In any event, while a fuller refection on the political philosophy underlying the international framework of accountability is beyond the scope of this preliminary exploration, it seems clear that recent developments in the struggle for justice call for a careful reexamination of the traditional assumptions about the nature and functions of international law.

CHAPTER 10

THE INTERNATIONAL CRIMINAL COURT AND THE CHALLENGE OF DETERRENCE

Gustavo Gallón

A. INTRODUCTION

Can an international criminal court deter future violations of human rights and humanitarian law? It would be pleasant to give a positive or optimistic answer to this question, but no one can predict that a potential violator of human rights will refrain from acting due to the existence of an international criminal tribunal. Yet most people in the world would agree that heinous human rights violations should not reoccur and must be prevented. It may be a universal hope that this goal can be achieved through deterrence produced by a criminal court. Nonetheless, the hope of significantly deterring violations of international human rights and humanitarian laws by means of an international criminal court may not be well-founded for several reasons.

First, in order to deter future violations, a system of justice must be effective in bringing to a halt current violations. This does not appear to be a likely role for the ICC. Secondly, no system of justice is able fully and completely to deter wrongdoing. Thirdly, the proposed international criminal court is still a weak project that needs to be strengthened before a minimum level of deterrence may be expected.

This initially negative conclusion does not mean that an international criminal court ultimately cannot deter violations, or that creating the court is a useless exercise. Instead, it means that the important advances made thus far towards establishment of an international criminal court must continue and be strengthened in order to assure the court's effectiveness, its capacity to bring about a cessation of violations through accountability, and its consequent ability to deter human rights violations.

B. CESSATION AS THE FIRST PURPOSE OF AN INTERNATIONAL CRIMINAL COURT

Redress and deterrence are commonly mentioned as the principal purposes of the judicial procedures instituted to respond to violations of human rights and humanitarian law. They also belong to the list of purposes attributed to criminal law generally, but the specific discussions about the rationale for punishing human rights violations tend to focus on the purposes of redress and deterrence. Moreover, they tend to produce a division between partisans of redress and partisans of deterrence.[1]

Victims are usually seen as partisans of redress or accountability for past violations. So are thinkers considered to be idealistic or fundamentalist. Governments, as well as scholars considered to be realists or pragmatists, are frequently identified as partisans of deterrence of future violations, looking forward rather than backward. This distinction would not be problematic if the preference for one purpose was not viewed as denigrating or eliminating fulfillment of the other. Unfortunately, many governments and pragmatists are viewed as sacrificing redress and accountability under the pretext of deterring future violations as a superior aim. Other times, victims and fundamentalist actors are accused of putting in danger emerging institutions, democracy, or social coexistence, by trying to obtain redress and accountability at any cost.

This supposed opposition between redress and deterrence has hidden the existence and importance of another purpose of the judicial human rights procedures: the cessation of ongoing violations. This purpose precedes that of redress and deterrence. It is a necessary pre-condition for the possibility of redress and deterrence. Cessation requires that the perpetrator be deprived of the power that allows him or her to commit further violations. Means to accomplish this purpose can be isolation, imprisonment, or other justified means of eliminating the power of the perpetrator.

1. Cessation as a Judicial Function

Cessation is part of the protection of public order,[2] important to the functioning of the judicial system, although it is rarely mentioned as a purpose of judicial action against human rights violations. One of the main explanations for that omission may be that most judicial activity concerned with human rights violations has taken place after the collapse of the regime responsible for the systematic violations. The Nuremberg and Tokyo tribunals prosecuted military and civilian leaders defeated in World War II. Greek and Argentine trials began after the military juntas lost their power in each country. In those cases and in similar instances, the question of how the judicial procedure could ensure cessation of the violations did

---

[1] CARLOS SALVADOR NINO, RADICAL EVIL ON TRIAL (1996), 135–148; JAIME MALAMUD-GOTI, GAME WITHOUT END (1996), 10–17.

[2] Michael Reisman identifies seven goals for the protection, restoration, and improvement of public order, the second one of which is *"suspending* current public order violations." This notion of suspension corresponds to our notion of cessation. *See* W. Michael Reisman, "Legal Responses to Genocide and Other Massive Violations of Human Rights," *in* Cherif Bassiouni and Madeline H. Morris, *Accountability for International Crime and Serious Violations of Fundamental Human Rights*, 59 LAW & CONTEMP. PROB. 75 (1996).

not occur because the activities had already ceased. Instead, the question became one of providing redress to victims and deterring future violators.

In the cases mentioned, cessation resulted from military or political action. At other times it has been the result of police action. It is not easy, in such circumstances, to see cessation as a part of the purpose of the judiciary, but it is integral to its functions. The efficacy and the rapidity of military, political, or police actions seeking to halt human rights violations can be substantially improved if there is a strong judicial system mandated to act against the violations and violators, beginning by halting their continuation.[3]

Experience teaches that, first of all, the cessation of human rights violations, especially massive violations, must be accomplished early. Without a strong international judicial mechanism, however, the international community is reluctant to act through intervention to bring about a halt to abuse. Multiple calculations made by governments, as well as risks of illegitimate intervention, make cessation difficult or dangerous if the process is not under the authority of a legitimate and strong international judicial mechanism.

2.   Cessation, Accountability, and Insufficient Deterrence

The United Nations may have tried to apply this lesson to the gross violations that occurred in the former Yugoslavia and in Rwanda when the Security Council decided to create the *ad-hoc* international criminal tribunals. Unfortunately, the material resources and the coercive support given to the *ad-hoc* tribunals have been inferior to the exigencies of the situation.[4] In these conditions, the inability to bring a halt to the human rights violations is not surprising. This inability obvi-

---

[3] As Professor Reisman says: "What can the enlightened sectors of the international community do to prevent and halt the proliferation of genocides and massive human rights violations around the planet? We evade the obvious, albeit costliest answer—to arrest them before, or at least while they are happening, by any means necessary: to stop them by stopping them." Nevertheless, he avoids considering judicial action to bring about such cessation, maybe because he is critical of "a judicial romanticism in which we imagine that merely by creating entities we call 'courts' we have prevented or solved major problems." *Id.* The advantage of including cessation or suspension of violations within the frame of action of the judiciary is to reduce the risk of arbitrariness involved in the need or the will of stopping violations "by any means necessary."

[4] In 1997, the President of the ICTFY summarized his conclusions as follows: "Eighteen public indictments have been issued by the Prosecutor and confirmed by the Judges, 11 indictees have been arrested and brought to The Hague for trial, one trial has been held . . . while two more trials are under way, a third is to commence later in 1997 and two others to start in 1998. . . . Despite these accomplishments, the Tribunal remains a partial failure—through no fault of its own—because the vast majority of indictees continue to remain free, seemingly enjoying absolute immunity. . . . [The] Tribunal has been created for the very purpose of rendering justice but has been left partially ineffective by the failure of states to make arrests." Antonio Cassese, Report of the International Tribunal for the Prosecution of Persons Responsible for Serious Violations of International Humanitarian Law Committed in the Territory of the Former Yugoslavia since 1991, United Nations, Document A/52/375 S/1997/729, paras. 173 and 175.

ously has been followed by inadequate deterrence and insufficient redress in Rwanda and in the former Yugoslavia.

Another example of insufficient action to halt violations is the case of Augusto Pinochet. Violations diminished in Chile during the late 1970s and the 1980s, thanks to the international political reaction among other factors. That partial cessation was complemented later by a domestic referendum that politically defeated the dictatorship. However, even if massive human rights violations ceased once the new democratic period began, there was never accountability of violators or true cessation. Those responsible for the wrongs continued to wield enormous power acquired from the terror created by the grave and numerous violations that remained almost entirely unpunished. Obviously, there was no redress for the victims of those violations. The trials against Pinochet in England in 1998 and 1999 demonstrate the aftermath, that there has been no deterrence in Chile. Pinochet and his numerous supporters—almost a third of Chileans—continue to justify the violations that were committed, seeing them as necessary to save the nation from the so-called danger of communism, and insisting that they would repeat the violations if necessary.[5] They have not been deterred at all because they never were held accountable through a judicial decision.

Cessation and accountability are thus conditions for deterring and providing redress to victims of human rights violations. It is not only the result of a military, political or police action, but is a judicial function. Cessation is, and has to be, the first purpose of the judicial action against human rights violations.

The problem is that stopping violations seems to be more difficult than is deterring future conduct, although in reality the first is a prerequisite to the second. It implies confronting the violator before the violations become massive and it may require confronting numerous perpetrators. That is a task that politics and societies find difficult. It seems more useful and more comfortable not to act directly against the violators—against all the violators—but to act against none or a few of them expecting that the rest will be deterred from committing violations again. The same rationale leads governments frequently to decide not to punish past violations but to declare at the same time the commitment to seriously punish any violations that occur in the future. The expectation is that there will be no new violations because the announced commitment to punish seriously will suffice to deter wrongdoing.

---

5 "While Communism has assassinated many millions of human beings during this century in this continent, and specifically in the countries that condemn me through spurious trials, I am persecuted because I defeated Communism in Chile, virtually saving the country from a civil war. That meant three thousand deaths, almost a third of which [was] uniformed and civilian people who fell victim to extremist terrorism." from the letter written by Pinochet in London in November 1996, published as "Carta de Pinochet a todos los chilenos" or "Pinochet rechaza cargos en carta a los chilenos," *in* La Tercera en Internet (*www.latercera.com*), section "Encrucijada judicial. Caso Pinochet. Documentos."

Deterrence is a normal and understandable wish of governments and of societies in order to prevent human rights violations. Deterrence also usually is a legitimate and an adequate approach to prevention. It is even called "the ultimate end of every good legislation" by Beccaria.[6] But deterrence of anonymous and potential violators can be a dangerous illusion with painful consequences if it is not preceded or accompanied by effective accountability of the known violators of the past and of the present.

C. TOTAL DETERRENCE AS AN UNATTAINABLE END

The goal of deterrence can be a dangerous illusion if it leads to an assumption that violations will cease after the establishment of an international criminal court, or that at least the most heinous crimes against humanity will not be repeated, thanks to the deterrent effect of such a court. Unfortunately, no legal system can totally eliminate crime. In fact, the existence of a criminal justice system in each society is not related to the expectation that crime will end, but to the assumption that crimes will continue to take place. No legal system has ever deterred every person from committing crimes. Such systems exist precisely to protect society by punishing criminals who, despite sanctions, continue to disrespect the rights of others. Criminal justice reflects a need to protect rights and to provide redress to victims whose rights are violated. Of course, an effective criminal system can also deter potential criminals,[7] but the level of deterrence of every criminal system is limited.

The existence of an international criminal court does not mean that the violations or crimes that occur in the future will be small or unimportant. Heinous, gross or horrendous human rights violations may reappear. People like Hitler or Pol Pot would not have abstained from massively violating human rights because of the creation of an international court. The court would have to act effectively. The capacity for such a court to enjoin violators, more than the dream of deterring them, is what should sustain the hope of people to confront and defeat in the future what it was not possible to face opportunely in the past.

1. Fictitious Accountability

If a deterrent effect—even limited or partial—is desired, the efforts at holding perpetrators accountable must be significant and serious. In fact, deterrence is directly proportional to accountability. That means that the more the violators are stopped and held accountable, the higher the deterrence effect. If many violators escape control by the court, there may be no deterrence effect at all. The same can happen if the control is fictitious, which is the case of prosecuting scapegoats.

---

[6] Because "[I]t is better to prevent crimes than to punish them," CESARE BECCARIA, ON CRIMES AND PUNISHMENTS 93 (1963).

[7] Concerning those conditions, *see* RICHARD A. POSNER, ECONOMIC ANALYSIS OF LAW 217–236 (4th ed. 1992).

Accountability can be fictitious even if the prosecuted are the actual perpetrators. There are at least three possible scenarios in which that can happen. First, it happens when only some, or many, supporters of violators, but not leaders, are prosecuted. It is evident that if leaders feel free from prosecution, they will be able to continue committing human rights violations, even if it is more difficult for them to recruit new supporters who risk being prosecuted. Second, when only leaders committing violations, but not their supporters or subordinates, are tried,[8] it is natural for former subordinates to attempt to replace the former chiefs and become new leaders who can continue the commission of human rights violations. They will try to avoid repeating the mistakes of their leaders, but they will not necessarily be deterred from committing new violations, if only to eliminate witnesses or investigators who represent a danger to the impunity they enjoy.

The third scenario occurs when prosecution focuses on a target—a person or a small group of people, considered to be the key element—to explain every violation. This is a frequent temptation in life and in the history of criminal law. Once a mastermind or leader is identified as the source of every evil, it is easy to conclude that eliminating that person suffices to resolve the problem. Hitler, Pol Pot, and Pinochet are important, but it is an over-simplification to concentrate on a particular individual. Reality is normally more complex. Massive or systematic human rights violations involve more than a leader, requiring enormous decentralization in action. Prosecuting only one individual will not deter other people from committing violations. Instead, other leaders can emerge to reproduce the machinery of violations. A non-fictitious policy has to face the challenge of stopping all leaders and key supporters by positive actions, instead of expecting them to be deterred as an automatic consequence of taking action against one leader.

2. Complementarity of Deterrence and Redress

If prevention or deterrence is not assumed as the effect of a passive situation—i.e., the mere existence of an international criminal court—but as the effect of positive actions oriented to hold accountable violators, it is likely that a certain level of deterrence can be achieved. A balance rather than an opposition has to be found between deterrence and redress, in order to halt violations and avoid the risk of fictitious accountability.

---

[8] "Prosecuting only leaders would, in many contexts, be a mistake. If the international community would likely be satisfied by a few prominent prosecutions, the likely presumption would be that those few prosecutions should be of top-level leaders. . . . These factors would likely make the leaders appear to the international community like the appropriate group to prosecute. Not necessarily so, however, in the perception of the victim population. . . . Obviously, not all leaders and not all followers can be prosecuted in most contexts of crimes of mass violence. But a prosecutorial design that includes followers as well as leaders would serve victim interests better than would a leaders-only design." Madeline Morris, *Complementarity and Its Discontents: States, Victims, and the International Criminal Court, infra* Chapter 15.

Policies based upon deterrence or prevention as the exclusive or the most important purpose tend to ignore or minimize the value of the aforementioned directly proportional relationship between accountability and deterrence. As achieving cessation is a difficult task, a normal or understandable ambition is to have a maximum of deterrence effect with a minimum of effort. That is, however, probably the surest method not to obtain deterrence and not to stop violations in a significant way. To obtain at least a minimum level of deterrence, a maximum effort of cessation and accountability has to be undertaken. This is not a comfortable conclusion, but the opposite does not lead to a more satisfactory performance. The results of the implementation of the law of minimum effort to reduce human rights violations have been disastrous, as the second half of the twentieth century witnesses.[9]

Building a judicial policy against human rights violations on redress, rather than deterrence, also poses problems. The nature of human rights violations that fall within criminal jurisdiction is so infamous that it is difficult or impossible to attain a degree of satisfactory redress. The quantity of violations is also so huge that it is difficult or impossible to assure redress for each one of them. The pain and the damage caused the victims are so deep that it is not always easy to avoid allowing vengeance to prevail over redress. Those and other problems related to redress do not mean that the reparative purpose of justice has to be eliminated, but that those problems have to be considered in a proper way.

The reparative purpose must not be eliminated because, first of all, it is a legitimate purpose. People whose rights have been violated by criminal actions have an undeniable right to truth, to justice, and to reparation, as has been clearly stated by the set of principles against impunity, currently in discussion by the U.N. Commission on Human Rights.[10] Secondly, redress is not only a legitimate purpose, but also a reliable guide to orient the purpose of accountability. Victims usu-

---

[9] ERIC HOBSBAWM, AGE OF EXTREMES: THE SHORT TWENTIETH CENTURY 1914–1991 (1994).

[10] By Resolution 1998/53, the Commission on Human Rights decided to ask the Secretary-General to invite states, international organizations, and non-governmental organizations to provide comments on the "Set of Principles for the Protection and Promotion of Human Rights through Action to Combat Impunity" prepared by the expert Louis Joinet (U.N. Doc. E/CN.4/Sub.2/1997/20/Rev.1). The set of principles identifies three main victims' legal rights: their right to know, to justice, and to reparations. According to Principle 3, "[i]rrespective of any legal proceedings, victims, their families and relatives have the imprescriptible right to know the truth about the circumstances in which violations took place and, in the event of death or disappearance, the victim's fate." Regarding the right of justice, Principle 18 reaffirms the obligation of the states "to investigate violations, to take appropriate measures in respect of the perpetrators, particularly in the area of justice, by ensuring that they are prosecuted, tried and duly punished, to provide victims with effective remedies and reparation for the injuries suffered, and to take steps to prevent any recurrence of such violations." "Any human rights violation gives rise to a right to reparation on the part of the victim or his or her beneficiaries, implying a duty on the part of the state to make reparation and the possibility for the victim to seek redress from the perpetrator," as Principle 33 states.

ally know, better than anybody, who the real perpetrators are. Their particular experience, based on their own tragedy, is useful to help in identifying and in acting against key violators. In this way—increasing the neutralization performances—the purpose of providing redress can contribute to the purpose of preventing or deterring future violations. If these two purposes are put in this order, they are not opposite but complementary.

If these two purposes are seen as opposite, they risk being unrealizable. Redress will be permanently reduced in favor of prevention or deterrence. And the preference for deterrence tends to fall permanently into fictitious accountability, which means also fictitious deterrence. In contrast, policies based on complementarity or balance between deterrence and redress seem to be more able to lead to a higher level of accountability. It is a very difficult challenge, but it could also mean a significant level of deterrence of human rights violations.

D. CONSTRAINTS AND POSSIBILITIES OF THE INTERNATIONAL CRIMINAL COURT

The Statute approved in Rome for the creation of the International Criminal Court no doubt aims at deterrence, with little consideration of redress. This is not a necessary consequence of the fact that its jurisdiction is restricted to "the most serious crimes of concern to the international community as a whole," as the Statute repeatedly states (Preamble, Article 1, Article 5). There is a general consensus on the need for an international court to focus exclusively on very serious crimes that are not prosecuted by domestic courts, according to the principle of complementarity. The international criminal court need not prosecute every crime committed in the world, but only those heinous crimes of genocide, crimes of war, crimes against humanity, and eventually crimes of aggression, that escape the jurisdiction of domestic tribunals. The problem is that some states have tried to reduce the consensus in order to preclude the ICC from exercising jurisdiction over all those crimes that meet the test of being "the most serious crimes of concern to the international community as a whole." They seek instead to limit the ICC's jurisdiction to a few of the most serious crimes. That means some—and perhaps many—of the most heinous crimes of concern to humanity will escape the jurisdiction of the Court.

1. Crimes of the Past

The first category of crimes that escape the activity of the Court are those committed in the past, everywhere in the world (Article 11 of the Rome Statute). The past begins with the entry into force of this treaty after ratification by sixty states, plus sixty days (Article 126). It may take some years before that happens, so it is not yet possible to indicate with precision when the future will begin. Clearly, many serious crimes of concern to the international community will continue to be committed before the International Criminal Court is able to prosecute and to deter them.

It is encouraging to know that a number of states close to the figure required for ratification have remained committed to the creation of the Court. It is likely that they will ratify the treaty in a short time. The Preparatory Commission has fixed June 30, 2000, as the date to finish the preliminary work: defining the elements of crimes, and drafting the rules of procedure and proof (Resolution F, adopted by the Rome's Conference). The ICC could be inaugurated as early as the middle of 2000.

The Court will have jurisdiction to decide whether it is competent to try a crime that began prior to but continued in its effects after the treaty's entry into force. The typical example is the forced disappearance of persons, a crime that ceases only when the victim reappears, dead or alive. Nothing in the Statute forbids the Court to try such cases, despite the fact that numerous states that approved the Statute are involved in cases of forced disappearances that remain unpunished. Their silence could be interpreted as a tacit acceptance on this point. The Court should apply the prevailing interpretation in international law on this issue, which would lead it to conclude that such unending crimes are within the jurisdiction of the Court. Such a conclusion could increase the Court's capacity to redress and deter heinous violations.

2. Crimes of the Future

Crimes committed in the territory of a state not party to the treaty remain outside the powers of the Court (Article 12). This is a serious deficiency because many violations committed in the territories of states, both weak and powerful ones, will continue unpunished. Fortunately, the potentially serious consequences of this restriction are limited. First, the Security Council of the United Nations can decide to present a case to the court on petition of the Prosecutor (Article 13(b)). This is a remote possibility, but something similar happened when the Security Council decided to create the *ad-hoc* tribunals for Rwanda and for the former Yugoslavia.

Second, if the violation is committed by a national of a State Party, the court can assume the case directly, even if the crime occurs in the territory of a state that has not accepted its competence. If, for instance, Spain accepts the treaty and a Spanish citizen in Colombia commits a crime within the jurisdiction of the Court, the Court can assume the case even though Colombia does not ratify the treaty.

Last, there is a possibility, also remote but not impossible, that a state not being party to the treaty accepts the jurisdiction of the Court, by petition of the Court itself, for specific acts committed prior to its acceptance (Articles 11.2 and 12.3). Inasmuch as the Rome Conference did not establish the universal jurisdiction of the Court, intense work has to be done by civil society in order to obtain ratification of the treaty or acceptance of the Court's jurisdiction for a specific case. Even if that does not happen, there remains the possibility that the Security Council may decide to submit to the Court crimes committed within a non-party state.

3. Some Crimes of War

A third category of crimes remains outside the jurisdiction of the Court. By a specific declaration of a state, some crimes of war, even committed in the territory of a State Party, or by a national of a State Party, can be excluded from the jurisdiction of the Court, for a period up to seven years after the ratification (Article124). This possibility applies to war crimes but not genocide or crimes against humanity, which cannot be subjected to this exception (Articles 124 and 8).

This exception seems unreasonable. A state can accept a part of the jurisdiction of the Court in relation to grave crimes and can delay it in relation to other crimes equally grave. It is likely, however, that it was only this concession that brought France to accept application of the Statute to its nationals. On the last day of the Conference the French government distanced itself from the position it had shared with the United States. The latter sought a Court that could never intervene in crimes committed by nationals of a state without the consent of that state.

Had the position of the United States prevailed, there would not be today even an embryo of a Court able to strengthen gradually its capacity to become independent, effective, and strong. But it is also true that the possibility to exclude crimes of war from the jurisdiction of the Court during seven years weakens and delays its capacity to redress and deter human rights violations.

4. Crimes at the Discretion of the Security Council

Grave crimes that the Security Council does not wish to prosecute can also escape the jurisdiction of the Court. This is a fourth possibility prescribed by the Statute and it allows the Security Council the prerogative of ordering the Prosecutor or the Court to abstain from initiating or following the investigation or the trial of a specific crime. This is a power the Council can execute for twelve months and can renew as many times as it wants for successive periods of twelve months (Article 16).

This option no doubt opens the door to impunity and to non-accountability of human rights violators and it should not have been accepted. The door also remains open, however, to the people of the world, and especially to those of the members of the Security Council, to ensure that this prerogative not be used.

In this respect, it must be taken into account that the detestable right to veto is still accorded to the five permanent members of the Security Council and can be used by them in this case. If one of them objects to halting the activity of the Prosecutor or that of the Court, the investigation or the trial can continue and can be concluded successfully. This is one of those paradoxes of life where an institution created for obstructing actions is transformed into the means of allowing them.

5. A Court with Wings but also with Strong Enemies

The victims of human rights violations have here a possibility to act that, while small, is greater than anything previously available. That possibility of action exists thanks to the fact that a key provision was kept in the Statute. It grants the Prosecutor permission to initiate investigations on his own (*proprio motu*) (Article 15). Some states did not want to allow the Prosecutor to receive complaints, nor to have the power to initiate inquiries. Had these states succeeded, the Prosecutor would have been reduced to an agent of the complaints formulated by the states or by the Security Council.

Fortunately, that was not the case, although the right of victims to be party to the processes before the Court was also rejected. The Prosecutor may obtain information from victims (Article 15.2) and they can "make representations to the Pre-Trial Chamber" that has to authorize the investigation of cases (Article 15.3). The Statute also clearly establishes the victims' right to reparation, including restitution, compensation, and rehabilitation (Article 75).

Many of the deficiencies of the treaty concerning the Prosecutor's competence can be corrected over time, although it will not be an easy task. The Prosecutor will remain subject to a labyrinth of norms which may allow any state to impede him in dealing with a case (Articles 17, 18, and 19). Complementary jurisdiction means that the treatment of a case by the Court is conditioned by the fact that the respective state did not try the case or is not able to try it.

An important requisite for the Court is the presence of effective, independent, and honorable judges, which courts sometimes fail to see appointed or elected. The Court also needs to be assured enough economic resources to accomplish its immense tasks. Finally, one of the most serious concerns for the success of the Court is state cooperation. The Statute clearly establishes the duty of states Parties to cooperate with investigations and prosecutions (Article 86) and carefully regulates this duty in detail (Articles 86–102). The Statute allows the Court to refer the matter to the Assembly of states Parties or to the Security Council when a state fails to comply with a request of cooperation (Article 88.7). These provisions are positive, but international relations have to evolve much further in order to assure the Court its own means for implementing its decisions, especially for arresting the persons prosecuted by the Court. Otherwise, its capacity to halt and deter human rights violators will be very weak, as the experience of the *ad-hoc* tribunals shows.

Future evolution is uncertain, taking into account the open opposition to the Court expressed by some states. Their attempt to reduce the already restricted competence of the Court can affect its capacity to restrain human rights violators. Therefore, it also risks reducing, if not eliminating, the Court's capacity to deter perpetrators of heinous abuses. Unfortunately, those capacities are currently very weak and they will continue to be weak for many years due to the Rome Statute.

On the other hand, fortunately, Rome also approved some restrictions on the restrictions. They can help to build—in a long and difficult process—the basis for the Court to be able to restrain and effectively deter human rights violations in the future, as well as to secure redress for the victims.

E. CONCLUSION

Undoubtedly, the independent, effective, and strong Court that humanity requires has not yet been created. An important decision has been taken, a first step, that does not preclude advancement towards achieving such a Court. The battle for creating an organism to hold individuals accountable for violations of human rights and of humanitarian law did not come to the end with the Rome Conference. In fact, this struggle is still beginning, but in terms that may allow future generations to have international legal tools for facing atrocities and countering impunity. These tools are better than what has existed so far. It is necessary to continue working in order to consolidate them in order to confront the most serious crimes of concern to the international community.

CHAPTER 11

THE PENALTY PROVISIONS
OF THE ICC STATUTE

William A. Schabas

Le châtiment est nécessaire afin de défendre l'honneur ou l'autorité de celui qui a été lésé, afin que l'absence de châtiment n'entraîne pas la dégradation de la victime.

—Hugo Grotius

The International Criminal Court would not be a criminal court if it could not impose punishment. Establishing the appropriate penalties and the guidelines for judicial discretion in making the punishment fit the crime take up relatively little space—a mere four articles—within the Rome Statute of the ICC. During the early stages of its drafting, at the *Ad Hoc* Committee and the Preparatory Committee of the General Assembly, sentencing matters were somewhat secondary and, by and large, uncontroversial.[1] At Rome, however, sharply differing value systems came into conflict. The debate, principally about the exclusion of capital punishment from the Statute, spilled over inevitably into the field of international human rights. In the end, the Rome Conference acted to abolish the death penalty in another jurisdiction, this one international.

The relevant provisions are Articles 77 to 80. According to Article 77, the maximum permissible prison sentence is life imprisonment. Additional penalties, namely fines and forfeiture of assets, are also allowed. Sentencing considerations, that is, the role of mitigating and aggravating factors, the relevance of time served in preventive detention, and the sentencing consequences with respect to conviction for more than one offence, are addressed in Article 78. Money and other assets collected as a result of fines or forfeiture are to be administered by a trust fund to be established pursuant to Article 79. Article 80 provides that the sentencing provisions are without prejudice to national criminal law. The detailed application of these principles is to be determined in the Rules of Procedure and Evidence.[2]

---

[1] For a general review of the penalties issues in the work prior to the Rome Conference, *see* William A. Schabas, *Penalties*, in THE INTERNATIONAL CRIMINAL COURT, COMMENTS ON THE DRAFT STATUTE 273–299 (Flavia Lattanzi ed., 1998).

[2] Pursuant to the Rome Statute of the International Criminal Court, art. 51, U.N. Doc. A/CONF.183/9 (1998), *reprinted in* 37 I.L.M. 999 *and in* the Appendix to this volume.

A. THE INTERNATIONAL LAW COMMISSION DRAFT

After a flurry of activity in the early 1950s, the International Law Commission suspended its study of the creation of an international criminal court for more than thirty-five years,[3] only resuming the work in 1990 in response to a request from the General Assembly.[4] An important discussion of the issue was held at the 1991 session of the ILC, in the context of debate on the companion project, the *Code of Crimes Against the Peace and Security of Mankind*.[5] In 1993, the Commission presented its first version of a draft statute for the court to the General Assembly.[6] The text stated that a person convicted under the statute would be subject to imprisonment, up to and including life imprisonment, and a fine of any amount.[7] The Commission added that in determining the sentence, the tribunal "may have regard to the penalties provided for by the law of the accused's own state, the state where the crime was committed, and the state which had custody of and jurisdiction over the accused." Provision also was made for return of property acquired during commission of the crime to the rightful owner or, if impossible, forfeiture of the proceeds of the crime.[8] An additional article, entitled "[a]ggravating and mitigating factors," stated: "[i]n imposing sentence, the Chamber should take into account such factors as the gravity of the crime and the individual circumstances of the convicted person."[9] The 1993 draft statute also allowed for a right of appeal against sentence if there was "manifest disproportion between the crime and the sentence."[10]

These texts were somewhat reworked in 1994, although the substance did not change significantly. The 1994 draft became the reference point for the General Assembly in its work on the permanent criminal court over the years 1995–1998. The sentencing provisions read as follows:

Article 46. Sentencing

1. In the event of a conviction, the Trial Chamber shall hold a further hearing to hear any evidence relevant to sentence, to allow the Prosecutor

---

[3] The history of the treatment of penalties issues in international criminal law is reviewed in William A. Schabas, *International Sentencing: From Leipzig (1923) to Arusha (1996)*, in III INTERNATIONAL CRIMINAL LAW 171–193 (M. Cherif Bassiouni ed., 2d rev. ed. 1999).

[4] YEARBOOK OF THE ILC1990, Vol. II, para. 100.

[5] Eighth Report on the Draft Code of Crimes Against the Peace and Security of Mankind, by Mr. Doudou Thiam, Special Rapporteur, U.N. Doc. A/CN.4/430 and Add.1, §§ 101–105.

[6] Report of the International Law Commission on the Work of Its Forty-Fifth Session, U.N. Doc. A/48/10, § 84 (1993).

[7] *Id.*, art. 53.

[8] *Id.* at 317–319.

[9] *Id.* at 320.

[10] *Id.*, art. 55(1)(c).

and the defense to make submissions and to consider the appropriate sentence to be imposed.

2.   In imposing sentence, the Trial Chamber should take into account such factors as the gravity of the crime and the individual circumstances of the convicted person.

Article 47. Applicable Penalties

1.   The Court may impose on a person convicted of a crime under this Statute one or more of the following penalties:

   a.   a term of life imprisonment, or of imprisonment for a specified number of years;
   b.   a fine.

2.   In determining the length of a term of imprisonment or the amount of a fine to be imposed, the Court may have regard to the penalties provided for by the law of:

   a.   the state of which the convicted person is a national;
   b.   the state where the crime was committed; and
   c.   the state which had custody of and jurisdiction over the accused.

3.   Fines paid may be transferred, by order of the Court, to one or more of the following:

   a.   the Registrar, to defray the costs of the trial;
   b.   a state the nationals of which were the victims of the crime;
   c.   a trust fund established by the secretary-general of the United Nations for the benefit of victims of crime.[11]

The commentary that accompanied the 1994 International Law Commission draft noted that the court was not authorized to impose the death penalty. It also pointed out a change from the 1993 version, which had provided for restitution or forfeiture of instrumentalities of crime. The private law issues this might raise, for instance in determining the rightful owner of property, troubled some members. The Commission thus decided to leave this matter to national jurisdictions and international cooperation agreements. Alternative forms of punishment, such as community service, found favor with some members of the Commission but provoked opposition from others who considered these inappropriate for the serious crimes that would be tried by the court.[12]

---

[11]   Report of the International Law Commission on the Work of Its Forty-Sixth Session, Vol. II, U.N. Doc, A/CN.4/SER.A/1994/Add.1, at 60.

[12]   *Id.*

B. FROM *AD HOC* COMMITTEE TO THE FINAL PREPCOM DRAFT

The U.N. General Assembly created an *ad hoc* committee in 1994 to consider the ILC draft. The *Ad Hoc* Committee's Working Group on general principles of criminal law considered that attention might be devoted to aggravating and mitigating circumstances, penalties in general, discrepancy between maximum penalties under domestic law and the court's statute, and the possible imposition of fines and other financial sanctions.[13] It gave little attention to draft Article 46, but there was much criticism of Article 47 based on an alleged failure to respect the *nulla poena sine lege* rule. The report stated that "[i]t was generally held there was a need for maximum penalties applicable to various types of crimes to be spelled out. The view was expressed that minimum penalties should also be made explicit in view of the seriousness of the crimes."[14] Exclusion of the death penalty was generally accepted, with one dissident delegation. There was debate about whether to include fines at all and, if so, how to address their enforcement. Provisions for confiscation, restitution of property, and compensation for victims were also advanced. Several delegations were concerned with the reference to national law in Article 47(2) of the draft.[15]

The Preparatory Committee or "PrepCom," established by the General Assembly in 1995, met twice during 1996. Its Working Group on General Principles of Criminal Law and Penalties dealt with penalties at the August 1996 session and considered a number of amendments to the International Law Commission draft.[16] There were two main issues, the type of penalties and the relevant law for their determination. Rigorous positivists, who felt the statute should set penalties with a precision comparable to that of national penal codes, continued to be opposed by those satisfied with somewhat more vague and general provisions, who argued that this did not fundamentally offend the *nulla poena* rule, and moreover that it would be the only way to reach consensus.[17] Some recommended that detailed provision be adopted for punishment of minors and for aggravating and mitigating factors in determining punishment.[18] Again, the majority favored exclusion of the death penalty, with a few states in opposition.[19]

---

[13] Report of the *Ad Hoc* Committee on the Establishment of an International Criminal Court, U.N. Doc. A/50/22, para. 89, at 19; also Annex II, at 59.

[14] *Id.* at 36, para. 187.

[15] *Id.*

[16] On the sentencing provisions, *see* Report of the Preparatory Committee on the Establishment of an International Criminal Court, GAOR, Fifty-First Session, Supp. No. 10 (A/51/10), Vol. I, at 228–234; U.N. Doc. A/AC.249/WP.35; U.N. Doc. A/AC.249/WP.44; U.N. Doc. A/AC.249/WP.46; U.N. Doc. A/AC.249/WP.53.

[17] Report of the Preparatory Committee on the Establishment of an International Criminal Court, *id.* at 63, para. 304.

[18] *Id.*

[19] *Id.*, para. 306.

Delegations generally accepted that imprisonment would be the basic sentence. A variety of views were expressed on other sanctions such as fines, forfeiture, and disenfranchisement.[20] The PrepCom also contemplated victims' rights and the problem of punishment for corporate entities.[21] Serious differences continued to be expressed on the role of national law in the determination of penalties.[22]

There was no time for discussion of penalties at the February 1998 session of the Working Group on General Principles.[23] Later that year, the PrepCom decided to establish a distinct Working Group on Penalties, and named Norwegian diplomat Rolf Einar Fife as its chair.[24] At the December 1998 session, Fife avoided all discussion of capital punishment, noting that agreement seemed difficult and this would be left for the diplomatic conference. During the session, delegations expressed disagreement about life imprisonment, juvenile penalties, the role of national law, penalties for corporate offenders, the significance of prior detention, forfeiture, fines and factors to be considered in determining sentence. The result was a lengthy series of provisions accompanied with the usual square brackets indicating lack of consensus. The text was reorganized early in 1998 in the Zutphen draft[25] and later adopted by the PrepCom in its final draft statute.[26]

C. PENALTIES AGREED TO AT THE ROME CONFERENCE

At the Rome Diplomatic Conference, a Working Group on Penalties was constituted, again chaired by the very able Rolf Einar Fife.[27] The Working Group first

---

[20] *Id.*, para. 305.

[21] *Id.*, para. 307.

[22] *Id.*, para. 308.

[23] Decisions Taken by the Preparatory Committee at Its Session Held from Feb. 11–21, 1997, Annex I, Report of the Working Group on General Principles of Criminal Law and Penalties, U.N. Doc. A/AC.249/1997/L.5, 18, para. 2.

[24] Decisions Taken by the Preparatory Committee at Its Session held from Dec. 1–12, 1997, Annex V, Report of the Working Group on Penalties, U.N. Doc. A/AC.249/1997/L.9/Rev.1, at 18. *See also* U.N. Doc. A/AC.249/1997/WG.6/CRP.1/Rev.1; U.N. Doc. A/AC.249/1997/ WG.6/CRP.2/Rev.1; U.N. Doc. A/AC.249/1997/WG.6/CRP.3/Rev.1; U.N. Doc. A/AC.249/1997/ WG.6/CRP.4–13/Rev.1. For the chair's version of these negotiations, *see* Rolf Einar Fife, *Penalties*, in THE INTERNATIONAL CRIMINAL COURT: THE MAKING OF THE ROME STATUTE 319–344 (Roy S. Lee ed., 1999).

[25] Report of the Inter-Sessional Meeting from Jan. 19–30, 1998 in Zutphen, The Netherlands, U.N. Doc. A/AC.249/1998/L.13, at 126–133.

[26] Report of the Preparatory Committee on the Establishment of an International Criminal Court, U.N. Doc. A/CONF.183/2/Add.1, 142–148.

[27] There are no summary records of the Working Group on Penalties. Observations based on the debates in the Working Group are from the personal notes of the author, who attended the sessions. *See also* Rolf Einar Fife, *supra* note 25; Rolf Einar Fife, *Article 77*, COMMENTARY ON THE ROME STATUTE OF THE INTERNATIONAL CRIMINAL COURT, OBSERVERS' NOTES, ARTI-CLE BY ARTICLE 985–998 (Otto Triffterer ed., 1999); Rolf Einar Fife, *Article 80, id.* at 1089–1014.

met on June 30, more than two weeks into the Conference. It was expected that it could resolve its work with a handful of scheduled sessions over a few days, but, although some issues were disposed of quickly, it soon became apparent that finalizing the general provisions would be impossible until the debate over the death penalty was resolved. The obstinacy of some states who were determined to make this an issue meant that the Working Group did not complete its report until the final days of the Diplomatic Conference.

1. Applicable Penalties

Article 77 of the Rome Statute establishes three possible penalties: imprisonment, fines, and forfeiture of proceeds of crime. The other alternatives found in square brackets in the PrepCom draft—capital punishment, disqualification, and forfeiture of instrumentalities of crime—were deleted by the Working Group on Penalties at the Rome Conference. The final text states:

Article 77. Applicable Penalties

1.   Subject to Article 110, the Court may impose one of the following penalties on a person convicted of a crime under Article 5 of this Statute:

> a.   Imprisonment for a specified number of years, which may not exceed a maximum of 30 years; or
> b.   A term of life imprisonment when justified by the extreme gravity of the crime and the individual circumstances of the convicted person.

2.   In addition to imprisonment, the Court may order:

> a.   A fine under the criteria provided for in the Rules of Procedure and Evidence;
> b.   A forfeiture of proceeds, property and assets derived directly or indirectly from that crime, without prejudice to the rights of bona fide third parties.

a.   Terms of Imprisonment

The 1994 International Law Commission draft mentioned the possibility of "a term of life imprisonment, or of imprisonment for a specified number of years."[28] During debates in the International Law Commission, several of its members argued that life imprisonment was, like the death penalty, incompatible with contemporary approaches to sentencing and with international human rights norms.[29] The conference room paper adopted at the December 1997

---

[28]   Report of the Preparatory Committee on the Establishment of an International Criminal Court, *supra* note 26, art. 47(1)(a).

[29]   U.N. Doc. A/CN.4/SR.2208, § 10 (Graefrath); U.N. Doc. A/CN.4/SR.2208, § 21 (Calero Rodriguez); U.N. Doc. A/CN.4/SR.2209, § 19 (Barboza); U.N. Doc. A/CN.4/SR.2210, § 47

PrepCom left several options in square brackets: life imprisonment; imprisonment for a specified number of years; imprisonment for a maximum (thirty years was suggested); a definitive term of imprisonment (twenty to forty years was suggested), subject to a reduction in accordance with other provisions of the statute.[30] An additional clause, also in square brackets, said that the court could specify a minimum period to be served during which the convicted person would not be subject to provisional release or parole. Several states preferred defining maximum sentences only, while a majority felt that both maximum and minimum sentences should be clearly stated. Only a small group of countries considered it unnecessary to set either minimum or maximum penalties.

Out of respect for some of the views expressed, the conference room paper adopted at the December 1997 PrepCom included two footnotes. The first addressed the issue of lengthy sentences, and said that "[t]o meet concerns of several delegations regarding the serving of a life sentence or a long sentence of imprisonment," there should be a mandatory mechanism for reexamination of sentences by the Court after a certain period of time. "In this way, the Court could also ensure the uniform treatment of prisoners regardless of the state where they served their sentence."[31] The second note, in a similar vein, declared that an exhaustive list of factors that might reduce the minimum sentence should be included if a minimum sentence provision were to be included. Factors could include diminished mental capacity falling short of exclusion of criminal responsibility, age, duress, and subsequent conduct of the convicted person.[32] These texts were reproduced in the Zutphen draft and the final proposal of the Preparatory Commission submitted to the Diplomatic Conference.[33]

The chair of the Working Group on Penalties made clear in his opening remarks at the first session on June 30, 1998, that clear consensus existed on making imprisonment the basic penalty of the International Criminal Court. He attempted to review the difficulties encountered in "refining" the statute's

---

(Njenga); U.N. Doc. A/CN.4/SR.2212, § 4 (Solari Tudela). *See also* U.N. Doc. A/CN.4/Ser.A/1991/Add.1 (Part 2), A/46/10, § 88. The German Constitutional Court has suggested that life imprisonment without possibility of parole constitutes cruel, inhuman, and degrading punishment [1977] 45 BVerfGE 187, 228. *See* Dirk van Zyl Smit, *Is Life Imprisonment Constitutional? The German Experience*, [1992] PUBLIC LAW 263; Dirk van Zyl Smit, *Life Imprisonment as an Ultimate Penalty in International Law: A Human Rights Perspective*, 10 CRIM. L.F. 1.

[30] U.N. Doc. A/AC.249/1997/WG.6/CRP.2/Rev.1 (Dec. 10, 1997).

[31] *Id.*

[32] *Id.*

[33] Report of the Inter-Sessional Meeting from Jan. 19–30, 1998 in Zutphen, The Netherlands, U.N. Doc. A/AC.249/1998/L.13, at 231; Report of the Preparatory Committee on the Establishment of an International Criminal Court, Addendum, U.N. Doc. A/CONF.183/2/Add.1, at 119. *See also* Chairman's Working Paper on Article 75, U.N. Doc. A/CONF.183/C.1/WGP/L.3.

position on imprisonment. A "large number" of delegations had insisted on a reference to life imprisonment, noted Fife. Yet a "large number" had also objected to it, on the grounds that life imprisonment neglected rehabilitation and, in certain cases, raised constitutional problems. In the debate that followed, many states reiterated their opposition to life imprisonment, with several calling it a cruel, inhuman and degrading form of punishment, prohibited by international human rights norms.[34] A few delegations rejected life imprisonment because it was not a determinate penalty, preferring a term of a fixed number of years.[35] Several said simply that they supported life imprisonment.[36] Several states said they preferred a maximum of life imprisonment, but that they would agree to a maximum fixed term accompanied by a period without parole eligibility.[37] Others said they opposed life imprisonment, but could see it as a possible compromise with states that preferred capital punishment.[38] Another option proposed was to include both life imprisonment and fixed terms.[39] Summing up the debates, Fife said that there was a "general feeling" that "high sentences" should be allowed, adding that some delegations favored minimum sentences. When the Working Group met in informal session the following day, some states that had earlier opposed life imprisonment as too harsh now seemed to have softened their position.[40] Consensus appeared within reach. But when Fife suggested that life imprisonment with a review mechanism might be a basis for agreement, Mexico took the floor to say that this would not be acceptable.

The debate on imprisonment became inextricably entwined with the question of capital punishment. Predictably, those states that aggressively supported the death penalty also insisted upon heavy and inflexible terms of imprisonment. Abolitionist states, on the other hand, also tended towards a liberal approach to custodial sentences. It seemed likely that the price to pay for exclusion of the death penalty was going to be provisions on imprisonment that were more rigorous than many states would have liked. The concerns of the liberal states, which were driven in many cases by constitutional considerations, would be recognized by establishing a regime for mandatory review of sentences similarly to the parole schemes of domestic legal systems. That way, it could not be said that there were lengthy fixed terms of imprisonment without possibility of release. On July 6, the chair of the Working Group submitted a discussion paper on the imprisonment provision accompanied by a lengthy footnote reflecting the tone of the debates:

---

[34] Andorra, Chile, Cuba, Israel, Mexico, Spain, Portugal, Venezuela.

[35] Qatar, Saudi Arabia.

[36] Holy See, Iran, Kenya, Russian Federation.

[37] France, Dominican Republic, Hungary.

[38] Finland, Norway, Sweden, Switzerland.

[39] Egypt, Libya, Singapore.

[40] China, France, Germany, Norway, Portugal, Spain, Switzerland.

1.   To meet the concerns of a number of delegations regarding the severity of a life sentence or a long sentence of imprisonment, it would be necessary to provide for a *mandatory* mechanism in Part 10, Article 100, by which the prisoner's sentence would be re-examined *by the Court* after a certain period of time, in order to determine whether he or she should be released. In this way, the Court should also ensure the uniform treatment of prisoners regardless of the states where they served their sentence.

However, a number of other delegations linked their consideration of this proposal to a requirement for lengthy periods of imprisonment before such a review could take place, as well as strict criteria which would govern the Court's determination of the question. Among such criteria several delegations emphasized that evidence of the prisoner's early and continuing willingness to cooperate with the Court in investigations and prosecutions ought to be the principal or only ground upon which the Court would base its determination. Yet other delegations argued that the Court should be able to take other grounds into consideration for such a determination. Such grounds could include voluntarily assisting the Court in the enforcement of its judgments in other cases, and in particular providing information as to the location of assets, which may be used to the benefit of victims or their families. Clearly, any grounds for such a determination would have to be strictly defined.

With regard to the periods of imprisonment to be served before a review may take place, it is suggested that they be set at: (i) not less than 20 years in case of life imprisonment, and (ii) not less than two thirds of the term in case of imprisonment for a specified number of years. With regard to the period for life imprisonment, it is noted that some delegations supported this period being set at not less than 25 years.

Consideration should also be given to the issue of subsequent mandatory reviews following the initial one. In subsequent reviews other grounds besides those listed above may become more relevant, while the relevance of the stated grounds may diminish. For the purposes of establishing a system of periodic review, there would appear to be a need to distinguish between life imprisonment and imprisonment for a specified number of years. In the case of the former, it is suggested that subsequent reviews take place at three-year intervals. In relation to other terms of imprisonment, in view of the technical complexity of similar provisions, it is suggested that subsequent mandatory reviews take place according to a schedule specified in the Rules of Procedure and Evidence.[41]

---

[41] Chairman's Working Paper on Article 75, Paragraph 1, U.N. Doc. A/CONF.183/C.1/WGP/L.3/Rev.1, 1–2.

Two days later, Fife presented a compromise proposal on the subject of imprisonment, allowing for a life term but with a mandatory review mechanism.[42] Fife told the Working Group that the compromise addressed concerns expressed by Venezuela, El Salvador, Nicaragua, and Colombia, all of whom had constitutional prohibitions on life imprisonment. To address this, the report included a "Note," destined for the Working Group concerned with Article 100 of the Statute and, eventually, for judges called upon to interpret the Statute:

> To meet the concerns of a number of delegations regarding the severity of long sentences of imprisonment, it would be necessary to provide for a *mandatory* mechanism in Part 10, Article 100, by which the prisoner's sentence would be re-examined *by the Court* after a certain period of time. In this way, the Court should also ensure the uniform treatment of prisoners regardless of the state where they served their sentence.
>
> However, a number of other delegations linked their consideration of this proposal to a requirement for lengthy periods of imprisonment before such a review could take place, as well as strict criteria which would govern the Court's determination of the sentence. Among such criteria, several delegations emphasized that the behavior of the prisoner, including in particularly early and continuing willingness to cooperate with the Court in investigations and prosecutions ought to be the principal or only ground upon which the Court would base its determination. Yet other delegations argued that the Court should be able to take other grounds into consideration for such a determination. Such grounds could include voluntarily assisting the Court in the enforcement of its judgments in other cases, and in particular providing information as to the location of assets which may be used to the benefit of victims or their families. Clearly, any grounds for such a determination would have to be strictly defined.
>
> With regard to the periods of imprisonment to be served before a review may take place, it is suggested that they be set at not less than two thirds or the term of imprisonment, and, in any event, not more than 25 years.
>
> Article 100 should also provide for subsequent mandatory reviews following the initial one. In subsequent reviews other grounds besides those listed above may become more relevant, while the relevance of the stated grounds may diminish. In view of the technical complexity of such rules, it is suggested that subsequent mandatory reviews take place according to modalities specified in the Rules of Procedure and Evidence.[43]

---

[42] Report of the Working Group on Penalties, Addendum, U.N. Doc. A/CONF.183/C.1/WGP/L.14/Add.1. The report was never in fact adopted. *See also* Report of the Working Group on Penalties, Addendum, Corrigendum, U.N. Doc. A/CONF.183/C.1/WGP/L.14/Add.1, Corr.1.

[43] Report of the Working Group on Penalties, Addendum, *id.* at 3. The third paragraph was orally amended by the chair: "With regard to the periods of imprisonment to be served before a

Consensus was reached the following day.[44] Fife's proposal was accompanied by a footnote saying that it was "without prejudice to the issue of the inclusion or the non-inclusion of the death penalty," a matter which remained unresolved.[45]

Fife thus skillfully managed to separate the issue of life imprisonment from that of capital punishment, sending a consensus text on the basic sentencing provision to the Drafting Committee, despite a continuing impasse on the death penalty. The states opposed to life imprisonment had given ground, but with the proviso of mandatory review after a certain period of time, as well as the qualification that life imprisonment only be imposed "when justified by the extreme gravity of the crime and the individual circumstances of the convicted person." As a final gesture of respect for the feelings of the more liberal states, the report of the Working Group contained a footnote stating that "[s]ome delegations expressed concerns about an explicit reference to life imprisonment."[46]

The Rome Statute provides that the Court may impose imprisonment "for a specified number of years, which may not exceed a maximum of 30 years,"[47] and that it may impose "[a] term of life imprisonment when justified by the extreme gravity of the crime and the individual circumstances of the convicted person."[48] The expression "extreme gravity" is perplexing, because in any event the Court only has jurisdiction over crimes that meet this standard. (Article 1 affirms that the Court shall exercise jurisdiction over "the most serious crimes of international concern.") Nevertheless, there are several references to gravity within the Statute,[49] suggesting the drafters contemplated some hierarchy among the types of case that might come before the Court. Moreover, in a general sense genocide and crimes against humanity would seem to be of greater gravity than war crimes,

---

review may take place, it is suggested that they be set at not less than two thirds of the term of imprisonment. In case of life imprisonment, the period to be served before a review may take place would be not less than 25 years."

[44] Report of the Working Group on Penalties, U.N. Doc. A/CONF.183/C.1/WGP/L.14/Add.2* (July 10, 1998).

[45] *Id.*

[46] *Id.* at 2, n. 2. Allowance for the possibility of life imprisonment in the Rome Statute should not necessarily create an obstacle to ratification for states whose constitutions forbid this penalty. After all, it is not the state that is imposing such a term but rather the International Criminal Court. Some constitutional courts have accepted the notion that while their own constitutional instruments may forbid certain penalties, this should not foreclose the possibility of surrendering fugitives to a state that imposes those same penalties: Kindler v. Canada, [1991] 2 S.C.R. 779, 67 C.C.C. (3d) 1, 84 D.L.R. (4th) 438, 6 C.R.R. (2d) 193; Ng Extradition (Can.), [1991] 2 S.C.R. 856, 67 C.C.C. (3d) 61, 84 D.L.R. (4th) 498.

[47] Rome Statute of the International Criminal Court, *supra* note 2, art. 77(1)(a).

[48] *Id.*, art. 77(1)(b).

[49] *Id.*, arts. 7(1)(g), 17(1)(d), 53(1)(c), 53(2)(c), 59(6), 78(1), 90(7).

something implied by at least two provisions of the Statute. States may "opt out" of war crimes pursuant to Article 124, something forbidden them with respect to genocide and crimes against humanity. In addition, some defenses are available in the case of war crimes that are excluded with respect to the other categories of offence.[50] Also, and taking guidance from general principles of criminal law applicable in national systems, the Court may well decide that some of the inchoate offences described in Article 25, such as attempts and incitement to genocide where the crime itself is not actually carried out, are also at the low end of the gravity scale.

The Statute establishes mandatory rules for subsequent revision of any sentence. This is the key to understanding the relative gravity of the two options. The Rome Statute does not set up a conditional release or parole system, as in most domestic legal systems. Instead, Article 110 creates a form of permanent and irrevocable review of sentences. According to Article 110(3), the Court "shall review the sentence to determine whether it should be reduced" after the offender has served two-thirds of the sentence. Thus, someone sentenced to the maximum fixed term of thirty years will become eligible for review of sentence after serving twenty years in detention. The same paragraph declares that in the case of a life sentence, the review shall take place after twenty-five years. If initial review pursuant to the Rome Statute is unsuccessful, the offender is entitled to renew an application in accordance with terms to be established in the Rules of Procedure and Evidence.

b.   Capital Punishment

The exclusion of the death penalty from the International Law Commission draft statute, as well as from the statutes of the two *ad hoc* tribunals adopted by the Security Council, manifests a growing international consensus opposed to capital punishment, at least as far as international justice is concerned.[51] During preparation of the draft statute and the draft Code of Crimes, a few members of the International Law Commission argued that capital punishment should not be excluded,[52] but the vast majority considered it to be unthinkable, given the international trend in favor of abolition of the death penalty.[53]

---

[50]   *Id.*, arts. 31(1)(c), 33(2).

[51]   WILLIAM A. SCHABAS, THE ABOLITION OF THE DEATH PENALTY IN INTERNATIONAL LAW (2d ed. 1997).

[52]   U.N. Doc. A/CN.4/SR.2211, § 15; U.N. Doc. A/CN.4/SR.2212, § 19; U.N. Doc. A/CN.4/SR.2212, § 28; U.N. Doc. A/CN.4/SR.2213, § 55. Special Rapporteur Doudou Thiam promised that the Commission's report would state that "two or three of its members" had expressed reservations about exclusion of the death penalty: U.N. Doc. A/CN.4/SR.2213, § 59. The report eventually stated that "many members of the Commission" opposed the death penalty and "[s]ome other members" supported the death penalty: U.N. Doc. A/CN.4/Ser.A/1991/Add.1 (Part 2), A/46/10, §§ 85–85.

[53]   U.N. Doc. A/CN.4/SR.2207, §§ 23–24; U.N. Doc. A/CN.4/SR.2208, § 2; U.N. Doc.

The matter would not go away, however, and several states in North Africa, the Middle East and Asia sporadically returned to it during the PrepCom meetings. A proposal sponsored by Algeria, Libya, Egypt, Jordan and Kuwait sought to retain the death penalty in the statute "where there are aggravating circumstances."[54] At the August 1996 session of the PrepCom, some states argued that if the statute were to be considered representative of all legal systems, it should include the death penalty.[55] Citing the Islamic legal code of the Shari'a, the representative of Egypt said that the death penalty should be retained as an option, perhaps where there were aggravating circumstances.[56] Malaysia also urged recognition of the death penalty, which it said was included in many national legal jurisdictions.[57] Representatives of Italy, Portugal, Mexico, New Zealand, and Denmark spoke against including the death penalty in the court's statute.[58] According to the report of the 1996 PrepCom:

> Some delegations expressed their strong support for the exclusion of the death penalty from the penalties that the Court would be authorized to impose in accordance with Article 47 of the draft statute. While the death penalty was ruled out by those delegations, others suggested that the death penalty should not be excluded *a priori* since it was provided for in many legal systems, especially in connection with serious crimes.[59]

The conference room paper produced by the Working Group on Penalties at the December 1997 PrepCom outlined two options, one excluding the death penalty, the other allowing it, "as an option, in case of aggravating circumstances and when the Trial Chamber finds it necessary in the light of the gravity of the crime, the number of victims and the severity of the damage."[60] But the chair of the Working Group refused to allow debate on subject, stating that it was clear that there was no consensus, and that there were staunch supporters of both options. There would be no point discussing it "at the technical level," he said.

A/CN.4/SR.2208, § 21; U.N. Doc. A/CN.4/SR.2208, § 30; U.N. Doc. A/CN.4/SR.2209, § 5; U.N. Doc. A/CN.4/SR.2209, § 29; U.N. Doc. A/CN.4/SR.2210, § 25; U.N. Doc. A/CN.4/SR.2210, § 33; U.N. Doc. A/CN.4/SR.2210, § 46; U.N. Doc. A/CN.4/SR.2212, § 4; U.N. Doc. A/CN.4/SR.2213, § 12; U.N. Doc. A/CN.4/SR.2213, § 23; U.N. Doc. A/CN.4/SR.2213, § 33

54 U.N. Doc. A/AC.249/WP.44.

55 U.N. Doc. L/2805 (1996); *also* U.N. Doc. L/2813 (1996).

56 U.N. Doc. L/2805.

57 U.N. Doc. L/2806.

58 *Id.*

59 Report of the Preparatory Committee on the Establishment of an International Criminal Court, Vol. I, *supra* note 26, para. 306.

60 U.N. Doc. A/AC.249/1997/WG.6/CRP.1, at 3 (Dec. 2, 1997).

During the initial statements in the Working Group on Penalties at the Rome Conference many states spoke against any reference to the death penalty in the statute.[61] Most of those who explained their position invoked human rights norms.[62] A few noted problems with complementarity. Others said they had no firm position on the subject of capital punishment,[63] or implied this by saying nothing on the subject and noting that they preferred imprisonment.[64] The chair indicated his preference by submitting a text "proposed for consideration, in order to contribute to clarity as to a possible structure," that omitted the death penalty.[65]

Two geo-cultural blocs of states were vocal advocates of the death penalty, those of the Arab and Islamic group, and those of the English-speaking Caribbean states. In the case of the former, the justification was religious and cultural factors.[66] On July 3, a group of Arab states prepared a proposal that they described as an "honest, genuine effort to bridge the gap." It read:

> The Court may impose on a person convicted under this Statute one or more of the penalties provided for by the law of the state where the crime was committed.
>
> In cases where national law does not regulate a specific crime, the Court may apply one or more of the following penalties:
>
> a) . . . ;
>
> b) . . . ;
>
> c) . . . ;
>
> d) . . . ;[67]

The same day, the Caribbean states submitted a text that openly recognized the death penalty:

---

[61] Argentina, Dominican Republic, France, Hungary, Israel, Mexico, Samoa, Spain, Uruguay, Andorra, Chile, Finland, Greece, Holy See, Philippines, Russian Federation, Sweden, Switzerland, Ukraine, Venezuela.

[62] Ukraine, for example, said it was obliged to take this view as a member of the Council of Europe.

[63] Sierra Leone, Turkey.

[64] Congo (DR), Cuba, Japan, Kenya, Senegal.

[65] Chairman's Working Paper on Article 75, U.N. Doc. A/CONF.183/C.1/WGP/L.3 (June 30, 1998).

[66] Egypt.

[67] Proposal Submitted by Algeria, Bahrain, Comoros, Egypt, the Islamic Republic of Iran, Iraq, Kuwait, the Libyan Arab Jamahiriya, Nigeria, Oman, Qatar, Saudi Arabia, the Sudan, the Syrian Arab Republic, the United Arab Emirates and Yemen, U.N. Doc. A/CONF.183/C.1/WGP/L.11 & Corr. 2 (July 3, 1998).

The Court may impose upon a person convicted under this Statute one or more of the penalties:

a. The death penalty;

b. A term of life imprisonment;

c. A term of imprisonment not exceeding thirty (30) years.

The Court may attach to any sentence of imprisonment a minimum period during which the convicted person may not be granted any [release under relevant provisions of the Statute].[68]

Publicly, the two groups of states suggested it would be impossible to finalize not only the general text on imprisonment but also provisions dealing with the principle of legality,[69] fines,[70] and the role of national legislation,[71] without an agreement on capital punishment. Informally, the death penalty advocates admitted that they did not expect to succeed in inserting the death penalty in the statute's sentencing provisions. In parallel with the Caribbean proposal, Trinidad and Tobago hinted at a basis for compromise when it circulated informally a document entitled "Sample Understanding/Declaration by Trinidad and Tobago in lieu of Article 75(e)":

> UNDERSTANDING. Trinidad and Tobago understands that International Law does not prohibit the death penalty, and that this Statute does not restrict the right of Trinidad and Tobago to apply the death penalty to persons duly convicted and sentenced to that penalty under the existing laws of Trinidad and Tobago. It also follow that under the principle of complementarity, recognized by the Statute of the International Criminal Court, Trinidad and Tobago retains the sovereign right to impose the death penalty on persons duly tried and convicted in Trinidad and Tobago, of international crimes potentially falling within the complementary jurisdiction of the International Criminal Court.

> DECLARATION. Trinidad and Tobago declares that nothing in the Statute of the International Criminal Court and the Final Act of the Diplomatic Conference of Plenipotentiaries on the Establishment of an International Criminal Court affects the right of Trinidad and Tobago or of other states to impose the death penalty under their domestic law.

---

[68] Proposal Submitted by Barbados, Dominica, Jamaica, Singapore and Trinidad and Tobago, U.N. Doc. A/CONF.183/C.1/WGP/L.13 (July 3, 1998).

[69] Sudan.

[70] United Arab Emirates, Rwanda.

[71] Sudan.

The subject was aired at an informal session of the Working Group on the afternoon of July 3. The Chair of the Working Group explained that under the principle of complementarity, the penalties regime chosen for the international court would have no impact on the scheme in force within national courts. Fife said that including the death penalty in the statute, either directly, as in the Caribbean states proposal, or implicitly, as in the Arab and Islamic states proposal, would make it impossible for a huge number of states to accede to the treaty. Many states spoke in support of the chair, some of them predictable, such as Chile, Costa Rica, Greece, France, Namibia, and New Zealand, others perhaps not so, such as Kenya. Slovenia and Colombia invoked constitutional problems if capital punishment were included.

The United States of America took the floor at the formal, public session of the Working Group on the evening of July 3, 1998, in an effort to assist the chair in his search for a workable solution. Ambassador David Scheffer focused on the concept of complementarity: "[W]e know the death penalty very well in the United States, where it is imposed in many jurisdictions including by the federal system, and where it is supported by the executive." Scheffer said he was confident that federal prosecutors would seek the death penalty in appropriate cases where genocide, crimes against humanity and war crimes were charged, citing U.S. legislation. The international criminal court should encourage national judicial systems to prosecute and punish the crimes within its jurisdiction, "and this will include the death penalty." But, said Scheffer, a second principle was the need to create a uniform penalty regime for the court, failing which the operation of the court would be diverse and unpredictable. "The United States believes that the language proposed by the chair achieves the goal of just and severe punishment on an international level," he concluded.

Three days later, on July 6, 1998, the chair of the Working Group issued a "position paper" containing a detailed assessment of the death penalty debate:

2. The Coordinator would like to stress the following:

> Extensive consultations, as well as statements in the Plenary of the Conference and in the Working Group on Penalties, have shown that a number of delegations strongly favor an inclusion of the death penalty as one of the penalties to be applied by the Court. On the other hand, the consultations as well as statements in the Plenary and in the Working Group have also shown that a number of other delegations are strongly opposed to such an inclusion. In this context, a number of delegations have stressed that cooperation between states and the Court would effectively be hindered should the Statute provide either directly or indirectly for an inclusion of the death penalty.
>
> On the basis of these consultations it is the opinion of the Coordinator that there are no grounds for establishing a consensus

on this issue. At the same time, a very substantial number of interventions of delegations in the course of the work of the Working Group have indicated a strong desire to achieve a balanced compromise on the main penalties to be included in the Statute. All delegations have indicated a willingness to find solutions which may be conducive to the shared goal of an early establishment of an International Criminal Court with a broad basis of support from the international community.

It should be noted that not including the death penalty in the Statute would have no bearing on national legislation and practices in this field. States have the primary responsibility for prosecuting and punishing individuals for crimes falling under the subject-matter jurisdiction of the Court. In accordance with the principle of complementarity between the Court and national jurisdictions, the Court would clearly have no say on national practices in this field.[72]

The Working Group reconvened on July 16, one day before the end of the Diplomatic Conference, with the death penalty issue still unresolved. Fife referred to "intense consultations" on the subject, citing an informal meeting held on July 11 where he was mandated to prepare a compromise position. It had three constituent elements. The first was deletion of any reference to the death penalty in the Statute, accompanied by a footnote in the report of the Working Group that said "[s]ome delegations do not agree with the decision to exclude the death penalty but they have decided to permit the Conference to proceed on the basis of the Chairman's proposal while reserving the right to put their views on record at appropriate stages of the Conference."[73] The second was the addition of a provision later to be numbered Article 80 of the Rome Statute:

Non-prejudice to national application of penalties and national laws

Nothing in this Part of the Statute affects the application by states of penalties prescribed by their national law, nor the law of states which do not provide for penalties prescribed in this Part.

The third element was a statement which the Working Group was to recommend be read by the President of the Conference, and that would be included in the official records of the conference:

The debate at this Conference on the issue of which penalties should be applied by the Court has shown that there is no international consensus

---

[72] Chairman's Working Paper on Article 75, Paragraph 1, U.N. Doc. A/CONF.183/C.1/WGP/L.3/Rev.1 (July 6, 1998), 2–3.

[73] Report of the Working Group on Penalties, U.N. Doc. A/CONF.183/C.1/WGP/L.14/Add.3/Rev.1 (July 17, 1998), 2.

on the inclusion or non-inclusion of the death penalty. However, in accordance with the principles of complementarity between the Court and national jurisdictions, national justice systems have the primary responsibility for investigating, prosecuting and punishing individuals, in accordance with their national laws, for crimes falling under the jurisdiction of the International Criminal Court. In this regard, the Court would clearly not be able to affect national policies in this field. It should be noted that not including the death penalty in the Statute would not in any way have a legal bearing on national legislations and practices with regard to the death penalty. Nor shall it be considered as influencing, in the development of customary international law or in any other way, the legality of penalties imposed by national systems for serious crimes.[74]

There were statements from some of the concerned delegations. The Minister of Justice of the Sudan, who was present, took the floor:

On behalf of the Arab group, which we chair, I thank you for your efforts. We accept, on behalf of our group, this compromise; we do not want this issue to be a stumbling block to the advancement of this conference; we should like to express clearly and unequivocally our views. This must not be interpreted as proof that it is an acceptance of worldwide abolition of the death penalty.

Trinidad and Tobago's Attorney General also made a statement:

We cannot agree with the decision to exclude the death penalty. But in order to permit the conference to proceed, we will not oppose this. We want to make it quite clear that we do not consider the death penalty to be a human rights issue.

His remarks were endorsed in brief comments by the delegations of Dominica, Ethiopia, Barbados, and Jamaica. Fife brought down his gavel for the last time, declaring the compromise adopted, to the great relief of the entire Diplomatic Conference.

The same afternoon, the Working Group's report was presented to the Committee of the Whole. Singapore had reserved its right to intervene during the morning session, and had a prepared statement to deliver:

In the exercise of our right under fn. 1 of L.14/Add.3/Rev.1, we make this statement. Penalties must be commensurate with the gravity of the crime. We co-sponsored the proposal to introduce the death penalty. No delegation made the mistaken assertion that the death penalty is prohib-

---

[74] *Id.*

ited under international law. Even the Second Optional Protocol allows the death penalty. It has been characterized by some as a human rights question. We should not overplay the right to life of the convicted person *vis à vis* the right to security of the victim. We do not want to impose our system of criminal justice on others. The decision not to include the death penalty would not impede the sovereign right of states to impose the death penalty. The record of this conference shows that there is no international consensus as to the abolition of the death penalty.

Trinidad and Tobago, Ethiopia, Lebanon, Saudi Arabia, and Rwanda also made declarations expressing their preference for the death penalty.

The next evening, when the final draft statute was presented in the plenary committee of the conference, President Giovanni Conso read the agreed statement. It was like a bone sticking in his throat, but he dutifully respected the will of the Working Group. Singapore took the floor once again to affirm that "the debate in the conference clearly demonstrates that there is no international consensus on abolition of the death penalty."

c.   *Fines*

The International Law Commission draft contemplated the possibility of fines, and implied that they may be imposed either as an alternative to a custodial sentence or in addition to one.[75] At the August 1996 PrepCom, several delegations questioned whether fines should be included, suggesting this was unsuitable considering the gravity of the crimes before the court.[76] Others did not oppose the idea, but said that they should always be accompanied by prison terms.[77] According to the report, "[i]t was recognized however that fines might be appropriate for such 'procedural' crimes as perjury or contempt of court or as supplementary to a penalty of imprisonment or as penalties to be applied to juridical persons."[78]

The text proposed at the December 1997 PrepCom envisaged two alternatives, but the entire section on fines was in square brackets. The first option was fines in addition to a sentence of imprisonment for specific crimes. The second allowed for fines upon conviction of perjury or contempt of court, or as an ordinary penalty, or as a penalty in addition to imprisonment. A footnote to the document stated that some delegations considered that fines should be limited to

---

[75] Report of the Preparatory Committee on the Establishment of an International Criminal Court, *supra* note 26, art. 47(1)(b).

[76] U.N. Doc. L/2805 (Sweden, Japan).

[77] *Id.* (Switzerland).

[78] Report of the Preparatory Committee on the Establishment of an International Criminal Court, Vol. I, *supra* note 26, para. 305.

so-called "procedural offences," such as contempt and perjury, and that they should be excluded in the case of "core" offences, such as genocide, crimes against humanity and war crimes.[79] The ensuing discussions in the Working Group of the PrepCom were unsuccessful in resolving differences on the subject.[80] The chair of the Working Group declared that "there was still no agreement as to whether fines should be a main penalty, or only a subsidiary penalty for core crimes," adding that "a very large majority" felt it should be a secondary penalty. A fines provision was included in the draft statute submitted to the Diplomatic Conference, but of course it was in square brackets.[81]

During the initial exchange of views in Rome at the June 30 session of the Working Group on Penalties, many states supported fines but only as a secondary penalty.[82] A small number were opposed altogether.[83] When delegations turned to the details, difficulties with administrative aspects emerged, principally the problem of execution. States asked how to deal with non-payment, and it was noted that international human rights law prohibits imprisonment for debt. One suggestion was to treat non-payment of fines as a form of contempt of court.[84] Fife subsequently presented an attempt at a compromise proposal: "2. In addition to imprisonment, the Court may order: (a) a fine, which is proportionate to the circumstances of the crime and not excessive to the means of the convicted person. Where a convicted person deliberately refuses to comply with an order imposed by the Court to pay a fine, the Court shall, in accordance with the Statute and the Rules of Procedure and Evidence, hold a hearing to consider the matter and may impose another penalty on the person."[85] Fife admitted that several delegations were unhappy with the idea of re-sentencing. After discussion, the provision was amended to read: "2. In addition to imprisonment, the Court may order: (a) a fine, under the criteria provided by the Rules of Procedure and Evidence." It was accompanied by a footnote drawing the attention of the Drafting Committee to the need to consider the Article in conjunction with Article 99, on enforcement of fines.[86] Thus, the Rome Statute allows the Court to impose a fine, but only "[i]n addition to imprisonment." The criteria in establishing fines are to be provided for in the Rules of Procedure and Evidence.[87]

---

[79] U.N. Doc. A/AC.249/1997/WG.6/CRP.1, at 2 (Dec. 2, 1997).

[80] U.N. Doc. A/AC.249/1997/WG.6/CRP.5 (Dec. 10, 1997).

[81] Report of the Preparatory Committee on the Establishment of an International Criminal Court, *supra* note 26, at 120.

[82] Dominican Republic, Egypt, France, Iraq, Israel, Kuwait, Libya.

[83] Cuba, Japan, Turkey.

[84] United States of America.

[85] Chairman's Working Paper, A/CONF.183/C.1/WGP/L.10 (July 2, 1998), amended orally.

[86] Report of the Working Group on Penalties, U.N. Doc. A/CONF.183/C.1/WGP/L.14 (July 4, 1998), 3.

[87] Rome Statute of the International Criminal Court, *supra* note 2, art. 77(2).

d. Forfeiture

There had been no mention, in the International Law Commission draft statute or the statutes of the *ad hoc* criminal tribunals, of sanctions other than imprisonment and fines, but forfeiture was provided for in the conference room paper of the December 1997 PrepCom.[88] The text authorized the court to order forfeiture or seizure of instruments and objects of crime, property and proceeds of crime, and, where confiscation was impossible, a sum of money equivalent thereto.[89] It was modified somewhat as a result of informal discussions.[90] According to a footnote, "[I]t was suggested that forfeiture not be included as a penalty, but instead be included as a mechanism which the Court would request states to use with regard to execution of an order for reparations. According to this view, a provision on forfeiture could be considered as a separate paragraph of this Article or elsewhere in the Statute."[91]

At the Rome Conference, many delegations distinguished between instrumentalities and proceeds. Fife pushed the debate along, explaining summarily the difficulties in the concept of forfeiture of instruments of crime and indicating that the issue was simply too complicated for any consensus text to emerge. It takes little imagination to conceive of the potentially enormous scope of such a provision, when war crimes committed by the state or with its complicity are involved. Theoretically, an instrumentality could include an aircraft carrier, a military base or a space station. On July 3, the chair presented his proposal providing for forfeiture of proceeds as a penalty additional to imprisonment. It was adopted without debate,[92] accompanied by a footnote: "The Working Group draws the attention of the Drafting Committee to the need to consider this Article in conjunction with Article 99, Enforcement of fines and forfeiture measures."[93]

e. Disqualification

Chile proposed at the August 1996 session of the PrepCom that the court might attach civil consequences to a conviction.[94] The conference room paper at

---

[88] Note that in the post-Second World War trials, forfeiture of property was declared only in the case of Alfred Krupp. The High Commissioner later found that this constituted "discrimination," and quashed the order. "General confiscation of property is not a usual element in our judicial system and is generally repugnant to American concepts of justice," he wrote. "Announcement of Decisions by the United States High Commissioner for Germany, Jan. 31, 1951, Upon Review of the Sentences Imposed by Tribunals Established Pursuant to Ordinance No. 7," in 15 TRIALS OF THE WAR CRIMINALS 1180–1191, at 1188.

[89] U.N. Doc. A/AC.249/1997/WG.6/CRP.1, at 3 (Dec. 2, 1997).

[90] U.N. Doc. A/AC.249/1997/WG.6/CRP.8 (Dec. 10, 1997).

[91] *Id.*

[92] Report of the Working Group on Penalties, U.N. Doc. A/CONF.183/C.1/WGP/L.14 (July 4, 1998), 3.

[93] *Id.* at 3, n. 2.

[94] U.N. L/2805 (Chile).

the December 1997 PrepCom suggested a reference to suspension or loss of rights that would allow the Court to disqualify, dismiss or suspend public officials. One option considered by delegates to the December 1997 meeting was to add that disqualification or suspension be effective "in the modality and to the extent such penalty could be imposed in accordance with the laws of either the state of which the convicted person is a national, the state where the crime was committed, [or] the state which had custody of and jurisdiction over the accused."[95] All of this was, of course, in square brackets. The December PrepCom simplified the proposal, and the reference to national laws that had appeared as an option in the earlier document eventually was relegated to a footnote.[96]

At the Rome Conference, the chair of the Working Group presented the question of disqualification as being "not central to our concerns." He noted that it had limited support, and that there were difficult issues involved that were unlikely to lead to consensus. At the July 1 meeting of the Working Group he proposed that it be simply deleted. Delegates indicated that they were flexible on the subject, and it was so decided.[97]

2. Determination of the Sentence

Article 78 concerns determination of the sentence and addresses three issues: mitigating and aggravating factors, the treatment of time served in detention prior to sentencing, and the imposition of sentences in the case of conviction for more than one offence. It states:

Article 78. Determination of the sentence

1. In determining the sentence, the Court shall, in accordance with the Rules of Procedure and Evidence, take into account such factors as the gravity of the crime and the individual circumstances of the convicted person.

2. In imposing a sentence of imprisonment, the Court shall deduct the time, if any, previously spent in detention in accordance with an order of the Court. The Court may deduct any time otherwise spent in detention in connection with conduct underlying the crime.

3. When a person has been convicted of more than one crime, the Court shall pronounce a sentence for each crime and a joint sentence specifying the total period of imprisonment. This period shall be no less

---

[95] U.N. Doc. A/AC.249/1997/WG.6/CRP.1, at 2–3 (Dec. 2, 1997).

[96] U.N. Doc. A/AC.249/1997/WG.6/CRP.6 (Dec. 10, 1997).

[97] Report of the Working Group on Penalties, U.N. Doc. A/CONF.183/C.1/WGP/L.14 (July 4, 1998), 2.

than the highest individual sentence pronounced and shall not exceed 30 years' imprisonment or a sentence of life imprisonment in conformity with Article 77, paragraph 1 (b).

a. Mitigating and Aggravating Factors

Two options on mitigating and aggravating factors were presented at the December 1997 PrepCom.[98] The first was worded in general terms, inviting the Court, when determining sentence, to take into account such aspects as the gravity of the crime, the extent and severity of the damage or injury caused and the impact of the crime on the victims, and the individual circumstances of the convicted person, including any previous conviction as well as the degree of intervention of the convicted person in the commission of the crime. The second was considerably more detailed in its enumeration of aggravating and mitigating factors. It included, in addition to the factors set out in the first option, the nature of the illicit behavior and the means employed to execute the crime, the form or degree of intervention of the agent in the commission of the crime, as well as his or her capacity and that of the victim, the circumstances of time, mode and place of the act executed, the age, education, culture, customs, social and economic condition of the agent, the motives which induced him or her to commit the crime, and the substantial cooperation with the Prosecutor by the convicted person before or after conviction.[99]

After informal consultations, the text was revised into a more simple formulation authorizing the Court simply "to take into account such factors as the gravity of the crime and the individual circumstances of the convicted person." The conference room paper noted the impossibility of foreseeing all relevant aggravating and mitigating circumstances. Many delegations considered that the matter was better left to the rules of the Court, although for some this would depend upon how the rules were to be adopted.[100] There were no square brackets, a considerable accomplishment. For this reason, there was no real debate on the subject in the Working Group at the Rome Conference. At Rome, the text was adopted early in the debates of the Working Group on Penalties,[101] accompanied by a footnote:

---

[98] In the course of discussions on general principles of criminal law within the Preparatory Committee, the usefulness of a text covering factors insufficient to constitute a full-fledged defense to charges became apparent. In the specific case of mental disorder, the Working Group on General Principles of Criminal Law considered adding language along the following lines: "If a mental disease or defect merely influences his judgment or his control over his actions without destroying it, the person shall remain criminally responsible but his punishment may be reduced." U.N. Doc. A/AC.249/1997/WG.2/DP3.

[99] U.N. Doc. A/AC.249/1997/WG.6/CRP.1, 4 (Dec. 2, 1997).

[100] U.N. Doc. A/AC.249/1997/WG.6/CRP.3 (Dec. 10, 1997).

[101] Report of the Working Group on Penalties," U.N. Doc. A/CONF.183/C.1/WGP/L.14 (July 4, 1998), 3.

It may be impossible to foresee all of the relevant aggravating and miti- gating circumstances at this stage. Many delegations felt that factors should be elaborated and developed in the Rules of Procedure and Evidence, while several other delegations expressed the view that a final decision on this approach would depend upon the mechanism agreed for adopting the Rules. Among the factors suggested by various delegations as having relevance were: the impact of the crime on the victims and their families; the extent of damage caused or the danger posed by the convicted person's conduct; the degree of participation of the convicted person in the commission of the crime; the circumstances falling short of exclusion of criminal responsibility such as substantially diminished mental capacity or, as appropriate, duress; the age of the convicted per- son; the social and economic condition of the convicted person; the motive for the commission of the crime; the subsequent conduct of the person who committed the crime; superior orders; the use of minors in the commission of the crime.[102]

The Statute also declares, in Article 27, that official capacity shall not, "in and of itself, constitute a ground for reduction of sentence." The opposite would be more logical. The fact that a convicted person held a senior government posi- tion will generally be an aggravating factor. The provision dealing with the defense of superior orders does not specify whether an accused may still invoke the fact that he or she acted under superior orders as a mitigating factor if the defense is rejected or is inadmissible. Formulations to this effect appear in a num- ber of international criminal law instruments.[103] The silence of the Statute on this subject should not be taken to imply that superior orders cannot be a mitigating factor in certain cases.

b. Credit for Time Served

In early versions of the PrepCom text, credit for time served was addressed under the heading of mitigating factors. Several delegations felt that this was inap- propriate, however, and it was agreed to approach the matter distinctly.[104] At its December 1997 session, the PrepCom decided that a specific provision in the Statute should address this point. It recommended the following: "[t]ime spent in detention in accordance with an order of the Court prior to final sentencing shall be deducted by the Court from any term of imprisonment to be served. Time oth-

---

[102] *Id.* at 3; Report of the Working Group on Penalties, U.N. Doc. A/CONF.183/C.1/WGP/ L.14/Corr.2 (July 6, 1998), 1, para. 2.

[103] For example, art. 7(4) of the Statute of the International Criminal Tribunal for the Former Yugoslavia: "4. The fact that an accused person acted pursuant to an order of a Government or of a superior shall not relieve him or her of criminal responsibility, but may be considered in mitigation of punishment if the International Tribunal for Rwanda determines that justice so requires."

[104] U.N. Doc. A/AC.249/1997/WG.6/CRP.1, at 5 (Dec. 2, 1997).

erwise spent in detention in connection with conduct underlying the crime may also be deducted."[105] The text was not in square brackets, and was easily adopted at the first meeting of the Working Group on Penalties of the Diplomatic Conference, on June 30, 1998.[106]

c. Multiple Convictions

When sentence is pronounced for more than one offence, the Court must specify the sentence for each offence as well as a total period of imprisonment. Of course, the total period cannot be less than the highest individual sentence pronounced, nor may it exceed the total set out in Article 77(1)(b), that is, life imprisonment or a total of thirty years. This was a hybrid of the two options considered by the PrepCom in December 1997 and included in the final draft statute submitted to the Rome Conference.[107] According to one variant, the Court would pronounce a single sentence that could be increased up to the maximum allowable penalty in the case of multiple convictions. The second option was to allow the Court to specify whether multiple sentences would be consecutive or concurrent.[108]

At the Rome Conference, the matter was discussed in the informal session of the Working Group on Penalties of July 1, 1998. The chair observed that some states considered it important that there be a ceiling on the punishment to be meted out.[109] Others felt the penalty should "fit the crime." Fife made a verbal proposal: "[w]hen a person has been convicted of more than one crime, the Court shall indicate a sentence for each crime and pronounce on the total period of imprisonment to be served, which shall not exceed half of the longest term of imprisonment prescribed for the gravest crime."[110] On July 6, he submitted a new version that, with minor changes, constituted the final text.[111]

3. Trust Fund

Article 79 mandates creation of a Trust Fund:

---

[105] U.N. Doc. A/AC.249/1997/WG.6/CRP.7 (Dec. 10, 1997).

[106] Report of the Working Group on Penalties, U.N. Doc. A/CONF.183/C.1/WGP/L.14 (July 4, 1998), 3.

[107] U.N. Doc. A/AC.249/1997/WG.6/CRP.10 (Dec. 10, 1997).

[108] Report of the Preparatory Committee on the Establishment of an International Criminal Court, *supra* note 26, at 122–123.

[109] There were two submissions along these lines : Proposal Submitted by Austria, U.N. Doc. A/CONF.183/C.1/WGP/L.5 (July 1, 1998); Proposal Submitted by Ukraine, U.N. Doc. A/CONF.183/C.1/WGP/L.6 (July 1, 1998).

[110] Later issued as Chairman's Working Paper on Article 77, U.N. Doc. A/CONF.183/C.1/WGP/L.9 (July 2, 1998).

[111] Chairman's Working Paper on Article 77, U.N. Doc. A/CONF.183/C.1/WGP/L.9/Rev. 1 (July 6, 1998).

Article 79. Trust Fund

1. A Trust Fund shall be established by decision of the Assembly of states Parties for the benefit of victims of crimes within the jurisdiction of the Court, and of the families of such victims.

2. The Court may order money and other property collected through fines or forfeiture to be transferred, by order of the Court, to the Trust Fund.

3. The Trust Fund shall be managed according to criteria to be determined by the Assembly of States Parties.

The International Law Commission draft said that the Court should be empowered to order that fines paid be transferred to a trust fund established by the United Nations Secretary-General for the benefit of victims of crime.[112] At Rome, the Trust Fund provision grew out of a proposal entitled "Fines [and assets] collected by the Court."[113] Three options were presented: creation of a trust fund, return the assets to the state of the victims, remit them to the Registrar to defray costs of the trial.

The initial debate in the Working Group on Penalties showed a very strong preference for the first of the three proposals. The June 30 session of the Working Group mandated the chair to prepare a new proposal based on that option. The next day, the chair submitted a new text: "Article 79. Fines and assets collected by the Court. Fines and assets collected by the Court may be transferred, by order of the Court, to a trust fund established by the Secretary-General of the United Nations for the benefit of victims of the crime and their families."[114] At Japan's suggestion, Fife replaced the word "assets" with "proceeds, property and assets obtained through forfeiture." The words "by the Secretary-General of the United Nations" were changed to "pursuant to a decision of the states Parties." France, which was a strong advocate of the cause of victims at the Conference, said that there should be some criteria for distribution. The chair prepared yet another version:

Fines collected by the Court.

1. A Trust Fund shall be established by decision of the Assembly of States Parties, for the benefit of victims of crimes within the jurisdiction of the Court and of their families.

---

[112] Report of the Preparatory Committee on the Establishment of an International Criminal Court, *supra* note 26, art. 47(3)(C); Report of the Commission to the General Assembly on the Work of Its Forty-Sixth Session, U.N. Doc. A/CN.4/SER.A/1994/Add.1 (Part 2), 60, para. 91.

[113] Report of the Preparatory Committee on the Establishment of an International Criminal Court, *supra* note 26, at 123–124.

[114] Chairman's Working Paper on Article 79, U.N. Doc. A/CONF.183/C.1/WGP/L.2 (June 30, 1998).

2. Money and proceeds of other property collected by the Court through fines or forfeiture may be transferred, by order of the Court, to the Trust Fund.

3. The Trust Fund shall be managed according to criteria to be determined by the Assembly of States Parties.[115]

During discussion that day, the phrase "by the Court" was eliminated from the heading because some assets might be collected by states. The terms "proceeds of" and "by the Court" in paragraph 2 were also deleted. The chair drew the attention of the Working Group to the use of the term "may" in paragraph 2. He said this was to avoid obliging the Court to put the assets in the Trust Fund, and to permit restitution directly to the victims in some cases. As for the criteria in paragraph 3, he explained that this meant criteria for use and distribution.[116]

Article 79 is all that remains of more ambitious proposals to provide for compensation, restitution and reparation within the penalties provisions of the Statute. Although nobody contested the importance of these goals,[117] there were serious questions as to whether this function should fall to the International Criminal Court. The December 1997 PrepCom considered a draft proposal enabling the court to order "appropriate forms of reparation," although it was to be without prejudice "to the obligation on every state to provide reparation in respect of conduct engaging the responsibility of the state."[118] In deciding to drop reference to reparation, the Working Group on Penalties recalled that this matter was addressed elsewhere in the Statute.[119]

4. Draft Provisions Deleted by the Rome Conference

The International Law Commission draft statute gave no consideration to the case of juvenile offenders. All national criminal law systems provide for the possibility of reduced sentences in the case of adolescents, and this is assuredly a general principle of law, reflected in Article 37 of the Convention on the Rights of the Child.[120] During the drafting, many delegations requested a specific provi-

---

[115] Chairman's Working Paper on Article 79, U.N. Doc. A/CONF.183/C.1/WGP/L.7 (July 2, 1998).

[116] Report of the Working Group on Penalties, U.N. Doc. A/CONF.183/C.1/WGP/L.14, 4; Report of the Working Group on Penalties, U.N. Doc. A/CONF.182/C.1/WGP/L,14/Corr.2, 2.

[117] U.N. Doc. E/CN.4/Sub.2/1993/8.

[118] U.N. Doc. A/AC.249/1997/WG.6/CRP.1, 2 (Dec. 2, 1997). *See, on this point,* WOMEN'S CAUCUS FOR GENDER JUSTICE IN THE INTERNATIONAL CRIMINAL COURT, RECOMMENDATIONS & COMMENTARY, ARTICLE 47, PENALTIES & REPARATIONS (DEC. 10, 1997), 1.

[119] Rome Statute of the International Criminal Court, *supra* note 2, art. 75.

[120] Convention on the Rights of the Child, G.A. Res. 44/25, Annex. *Also* United Nations Standard Minimum Rules for the Administration of Juvenile Justice, U.N. Doc. A/CONF.121/22/Rev.1 (1986), G.A. Res. 40/33; United Nations Rules for the Protection of Juveniles Deprived of Their Liberty, G.A. Res. 45/113.

sion for juvenile offenders. The conference room paper prepared in anticipation of the December 1997 PrepCom set the age of criminal responsibility at thirteen, and stated that offenders under the age of eighteen could not be sentenced to more than twenty years in detention, unless the Court decided otherwise for "specified reasons."[121] Following informal discussions, two options emerged, the first echoing the earlier version, and the second leaving the entire matter to the discretion of the court, which would be charged with determining "the appropriate measures to ensure the rehabilitation of the offender." A third option, mentioned only in a footnote, suggested that the Court could exercise jurisdiction over persons aged sixteen to eighteen, provided it had determined the person was capable of understanding the unlawfulness of his or her criminal conduct at the time of the offense.[122]

The question of juvenile penalties hinged on whether or not the Court would actually exercise jurisdiction in such cases. At Rome, the Working Group on Penalties merely waited while this issue was considered by the Working Group on General Principles. Austria, the United States and Israel argued that the age of criminal responsibility should be set between sixteen and eighteen. Israel explained that the age of responsibility should correspond to the age permitted for recruitment into the armed forces. This view did not prevail, however. Eventually, the Working Group on General Principles agreed to a text entitled "[n]on-jurisdiction over minors," which read: "[t]he Court shall have no jurisdiction over persons who were under the age of eighteen at the time of the alleged commission of a crime." A slightly modified text was adopted by the Drafting Committee, resolving the issue for the Working Group on Penalties, which in fact never considered the question.[123]

Like sentences for juveniles, the subject of the appropriate penalty for legal persons was also contingent on a decision of the Working Group on General Principles with respect to their treatment by the Statute. Ultimately, legal persons were excluded from the jurisdiction of the Court, after the Working Group on General Principles recognized the impossibility of consensus on the subject. This settled yet another potential difficulty for the Working Group on Penalties.[124]

---

[121] U.N. Doc. A/AC.249/1997/WG.6/CRP.1, AT 2 (Dec. 2, 1997).

[122] U.N. Doc. A/AC.249/1997/WG.6/CRP.4 (Dec. 10, 1997).

[123] Report of the Working Group on Penalties, U.N. Doc. A/CONF.183/C.1/WGP/L.14 (July 4, 1998), AT 1–2.

[124] Report of the Working Group on Penalties, U.N. Doc. A/CONF.183/C.1/WGP/L.14/Add 1 (July 7, 1998), AT 1, 4. A draft provision on penalties for legal persons had been added by the 1998 session of the PrepCom: U.N. Doc. A/AC.249/1998/CRP.13, art. 69 [47 *bis*]. This became art. 76 in the draft statute: U.N. Doc. A/CONF.183/2/Add.1, p. 121. A proposal on the subject was also submitted at the Diplomatic Conference: Proposal on Article 76 Submitted by Belgium, Benin, Brazil, Burundi, the Dominican Republic, Egypt, France, Oman, Portugal, the Republic of Korea, Romania, Samoa, Slovenia, South Africa, Thailand, Togo, the United Kingdom of Great Britain and Northern Ireland, and the United Republic of Tanzania, U.N. Doc. A/CONF.183/C.1/WGP/L.12 (July 2, 1998).

A third provision that the Working Group on Penalties chose to delete concerned the use of national law in determining sentences. The draft statute prepared by the International Law Commission states that the Court "may" have regard to penalties provided in the national law of the state of which the convicted person is a national, the state where the crime was committed, and the state having custody of and jurisdiction over the accused.[125] These terms echoed the statutes of the *ad hoc* tribunals for the former Yugoslavia and Rwanda.[126] It was felt that if it could be shown that penalties similar to those imposed by the Court were also in effect in states having some connection with the crime or the offender, then the *nulla poena sine lege* argument would be appropriately addressed.

When the International Law Commission text on national law was studied by the August 1996 PrepCom, some delegations considered it might lead to vagueness and imprecision, which could be contrary to the principle of legality. In addition, they cited the danger of inequality and inconsistency, because national laws vary considerably as to sentences, even for the most severe crimes. Others urged recourse to national law on a subsidiary basis, and only if it did not run counter to international criminal law. The report notes: "[o]ne suggestion was that the draft statute should include an international standard for the various crimes; the jurisprudence and the experience of the Court could gradually expand this area. Another view, however, considered that the *renvoi* (referral) to national legislation could constitute a compromise among differing concepts and a solution to the difficult problem of determining the gravity of penalties."[127] The December 1997 PrepCom decided to include an option allowing the Court to consider national law.[128]

In the initial debate in the Working Group on Penalties at the Rome Conference, some states advocated reference to national legal standards[129] although many more were opposed, urging that any such reference be deleted.[130] Some said it raised problems with the right to equality. At the Working Group's July 3 session, the chair noted that there were "widely differing views" on the provision, and he proposed it be deleted "because there is no consensual basis." This met with general agreement.[131]

---

[125] Report of the Preparatory Committee on the Establishment of an International Criminal Court, *supra* note 26, at art. 47(2).

[126] Statute of the International Criminal Tribunal for the Former Yugoslavia, art. 24, § 1; Statute of the International Criminal Tribunal for Rwanda, art. 23, § 1.

[127] Report of the Preparatory Committee on the Establishment of an International Criminal Court, Vol. I, *supra* note 26, at para. 308.

[128] U.N. Doc. A/AC.249/1997/WG.6/CRP.9 (Dec. 10, 1997). *Also* Report of the Preparatory Committee on the Establishment of an International Criminal Court, *supra* note 26, at 123.

[129] Oman, Kuwait.

[130] Congo (DR), Cuba, France, Hungary, Israel, Portugal, Sierra Leone, Singapore, Uruguay, Chile, Philippines, Russian Federation.

[131] Report of the Working Group on Penalties, U.N. Doc. A/CONF.183/C.1/WGP/L.14 (July 4, 1998), 1–2.

There is another avenue by which to introduce national law into sentencing considerations. Article 21 of the Statute, entitled "Applicable Law," entitles the Court to consider "general principles of law derived by the Court from national laws of legal systems of the world including, as appropriate, the national laws of states that would normally exercise jurisdiction over the crime, provided that those principles are not inconsistent with this Statute and with international law and internationally recognized norms and standards." In reality, however, this is unlikely to prove terribly helpful. The *ad hoc* tribunals have quickly recognized the difficulties in applying the concept and have accorded only perfunctory attention to domestic norms and practice.[132]

D. CONCLUSION

One of the great difficulties in drafting the Rome Statute was convincing delegates that the exercise was not one of comparative criminal law. Many participants saw the drafting process as a chance to convince others of the merits of their own domestic legal system, rather than a forum for compromise and, possibly, an opportunity to learn about the strengths of other legal cultures. While these problems were present in the preparation of the penalties provisions, the final result is a regime that potentially leaves great discretion in the hands of the judges of the new Court. Some of the pieces remain to be put in place in the Rules of Procedure and Evidence, particularly the identification of mitigating and aggravating factors, but if the debates at Rome are indicative of the tone that will be taken in the Preparatory Commission, the tendency will be towards a lowest common denominator based on general principles of law derived from domestic legal systems.

If there is an overall picture that emerges from the four articles of part 7 of the Statute, it is of a relatively humane and enlightened sentencing scheme. The death penalty, of course, is excluded, as are other forms of corporal punishment. The basic penalty is imprisonment, but couched in terms that imply life imprisonment is applicable only in the most serious cases. Both the text of the provisions and the *travaux préparatoires* send messages to the judges of relative clemency. This can only have salutary effects on domestic judicial systems. Penal reformers, judges and lawyers, parliamentarians and journalists will all turn to the Statute as a model in debates on sentencing policy. The majority will find that the Statute is more liberal than what is offered by their own legal system.

The Statute says nothing about the principles of sentencing. Is the Court to focus principally on retribution or rather on deterrence, on some combination of the two, or on other factors? The question is certainly one that interests judges, as the evolving case law of the *ad hoc* tribunals indicates. The obvious explanation for the Statute's silence on this point is that agreement would have been impossi-

---

[132] Prosecutor v. Erdemovic (Case No. IT–96–22–T), Sentencing Judgment of Nov. 29, 1996, para. 35; Prosecutor v. Serushago (Case No. ICTR–98–39–S), Sentence, Feb. 2, 1999, para. 18.

ble, but it is also clear from the *travaux,* as well as the work in the International Law Commission, that the question rarely arose.

The failure to discuss, let alone identify, relevant factors in sentencing may show that those who created the International Criminal Court took them for granted, but this is unlikely. The debates revealed fundamentally different attitudes towards the purposes of criminal punishment, indicated by attitudes toward such questions as life imprisonment, mandatory review and capital punishment. The failure to address the purposes of sentencing directly may also reveal the fact that it seems to be more on the periphery than at the core of the work of the Court. Sentences must be imposed, of course, and therefore the Statute must contain sentencing provisions, but the silence on the objectives that sentences are expected to accomplish quite possibly indicates an implicit assumption, shared by many states from a variety of legal cultures, that the work of the Court is more about a search for truth than about sending people to prison.

CHAPTER 12
REPARATIONS FOR VICTIMS OF INTERNATIONAL CRIMES

Dinah L. Shelton[1]

A. INTRODUCTION

Article 75.1 of the Rome Statute mandates the Court to:

> establish principles relating to reparations to, or in respect of, victims, including restitution, compensation and rehabilitation. On this basis, in its decision the Court may, either upon request or on its own motion in exceptional circumstances, determine the scope and extent of any damage, loss and injury to, or in respect of, victims and will state the principles on which it is acting.

The application of this provision must be based on respect for the internationally guaranteed human rights of every person appearing before the Court, whether victim or defendant. Human rights law establishes a minimum standard of treatment that must inform the Court's work. Given the concurrence of jurisdiction between national tribunals and the International Criminal Court, individuals should receive no less favorable treatment at the International Criminal Court than that guaranteed them in national courts under the international customary and treaty law of human rights.

B. LESSONS FROM INTERNATIONAL HUMAN RIGHTS LAW

1. The Right to a Remedy

The right to a remedy when rights are violated is expressly guaranteed by global and regional human rights instruments. Most texts guarantee both the procedural right of effective access to a fair hearing and the substantive right to a remedy. The Universal Declaration of Human Rights provides that "[e]veryone has the right to an effective remedy by the competent national tribunals for acts

---

[1] An earlier version of this contribution was prepared for and distributed by The Center on International Cooperation of New York University to the July 26–Aug. 13, 1999, Meeting of the Preparatory Commission for the International Criminal Court. Further information on the Center is available, along with its publications and working papers, on the Center's web site <www.nyu.edu/pages/cic>.

violating the fundamental rights granted him by the constitution or laws" (Article 8). The International Covenant on Civil and Political Rights contains three separate articles on remedies. Article 2.3 calls on States Parties to ensure that any person whose rights or freedoms recognized in the Covenant are violated shall have an effective remedy notwithstanding that the violation has been committed by persons acting in an official capacity; to ensure that any person claiming such a remedy shall have the right thereto determined by competent judicial, administrative or legislative authorities, or by any other competent authority provided for by the legal system of the state, and to develop the possibilities of judicial remedy; and to ensure that the competent authorities shall enforce such remedies when granted. The Convention on the Elimination of Racial Discrimination also contains broad guarantees of an effective remedy (Article 6), like the Convention on the Elimination of All Forms of Discrimination against Women, which requires competent national tribunals and other public institutions to ensure "the effective protection of women against any act of discrimination." (Article 2.c).

The United Nations Convention against Torture refers in Article 14 to redress and compensation for torture victims: "Each State Party shall ensure in its legal system that the victim of an act of torture obtains redress and has an enforceable right to fair and adequate compensation, including the means for as full rehabilitation as possible. In the event of the death of the victim as a result of an act of torture, his dependents shall be entitled to compensation."

Declarations, resolutions and other non-treaty texts also address the right to a remedy. In some instances, the issue is raised by human rights organs when issuing "general comments." In 1998, the Working Group on Involuntary or Enforced Disappearances issued a General Comment to Article 19 of the 1992 Declaration on the Protection of All Persons from Enforced Disappearance. The Working Group elaborated on the obligation to provide adequate compensation. Compensation is deemed "adequate" if it is "proportionate to the gravity of the human rights violation (e.g., the period of disappearance, the conditions of detention, etc.) and to the suffering of the victim and the family." Amounts shall be provided for any damage, including physical or mental harm, lost opportunities, material damages and loss of earnings, harm to reputation, and costs required for legal or expert assistance. In the event of the death of the victim, as a result of an act of enforced disappearance, the victims are entitled to additional compensation. Measures of rehabilitation should be provided, including medical and psychological care, rehabilitation for any form of physical or mental damage, legal and social rehabilitation, guarantees of non-repetition, restoration of personal liberty, family life, citizenship, employment or property, return to the place of residence, and similar forms of restitution, satisfaction and reparation that may remove the consequences of the enforced disappearance.

Norms adopted in the area of crime prevention and criminal justice also mandate remedies. The United Nations Declaration of Basic Principles of Justice for

Victims of Crime and Abuse of Power[2] contains broad guarantees for those who suffer pecuniary losses, physical or mental harm, and "substantial impairment of their fundamental rights" through acts or omissions, including abuse of power. Victims are entitled to redress and to be informed of their right to seek redress. The Declaration specifically provides that victims of public officials or other agents who, acting in an official or quasi-official capacity, violate national criminal laws, should receive restitution from the state whose officials or agents are responsible for the harm inflicted. Abuse of power that is not criminal under national law but that violates internationally recognized norms relating to human rights should be sanctioned and remedies provided, including restitution and/or compensation, and all necessary material, medical, psychological, and social assistance and support.

Regional instruments also contain provisions requiring legal remedies for violations of human rights. The commissions and courts have interpreted and applied these guarantees in several cases. The European Convention on Human Rights modeled its general remedial provision, contained in Article 13, on Article 8 of the Universal Declaration of Human Rights. The American Convention on Human Rights goes further, entitling everyone to effective recourse to protection against acts that violate the fundamental rights recognized by the constitution "or laws of the state or by the Convention," even when the act is committed by persons acting in the course of their official duties (Article 25). The African Charter has several provisions on remedies. Article 7 guarantees every individual the right to have her/his cause heard, including "the right to an appeal to competent national organs against acts violating his fundamental rights as recognized and guaranteed by conventions, laws, regulations and customs in force."

In sum, it is clear that the existence of effective remedies is an essential component of international human rights law.

2. The Purpose of Remedies

The primary function of corrective or remedial justice is to rectify the wrong done to a victim. Compensation can only provide something equivalent in value

---

[2] U.N.G.A. Res. 40/34 of Nov. 29, 1985. Paragraph 4 states that victims are entitled to access to the mechanisms of justice and prompt redress for the harm they have suffered. Procedures are to be expeditious, fair, inexpensive and accessible. Where appropriate, restitution should be made to victims, their families or dependents by offenders or third parties responsible for their behavior. (Para. 8) Victims of abuse of power are defined as those harmed by acts which do not yet constitute violations of national criminal laws. In 1990, the Eighth United Nations Congress on the Prevention of Crime and the Treatment of Offenders (Havana, Cuba, Aug. 27–Sept. 7, 1990), recommended that states base national legislation upon the Declaration and requested the UN Secretary General to study the feasibility of establishing an international fund for victims of transnational crimes. Report of the Congress, A/CONF.144/28. The Council of Europe produced the European Convention on the Compensation of Victims of Violent Crimes (1983), a 1985 recommendation R(85) 11 on the position of the victim in the framework of criminal law and procedure, and a 1987 recommendation R(87)21 on assistance to victims and prevention of victimization.

to that which is lost; rectification or restitution restores precisely that which is taken. Where restitution or rectification is not possible, substitute remedies, including damages, are required. In fact, monetary compensation is the most common form of reparation because, as Grotius says, "money is the common measure of valuable things." The amount of compensation must correspond to the value of restitution in kind. Arbitral tribunals frequently restate the theory that reparations "must wipe out all the consequences" of the illegal act. In the *Lusitania* cases, the arbiter Parker stated that the "remedy must be commensurate with the injury received. . . . The compensation must be adequate and balance as near as may be the injury suffered."[3]

Human rights violations committed by state officials are qualitatively different from private injury because of the motives and nature of the conduct as well as the identity of the wrongdoer. Individuals expect protection from the state; one of its fundamental purposes is to secure the safety and well-being of those within its power. For the government itself to cause harm adds an element of outrage generally not present in purely private wrongdoing. The Inter American Court of Human Rights recognized the profound impact that such violations can have. In the *Loayza Tomayo v. Peru (Reparations)*[4] decision, it pointed out that the very existence and conditions of the life of a person are altered by unfairly and arbitrarily imposed official actions taken in violation of existing norms and of the trust that is placed in the hands of public power, whose duty is to protect and provide security in order for individuals to exercise their rights and satisfy their legitimate personal interests. The remedies afforded should reflect the breach of trust involved because, in general, the more outrageous the wrongdoer's conduct, the more outraged and distressed the victim will be and the greater the harm that will be suffered.

Remedies should provide the important psychological and social functions of reintegration and rehabilitation of the victimized. Victims of abuse often are blamed for their victimization or avoided because of the horrific nature of the stories they have to tell. Bystander's guilt may also lead to rejecting the victims. Not infrequently, the social reaction is indifference or avoidance leading to a silence that is detrimental to the victims, producing isolation and mistrust. Children of victims may adopt these reactions and themselves become victims over time. The need to re-adapt to normal society and return to pre-victim ways of living and functioning is crucial.

As compensation is the most common remedy, every legal system should strive for certainty in calculating damages to avoid under- or over-compensating a victim. Uncertainty and arbitrariness in awards undermines respect for the law; legal certainty represents one of modern jurisprudence's central concerns as the

---

³ *Lusitania* cases, 7 R.I.A.A. 35, 36.

⁴ Loayza Tomayo v. Peru, Judgment of Nov. 27, 1998, 43 Inter-Am. Ct. H.R. (ser.C) (1998).

law searches for order and predictability. The rule of law implies that society administers justice by fixing standards that individuals may determine prior to controversy and that reasonably guarantee all individuals like treatment. Accurate assessment is also necessary because inadequate or excessive awards frustrate the compensatory, retributive and deterrent functions of the law.

The prevalence of compensation as a remedy should not diminish consideration of the need for other kinds of redress. When rights are infringed, someone has been victimized because of an unwarranted act of interference and therefore justifiably has the right to reclaim her/his prior position. This focus on the victim demands provision of something equivalent in value to that which was lost, or restoring precisely that which was removed. The primary goal of remedies thus should be rectification or restitution rather than compensation. When rights are violated, the ability of the victim to pursue self-determination is impaired and it is not justifiable generally to assume that compensation restores the moral balance *ex ante*. A morally adequate response addresses itself in the first instance to restoring what was taken.

3. Who May Claim Remedies

International tribunals have adopted rules and decided cases setting forth the procedural requirements to claim remedies, including standing to file claims, presentation of claims, and the power of the tribunals to oversee the execution of judgments. The designation of a "victim" is an international legal question and at a minimum includes the individual whose right or freedom has been violated. It generally is not necessary for the victim to be a national or resident of the defendant state. When the victim is deceased or the injury has consequences for other persons, third parties also may be characterized as victims of the violation. The former European Commission on Human Rights defined the term "victim" as including "not only the direct victim or victims of the alleged violation, but also any person who would indirectly suffer prejudice as a result of such violation or who would have a valid personal interest in securing the cessation of such violation."[5]

Among the cases decided by the Inter-American Court of Human Rights by the end of 1998, few direct victims had survived the breaches to bring an international complaint. In all remaining cases, various family members and other dependents of the deceased were the claimants. In such cases they sought remedies for injuries to the deceased prior to death, wrongful death, and consequential damages they have suffered in their own right. The Inter-American Court has held that both pecuniary and non-pecuniary claims survive and automatically pass

---

[5] X v. Federal Republic of Germany, App.4185/69, 35 Eur. Comm'n H.R. Dec. & Rep. 140, 142 (1970). *See also* Koolen v. Belgium, 1478/62 13 Eur. Comm'n H.R. Dec. & Rep. 89; X v Germany, 282/57, I Y.B. Eur. Conv. on H.R.166; Andronicou and Constantinou v. Cyprus (Admissibility), 82B Eur. Comm'n H.R. Dec. & Rep. 112 (1995).

to the victim's heirs or successors. In general, the Court requires the state to remedy the harm caused to those who suffer the "immediate effects" of its breaches of human rights guarantees when those effects are sufficiently direct and proximate. In *Loayza Tamayo v. Peru*, the Court held that the victim's family members were also "injured parties" within the meaning of Article 63.1 and could present their own claims during the reparations phase of the case. The Court considered that the term "family members" should be understood in a broad sense to include all those persons linked by a close relationship, including the children, the parents and the siblings. Similarly, in *Blake v. Guatemala*, the parents and siblings of the disappeared all claimed to be directly injured by Blake's disappearance and death. The Court referred to the especially grave context of forced disappearance that caused the family anguish and suffering, together with insecurity, frustration and impotence in the face of the government's failure to investigate. Finding that the family had experienced grave moral damage and suffering as a result of the violations, it awarded each member of the family $30,000. Finally, in *Suarez Rosero v. Ecuador*, the applicant sought $20,000 in moral damages for himself, and $20,000 for his wife and daughter. The Court awarded $20,000 each to him and his wife, and $10,000 to the daughter, holding that it is human nature to suffer in the circumstances he had been through and that no proof was required. Further, there must be presumed repercussions for his wife and daughter. The Court based its award on the totality of the circumstances and awards made in similar cases.

The Human Rights Committee has also indicated that family members may be considered victims of violations perpetrated on one of their relatives. In the case of a disappearance, the Committee found that the mother of the disappeared was a victim.

Standing to claim remedies thus will extend to all direct and indirect victims of crimes within the jurisdiction of the ICC. This will necessarily include legal as well as natural persons. Article 8 of the Statute includes crimes whose victims most often are legal persons. These crimes include extensive destruction and appropriation of property (Article 8.2.a.iv), attacking or bombarding towns, villages, dwellings or buildings (Article 8.2.b.v), and intentionally directing attacks against buildings dedicated to religion, education, art, science or charitable purposes, and historic monuments (Article 8.2.b.ix). The last, in particular, is likely to involve claimants from municipalities to foundations, religious institutions and museums. Looting of cultural property and the destruction of cultural monuments is a war crime and contrary to the 1954 Hague Convention on the Protection of Cultural Property During Armed Conflict. It is a crime that has become particularly significant during ethnic and religious conflicts. Examples abound of such attacks and efforts to recover such property by the legal entities entitled to the property, from the Greek Cypriot church lawsuits to recover stolen mosaics from churches in occupied Cyprus, to the looting of the museum of Kabul, to the taking of temple artifacts in Cambodia, to on-going efforts to recover art stolen during the Second World War. If legal persons are not permitted to make claims at the ICC, there will be many instances of looted or destroyed cultural property in which no one will have standing to seek restitution or compensation, thus rendering a portion of the Court's jurisdiction moot.

4. Kinds of Remedies

The law of remedies in legal systems throughout the world seeks to undo the effects of wrongdoing and restore what was taken from the victim. Thus, restitution is preferred when possible and money is awarded as a substitute when the victim cannot be restored to her/his pre-injury position. In practice, restitution is generally limited to claims of stolen property, unlawful termination of employment or arbitrary detention, and similar cases where the exact thing taken can be returned. For personal injury and death no restoration is possible, however. Life cannot be recovered, nor can a rape or torture victim have the rape or torture expunged. In such cases, money becomes a substitute for the pre-injury status.

A sum of money awarded as damages is designed to compensate victims for harm they have suffered, with the intention of making the victim as well off as he or she would have been if the injury had never occurred. It must be recognized that large amounts of money may be necessary to place the victim in the same position of relative satisfaction that he or she occupied before the event. The assessment or calculation of damages is complex. Physical injury, for example, can cause harm in two ways. First, it lowers the level of income received, and second it usually lowers the value of any income received because of the loss of possibilities to enjoy it.

Human rights tribunals classify monetary compensation under three headings: pecuniary losses, non-pecuniary damage, and costs and expenses.

Intangible injuries such as physical pain and suffering have long been recognized as legitimate elements of damages. Mental anguish independent of physical injury is also now recognized as an element of recovery, including humiliation, loss of enjoyment of life and other non-pecuniary losses. Loss of consortium when one is deprived of a spouse may include loss of love and companionship as well as services in the home, society, and sexual relations. The impairment of any of these gives a right to damages. Interference with parent/child relations may lead to damages for loss of companionship, comfort, guidance, affection and aid. All these factors represent the irreplaceable intangibles of family life. In civil law systems, "*préjudice moral*" includes pain and suffering, sadness and humiliation caused by disfigurement, loss of amenities, loss of recreational ability, loss of any of the five senses, inability to enjoy sexual relations, harm to marriage possibilities, and generally damage to the enjoyment of life. Overall, where there has been an injury, the focus is at least in part on diminution of the injured person's expectations of life.

In sum, national and international tribunals award compensation for violations of basic rights and provide numerous examples of expansive remedies
designed to ensure the restoration, as nearly as possible, of the situation that
would have existed had the wrongful conduct not occurred.

5. Remedies When There Are Large Numbers of Cases

Actions within the jurisdiction of the Court are likely to accompany internal armed conflicts, where the sheer number of victims and perpetrators may
overwhelm the best efforts to provide full redress to victims. When there are thousands of victims in need of justice, both the procedures and the substance
inevitably alter. Administrative solutions like sampling, or summary procedures
can assist in affording swifter resolution of claims for compensation. Compensation and other remedies are part of the rehabilitation process of torture victims and other survivors of gross misconduct. In balancing needs and ability to
pay, compromise is probably necessary in many cases because there are insufficient funds to provide full compensation to all victims. In the context of state
action, a U.N. Victims of Crime report recommended that "if it is uncertain whether
the budgetary means of the state will be sufficient to cover an unknown number
of claimants, a fund should be established to limit the financial burden. A basic
amount should be paid out immediately and the difference paid later, the final
amount payable to each claimant being known only at the time when it is clear
how many claimants filed claims and the amounts distributable out of the fund."[6]

The 1990 conflict in the Persian Gulf created new laws and procedures on
reparations for mass violations during armed conflict.[7] The United Nations
Compensation Commission has built upon the practice of international tribunals
hearing claims of state responsibility for injury to aliens. It also has looked to U.S.
mass tort claims administration as a model for the Iraqi claims process. It has
used "some of the techniques and arts of sampling that were developed in the
[U.S.] asbestos and Dalkon Shield cases."[8] The Commission is limited to awarding monetary compensation, and cannot impose restitution or punitive damages.

The UNCC has determined that pecuniary losses include loss of income and
medical expenses, mental pain and anguish due to the death of a spouse, child or
parent of the individual, or the individual's serious personal injury or suffering of
a sexual assault, aggravated assault or torture. Compensation may be awarded for
mental pain and anguish to individuals for dismemberment, disfigurement, loss

---

6   Victims of Crimes: Working Paper Prepared by the Secretariat, Seventh United Nations
Congress on the Prevention of Crime and the Treatment of Offenders, A/CONF.121/6 at 39
(1985). *See also* United Nations Declaration of Basic Principles of Justice for Victims of Crime
and Abuse of Power, para. 13, G.A. Res. 40/34, 29 Nov. 1985, Annex.

7   David J. Bederman, *The United Nations Compensation Commission and the Tradition of
International Claims Settlement*, 27 INT'L L. & POL. 1 (1994).

8   N. C. Ulmer, *The Gulf War Claims Institution*, 10 J. INT'L ARB. 85, 88 (1993).

of use of a body part, being taken hostage, being illegally detained, having a well-founded fear for one's life, and being deprived of all economic resources such as to threaten one's survival. The U.N. has published a scale of mental pain and anguish for most of the situations faced by individuals during the conflict. Victims of aggravated assault, sexual assault or torture may claim up to $5,000 per incident.[9]

In the United States, the *Marcos* litigation exemplifies the problems associated with efforts to afford all victims some remedy. In the class action suit, the large numbers of victims necessitated innovative procedures that limited the individualized decision-making, taking of evidence, and procedural fairness to both sides that would normally be required in litigation. Rather than hold separate hearings on each of the 10,059 claims, the U.S. District Court allowed the use of a statistical sample of the claims in determining compensatory damages. After an initial review, 518 claims were ruled facially invalid, leaving a pool of 9,541, of which 137 were randomly selected by computer. The number chosen was based on the testimony of a statistical expert who stated that a random sample of 137 claims would achieve a 95 percent statistical probability that the same percentage determined to be valid among the examined claims would be applicable to the totality of claims filed.[10]

The 137 claimants randomly sampled, which included torture victims, families of those summarily executed, and those who disappeared, were deposed and the expert reviewed the depositions to determine the claims. Five percent of the claims were determined to be invalid. Based on the sample, the expert recommended that the sixty-four torture claimants get $3,310,000, an average of $52,719 per valid claim. For summary execution, the recommendation was $6,425,767 for fifty valid claims, an average of $128,515 per valid claim. For the disappearances, the expert recommended $1,833,515, an average of $107,853 per valid claim. The court applied the 5 percent invalidity rate found in the random samples in making its awards to the entire class of 10,059 remaining claims.

In calculating the amounts due for torture, the expert ranked the claims on a scale from one to five, with five representing the worst abuses and suffering. Consideration was given to: (1) physical torture, including methods used and/or abuses suffered; (2) mental abuse, including fright and anguish; (3) duration of the torture; (4) length of detention, if any; (5) physical and/or mental injuries; (6) victim's age; and (7) actual losses, including medical bills. "Although each claim of torture was unique," the expert determined "that there were sufficient similarities within a rating category to recommend a standard damage amount to each victim within that grouping." The amount ranged from $20,000 for category one to $100,000 for category five.

---

[9] *Id.*

[10] In re Estate of Marcos, 103 F.3d 767, 782.

For summary executions and disappearances, the existence of torture prior to the death or disappearance was weighed in the damages. Loss of earnings was also factored in, using the formula of 2/3 × (80–age of death) × annual income, a formula adopted by the Philippine Supreme Court. A cap of $120,000 was placed on lost earnings. When there was no evidence of earnings, the average for the occupation was utilized.

The *Marcos* cases and the international experiences described above demonstrate the unlikelihood of full compensation even when the desire to provide redress is present. Given the limited resources available, the courts and states have sought a fair way of prorating the claims based on the severity of injury. Such an approach maximizes the recovery of all of the victims who came forward, but should be coupled with other remedies, from prosecution to rehabilitation.

If the International Criminal Court decides upon a sampling or other summary procedure, it should consider utilizing its authority under Article 76.3 to afford an appellate hearing to those who claim error in the application of the procedure to their claims.

B. RECOMMENDATIONS FOR THE PROCESSING OF CLAIMS UNDER THE ROME STATUTE

The Court will need to develop processes for the filing of claims early on and maintain them throughout the criminal proceeding. This process should begin as soon as an individual is accused of crimes within the jurisdiction of the Court, in order to allow the marshaling and preservation of evidence. Files can be maintained of those who wish to seek compensation for abuse perpetrated by the defendant. The actual hearing on reparations cannot take place until the conviction is obtained. During the criminal phase, the role of victims will be primarily as witnesses for the prosecution.

The Statute foresees that a hearing may be held in connection with sentencing, and this will require that claims be submitted within a reasonable time prior to the hearing. At the hearing, if there are a manageable number of claimants, the Court may accept oral arguments or evidence from each of them. If there are large numbers involved, proceedings similar to those used in the UNCC or the *Marcos* case will be required, perhaps using sampling techniques or designating a representative for the victims.

The issues of evidence and standards of proof will be extremely important. While the requisite standard for conviction is proof beyond a reasonable doubt, this is not an appropriate standard for claims of reparation after the conviction has been obtained. In essence, the claim of redress is a civil claim heard in the criminal jurisdiction. Different legal systems use different terminology, but all utilize a lower standard of proof for civil claims, usually preponderance of the evidence, a balance of probabilities, or *"conviction intime."* It would be unjust to require a high standard of proof of loss or injury, given the circumstances in which many of the victims will find themselves, including refugee status, homelessness, and lack of medical care where certificates or evidence of injury could be obtained.

Inevitably, there will be injuries that emerge or continue after the completion of the criminal proceedings. It seems unreasonable and unmanageable for the Court to continue reopening cases or retaining jurisdiction to hear all claims that may emerge after the date of conviction. In such instances, the Rules of Procedure and Evidence might provide that claims have to be presented to the Trust Fund and not to the Court itself. If the national courts are functioning, there could be an added requirement of seeking relief in the domestic jurisdiction prior to filing the international claims against the defendant.

C. CONCLUSION

The inclusion of a provision on victim reparations in the Statute of the Court confers an opportunity and a responsibility on the Court to afford justice to those who have suffered from the heinous crimes committed by those indicted and convicted of crimes within the Court's jurisdiction. A moral imbalance is created by the wrongs done, and the direct means of correcting that imbalance is for the wrongdoer to restore what was taken or to pay full compensation in lieu of restitution. While criminal prosecution of the guilty serves the needs of international society to deter and punish, victims require more if they are to be rehabilitated and reintegrated into society. To fulfill the goals of Article 75, the Court Rules of Procedure and Evidence should recognize that there are direct and indirect victims, and that the term "victims" includes both natural and legal persons. All victims should be afforded full redress when possible, but at least some redress in every case. Methods of sampling, representation and other innovative mechanisms can assist in achieving this goal when the number of claimants is too large to allow individualized hearings and determinations of reparations. Finally, it is essential to recognize that the failure to provide justice would risk further cycles of violence, thus undermining one of the purposes for the creation of the Court.

CHAPTER 13
THE TRUST FUND OF THE ICC

Thordis Ingadottir[1]

A. INTRODUCTION

According to Article 79 of the Rome Statute:

1. A Trust Fund shall be established by decision of the Assembly of States Parties for the benefit of victims of crimes within the jurisdiction of the Court, and of the families of such victims.

2. The Court may order money and other property collected through fines or forfeiture to be transferred, by order of the Court, to the Trust Fund.

3. The Trust Fund shall be managed according to criteria to be determined by the Assembly of states Parties.

Article 75.2 indicates that:

2. The Court may make an order directly against a convicted person specifying appropriate reparations to, or in respect of, victims, including restitution, compensation and rehabilitation. Where appropriate, the Court may order that the award for reparations be made through the Trust Fund provided for in Article 79.

The Rome Statute does not describe the structure of the Trust Fund. Article 79 leaves to the Assembly of States Parties the task of deciding crucial issues such as who will control it (e.g., whether it is going to be a fully independent entity, subordinate to the Court, or administered by the U.N. Secretary-General), how it will be composed (e.g., trustees' nature and capacity), how it will function, and what criteria will govern disbursements.[2] The Rome Statute does prescribe that the Trust Fund is to have two sources of income: awards for reparations made by

---

[1] The author wishes to thank Dinah Shelton, Dirk Solomons, Cesare Romano and Shepard Forman for their comments. However, any errors or omissions are the sole responsibility of the author. An earlier version of this contribution was prepared for and distributed by the Center on International Cooperation of New York University.

[2] The discussion herein does not address the issues the Rome Statute has left to the Assembly of states Parties.

the Court (Article 75.2); and money and other property collected through fines or forfeiture (Article 79.2). In both instances, the Court is free to decide whether to disburse funds and property itself or to entrust the task to the Trust Fund.[3] The Rome Statute also indicates that the Court can resort to the Trust Fund to carry out the fundamental task of awarding victims reparations and to handle money and other property collected through fines or forfeiture. The Preparatory Commission of the International Criminal Court therefore must consider such arrangements in drafting the Court's Rules of Procedure and Evidence.

If the Court is eventually to resort to the Trust Fund, which it should to the maximum extent possible, then its Rules of Procedure and Evidence will necessarily discipline how it will do so. The Preparatory Commission should keep in mind what the Trust Fund can and can not do under the Rome Statute, and what is left to the Assembly of States Parties to decide. Statutory provisions on the Trust Fund are extremely brief (Articles 75.2 and 79) and somewhat ambiguous.

B.   THE TRUST FUND

Under the Rome Statute, the function of the Trust Fund is twofold:[4]

1.   It can be used by the Court as *depository*, i.e., the Court can order money and other property collected through fines or forfeiture to be transferred to the Trust Fund. The Trust Fund collects these funds, pools them together and utilizes them for the benefit of victims (Article 79.2); and
2.   It can be used by the Court as *intermediary* (i.e., when the Court "makes an order directly against a convicted person specifying appropriate reparations to, or in respect of, victims . . . ," it can also order that the award of such reparations be made through the Trust Fund) (Article 75.2).

There is a substantial difference between the funds the Trust Fund will manage under Article 75.2 and those under Article 79.2. Indeed, it is only in the case of funds deriving from fines and forfeiture (Article 79.2) that the Trust Fund will actually act as a trustee (i.e., one who holds legal title to property in trust for the benefit of another person). The wording of Article 75.2 clearly indicates that reparations can be awarded by the Court's order *through* rather than *into* the Trust Fund.[5] This means that the Trust Fund never acquires proprietary rights to com-

---

[3] "The Court may order money. . . ." (art. 79.2); "Where appropriate, the Court may order. . . ." (art. 75.2).

[4] Of course, the Assembly of States Parties might extend the competencies of the Trust Fund beyond these two aspects to benefit victims of crime within the jurisdiction of the Court and of the families of such victims.

[5] Indeed, the Preparatory Committees Draft Statute authorized the Court to order that the award of reparations be made *into* the Trust Fund. *See* Report of the Preparatory Committee on

pensation awarded for the benefit of victims. It merely acts as an intermediary. It follows that while the Trust Fund can use funds deriving from fines and forfeiture for anything it might consider beneficial for victims, awards for reparations are different. The Trust Fund is bound to disburse an award solely to the victims of that particular convicted individual at the time and in the forms decided by the Court. This fundamental difference in functions has an enormous impact on the way the Trust Fund will be structured, managed and financed, and on its relations with the Court.

1. The Trust Fund as "Depository" (Article 79.2)

Under Article 77.2, in addition to imprisonment, the Court may order fines and forfeiture of proceeds, property and assets derived directly or indirectly from the adjudged crime, without prejudice to the rights of bona fide third parties. Fines will be collected and property will be forfeited by States Parties, in accordance with the procedure of their national law, and they will transfer those funds to the Court (Article 109). The Court may eventually order money and any other property collected through fines or forfeiture to be transferred to the Trust Fund (Article 79.2).

The significance of this funding source for the Trust Fund will largely depend on the amount of fines imposed.[6] In determining fines, in accordance with criteria provided for in the Rules of Procedure and Evidence, the Court shall take into account such factors as the gravity of the crime and the individual circumstances of the convicted person (e.g., age or social and economic conditions of the convicted person, the motive of crime, or superior orders) (Article 78.1).[7] A proposal has been made to let the Rules of Procedure and Evidence decide a maximum fine which can be imposed by the Court.[8]

The Rome Statute does not give further directions on how they can be used, or who will have the power of decision, after these funds are transferred to the

---

the Establishment of an International Criminal Court, Draft Statute & Draft Final Act, U.N. Doc. A/Conf.183/2/Add.1, 1998, art. 73. In any event, the French text of Article 75.2 leaves no room for doubt. It reads: *"La Cour peut rendre contre une personne condamnée une ordonnance indiquant la réparation qu'il convient d'accorder aux victimes ou à leurs ayants droit. Cette réparation peut prendre notamment la forme de la restitution, de l'indemnisation ou de la réhabilitation. Le cas échéant, la Cour peut décider que L'indemnité accordée à titre de réparation est versée par l'intermédiaire du Fonds visé à l'Article 79."*

[6] The International Criminal Tribunals for the Former Yugoslavia and Rwanda offer no guidance as they do not have provisions for the imposition of fines in their statutes.

[7] Note included in the Report of the Working Group on Penalties at the Rome Conference, U.N. Doc. A/CONF.183/C.1/WGP/L.14/Corr. 2.

[8] Proposal submitted to the Preparatory Commission for the International Criminal Court by Australia, Draft Rules of Procedure and Evidence of the International Criminal Court, Jan. 26, 1999, Rule 104, U.N. Doc. PCNICC/1999/DP.1. Proposal submitted by France, General Outline of the Rules of Procedure and Evidence, U.N. Doc. PCNICC/1999/DP.2, Rule 110.

Trust Fund. This is a critical gap that should be addressed in the Court's Rules of Evidence and Procedure. The power to decide how to allocate money and any other property collected through fines or forfeiture could rest either with the Court or with the Trust Fund. The better solution is to give the Court the primary responsibility to determine allocation in its order of transfer to the Trust Fund. The Trust Fund should be allowed to determine the destination and use of such funds only when the Court has declined to do so. In the Rome Statute the power to decide on the amount, management and destination of compensation rests with the Court. If money and any other property collected through fines or forfeiture is eventually to be used also to supplement inadequate reparations that victims of crimes can obtain from the convicted person (i.e., inadequate because assets could not be seized or because they are insufficient), then the Court must have full control of these resources.[9]

Regardless of whether the decision on the use of funds deriving from fines and forfeiture is taken by the Trust Fund or the Court, the funds should be used for the benefit of victims only. Under no circumstances should they be used to support operational costs of the Court. The legislative history of the Article supports such interpretation.[10] The fact that funds deriving from fines and forfeiture are not included as sources of the Court's funding listed in Article 115 also strongly supports such a conclusion. Having said this, it remains to be seen which victims should benefit, and how, from money and other property collected through fines or forfeiture.

Clear policies on the allocation of such funds between cases will have to be adopted. Indeed, in the Rome Statute Article 79.2, funds are not earmarked exclusively for the benefit of the victims of the case from which they originate.

Nothing in the Statute prohibits the use of money and other property collected through fines or forfeiture for purposes other than financing compensation.

---

[9] *See infra* p. 155.

[10] Article 79, providing for the establishment of the Trust Fund, is in Part 7 of the Rome Statute (Penalties). In earlier drafts the Trust Fund was part of the provision on fines collected by the Court. Both the International Law Commission Draft Statute and the Preparatory Committee Draft Statute indicated that fines could either be transferred to a trust fund, to the state of which the victims were nationals, or to the Registry to defray the costs of the trial. Conversely, during the negotiations in Rome, preference was given to using the funds collected through fines and forfeiture to benefit victims through a trust fund and other options were accordingly dropped from the text. *See* Report of the International Law Commission on Its Forty-Sixth Session, Draft Statute for an International Criminal Court, May 2–July 22, 1994 (U.N.G.A., 49th Sess., Supp. No. 10, U.N. Doc. A/49/10 (1994)), art. 47, and Report of the Preparatory Committee on the Establishment of an International Criminal Court, Draft Statute & Draft Final Act, *supra* note 3, art. 79. In 1996, the Preparatory Committee on the Establishment of an International Criminal Court, debated whether "the International Criminal Court should concern itself with the collection of pecuniary sanctions, other than for the purpose of compensating victims." *See* U.N.G.A., 51st Sess., Supp. No 22, U.N. Doc. A/51/22 (1996), n. 69, at 228.

The Rules of Procedure and Evidence should clearly indicate that the Court (or the Trust Fund, if the Court declines to do so) may designate such funds for purposes other than financial compensation.

In the first place, the Court should be allowed to designate money and other property collected through fines or forfeiture for victims' *legal assistance*. Legal expenses incurred by victims in filing their claims and having them adjudicated should be included in reparations. As an alternative, the Trust Fund could fund legal assistance to individuals who wish to file claims but are unable to do so because they cannot afford the legal expertise to prepare them, or to defray legal costs for those who file claims and whose cases are pending. Legal aid should be granted not only in proceedings before the Court itself, but also for any other proceedings in national fora aimed at obtaining reparations when the Court has failed to provide them. Since the Rome Statute leaves the Court discretion to decide whether to order reparations, victims should receive help in pursuing remedial justice in national or regional human rights courts in those cases where proceedings result in conviction but the Court does not order reparations. The right to a remedy is a fundamental human right, and the discretionary powers conferred upon the Court should not thwart it. Nothing in the Rome Statute's provisions on reparations to victims can be interpreted as prejudicing the rights of victims under national or international law (Article 75.6).

Secondly, the Court should be allowed to designate funds derived from fines and forfeiture for individual victims' interim relief. Years are likely to pass between the time when crimes are committed and the time when victims might be awarded reparations (i.e., time for a full trial, conviction and the seizure of assets). The use of funds from fines and forfeiture might help victims sustain themselves, especially when expensive medical and/or psychological support is severely needed.

Thirdly, the Court should be able to designate funds deriving from fines and forfeiture for humanitarian aid. Such funds could be allocated to victims directly or through established channels of humanitarian assistance.[11] The Trust Fund can engage directly or indirectly in activities benefitting groups of victims (e.g., by helping establish orphan centers, psychological assistance, and medical assistance training programs).[12] This form of aid could reach unidentified victims who, due

---

[11] Both the U.N. Voluntary Fund for Victims of Torture and the U.N. Voluntary Trust Fund on Contemporary Forms of Slavery provide financial assistance "through established channels of assistance," U.N. Doc. A/RES/36/151 (1981) and U.N. Doc. A/RES/46/122 (1991). At the U.N. Voluntary Fund for Victims of Torture "this has been interpreted to mean that the assistance will be provided though existing humanitarian organizations to projects or to initiate projects sponsored or administered by these humanitarian organizations. The fund does not directly administer projects nor does it give assistance directly to individuals," U.N. Doc. A/48/520, App. II.

[12] The U.N. Voluntary Fund for Victims of Torture finances programs which provide medical, psychological, social or legal assistance as directly as possible to the victims of torture and their relatives. Examples of this include the establishment of treatment centers, meetings of

to their victimization and/or social situation, cannot claim their right to reparation through formal procedures.

2. The Trust Fund as "Intermediary" (Article 75.2)

According to Article 75.3 of the Rome Statute:

> Before making an order under this Article [i.e., an order to repair and/or to award reparations through the Trust Fund], the Court may invite and shall take account of representations from or on behalf of the convicted person, victims, other interested persons or interested states.

The Court is not required to consult the convicted person, victims, other interested persons or interested states before ordering and/or awarding reparations, since it is given a discretionary power to do so ("may"). However, once the position of these participants has been ascertained, the Court shall take it into account. What is missing from this reference is the Trust Fund. Nothing seems to bar the Court from inviting representations from the Trust Fund for this purpose. To ensure the competent management and control of funds entrusted to the Trust Fund, it is crucial that the Rules of Procedure and Evidence mandate the Court to consult the Trust Fund before any order on reparations is made. The Trust Fund can best assess its capacity to fulfil reparations orders. Admittedly, an award of reparations by the Court will be based first and foremost on abstract legal principles relating to reparations for victims. Yet, the Trust Fund's actual capacity to obtain such awards must be considered. Moreover, the Trust Fund will be bound by its own regulations and operational policies which might prevent it from transferring funds in the terms requested by the Court.[13]

Once the Court has ordered the convicted person to make reparations, it can also order the award to be made through the Trust Fund. The actual use of the Trust Fund as a means of transferring reparations from the convicted person to victims is optional. Reparations are transferred to the Court first, and the Court can decide to transfer them directly to the victims. Yet direct transfer is likely to take place only in those cases where reparations do not take the form of monetary compensation but rather of restitution. When reparations take the form of compensation, preference should be given to using the Trust Fund.

---

experts, aid to indirect child victims, publications, legal assistance and economic and social rehabilitation. *See* U.N. Doc. A/48/520, Annex I.

[13] For instance, trust funds under the management of the United Nations Secretary-General have rules requiring the preparation of a cost plan and spending authority. *See* Secretary-Generals Bulletin, *Establishment and Management of Trust Funds*, U.N. Doc. ST/SGB/188 (Mar. 1, 1982); *Administrative Instruction, General Trust Funds*, U.N. Doc. ST/AI/284 (Mar.1, 1982); Secretary-Generals Bulletin, *Financial Regulations and Rules of the United Nations*, U.N. Doc. ST/SGB/Financial Rules/1/Rev.3 (1985).

As the experience of the 1990 Gulf War demonstrates, it is unlikely that sufficient funds will be exacted from convicted persons to pay all claims.[14] Fines and forfeiture transferred to the Trust Fund could provide additional funding for these awards. It might actually be easier for the Court to levy fines and seize forfeited property or assets than to get reparations. The Rome Statute provides that upon warrant of arrest or summons, the Court may ask States Parties to identify, trace and freeze proceeds, property and assets and instrumentalities of crimes for the purpose of eventual forfeiture, should the person indicted be found guilty (Articles 57.3.e and 93.1.k).[15] However, under the Statute the Court cannot take similar provisional measures with regard to reparations until it has actually convicted the accused person.[16] This makes the collection of forfeited assets and property more likely than that obtaining reparations and explains why Article 79.2 funds should also be used to finance reparations.

Even if funds derived from fines and forfeiture are drawn upon, it is still unlikely that the Trust Fund will have sufficient resources to pay all claims. Criteria on priority of payments should be set. Various factors could be taken into account, such as the kind of injury to be repaired, or the nature of the claimant (natural or legal person).[17] Another issue is whether to resort to installment payments for all or certain groups of victims.[18] Finally, when awards are financed by Article 79.2 funds because they are not earmarked for the benefit of the victims of the case from which they originate, it should be decided whether all awards in one case should be paid out before payment of those claimed in another case, or only some (and which) of them.

---

[14] This is even more true given that while U.N.S.C. Resolution 687 established state responsibility, in the case of the ICC only individual responsibility applies. Since 1991, the United Nations Compensation Commission has received approximately 2.6 million claims seeking compensation in excess of $300 billion. As of April 1999, the fund has been able to pay $2.7 billion. As it was clear that available funding would not be enough to pay all claims, the United Nations Compensation Commission adopted the *Priority of Payment and Payment Mechanism Guiding Principles*, U.N. Doc. S/AC.26 (Dec. 17, 1994).

[15] Of course, assistance in the identification and tracing of assets by states which are not party to the Rome Statute would depend on their national law; e.g., the U.S. Statutes on International Judicial Assistance provides that the "district court of the district in which a person resides or is found may order him to give his testimony or statement or to produce a document or other thing for use in a proceeding in a foreign or international tribunal," 28 U.S.C. § 1782.

[16] "In exercising its power under [Article 75: Reparations to Victims], the Court may, *after* a person is convicted of a crime within the jurisdiction of the Court, determine whether, in order to give effect to an order which it may make under this Article, it is necessary to seek measures under Article 93, paragraph 1." [Emphasis added.]

[17] For instance, in the U.N.C.C., compensation of claims under categories "A" (Claims for departure), "B" (personal injuries) and "C" (damages up to $100,000) has been given priority over state and corporate claims. U.N.C.C. Dec. No. 1, *Criteria for Expedite Processing of Urgent Claims*, U.N. Doc. S/AC.26/1991/1 (1991). The first award paid went to category B.

[18] The U.N.C.C. made pro rata payments to governments as funds became available, *id.*

3.   Other Possible Sources of Funding for the Trust Fund

The Court will likely experience difficulties in securing payment of fines and reparations, and it will likely have inadequate funds to compensate victims and pay essential support activities. Thus, alternative sources of financing for the Trust Fund, not listed in the Rome Statute, need to be considered.

Unlike the ICTY and the ICTR, which are subsidiary organs of the U.N. Security Council and whose expenses are covered by the core budget of the United Nations and by voluntary contributions, the International Criminal Court is to be funded by States Parties (Article 115.a). Funds may be provided by the United Nations, but only in particular in relation to the expenses incurred due to referrals by the Security Council and subject to the approval of the General Assembly (Article 115.b). Third, voluntary contributions from governments, international organizations, individuals, corporations or other entities may be accepted (Article 116). Compared to the International Criminal Court therefore, the two ad hoc tribunals benefit from a larger and more secure financial footing. The Court will require significant resources.[19] The 1998 budget of the International Criminal Tribunal for Former Yugoslavia was $64 million, while the same year the International Criminal Tribunal for Rwanda was slightly less than $59 million. Among international courts and tribunals only the European Court of Justice has a higher budget (about $140 million in 1998), while that of other international judicial fora is just a fraction of that of the two ad hoc criminal jurisdictions.[20]

The reason for the high cost of international criminal justice is that the prosecutor's office, hence by the tribunal itself, bears the costs of investigating cases and evidence-gathering, in contrast to other tribunals, where plaintiffs and defendants bear the costs associated with preparing their cases. Moreover, any international criminal tribunal will also invariably bear the costs, wholly or in part, of the defense of those indicted, their maintenance while in detention, and protection of the witnesses. These items do not exist in other international courts and tribunals (with some exceptions in the case of human rights courts).[21]

---

[19]   In an estimate made by Thomas S. Warrick in 1997, an initial fund of $60 million was considered adequate to finance startup costs and one large or two small active matters during the first year or two of operations of the International Criminal Court, *(Observation) of the International Criminal Court: Administrative and Financial Issues, in* THE INTERNATIONAL CRIMINAL COURT: OBSERVATIONS AND ISSUES BEFORE THE 1997–98 PREPARATORY COMMITTEE; AND ADMINISTRATIVE AND FINANCIAL IMPLICATIONS 37 (M. Cherif Bassiouni ed., 1997).

[20]   E.g., in 1998, the budget of the International Court of Justice was about $10 million (half of the biannual 1998–1999 budget), the International Tribunal for the Law of the Sea $5.7 million, the Dispute Settlement System of the World Trade Organization $1.2 million and the European Court of Human Rights $25 million. Note that the higher budget of the ECJ stems in large part from the high translation costs involved in having a dozen official languages.

[21]   In the case of the international criminal tribunals for former Yugoslavia and Rwanda only indigent indictees can request the assignment of a counsel. Most indicted persons have done so, fulfilling the tribunals' requirements.

Because the Court will require large amounts to finance its core activities, and because securing such financing is by itself arduous, as the experience of the two ad hoc criminal tribunals demonstrates, the Trust Fund should not encumber the Court's budget. The Rome Statute does not allocate funds for the Trust Fund from the budget of the Court and of the Assembly of State Parties. Article 114 merely provides that "[e]xpenses of the Court and the Assembly of the States Parties, including its Bureau and subsidiary bodies, shall be paid from the funds of the Court." If the Trust Fund is also to be financed with resources from the Court's budget, the Assembly of States Parties will need to amend the Statute, a politically arduous operation.

Subsuming the Trust Fund under the Court and Assembly of States Parties' budget also goes against the very nature of trust funds. A trust fund is money or property set aside for the benefit of another and held by a trustee.[22] One of the essential characteristics of any trust is self-sufficiency. A trust must have its own separate and sustainable budget, and funds must be sufficiently identifiable to enable legal title to pass to the trustee and from the trustee to the beneficiary.[23]

The Rome Statute also omits voluntary contributions as one of the Trust Fund's means of funding.[24] This omission is even more striking when considering that voluntary contributions of Governments, international organizations, individuals, corporations and other entities, can be used by the Court in accordance with criteria adopted by the Assembly of States Parties (Article 116). Despite this, nothing prohibits the Assembly of States Parties from allowing voluntary contributions to be made to the Trust Fund.

If the Trust Fund is going to accept voluntary contributions, the Assembly of States Parties will need to adopt criteria deciding when, from whom and in which form donations can be accepted.[25] It would also need to establish clear policies for the allocation of these contributions. Donors might want to earmark their contributions for the benefit of victims of certain crimes, or for certain cases, regions, or activities. The form of acceptable contributions would also need to be decided (e.g., whether contributions will be limited to funds, goods or professional assistance).[26]

---

[22] BLACKS LAW DICTIONARY (6th ed. 1990), at 1508–1509.

[23] *Id.* All general trust funds under the administration of the Secretary-General are charged for the program support function carried out by the organization. *Administrative Instructions: General Trust Funds, supra* note 13.

[24] *See, for comparison*, the United Nations Voluntary Trust Fund on Contemporary Forms of Slavery: "Funding shall be obtained by means of voluntary contributions from Governments, non-governmental organizations and other private or public entities," U.N. Doc. A/RES/46/12 (1991).

[25] *See, for instance*, policies on acceptance of pledges in the Secretary-General Bulletin, *Establishment and Management of Trust funds, supra* note 13, Rule 17.c.

[26] *See* here in this regard the following footnote made by the Committee of the Whole at

The criteria on voluntary contributions to the Trust Fund should be broader than those for contributions to the Court. Two considerations lead to this conclusion. First, while voluntary contributions to the Court might raise questions about its ultimate independence and impartiality, those to the Trust Fund, because they will eventually benefit only victims, do not. Secondly, although it is impossible to estimate income from voluntary contributions, it is not unlikely that it will involve considerable resources, possibly surpassing funds collected under Articles 75.2 and 79.2. Indeed, during the biennium 1996–1997, total income for all general trust funds under the direct responsibility of the U.N. Secretary-General was $408.9 million, of which $315.2 million represented contributions by Governments.[27] Total expenditures of these funds was $356.2 million for the same period, 25.2 percent lower than in the biennium of 1994–1995.[28]

Among other trust funds with competencies which might eventually overlap with those of the Trust Fund,[29] the U.N. Voluntary Fund for Victims of Torture receives voluntary contributions from governments, non-governmental organizations, and private individuals. The number of states contributing to the U.N. Voluntary Fund for Victims of Torture rose from five in 1982 to fourteen in 1990, and 37 in 1998. In 1998, the U.N. Voluntary Fund for Victims of Torture awarded grants to 114 projects by 105 organizations for $4.1 million, and in 1999 it awarded grants to about 130 organizations for $5.1 million. Requests for assistance for victims of torture are constantly increasing. In 1996, more than $5 million was requested from the Voluntary Fund for Victims of Torture; in 1998 this amount was $6.8 million and in 1999 it was more than $8 million.[30] It has been estimated that about 60,000 victims and members of their families were assisted in 1997 through the support of the U.N. Voluntary Fund for Victims of Torture.[31]

---

the Rome Conference on Voluntary Contribution to the Court: "The view was expressed that the Court may only receive contributions in kind from individuals and corporations," U.N. Doc. A/CONF.183/C.1/L.78 (July 15, 1998).

[27] Income of general trust funds for humanitarian activities was $220 million. Six large funds accounted for 49.8 percent of total expenditures for these trust funds: the Trust Fund for Disaster Relief ($60.3 million), the Afghanistan Emergency Trust Fund ($39.1 million), the Trust Fund for Enhancement of the Capacity of the United Nations Support Mission in Haiti ($27.0 million), the Voluntary Trust Fund for Assistance in Mine Clearance ($17.3 million), the Trust Fund for the Restoration of Essential Services in Sarajevo ($18.7 million), and the Trust Fund for Humanitarian Relief in Iraq ($19.7 million), Financial report and audited financial statements for the biennium ended Dec. 31, 1997 and Report of Board of Auditors, U.N. Doc. A/53/5 (1998).

[28] This decrease was due primarily to decreases in expenditures for humanitarian activities.

[29] Trust funds are not the only way through which victims of crimes might receive humanitarian assistance. For instance, during 1994–1998 the former Yugoslavia received $2.4 billion in emergency assistance though U.N. Consolidated Inter-Agency Humanitarian Assistance Appeals. *See* <www.reliefweb.int/fts/fintrak.html>.

[30] U.N. Doc. A/53/283 (Aug. 20, 1998) and the High Commissioner for Human Rights, Press Release of June 23, 1999, available at <www.un.org/news> (last visited July 18, 1999).

[31] *Id.*

While potentially considerable in amount, voluntary contributions are by their very nature highly volatile and tend to be emergency driven. The Trust Fund should be allowed to engage in negotiations with governments and other potential contributors. Direct negotiations with States Parties and Non-Parties is essential to obtain long-term voluntary pledges to ensure stability for the fund and greater effectiveness of the Trust Fund. The Trust Fund should also be able to negotiate with governments *ex gratia* contributions. Under the Rome Statute only individuals can be held responsible for crimes.[32] However, while not legally responsible under the Rome Statute, states might nonetheless feel the moral obligation to contribute to the reparation of certain crimes (e.g., when the convicted person is a national, or when crimes have been committed under a previous government which has been overthrown).

Finally, should voluntary contributions be excluded from the Trust Fund, the Court should nonetheless consider whether it should share some of the voluntary contributions it might receive under Article 116 of the Rome Statute with the Trust Fund. Voluntary contributions to the Court are "additional funds,"[33] This seems to indicate that while core expenses of the Court are to be covered by States Parties' assessed contributions, voluntary contributions could be used for collateral activities such as those to be funded by the Trust Fund.

C. CONCLUSION

The primary rationale for the provision of the Trust Fund in the Rome Statute was originally to endow the Court with a mechanism to collect, pool together and redistribute funds deriving from the enforcement of fines and forfeiture. Beside this core function, the Court might use the Trust Fund as an intermediary for the financing of reparations. The use of the Trust Fund for these functions is not mandatory, but this paper suggests that the Court should use the Trust Fund to the maximum extent possible. This will free the Court from routine tasks and allow it to concentrate on its judicial functions.

---

[32] An unsuccessful proposal was advanced in Rome to include state responsibility for reparation to victims. The Preparatory Committee Draft Statute had a provision that "[b]The Court may also [make an order][recommend] that an appropriate form of reparations to, or in respect of victims, including restitution, compensation and rehabilitation, be made by a state]: [if the convicted person is unable to do so himself/herself; [and if the convicted person was, in committing the offence, acting on behalf of that state in an official capacity, and within the course and scope of his/her authority]]; c) [in any case other than those referred in subparagraph b), the Court may also recommend that states grant an appropriate form of reparations to, or in respect of, victims, including restitution, compensation and rehabilitation]." *See* Report on the Establishment of an International Criminal Court, Draft Statute and Draft Final Act, *supra* note 3, art. 73.

[33] "Without prejudice to Article 115, The Court may receive and utilize, as additional funds, voluntary contributions. . . ." Rome Statute, art. 116.

The Rome Statute does not give directions on how funds derived from money and any other property collected through fines or forfeiture should be allocated, nor regarding who will have the power to make such decisions. This is a critical gap that should be addressed in the Court's Rules of Evidence and Procedure. The Court should be given the primary responsibility to decide on the use of funds deriving from fines and forfeiture. The Trust Fund should be allowed to determine the destination and use of such funds only when the Court has declined to do so.

Article 79.2 funds (fines and forfeiture) should be used for the benefit of victims only. Under no circumstances should they be used to support operational costs of the Court. They should be used to finance compensation first. However, the Rules of Procedure and Evidence should further indicate that the Court (or the Trust Fund, if the Court declines to do so) may use such funds for purposes other than compensation, such as legal aid of victims, interim relief, or humanitarian assistance. In particular, legal aid should be granted not only in proceedings before the Court itself, but also for any other proceedings in national fora aimed at obtaining reparations when the Court has declined to do so.

It is the responsibility of the Assembly of States Parties to decide whether the Trust Fund should take on a broad role and assist all victims within the jurisdiction of the Court and their families by various means. Nevertheless, the Trust Fund's non-judicial nature will need to be clearly stressed to avoid any misgivings on the effects of its various engagements.

The Court's use of the Trust Fund to award reparations needs to be carefully considered. First, the legal implications of the Court's order under Article 75.2 need to be elaborated, and the eventual extent of the Trust Fund's obligations has to be specified. Secondly, the Court will need to establish a mechanism or organ (perhaps a "Claims Bureau") to keep track of and process claims for reparations. The Trust Fund should be allowed to rely on such an organ as much as possible. Because of its relatively limited assets, the Trust Fund should not be burdened with procedural costs which could otherwise be handled by other bodies financed from the regular budget of the Court. Thus, the Trust Fund should only be used for distribution of available funds but not as a claim-processing instrument. Reasons of efficiency, economy and specialty argue against a dual system.

Criteria on setting priorities for payment of reparations need to be set, possibly as early as in the Rules of Procedure and Evidence. Moreover, to ensure the competent management and control of funds entrusted to the Trust Fund, it is crucial that the Rules of Procedure and Evidence mandate the Court to consult the Trust Fund before an order on reparations is made.

Finally, the Trust Fund should not encumber the Court's budget and vice versa. The two should remain as separate as possible. The Trust Fund should be allowed to receive voluntary contributions, and the Assembly of States Parties will need to adopt criteria deciding when, from whom and in which form donations can be accepted and how these funds will be used. These criteria should be broader than those of the Court, and the Trust Fund should be allowed to engage in negotiations with governments and other potential contributors. However, should voluntary contributions be excluded from the Trust Fund's funding sources, it should nonetheless be considered whether the Court should share with the Trust Fund some of the voluntary contributions it might receive under Article 116 of the Rome Statute.

CHAPTER 14

ARE REPARATIONS APPROPRIATELY ADDRESSED IN THE ICC STATUTE?

Fiona McKay

The Rome Statute of the International Criminal Court (ICC) made history in several ways, one of which was the adoption of provisions aimed at providing reparation for the victims of crimes within the ICC's jurisdiction. Article 75 of the Statute and related articles set out the framework for the reparations regime. The two core elements of this regime are as follows:

1. The Court *shall* establish principles relating to reparation and in so doing *may* determine the scope and extent of any damage, loss and injury; and
2. The Court *may* make a reparation order directly against a convicted person.[1]

In addition, Article 75 sets out certain principles aimed at making this regime workable. It provides for:

1. Representations to be made by the convicted person, victims, other interested parties or interested states;
2. Protective measures to be taken under Article 93, including the identification, tracing and freezing or seizure of assets;
3. Enforcement pursuant to Article 109, according to which States Parties shall give effect to orders of the court, without prejudice to the rights of *bona fide* third parties and in accordance with the procedure of their national law.

Finally, Article 79 provides that the Assembly of State Parties will establish and set criteria for a Trust Fund "for the benefit of victims of crimes within the jurisdiction of the Court, and of the families of such victims." The Court may order fines and forfeitures imposed as penalties to be paid into this Trust Fund.

This was the first real attempt to develop a reparation regime in the context of international criminal justice and thus its content had to be built largely from

---

[1]   Art. 75.1 and .2 (emphasis added).

first principles. While national practice provided some assistance, the reparation regime which was created was, as with the Statute as a whole, *sui generis* and not a reproduction of any national system.

The provisions concerning reparations in the ICC Statute can be regarded as a recognition by the states involved in the drafting process that individual criminal responsibility in international law carries with it the responsibility to repair so far as is possible the damage caused by the international crime. The International Criminal Court will be dealing only with cases in which domestic criminal justice systems have proved unwilling or unable to prosecute. In such situations, it is likely that reparation also will not be available domestically. Just as national systems have often failed to prosecute and punish perpetrators, so have they failed to adequately ensure reparation for victims.

The inclusion in the ICC Statute of powers relating to reparation also represents a major step forward in making international criminal justice more responsive to the rights and interests of victims, reflecting a trend which can be discerned in national practice and in current initiatives to develop international standards.

A. RELEVANT INTERNATIONAL STANDARDS

Recent years have seen a growing concern in the international community for the need to more effectively do justice for victims, and a growing recognition that this includes ensuring that appropriate reparation is provided. Such an evolution has been reflected in initiatives taken in two U.N. spheres of interest: criminal justice and human rights. In 1985, the U.N. General Assembly adopted a Declaration of Basic Principles of Justice for Victims of Crime and Abuse of Power,[2] developed by the U.N. Commission on Crime Prevention and Criminal Justice. This agency later developed a guidebook for policy makers and a handbook on the application of the Declaration.[3] One of the principles set out in the Declaration is that victims should receive restitution, compensation and assistance.

A second initiative was taken by the U.N. Sub-Commission on Prevention of Discrimination and Protection of Minorities which in 1989 requested a Special Rapporteur, Professor Theodoor van Boven, to undertake a study concerning the right to restitution, compensation and rehabilitation for victims of gross violations of human rights and fundamental freedoms.[4] In 1993, Professor van Boven submitted his final report, together with a draft set of U.N. Basic Principles and Guidelines on the right to reparation for victims of violations of human rights and international humanitarian law (these will be referred to as the draft Principles

---

[2] Adopted by the U.N. General Assembly on Nov. 29, 1985, Resolution 40/34.

[3] U.N. Docs. E/CN.15/1998/CRP.4 (Apr. 17, 1998) and E/CN.15/1998/CRP.4/Add.1 (Apr. 17, 1998).

[4] Resolution 1989/13, Forty-First Session.

and Guidelines).[5] This was subsequently revised in light of views and comments by states and others, and a later version[6] was presented to the U.N. Commission on Human Rights.

The draft Principles and Guidelines attempt to set out the scope and form of the right to reparation and to define state responsibilities in this regard. Based on the International Law Commission's Draft Articles on state Responsibility,[7] five main forms of reparation are identified, although it is emphasized that the list is not exhaustive. The five forms of reparation are:

1. restitution, including restoration of liberty, family life, citizenship, return to one's place of residence, and restoration of employment or property;
2. compensation for any economically assessable damage such as physical or mental harm, including pain, suffering and emotional distress, lost opportunities, material damages and loss of earnings, harm to reputation or dignity, legal and medical costs;
3. rehabilitation, including medical and psychological care as well as legal and social services;
4. satisfaction, including cessation of continuing violations, verification of the facts and disclosure of the truth, apology, and commemorations;
5. guarantees of non-repetition, including measures to prevent the recurrence of violations.

The approach is an important recognition of the fact that the starting point for reparation should be the needs and desires of victims, and that the form of reparation which will satisfy a victim will vary considerably from one case to another. In many instances, monetary compensation will not be sufficient or even desirable: an offer of payment to a bereaved family of a disappeared person can be viewed as insulting. Moral forms of reparation, such as disclosure of the truth and acknowledgment of responsibility, are often perceived as most important in the context of violations of human rights, a position that has been reiterated time and time again by groups representing families of the disappeared and other victims.

Although drafted primarily in the context of state responsibility, the framework set out in the draft Principles and Guidelines was considered by the states negotiating the ICC Statute to constitute an appropriate basis for defining reparation in the context of individual responsibility for international crimes. A wide and victim-centered approach to reparation also can be seen in some decisions of

---

5 U.N. Doc E/CN.4/Sub.2/1993/8 (July 2, 1993).

6 U.N. Doc E/CN.4/1997/104.

7 U.N. Doc A/51/10, 1996, arts. 42–46.

international and regional human rights bodies, such as the Inter-American Court of Human Rights and the U.N. Committee against Torture.

B. REPARATION IN INTERNATIONAL CRIMINAL JUSTICE

Previous international criminal tribunals have not attempted to deal fully with the question of reparation. The Statutes for the two ad hoc international criminal tribunals for former Yugoslavia and Rwanda do not give these tribunals the power to award reparation to victims, although the Rules of Procedure and Evidence have developed a limited capacity for the tribunals in this area. The Rules for the Tribunal for former Yugoslavia provide for restitution of property (Rule 105) and compensation to victims (Rule 106).[8] Rule 105(A) states:

> After a judgement of conviction containing a specific finding as provided in Sub-rule 98 ter (B), the Trial Chamber shall, at the request of the Prosecutor, or may, proprio motu, hold a special hearing to determine the matter of the restitution of the property or the proceeds thereof, and may in the meantime order such provisional measures for the preservation and protection of the property or proceeds as it considers appropriate.

This Rule further allows the Tribunal to seek assistance from the competent national authorities in determining ownership.

Rule 106 states that the Registrar shall transmit a judgment finding a person guilty to the competent national authorities, and that a victim may bring an action in a national court or other competent body to obtain reparation, pursuant to relevant national legislation. For this purpose, the Tribunal's judgment shall be considered binding as to the criminal responsibility of the convicted person. For their part, the Rules of Procedure and Evidence of the Tribunal for Rwanda, in their 1998 revised version, include among the functions of the Victims and Witnesses Support Unit the function of ensuring that victims and witnesses "receive relevant support, including physical and psychological rehabilitation, especially counseling in cases of rape and sexual assault."[9]

When it came to negotiating a treaty for the establishment of an international criminal court, there was therefore little precedent to draw upon, but a strong sense that a primary purpose of the ICC was to do justice for victims. U.N. Secretary-General Kofi Annan, in his opening address to the Diplomatic Conference in Rome on June 15, 1998, said that the overriding interest must be that of the victims. This sentiment is reflected in the Preamble to the Rome Statute, in which parties express that they are "mindful that during this century

---

[8] Rules of Procedure and Evidence of the International Criminal Tribunal for the Former Yugoslavia, as amended Mar. 11, 1999.

[9] Rule 34(A)(ii).

millions of children, women and men have been victims of unimaginable atrocities that deeply shock the conscience of humanity."

C. REPARATION IN THE DRAFTING HISTORY OF THE ICC STATUTE

The original draft Statute for an international criminal court submitted by the International Law Commission to the U.N. in 1994 contained no provision directly bearing on reparation.[10] The working group of the ILC discussed the issue of reparation and restitution, but deleted a draft article on restitution because of concern that determining the ownership of stolen property would require separate proceedings and was more appropriate for a civil than a criminal case. It was suggested that allowing the Court to consider such matters would be inconsistent with its primary function and contrary to its fundamental purpose, which was to prosecute and punish, without delay, perpetrators of the crimes in the Statute.[11] Nevertheless some members of the working group expressed the view that the Court should have power to provide reparation to victims. The draft that was eventually submitted to the General Assembly contained only an indirect reference to reparation: Article 47, which dealt with applicable penalties, authorised the Court to impose a fine as well as imprisonment on a convicted person, and provided that fines could be transferred to, *inter alia*, "a trust fund established by the Secretary-General of the United Nations for the benefit of victims of crime."

The Preparatory Committee on the Establishment of an International Criminal Court ("PrepCom") was charged by the U.N. General Assembly in 1995 with further discussing the ILC's draft statute, and drafting the text for a Diplomatic Conference.[12] The PrepCom met in New York in up to three sessions a year until the Diplomatic Conference in Rome in June–July 1998.

A compilation of states' proposals for consideration by the PrepCom published in 1996 included two proposals on reparation. First, a proposal entitled "Compensation for the Victims" echoed Rule 106 of the Rules of Procedure and Evidence of the Tribunal for former Yugoslavia. It required the Registrar to transmit judgments of the Court to the competent national authorities of the states concerned, stated that victims may institute proceedings in a national court, and provided that the judgment of the Court shall be binding on national jurisdictions as regards the criminal liability of the convicted person and the principles relating to compensation and restitution.[13] Second, a French proposal went further and gave the Court itself some direct role in reparation. It provided that in its judg-

---

[10] Draft Statute for a Permanent International Criminal Court, U.N.G.A. Doc. A/49/355 (Sept. 1, 1994).

[11] [1993] II Y.B. INT'L L. COMM'N 125, Part Two.

[12] U.N. GAOR 50/46 (Dec. 11, 1995).

[13] Report of the Preparatory Committee on the Establishment of an International Criminal Court, Vol. II, Compilation of Proposals, U.N. Doc. A/51/22, at 224.

ment the Court "may, where necessary, establish principles relating to compensation for damage caused to the victims and to restitution of property unlawfully acquired by the persons convicted."[14]

Proposals put forward by non-governmental organizations urged the PrepCom to give greater recognition to the needs and rights of victims. REDRESS, for example, proposed in June 1997, that in sentencing convicted persons, the Court may impose "other appropriate forms of reparation" as one of the possible sentences, "without prejudice to the obligation on every state to provide reparation in respect of conduct engaging the responsibility of the state."[15] REDRESS and other non-governmental organizations, supported by an increasing number of states, urged the PrepCom to adopt the term "reparation" rather than the narrower term "compensation" in line with developing international standards, and to give the Court power to make awards of various forms of reparation.

Initially, the idea of the Court playing a role in providing reparation to victims raised concern among some states about the danger of overwhelming the Court with claims. They also argued that their own legal systems did not allow reparation to be dealt with by a criminal court. In the draft text that went to Rome, the entire article was in square brackets, indicating the lack of agreement that reparation should be dealt with in the Statute at all. Nevertheless, in the debates in the Working Groups very few states spoke against the principle of the Court dealing with reparation. A willingness to look for a workable role for the Court in ensuring reparation for victims developed. This was due in no small measure to the willingness of common law countries, which had less of a tradition of victims obtaining reparation through criminal proceedings, and in particular the United Kingdom, to work hard to reach agreement with countries, such as France, which did have this tradition.

Nevertheless a number of states did raise specific concerns and there were very lengthy discussions held during the PrepComs relating to reparation. Some of the fiercest debates concerned whether or not the Court should have the power to make reparation orders against states as well as against convicted persons. Another area of concern was how to avoid turning the Court into a social service agency. The PrepCom initially discussed proposals relating to reparation in two Working Groups, that on penalties and that on procedures. The Working Group on Penalties included "appropriate forms of reparation . . . such as restitution, compensation and rehabilitation"—albeit in square brackets—as one of the lists of penalties that could be imposed on convicted persons by the Court.[16] While

---

[14] *Id.* at 223.

[15] *Promoting the Right to Reparation for Survivors of Torture: What Role for a Permanent International Criminal Court?*, REDRESS 43 (London, June 1997).

[16] *See* rolling text of the Working Group on Penalties, U.N. Doc. A/AC.249/1997/ WG.6/CRP.1 (Dec. 2, 1997) .

there was overwhelming support among states' delegates who spoke in the debates for the principle that the Court should be able to address issues of reparation, a significant number of states expressed unease with the inclusion of awards of reparation as a form of penalty rather than as a distinct power of the Court. Others believed that it was best to consolidate all matters relating to reparation in one place in the Statute, and that since reparation was dealt with elsewhere, it was not necessary to include it also as a penalty.[17] This view eventually prevailed. Although the text forwarded to the Rome conference still included the option of having reparation among the list of applicable penalties, this was only at the insistence of a few states, and even fewer states spoke in favour of its inclusion during the Rome conference.

Consensus was reached on one further important matter for the rights of victims at the December 1997 PrepCom, namely that victims would be listed as the primary beneficiaries of fines and confiscated assets. Previously, the relevant article had provided that such funds could go to meet the costs of the trial, to a state the nationals of which were victims of the crime, or to a trust fund for the benefit of victims. The new text made it clear that funds collected by way of fines or confiscated assets would go as a matter of priority to the trust fund.[18]

Meanwhile, the Working Group on procedures of the PrepComs continued to develop and discuss a free-standing article which would give the Court power to make determinations relating to reparation. Like the Working Group on Penalties, this Working Group was now using the term "reparation" rather than the term "compensation." The draft text discussed during the PrepCom of December 1997 still did not provide that the Court itself would become involved in actually making reparation orders against convicted persons. Instead it was envisaged that the burden would fall primarily on national courts to make and enforce such orders. The Court itself might determine the scope and extent of victimization, and determine that reparation should be made.[19]

Before, during, and after the last PrepCom, which took place in March and April 1998, the draft text improved significantly from the point of view of access to reparation for victims, so that the text forwarded to the Rome conference was considerably stronger than its predecessors. The draft article on reparation now explicitly provided for the Court itself to make an order regarding reparation directly against a convicted person. There was even language in the draft containing the possibility of the Court ordering that an appropriate form

---

[17] There is no formal record of these debates, and these comments are based on informal notes taken by REDRESS of sessions of the PrepCom where issues relevant to reparation were discussed.

[18] *See* U.N. Doc. A/AC.249/1997/WG.6/CRP.12 (Dec. 11, 1997).

[19] *See* Proposal of France of Dec. 5, 1997, U.N. Doc. A/AC.249/1997/WG.4/DP.3; and Proposal of the United Kingdom of December 10, 1997, U.N. Doc. A/AC.249/1997/WG.4/DP.13.

of reparation be made by a state. While this proposal had support from a number of states, a significant number were strongly opposed, and this provision did not survive the Rome conference.

The draft Statute before the negotiators at the Diplomatic Conference held in Rome in the summer of 1998 therefore contained the ingredients for a strong reparation regime for the Court. Deep disagreements remained between states regarding specific language, and the entire reparation article remained in square brackets, but early on the one state which had openly opposed the inclusion of a reparation regime for the Court dropped its objection. The issue thus became how strong a reparation article there would be, not whether there would be one at all. Outstanding issues included: whether the Court would consider making orders regarding reparation only at the request of victims, or whether it could do so on its own motion; whether the Court should be able to order reparation to be paid into the Trust Fund; and whether protective measures such as the tracing and freezing of assets could be made prior to or only following conviction.

The debate continued in informal sessions and in late night sessions of the Working Group on Procedures. Only in the last week of the Diplomatic Conference were all outstanding issues resolved and the article on reparation was finally adopted.

D. ANALYSIS OF THE REPARATIONS PROVISIONS OF THE STATUTE

Article 75.1— Establishing principles

The Court *shall* establish principles relating to reparations to, or in respect of, victims, including restitution, compensation and rehabilitation. On this basis, in its decision the Court *may*, either upon request or on its own motion in exceptional circumstances, determine the scope and extent of any damage, loss and injury to, or in respect of, victims and will state the principles on which it is acting.

One of the most significant developments brought about by the Court's reparation provision is the adoption of definitions for "reparation" and "victim" which are broadly in line with developing international standards. The use of the language "reparation . . . including restitution, compensation and rehabilitation," replacing the narrower term "compensation," was specifically intended to reflect the draft U.N. Basic Principles and Guidelines on the Right to Reparation for Victims of Violations of Human Rights and International Humanitarian Law (the "van Boven principles"). This intention was reflected in a footnote to (then) draft Article 73, which stated that for the purposes of interpreting the terms "victims" and "reparations," reference should be made to the definitions contained in the Declaration of Basic Principles of Justice for Victims of Crime and Abuse of Power and in the draft Principles and Guidelines on the Right to Reparation.[20] The

---

[20] U.N. Doc. A/CONF.183/C.1/WGPM/L.2/Add.7, of July 13, 1998, n. 5.

same footnote stated that those entitled to reparation would include not only direct victims but also others such as victims' families and successors.

One element of reparation is "rehabilitation." During the negotiations some states expressed concern at how the Court could be expected to deal with this issue and avoid becoming a social service agency. However, it became clear that allowing the Court to establish principles and make orders relating to rehabilitation did not mean that the Court itself would necessarily be involved in actually providing medical and other services to victims.

In order to resolve a dispute over how far the Court should go in assessing and determining individual claims, a footnote was inserted to reflect the views of some delegations that Article 75.1 was intended to allow the Trial Chamber to make determinations regarding the damage, loss, and injury of individual victims when there are only a few victims.[21] Where there are more than a few victims, however, the Trial Chamber may make findings as to whether reparations are due but not consider and decide individual claims.

Article 75.2—Orders against convicted persons

The Court *may* make an order directly against a convicted person specifying appropriate reparations to, or in respect of, victims, including restitution, compensation and rehabilitation. Where appropriate, the Court may order that the award for reparations be made through the Trust Fund provided for in Article 79.

Article 79: The Assembly of State Parties will establish and set criteria for a Trust Fund "for the benefit of victims of crimes within the jurisdiction of the Court, and of the families of such victims." The Court may order fines and forfeitures imposed as penalties to be paid into this Trust Fund.

The possibility for reparation to be paid through the Trust Fund will be important particularly where the defendant has insufficient assets or where there are multiple victims. It is expected that the Trust Fund will be augmented by contributions from states and others.

Article 75.3—Hearing representations

Before making an order under this article, the Court may invite and shall take account of representations from or on behalf of the convicted person, victims, other interested persons or interested states.

Such a provision protects due process rights, and gives due recognition to the involvement of victims in the process.

---

[21] *Id.* at n. 6.

Article 75.4—Protective measures regarding assets

In exercising its power under this article, the Court may, after a person is convicted of a crime within the jurisdiction of the Court, determine whether, in order to give effect to an order which it may make under this article, it is necessary to seek measures under article 93, paragraph 1.

Article 93.1: "States Parties shall, in accordance with the provisions of this Part and under procedures of national law, comply with requests by the Court to provide the following assistance in relation to investigations or prosecutions: . . . (k) The identification, tracing and freezing or seizure of proceeds, property and assets and instrumentalities of crimes for the purpose of eventual forfeiture, without prejudice to the rights of bona fide third parties."

While Article 75 itself only provides for provisional measures after conviction, Article 57.3(e) provides for protective measures pursuant to Article 93.1 where a warrant for arrest or summons has been issued, "and having due regard to the strength of the evidence and the rights of the parties concerned." This gives the Court an all important power to make such orders early in the process, in order to preempt so far as possible any steps by an accused person aimed at placing assets beyond reach of the victims.

Article 75.5—Enforcement

A State Party shall give effect to a decision under this article as if the provisions of Article 109 were applicable to this article.

Article 109: "States Parties shall give effect to fines or forfeitures ordered by the Court under Part 7, without prejudice to the rights of bona fide third parties, and in accordance with the procedure of their national law." If unable to do so, "it shall take measures to recover the value of the proceeds, property or assets ordered by the Court to be forfeited." Furthermore, property or its proceeds which are obtained by a state through enforcement of a judgment of the Court shall be transferred to the Court.

It is crucial to the effectiveness of a reparations regime that available enforcement procedures be as strong as possible. It is to be expected that in many instances it will not be possible to enforce reparation orders without the active cooperation of national authorities. The requirement for states to give effect to the Court's reparation orders is therefore important.

Finally, Article 75.6 states that "Nothing in this article shall be interpreted as prejudicing the rights of victims under national or international law."

The Statute, then, goes a long way toward recognizing the need for a wide and sensitive response to victims of violations of the type that will come before the Court.

E. NEGATIVE OR UNCERTAIN ASPECTS OF THE REPARATIONS PROVISIONS IN THE STATUTE

Despite the many positive elements of the reparations provisions in the Statute, they do not include everything victims rights advocates would have wished. Some were disappointed that the Court will not have power to order states to provide reparation, or even to recommend them to do so. Such a suggestion was contained in bracketed language in the draft article which came to Rome, but it was deleted. Many states took the view that the question of state responsibility was not for the ICC, which was being established for the purpose of prosecuting individuals only. This result made the enforcement provisions relating to the reparation regime all the more important.

The experience of human rights litigation, for example in the Inter-American human rights system and in United States courts, has demonstrated that obtaining a reparation judgment is one thing, enforcing it is quite another. Much will depend on the extent of state cooperation in the tracing and freezing of assets under Articles 57.3 and 93.1, and the effectiveness of the enforcement provisions. In relation to both protective measures and enforcement, victims may be forced to rely on national states where law and order may have broken down and judicial institutions may not be functioning effectively.

The draft Statute submitted to the Rome conference contained bracketed language which would have added reparation to the list of possible penalties which could have been imposed on convicted persons in addition to imprisonment or fines. Many groups campaigning for victims rights believed that this would constitute an important acknowledgement of the rights of victims in the criminal process in line with principles of restorative justice, particularly since some forms of reparation—such as the obligation to leave public office—are by their nature a form of penalty. In reality, however, the exclusion of reparation as a penalty was a symbolic rather than a substantive defeat.

F. CONCLUSION

The positive aspects of the reparations regime for the Court, as set out in the Rome Statute, definitely outweigh the negative aspects. The Court has been given the flexibility and capacity to take a holistic view of what reparation is needed in any particular case, and make appropriate orders. The power both to establish principles—including determining the scope and extent of damage—and to make orders against individuals, in combination with the possibility to draw from a Trust Fund, should combine to equip the Court with sufficient tools to examine what is needed to do justice to victims, even in situations involving large numbers of victims.

It should not be forgotten that the bringing of criminal proceedings itself and empowerment of victims to participate in the proceedings as more than mere bystanders[22] are also important elements of reparation for victims. But the Statute goes much further than that. The evolution of the far-reaching Article 75 from an original proposal that victims could take a judgment back to a national court to help them obtain "compensation" against a convicted person is a remarkable achievement.

The reparation provisions in the Statute mark an important stage in the evolution of accepted international standards governing the right to reparation for violations of human rights and humanitarian law, as elaborated in the draft U.N. Principles and Guidelines. It is hoped that the reliance placed on the draft Principles and Guidelines in arriving at a definition of reparation in the Statute will itself contribute to the early adoption of the Principles and Guidelines by the U.N. General Assembly. Article 75 is also a landmark in the increasing recognition of the rights of victims in the criminal justice process. In addition to the right to reparation, victims have gained a role in triggering investigations and prosecutions by the Court, and will be able to participate in the proceedings at appropriate stages.

The process by which the reparation provisions in the Statute were developed, with very little by way of precedent, is also a good example of effective cooperation and consultation between states, non-governmental organizations and experts. It is hoped that this experience could serve as a useful model for work in other areas.

The challenge ahead is to translate the principles set out in the Statute into Rules of Procedure in a way that does not weaken them, and which will prove to be workable and effective. At the same time, it will be important that states, in adopting legislation enabling them to implement the provisions of the Statute, include measures to ensure that they are able to cooperate fully with any orders of the Court relating to reparation, and to give effect to such orders. Finally, the real test of the effectiveness of the reparation provisions will come when the Court is established and dealing with its first case.

---

[22] *See* art. 68.3 ("Where the personal interests of the victims are affected, the Court shall permit their views and concerns to be presented and considered at stages of the proceedings determined to be appropriate by the Court.")

PART IV
PROBLEMS OF JURISDICTION
AND EFFECTIVENESS

CHAPTER 15

COMPLEMENTARITY AND ITS DISCONTENTS: STATES, VICTIMS, AND THE INTERNATIONAL CRIMINAL COURT

Madeline Morris

A. INTRODUCTION

The Rome Treaty for an International Criminal Court promises a Court that will be complementary to national jurisdictions. But the Treaty does not adequately define the purposes that the ICC is to be complementary in achieving. The Treaty reflects an intention that the Court shall serve the justice interests of the victims of genocide, war crimes and crimes against humanity,[1] the interests of the states principally affected by those crimes, and the interests of the broader community of states in relation to those crimes. But while the ICC Treaty includes some provisions to foster the interests of each of those three categories of intended beneficiaries, it fails to address the reality that, on many issues, the interests of these three groups will diverge.

Because the ICC Treaty articulates no principles or policies to govern such divergences of interests, decision making on fundamental issues that require prioritization of the interests of the three categories of intended beneficiaries will fall by default largely to the ICC prosecutor. The prosecutor will operate within a structure, framed by the Treaty, that encourages him or her to be attentive to the interests of the majority of States Parties to the ICC Treaty and to certain elements of the Court's broader international audience, but much less so to the interests of principally affected states or victim populations.

---

[1] *See* ICC Treaty, art. 5 (providing for ICC jurisdiction over those crimes). The Treaty provides for the Court eventually to have jurisdiction over the crime of "aggression" as well, but precludes the Court's exercising jurisdiction over that crime until such time as the Treaty is amended to include a definition of aggression and provisions specifying the conditions under which the Court shall exercise jurisdiction over that crime.

It is argued in the first part of this chapter that the structure put in place by the ICC Treaty fails to ensure that the interests of two of the three categories of intended ICC beneficiaries will in fact be served. The second part examines in some detail the nature of the divergences of interests likely to arise among the Court's intended beneficiaries, and suggests approaches to resolving the dilemmas posed. The conclusion suggests that the fundamental policy issues at stake may not appropriately be relegated to prosecutorial discretion but instead should be addressed by a representative and deliberative policy-making body if the ICC is ultimately to foster its intended purposes.

B. INTERESTS AND INFLUENCE

The ICC Treaty creates the framework for a permanent international institution with jurisdiction over the most serious international crimes. The Treaty's preamble states that the reason for creating the Court is that "the most serious crimes of concern to the international community as a whole must not go unpunished and . . . their effective prosecution must be ensured by taking measures at the national level and by enhancing international cooperation. . . ."[2] The Parties, the Treaty states, are "[d]etermined to put an end to impunity for the perpetrators of these crimes and thus to contribute to the prevention of such crimes. . . ."[3]

The Treaty emphasizes that, in pursuing those purposes, the Court "shall be complementary to national criminal jurisdictions."[4] The intended meaning of ICC complementarity with national jurisdictions, however, is not clearly elaborated in the Treaty. Articles 17–19 provide some technical specification of the ICC's relationship with national courts, as shall be discussed below, but the essential nature of the relationship is not addressed. In what sense is the ICC to complement national jurisdictions? Is it, at a minimum, not to impede their operations? Is it intended to support or assist national jurisdictions? Is it intended strictly as a substitute for national courts, to fulfill their functions when they are unavailable?

Underlying an inquiry into the meaning of ICC complementarity is the fundamental question of whose interests the Court is intended to serve. To focus this issue somewhat more sharply, it may be useful to conceptualize courts and prosecutors as analogous to fiduciaries entrusted with faithfully serving the interests of specified others.[5] In national jurisdictions, courts and prosecutors are bound to serve the interests of society in general and, to some ambiguous and debated degree, the interests of victims. In that debate, it is recognized that victims have interests that are in part distinct from the broader societal interests

---

[2] ICC Treaty, Preamble.

[3] *Id.*

[4] *Id.*, Preamble, art. 1.

[5] *Cf.* Kathleen Clark, *Do We Have Enough Ethics in Government Yet? An Answer from Fiduciary Theory*, 1996 U. ILL. L. REV. 57.

in criminal justice.[6] The balancing of those two sometimes divergent sets of interests is a chronic source of complexity in the administration of criminal law. The balancing is even more complex and problematic at the international level than it is in the national context because, in the operations of an international court, there is an additional layer of interests at stake: not only the principally affected state and the victims, but also the broader community of States Parties to the ICC Treaty will have potentially divergent interests in the handling of crimes within ICC jurisdiction. Because of the array of overlapping but also divergent interests at stake, the meaning of the ICC's complementarity with national courts is neither obvious nor inconsequential.

The potential divergence of interests between the different categories of ICC beneficiaries has significant implications for ICC prosecutorial policy and practice. The purposes of penal sanctions are commonly identified as deterrence, retribution, incapacitation, and rehabilitation.[7] The interests of victim populations may feature retribution—a just punishment for a wrong committed—more prominently than would the interests of the majority of States Parties to the Rome Treaty ("majority states"), which may tend more to focus on deterrence.[8] In addition, the interests of majority states may focus heavily on prosecution of political leaders, while the interests of victims may emphatically include prosecution not only of leaders but also of those lower in the hierarchy who personally committed the atrocities. Consistent with those differences in emphasis, the interests of victim populations may require a larger number of prosecutions and, possibly, a broader cross-section of defendants than would those of majority states. The interests of the state most affected by a particular context of mass crimes (the "principally affected state") will in some instances be largely consistent with those of the victim population, but in other situations those two sets of interests may

---

6 *See* Robert Mosteller, *Victims' Rights and the Constitution: Moving from Guaranteeing Participatory Rights to Benefitting the Prosecution*, 29 ST. MARY'S L.J. 1053 (1998); DEAN G. KILPATRICK, DAVID BEATTY, AND SUSAN SMITH HOWLEY, THE RIGHTS OF CRIME VICTIMS: DOES LEGAL PROTECTION MAKE A DIFFERENCE? (U.S. Dep't of Justice, Office of Justice Programs, National Institute of Justice, 1998) [hereinafter KILPATRICK, BEATTY, AND HOWLEY] and sources cited therein; Robert Mosteller, *Victims' Rights and the United States Constitution: An Effort to Recast the Battle in Criminal Litigation*, 85 GEO. L.J. 1691 (1997).

7 *See* ARYEH NEIER, WAR CRIMES 81–84 (1998) (proposing deterrence, retribution and incapacitation as purposes of criminal punishment); RICHARD G. SINGER & MARTIN R. GARDNER, CRIMES AND PUNISHMENT: CASES, MATERIALS, AND READINGS IN CRIMINAL LAW § 2.03 (1989) (discussing deterrence, retribution, incapacitation and rehabilitation as justifications for penal sanctions).

8 Incapacitation also would likely be a concern of victims, principally affected states, and majority states in situations where individual defendants pose a continuing threat. Rehabilitation may in some instances be of importance to majority states and perhaps principally affected states, but less so to victims. *Cf.* The Prosecutor v. Drazen Erdemovic, Case No. IT–96–22–T (Trial Chamber, Sentence) (1998) ("[The defendant's] circumstances and character . . . indicate that he is reformable and should be given a second chance to start life afresh upon release, while still young enough to do so.")

diverge. For example, principally affected states may wish to confer amnesties to which victim populations may object. Majority states may have yet a third set of interests relative to amnesties. Majority states may not wish to honor national amnesties. Or majority states may favor an amnesty arrangement that is not desired by the principally affected state. Short of a full amnesty, the principally affected state may wish to utilize plea bargaining arrangements. But the functioning of national plea bargaining systems may be impeded by the operation of the ICC, as I shall demonstrate. Because the interests of majority states, principally affected states, and victims populations may diverge in these and other ways, clear policy must be articulated as to the combination and priority of interests that the ICC is intended to serve. Without the clear articulation of policy on this fundamental point, it will be impossible to develop coherent policy at the level of prosecutorial practice.

It appears that the intention of the signatory states to the Rome Treaty is for the ICC to serve the interests of victims and principally affected states as well as those of majority states.[9] Although the issue of divergent international, national, and victim interests was not directly addressed in the discourse preceding adoption of the Rome Treaty, discussions concerning creation of an ICC routinely invoked the interests of victims in seeing justice done and reiterated the importance of promoting the functioning of national justice systems.[10] James Crawford, Chairman of the International Law Commission Working Group that prepared the draft ICC Treaty, emphasized in his speech at the opening of the Rome Conference that the Court is "not intended to displace existing national systems in cases where those systems are capable of working properly."[11] And U.N. Secretary-General Kofi Annan stressed in his speech opening the Rome Conference, and repeatedly thereafter, that "[s]uch a court should serve the overriding interest of the victims, and of the international community as a whole."[12]

The provisions of the Rome Treaty do, in important respects, reflect that the ICC's intended beneficiaries include victim populations and principally affected

---

[9] *Cf. UN Secretary-General Declares Overriding Interest of International Criminal Court Conference Must Be That of Victims and World Community as a Whole*, U.N. Press Release L/ROM/6.rl (June 15, 1998), *found at* <http:www.un.org/icc/pressrel/lrom6rl.htm.> (text of address by U.N. Secretary-General Kofi Annan stressing the interests of both victims and the international community in the establishment of an International Criminal Court) [hereinafter U.N. Press Release June 15]; Frank Jensen, Minister of Justice Denmark, Statement, Rome Conference (June 18, 1998), *found at* <http://www.un.org/icc/speeches/618den.htm> (highlighting the ICC Treaty's innovations regarding national courts and international jurisdiction).

[10] *See, e.g.*, U.N. Press Release June 15, *supra* note 9.

[11] James Crawford, Chairman, International Law Commission Working Group on an International Criminal Court, Statement, Rome Conference (June 15, 1998), *found at* <http://www.un.org/icc/speeches615>.

[12] Kofi Annan, *At Last, a Court to Deter Despots and Defend Victims*, INT'L HERALD TRIB., July 28, 1998, at 8.

states as well as those of majority states. Reflecting an intention that the Court should serve the interests of victims, Article 75 of the Treaty provides that the Court shall establish and implement principles for victim reparations. Article 79 provides that the States Parties shall establish a Trust Fund for the benefit of victims and their families. Article 53 provides that, if the prosecutor concludes "that there is not sufficient basis for a prosecution because . . . prosecution is not in the interests of justice, taking into account all circumstances, including . . . *the interests of victims*" then the prosecutor shall so inform the Court's pre-trial chamber as well as the state that referred the case or the Security Council if it referred the matter.[13] The prosecutor's decision not to proceed may then be reviewed by the pre-trial chamber.[14] Finally, Article 68 provides that, in the course of a trial, "[w]here the personal interests of the victims are affected, the Court shall permit their views and concerns to be presented. . . ."

Reflecting deference to the interests of principally affected states, the Treaty provides that the ICC will operate only where national justice systems are "unable" or "unwilling" genuinely to prosecute the cases in question.[15] Article 17 of the Treaty states that a case will be "inadmissible" before the ICC if the case is being investigated or prosecuted by a state with jurisdiction and with the ability and willingness genuinely to carry out the investigation or prosecution; or has been investigated by such a state after which that state decided not to prosecute; or has already been duly tried by such a state.[16] This positions the ICC essentially as a substitute for national courts, to fulfill their functions when they are unavailable, and would seem to imply that priority of place is given to national level justice interests, at least in some respects.

It is appropriate that the ICC should serve the interests of victims and principally affected states as well as those of majority states. The evils of genocide, war crimes and crimes against humanity inhere in the harm that they do to their victims and to the states they most affect, as well as in the fact that the threat of their repetition endangers international peace and security. It would make little sense to protect the welfare of potential future victims and states potentially affected but to ignore the welfare of present victims and their states by creating a court that is unresponsive to their interests. Victims' interests increasingly are the focus of some solicitude within national justice systems,[17] for moral and philosophical reasons and in recognition of the fact that one function of criminal justice is to avoid victims' taking justice into their own hands. This latter, practical reason for taking victims' interests into account is particularly relevant in the con-

---

[13] ICC Treaty, art. 53 (emphasis added).

[14] *Id.*

[15] ICC Treaty, art. 17.

[16] *See id.*, art.17(1)(a)–(c).

[17] *See* KILPATRICK, BEATTY, AND HOWLEY, *supra* note 6.

text of the most serious international crimes that so often involve societal cycles of violence and revenge.

Even while the Treaty does, in the provisions just surveyed, reflect an intention that the ICC should serve the interests of victims and principally affected states as well as those of majority states, the Treaty's overall structure does not ensure that the Court will do so. Quite the reverse, the Treaty creates a structure in which the interests of victims and principally affected states are likely to be largely overlooked.

The Treaty is silent on the overall priority of interests to be served by the Court and on major policy issues such as the number and array of defendants to be prosecuted, the appropriate relationship between the ICC and active national courts, the ICC's posture relative to national amnesties, and other important questions. Decisions on these fundamental issues will fall by default largely to the ICC prosecutor. The Treaty creates an incentive structure in which that prosecutor will likely be attentive, to some extent, to the interests of majority states, but much less so to those of principally affected states or victims. The Treaty's provisions on election, removal, and discipline of the prosecutor and judges make the Court loosely accountable to the States Parties.[18] On these matters, the will of the majority (or super-majority) of States Parties will govern.[19]

The prosecutor is likely also to be somewhat attentive to the views of the Court's broader international audience. That broader audience would include the media that cover the Court's work and thereby shape international public opinion about the Court (and about the prosecutor). It would also include the international legal and diplomatic communities, of which the prosecutor will be a member. Non-governmental organizations (NGOs) also will watch the Court and attempt to influence its policies. The broader audience to which the prosecutor will be attentive may also include states (especially powerful states) that are not parties to the Rome Treaty, particularly when their cooperation with the Court may be important. None of these potential influences on the prosecutor, with the possible exception of some NGO lobbying, is likely to foster the interests of victims or principally affected states. The tendencies set in place by the Treaty's accountability structure and the prosecutor's likely attentiveness to the Court's broader international audience thus are unlikely to favor the interests of principally affected states or victims populations. The net result is that the ICC may largely fail to serve the interests of two of its three intended categories of beneficiaries—victims and principally affected states—and, as we shall see in the following section, may even impede efforts by states to serve those interests.

---

[18]   ICC Treaty, arts. 34–52.

[19]   *Id.*

C. COMPLEMENTARITY AND ITS DISCONTENTS

The complementarity provisions of the ICC Treaty will result in the Court's potentially operating in two distinct postures: (1) sole active jurisdiction, where international prosecutions before the ICC are carried out in the absence of national prosecutions; and (2) active concurrent jurisdiction, where international prosecutions before the ICC are carried out concurrently with national prosecution of other cases arising from the same context of mass crimes.

The particular manifestations of divergence of interest between victims, principally affected states, and majority states that are likely to arise in a given context will depend largely upon whether the Court is the sole active jurisdiction or is exercising jurisdiction concurrently with active national courts.

1. The ICC as the Sole Active Forum

When the ICC acts as the sole active forum for the prosecution of crimes committed in a given context of mass crimes, the cases that it handles will be, by definition, the only ones prosecuted. Sole active jurisdiction thus places on the ICC the exclusive responsibility of assuring that an adequate total number and an appropriate array of cases are tried. When the Court operates in this posture, certain divergences of interest are likely to arise among the Court's intended beneficiaries.

The first area of potential conflict concerns national amnesties. Many countries (Argentina, Chile, Haiti, Angola, Brazil, South Africa, and Sierra Leone, to name a few) have conferred amnesties on perpetrators of serious international crimes. When a principally affected state has issued an amnesty—perhaps over the objections of the victim population, and with or without the approval of majority states—the ICC prosecutor will have to decide whether to prosecute individuals who have received the national-level amnesty. Although the appropriate relationship of the ICC to national amnesties was debated intensively during the negotiations for the Rome Treaty, the Treaty itself is silent on the matter.[20] The ICC Treaty thus offers no guidance on the appropriate resolution of one of the most serious areas of potential conflict among the intended beneficiaries of the Court.[21]

Even in the absence of an amnesty, a number of divergences of interest are likely to arise. Where the ICC is the sole active jurisdiction, the problematic issues will primarily concern the number and array of defendants to be tried. When the ICC bears exclusive responsibility for prosecutions, the danger arises that the ICC

---

[20] The Treaty contains provisions, not directly relating to amnesties, that some have interpreted as leaving the matter to prosecutorial discretion on a case-by-case basis.

[21] The complex issues involving the ICC's relationship to amnesties will be dealt with more fully in a separate piece by this author.

will tend to bring too few cases to serve adequately the interests of victims and, perhaps, principally affected states. This tendency would spring from the fact that the prosecutor, attentive to the majority states and also to the Court's broader international audience, is likely to aim for a few high-profile trials, even though this may not fulfill the interests of the states most affected and, particularly, the victim populations.

The prosecutor is likely to be satisfied by a rather small number of trials for two reasons. First, the majority states and the Court's broader international audience may be focused only passingly on the crimes in question and, where that is true, will likely take the view that those responsible have been punished if a few prominent trials occur. Second, the interests of majority states in prosecuting genocide, war crimes, and crimes against humanity are likely to be heavily focused on deterrence. With the crimes already having been committed, the majority states are likely to focus upon the use of punishment to help ensure that such mass crimes do not occur again. Deterrence is exemplary, and a relatively few examples may be thought to suffice.[22]

By contrast, the victim population's interests are unlikely to be satisfied by a small number of trials. Retribution, meaning a just punishment for a wrong committed,[23] is a function of criminal justice that is likely to be of particular importance to victim populations.[24] Indeed, the "sense of justice" would seem to have a great deal to do with retribution—the condemnation and punishment of the perpetrator—and less to do with a forward-looking interest in deterring future crimes. The justice interests of victim populations are likely to include a substantial retributive element precisely because of the immediate and personal relationship of victims to the crimes committed. This does not make victims "vengeful," as has occasionally been implied. Rather, it means that those who have suffered enormously as the victims of genocide, war crimes, and crimes against humanity have legitimate interests that may differ in emphasis from those of the broader international community that, while not oblivious to the crimes, has not experienced them personally. Where crimes have been committed on a

---

[22] Of course, *too* few examples will not suffice, since every perpetrator who goes unpunished provides an example that it is possible to commit crimes with impunity. For a discussion of the optimal number of prosecutions to achieve an acceptable degree of deterrence given a particular severity of punishment, *see* Richard Posner, ECONOMIC ANALYSIS OF LAW 163–78 (2d ed.1977).

[23] *See* IMMANUEL KANT, THE METAPHYSICAL ELEMENTS OF JUSTICE 99–102 (J. Ladd trans., 1965); PAUL ROBINSON, CRIMINAL LAW 15 (1997).

[24] This is not to say that deterrence is unimportant to victims. Indeed, deterrence likely is a concern of victims, particularly if there is an imminent threat of the reemergence of violent persecution of their group. My point is not that victims have no interest in deterrence or that majority states have no interest in retribution but, rather, that there likely is a difference of emphasis in this regard.

mass scale, by numerous perpetrators against many victims, the interests of victims are unlikely to be met be a few trials.[25]

Provisions exist within the ICC Treaty that could be interpreted as providing a statutory basis for the ICC taking a low-volume prosecutorial approach. Article 1 of the Treaty states that the ICC is intended to "exercise its jurisdiction over persons for the most serious crimes of international concern . . . ."[26] Consistent with Article 1, Article 5 delineates the Court's subject-matter jurisdiction as encompassing genocide, crimes against humanity, particularly serious war crimes (as defined by the Treaty), and aggression.[27] Article 17 lists as a basis for inadmissibility of a case before the ICC that the case, even while coming within the Court's subject-matter jurisdiction, is "not of sufficient gravity to warrant further action by the Court."[28] The listing of insufficient gravity as a basis for inadmissibility of cases otherwise within the Court's jurisdiction necessarily implies that some instances of genocide, crimes against humanity, serious war crimes, and aggression are not sufficiently grave to warrant the Court's action. Reading Articles 1, 5, and 17 together suggests that the ICC is intended to exercise its jurisdiction only over *grave instances* of the (delineated) most serious crimes.[29] One not-implausible interpretation of this gravity requirement would be that the ICC should try only a small number of the most culpable perpetrators.

For reasons I have already mentioned, such an interpretation of the Treaty would be a damaging one. And, while it sounds plausible, the "minimalist" approach is by no means mandated by the Treaty. While the trial of a handful of notorious perpetrators would be consistent with the language of the Treaty, so equally would be the trial of a larger, quite substantial number of perpetrators who were responsible for the grave cases of the crimes covered. If some forms of collaboration or even some crimes of violence would be considered less than grave, multiple murders and tortures undoubtedly constitute grave cases of the crimes within the Court's jurisdiction.

Failure by the ICC to prosecute an adequate number of perpetrators would not only ill-serve the interests of victim populations, but also could transform

---

[25] Article 53 of the Treaty, which provides for judicial review of a prosecutor's decision not to prosecute after an investigation into a particular case has been initiated, does not solve this problem. In contexts of mass crimes, most victims' cases will never become the subject of ICC prosecutors' investigations, much less of Article 53 reviews. Decisions regarding the number of cases to be brought will occur in policy making well prior to the point at which Article 53 would apply.

[26] ICC Treaty, art. 1.

[27] *Id.*, art. 5. *See supra* note 1 regarding the ICC's jurisdiction over the crime of aggression.

[28] *Id.*, art. 17(1)(d).

[29] *Id.*, arts. 1, 5, 17.

what should have been a matter handled solely by the ICC (because of national judicial incapacity) into a matter in which the ICC and national courts actively exercise concurrent jurisdiction. A state, despairing of the ICC's sparing approach to prosecutions, may jump into the breach even if it is ill-prepared to handle the cases. This is particularly likely if the state is already holding a large number of prisoners in connection with the mass crimes (as was the case, for example, in Rwanda after the genocide there).[30]

Addressing the interests of victim populations and principally affected states may often require a greater number of prosecutions than would be required to satisfy the interests of majority states. Ultimately, in the ICC as in national courts, resource limitations will constrain the number of prosecutions that can be brought. The argument made here is not that resource constraints can or should be overlooked but, rather, that ICC budget projections and resource allocations should be made in a manner that reflects the full range of interests intended to be served.

A problem closely related to the prosecution of too few cases is the possibility that the ICC will fail to prosecute an appropriate array of cases. The provisions of the ICC Treaty discussed above, specifying in effect that the ICC should handle only grave instances of the most serious crimes could easily be interpreted—misinterpreted in my view—to mean that the ICC should prosecute only leadership-level defendants. Prosecuting only leaders would, in many contexts, be a mistake.

If majority states and the broader international audience would likely be satisfied by a few prominent prosecutions, the presumption would be that those few prosecutions should be of top-level leaders. They generally are the most notorious, widely-known wrongdoers. In political terms, they bear the broadest responsibility because, while they may not be the individuals who directly committed specific atrocities (specific rapes, tortures, and murders may have been the creations of followers), the leaders created the political context in which the crimes were fostered. The leaders would bear the broadest responsibility for the mass crimes in the aggregate and would bear the political responsibility for the mass crimes overall. These factors would likely make the leaders appear to the international community like the appropriate group to prosecute.[31]

---

[30] *See* Madeline H. Morris, *The Trials of Concurrent Jurisdiction: The Case of Rwanda*, 7 DUKE J. COMP. & INT'L L. 352 (1997).

[31] This certainly has been the prevailing view within the International Criminal Tribunals for the former Yugoslavia and Rwanda (ICTY/R). Numerous statements indicate that personnel at the ICTY/R view the Tribunals' mandate as prosecution of the top-level leaders. Richard Goldstone states, for example, that "I still remain unpersuaded that there would be any advantage were the ICTR, as a policy, to pursue the 'small fish'." Letter from Richard Goldstone, Prosecutor, ICTY/R 1993–96, to Madeline Morris, Professor of Law, Duke University (Dec. 22, 1996) (on file with author). My conversations with ICTY/R personnel, almost without excep-

Not necessarily so, however, in the perception of the victim population. In addition to being concerned with leaders, victims pervasively express a deep and heartfelt desire that their particular perpetrators be brought to justice.[32] It is familiar to hear of a holocaust survivor, for instance, who has spent a lifetime longing for (and perhaps working for) the discovery and punishment of a particular camp guard, the punishment not only of a Hitler or an Eichmann but of the person who tortured him or killed his loved ones, the one whose face he cannot forget. Addressing the justice interests of victims, Judge Gabrielle McDonald, President of the International Criminal Tribunal for the former Yugoslavia (ICTY), has said, "I've never heard a witness say, 'That person is not important enough.' I've never heard a victim say, 'I want someone with a higher rank.' Every individual wants justice in their own case."[33]

Obviously, not all leaders and not all followers can be prosecuted in most contexts of crimes of mass violence. But a prosecutorial design that includes followers as well as leaders may often serve victim interests better than would a leaders-only design. It is true that since retribution (in contrast to deterrence) is not fundamentally an exemplary matter, prosecuting one camp guard, for instance, would not satisfy the interests of victims who were in a different camp. But at least some victims' needs would be met and, more to the point, such prosecutions would constitute an acknowledgment of the interests of victims and of their legitimacy. In addition, even for victims whose own individual perpetrators are not prosecuted, there may be symbolic retributive value in the prosecution, condemnation and punishment of a full cross-section of perpetrators, including followers as well as leaders.

It has been suggested that it is not worthwhile to prosecute followers because they have merely been led astray by leaders, through propaganda and other forms of manipulation. However, while large numbers of actors in mass violence may be caught up in the current and commit heinous crimes, there are also always large numbers of individuals who refrain, and even a few heroes who save others. It is demeaning to common people—to *people*—to suggest that, while leaders are worth prosecuting, followers are not responsible moral agents.

---

tion, reflect a presumption within the ICTY/R that the Tribunals' role is to try top-level leaders. The view expressed recurrently is that the trials of lower-level perpetrators before the ICTY/R are to be viewed either as second-best outcomes that were necessitated by the lack of higher-level defendants in custody or as "building blocks" whose purpose is to lead to the prosecution of "higher-ups."

[32] *See, e.g.*, Conversation of author with Alex Boraine and Paul VanZyl, Vice Chair and Executive Secretary, respectively, South African Truth and Reconciliation Commission (TRC), in New York, N.Y. (Nov. 8, 1998) (regarding the interests of victims who testified before the TRC) (notes on file with author).

[33] Marlise Simons, *Then It Was the Klan, Now It's the Balkan Agony*, N.Y. TIMES, Jan. 13, 1999, at A4 (quoting Judge McDonald).

The intention here is not to reject the possibility of a duress defense. Where the elements of that defense are met (essentially, that the crime was committed to avoid the imminent threat of grave physical injury or death),[34] duress is an appropriate defense. What is rejected, rather, is the suggestion that, even in the absence of duress, followers should be presumed not to be responsible actors.

Prosecuting a cross-section of perpetrators may be desirable in terms not only of retribution but also of deterrence. In support of the strategy of prosecuting only the top leaders, the argument often is made that it is most important to prosecute the leaders because "without the leaders, these crimes would not occur." It is equally true, however, that without the followers these crimes would not occur. Indeed, there are probably more than a handful of would-be leaders of crimes of mass violence whose dangerous aspirations are never realized for lack of followers. Applying deterrents at top, middle and lower levels of criminal hierarchies may be a more effective deterrence strategy, ultimately, than exclusive prosecution of those in leadership positions. This is not to say that the leaders should not be prosecuted. Indeed, their prosecution is essential. Rather, the point is that applying deterrents only to the leaders may be a poor approach. Prosecuting a cross-section of defendants may in many contexts be a preferable policy both for deterrence and for providing to the victim population a sense that justice has been done.

Peripheral collaborators clearly would not be a high priority for prosecution. Such cases would be "not of sufficient gravity to warrant further action by the Court."[35] But other followers, who themselves carried out murder, rape, torture and the like, have committed serious instances of the serious crimes that are the concern of the ICC.

When the ICC operates as the sole active forum, it will bear sole responsibility for achieving justice in the context in question. If the ICC is to serve the interests of all of its intended beneficiaries when operating in this posture, the ICC's prosecutorial strategy must entail an adequate number and array of prosecutions reflecting the goals both of deterrence and of retribution and the responsibilities both of leadership and of followership.

2. Active Concurrent Jurisdiction

The second posture in which divergences of interest between majority states, principally affected states, and victim populations will be manifested is when the ICC exercises jurisdiction concurrently with active national courts. There are a variety of reasons for which a state might pursue cases arising from the same situation with which the ICC is occupied. These different states' motives and the political contexts in which they appear will warrant different ICC responses in

---

[34] WAYNE LAFAVE & AUSTIN SCOTT, CRIMINAL LAW 432–41 (2d ed.1986).

[35] ICC Treaty, art. 17(1)(d); *supra* text accompanying notes 28–31.

accommodating the interests of victims, principally affected states, and majority states.

a. Variations in States' Motives

There are at least four reasons for which a state might pursue cases arising from the same situation with which the ICC is occupied:

1. although the state has a functioning judiciary, it is unable to pursue the particular cases being brought before the ICC because the state cannot obtain extradition of those defendants or cannot obtain necessary evidence abroad for those cases;
2. while the ICC considers the state unable to prosecute because of a collapsed justice system, the government's constituencies, including victim populations, view as inadequate the number or character of the prosecutions being brought by the ICC, and the state therefore considers it worthwhile to proceed with prosecutions notwithstanding the impaired condition of its justice system;
3. while the ICC considers the state unable to prosecute because of a collapsed justice system, the government desires to consolidate the rule of law or reinforce national judicial authority and therefore, on balance, considers it worthwhile to proceed notwithstanding the impaired condition of its justice system; and
4. state actors seek to suppress, discredit, or wreak vengeance upon political adversaries and can accomplish this through prosecutions, regardless of whether the national justice system has collapsed.[36]

We can identify examples of situations in which each of these four states' motives for actively exercising concurrent jurisdiction would arise. The first motive (that, although the state has a functioning judiciary, it is unable to pursue the cases being brought before the ICC because the state cannot obtain extradition or cannot obtain necessary evidence abroad) would likely have featured significantly in the case of Mengistu Haile-Mariam had an ICC been in existence at the relevant time. The current government of Ethiopia, several months after taking power in 1991, appointed a special prosecutor to prosecute genocide, war crimes and crimes against humanity committed under the deposed Mengistu

---

[36] A state might also be inclined to conduct sham prosecutions to shield potential defendants from real prosecution before the ICC by invoking the ICC Treaty's *ne bis in idem* provisions which state that, "No person who has been tried by another court for conduct also proscribed under [this Treaty] shall be tried by the Court with respect to the same conduct. . . ." ICC Treaty, art. 20(3). However, while the *ne bis in idem* provisions prohibit ICC retrial after national trial in most cases, they allow ICC prosecution of defendants whose trials at the national level were conducted for the purpose of shielding the defendant from justice. *See id.*, art. 20(3)(a). That safeguard presumably would deter most sham prosecutions and would provide an appropriate remedy for any that did occur.

regime.[37] In February 1997, when the special prosecutor announced that the charging process was complete, there were 5,198 individuals charged, including 2,246 defendants then in custody and 2,952 defendants charged *in absentia*.[38] Certain key figures in the former regime, including Mengistu himself, had found refuge in countries that refused Ethiopian extradition requests.[39] Had an international court been available for the prosecution of Mengistu and the others whom Ethiopia was unable to have extradited, then the international court might appropriately have tried those defendants while Ethiopian national courts tried the cases where lack of intergovernmental cooperation did not pose a problem.

The second of the states' motives for exercising concurrent jurisdiction (that the government's constituencies consider inadequate the number or array of prosecutions being brought by the international tribunal, and the state therefore considers it worthwhile to proceed with prosecutions notwithstanding the impaired condition of its justice system) is illustrated by the situation in post-genocide Rwanda. There, tens of thousands were implicated in the 1994 genocide.[40] The International Criminal Tribunal for Rwanda (ICTR) was created to prosecute crimes committed in that genocide and the war that ensued.[41] The number of cases prosecuted before the ICTR will be in the hundreds at most.[42] The prosecutions are focused, to the extent the ICTR finds possible, on leadership-level defendants.[43]

The Rwandan justice system had entirely collapsed when the current government took power in the summer of 1994.[44] The government of Rwanda has nevertheless chosen to proceed with mass-scale prosecutions.[45] It was unlikely that the government of Rwanda would have chosen otherwise, given the facts of Rwandan politics. The primary constituencies of the current Rwandan government are the minority Tutsi population that was the target of the 1994 genocide

---

[37] *See* Government of Ethiopia, Proclamation 22/1992 (1992). *See also*, THE OFFICE OF THE SPECIAL PROSECUTOR, THE TRANSITIONAL GOVERNMENT OF ETHIOPIA, THE SPECIAL PROSECUTION PROCESS OF WAR CRIMINALS AND HUMAN RIGHTS VIOLATORS IN ETHIOPIA 2 (1994) (discussing Proclamation 22/1992).

[38] *See* Martin Hill, "Ethiopia: The Dergue Trials," paper presented at the African Studies Ass'n of the UK, Biennial Conference, SOAS, University of London (Sept. 14–16, 1998): 9 (on file with author).

[39] *See id.* at 8.

[40] *See* Morris, *supra* note 30, at 350–52.

[41] *Id.* at 353.

[42] *Id.* at 357.

[43] *Id.* at 363 n.80.

[44] *Id.* at 357–61.

[45] *Id.* As of early 2000, Rwanda was holding 135,000 prisoners in connection with the genocide.

and the population of Tutsi refugees who had fled Rwanda three decades earlier and have returned to Rwanda since the current government took power in 1994. These populations, on whose support the Kigali government depends, have vocally condemned features of ICTR policy including the number and array of defendants to be prosecuted and have demanded that large-scale national prosecutions be pursued. It is impossible to say to what extent the demands for national prosecutions would have been diminished had the ICTR been prepared to handle a larger number of cases or to try followers as well as leaders. What is clear is that the number and character of prosecutions undertaken by the ICTR were insufficient to satisfy the Rwandan government's constituencies, particularly the victim population. It is predictable that, when a government is dependent upon constituencies who view the number or array of prosecutions brought by the international tribunal to be inadequate, the state will actively exercise jurisdiction concurrently with the international tribunal, notwithstanding the impaired condition of the national justice system.

The third state motive for exercising concurrent jurisdiction is to consolidate the rule of law and reinforce national judicial authority. The importance of consolidating the rule of law at the national level featured prominently in the 1991 debate in Ethiopia over whether to request establishment of an international tribunal or, instead, to conduct exclusively national prosecutions of the crimes committed under the Mengistu regime.[46] Ultimately, the decision to conduct exclusively national prosecutions was explicitly based in part on a desire to develop and reinforce the authority and legitimacy of the Ethiopian judiciary.[47] Had an ICC then been in existence and exercised jurisdiction on the ground that the Ethiopian judiciary was unable to do so (an unlikely but not inconceivable ICC decision, in light of the state of the Ethiopian judiciary in 1991), Ethiopia might well have chosen to proceed with national prosecutions concurrent with those of the international court.

Concerns regarding the fourth of the motives for concurrent jurisdiction (that state actors seek to suppress, discredit, or wreak vengeance upon political adversaries and can accomplish this through prosecutions regardless of whether the national justice system has collapsed) formed the impetus for establishment of the so-called "rules of the road" governing exercise of domestic jurisdiction for war crimes in Bosnia. On January 30, 1996, Bosnian Serb military officers General Djordje Djukic and Colonel Aleksa Krsmanovic were arrested by Bosnian government authorities on suspicion of war crimes.[48] Subsequent prosecution of those individuals by Bosnia would have been an exercise of national jurisdiction con-

---

[46] Conversations of author with Dawit Yohannes, Speaker, Parliament of Peoples' Representatives of Ethiopia, in Addis Ababa (Dec. 1995) (notes on file with author).

[47] *Id.*

[48] Chris Hedges, *Bosnia Limits War Crimes Arrests After NATO Delivers 2 Suspects*, N.Y. TIMES, Feb. 13, 1996, at A1.

current with that of the ICTY. The conflict between the Bosnian Serbs and the Bosnian government that followed the arrests centered on accusations of political prosecutions. The situation was defused only by the creation of a mechanism, dubbed "the rules of the road," whereby the Bosnian government submits for screening by the ICTY any prosecutions for war crimes that it intends to bring.[49] The Bosnian government may pursue a proposed prosecution only if the case is determined by the ICTY to be "consistent with international legal standards."[50]

The Bosnian government was willing to agree to such a screening mechanism because the arrangement, while ceding power to the ICTY, also potentially protected its own constituents from political prosecutions by other parties and averted a risk of reigniting armed hostilities.[51] In contexts where such reciprocal threats do not exist, however, states will be unimpeded in pursuing political prosecutions concurrently with prosecutions brought by an international tribunal.

The foregoing typology of four states' motives for active exercise of concurrent jurisdiction identifies themes rather than pure types. It is likely that variations on or combinations of these motives will underlie states' actions in many instances. Where states have any of the motives discussed, they are likely actively to exercise jurisdiction concurrently with the ICC.

The appropriate response of the ICC to divergences of interest arising in the application of active concurrent jurisdiction will depend, in part, upon the reasons for which national courts are operating concurrently with the ICC in a given instance. In serving the interests of victims and principally affected states as well as majority states, the ICC will have to be mindful of the interaction of its jurisdiction with that of active national courts. If a state is making *bona fide* efforts to achieve justice at the national level, then the ICC should take care to operate in a manner that is indeed complementary to those national efforts. If, on the other hand, the state's exercise of jurisdiction is not *bona fide*, then complementarity may require non-cooperation with the national jurisdiction. In considering the types of divergence of interest that may arise when the ICC is operating in a posture of active concurrent jurisdiction, it will be helpful to begin by drawing certain lessons from the interactions between the International Criminal Tribunals for the former Yugoslavia and Rwanda (ICTY/R) and the national courts with which those tribunals share active concurrent jurisdiction.

b.   The Vestiges of Primacy

The complementarity framework set forth in the Rome Treaty is intended to avoid problems that were associated with the jurisdictional "primacy" governing

---

[49]   *Id.*

[50]   Agreed Measures, Feb. 18, 1996 (on file with author).

[51]   The Bosnian parties also were under enormous international pressure, particularly from the United States, to accept the rules of the road arrangement. *See* Hedges, *supra* note 48.

the concurrent jurisdiction of the ICTY/R.[52] But ICC complementarity, while a definite improvement, retains certain pitfalls of the old primacy regime. Those pitfalls may be averted, but only with the use of carefully constructed prosecutorial policies designed to avert the potential problems.

The Statutes of the ICTY/R grant the tribunals jurisdictional primacy, meaning that the ICTY/R may require national courts to relinquish jurisdiction over cases which the ICTY/R wish to prosecute.[53] In some instances, this arrangement has engendered acrimony between the ICTY/R and states wishing to prosecute defendants over whom the ICTY/R has taken jurisdiction.[54] Primacy, as applied by the ICTY/R, has also created anomalous outcomes as leaders, tried before the international tribunals, have received more favorable treatment than followers, who have been tried in national courts. Primacy, as applied by the ICTR, also has created political obstacles to national plea bargaining arrangements in Rwanda. There, the removal of leaders from the state's jurisdiction to the ICTR precluded the possibility of allowing the state to punish leaders severely and, thereby, to ameliorate the affront to some constituencies caused by according lenient treatment to followers pursuant to plea bargains.

ICC complementarity incorporates a vestigial form of the primacy of jurisdiction exercised by the ICTY/R. Under the ICC Treaty, the Court is to determine whether a case otherwise within its jurisdiction[55] is "admissible." A case is inadmissible before the ICC if it has been or will be appropriately handled by a national jurisdiction.[56] Article 17 of the ICC Treaty provides:

1.   [T]he Court shall determine that a case is inadmissible where:

     a.   The case is being investigated or prosecuted by a state which has jurisdiction over it, unless the state is unwilling or unable genuinely to carry out the investigation or prosecution;

---

[52] For an examination of the problems involving the concurrent jurisdiction of the ICTR, *see* Morris, *supra* note 30, at 349, 362–72.

The problems of active concurrent jurisdiction confronted by the ICTY/R have arisen primarily in the Rwandan rather than the former-Yugoslav context. This is unsurprising since the Rwandan government has attempted more actively to conduct extensive national prosecutions than have the former-Yugoslav countries. *See* Fionnuala Ni Alain, *The Fractured Soul of the Dayton Peace Agreement: A Legal Analysis*, 19 MICH. J. INT'L L. 957, 996 (1998).

[53] *See* Statute of the International Criminal Tribunal for the Prosecution of Persons Responsible for Serious Violations of International Humanitarian Law Committed in the Territory of the Former Yugoslavia Since 1991, *in* Report of the Secretary-General Pursuant to Paragraph 2 of Security Council Resolution 808, Annex, art. 9(2), at 39, U.N. Doc. S/25704 (1993); Statute of the International Criminal Tribunal for Rwanda, S.C. Res. 955, U.N. SCOR 49th Sess., 3453rd mtg., Annex, art. 8(2), U.N. Doc. S/RES/955 (1994), *reprinted in* 33 I.L.M. 1598, 1605 (1994).

[54] *See* Morris, *supra* note 30 at 362–65.

[55] *See* ICC Treaty, arts. 5–12.

[56] *See id.*, art. 17.

b. The case has been investigated by a state which has jurisdiction over it and the state has decided not to prosecute the person concerned, unless the decision resulted from the unwillingness or inability of the state genuinely to prosecute;

c. The person concerned has already been tried for conduct which is the subject of the complaint, and a trial by the Court is not permitted under article 20, paragraph 3;

d. The case is not of sufficient gravity to justify further action by the Court.[57]

If admissibility is challenged,[58] the International Court will make the final determination of admissibility.[59] Pursuant to the Treaty, the ICC may exercise jurisdiction if it determines that the admissibility criteria are met, even over the objection of a state that would otherwise have jurisdiction.[60] Under the Treaty's *ne bis in idem* provisions, ICC jurisdiction over an admissible case is exclusive, precluding national prosecution of the case.[61] ICC complementarity thus incorporates a revised form of primacy in the sense that the ICC may assert exclusive jurisdiction even over the objection of a state. ICC primacy differs significantly from ICTY/R primacy in that the ICC Treaty articulates narrow criteria to be employed in exercising that primacy. ICC primacy is to be exercised only in the absence of adequate handling of the case by a state. In contrast, the ICTY/R exercises its power to prosecute and preclude national prosecution without statutory

---

[57] *Id.*, art. 17(1). Article 17 goes on to specify that:

2. In order to determine unwillingness in a particular case, the Court shall consider, having regard to the principles of due process recognized by international law, whether one or more of the following exist, as applicable:

a. The proceedings were or are being undertaken or the national decision was made for the purpose of shielding the person concerned from criminal responsibility for crimes within the jurisdiction of the Court referred to in article 5;

b. There has been an unjustified delay in the proceedings which in the circumstances is inconsistent with an intent to bring the person concerned to justice;

c. The proceedings were not or are not being conducted independently or impartially, and they were or are being conducted in a manner which, in the circumstances, is inconsistent with an intent to bring the person concerned to justice;

3. In order to determine inability in a particular case, the Court shall consider whether, due to a total or substantial collapse or unavailability of its national judicial system, the state is unable to obtain the accused or the necessary evidence and testimony or otherwise unable to carry out its proceedings.

[58] Challenges to admissibility may be brought by a state or other party. *See id.*, art. 19.

[59] *Id.*

[60] *Id.*, arts. 17–19.

[61] The *ne bis in idem* provisions state, "No person shall be tried before another court for a crime . . . for which that person has already been convicted or acquitted by the Court." *Id.*, art. 20(2).

guidance as to when that power should be applied.[62] Nevertheless, in the ICC as in the ICTY/R, the international tribunal ultimately determines whether it will exercise jurisdiction over a particular case to the exclusion of national courts.[63]

The ICC thus will have a vestigial form of primacy; the Court will have the power to insist upon taking a particular case if it determines that the case is admissible. By taking some cases and leaving others to national courts, the ICC will largely control the distribution of defendants between the national and international fora in contexts of active concurrent jurisdiction. It is the distribution of defendants that largely determines whether there will be anomalous outcomes in the handling of leaders and followers and whether the operation of the international tribunal will pose impediments to national plea bargaining arrangements or undermine national judicial authority. ICC prosecutorial policies governing the distribution of defendants will, therefore, be a crucial determinant of whether the ICC's intended "complementarity" operates in a constructive or a destructive manner relative to national jurisdictions.

The ICC's admissibility rules (that national courts have priority of jurisdiction unless they are unwilling or unable to handle the cases appropriately) will limit the ICC's choice of defendants when the ICC determines that national courts are functioning adequately. However, in other situations, where the ICC determines that a national justice system has collapsed or that a government is unwilling genuinely to prosecute, all potential cases would be admissible before the ICC.[64] The ICC will operate most often in this posture because, if the national justice system were neither defunct nor unwilling, then, in most situations, no cases would be admissible before the ICC.[65] The only exception would occur where a national jurisdiction were able and willing to try cases arising from the context of mass crimes but could not obtain extradition of a given defendant or could not obtain necessary evidence abroad. In all other instances, in situations where any cases were admissible before the ICC, all potential cases would be admissible before the ICC. In this posture, the ICC's choice of defendants will be constrained only by its own prosecutorial policies.

---

[62] *See* Morris, *supra* note 30, at 365.

[63] The ICC's taking jurisdiction over one prosecution, however, would not prevent a state from prosecuting other cases arising from the same context of mass crimes. Even if the ICC concludes that a state's justice system has collapsed or that the government is unwilling genuinely to prosecute—thus concluding, in effect, that the state is unable or unwilling to handle *any* cases arising from that context of mass crimes—the state may disagree and proceed with its own cases concurrently with those of the ICC. In such instances, the state and the ICC will exercise concurrent jurisdiction over the crimes committed within the overall context of the mass crimes in question.

[64] *See* ICC Treaty, art. 17.

[65] *Id.*

The prosecutorial policy embraced by the ICTY/R,[66] which appears likely to be adopted by the ICC, is a "stratified concurrent jurisdiction" approach to the distribution of defendants. Under this policy, the international forum seeks to prosecute the leadership stratum and leaves the lower strata defendants to be tried in national courts. This approach to the distribution of defendants predictably produces anomalous outcomes in the handling of leaders and followers, creates impediments to national plea bargaining arrangements, and may tend to undermine national judicial authority.

Stratified concurrent jurisdiction systematically produces anomalous outcomes in the handling of leaders and followers because the leaders, who are tried in the international forum, generally receive more favorable treatment than the followers, who are tried in national courts. The advantages for defendants of international prosecution include absence of the death penalty (applicable in many national courts but inapplicable under the ICC Treaty), greater due process protections (including appointed defense counsel) than many national fora offer, better conditions of incarceration than those in some countries, and, not infrequently in post-conflict contexts, greater assurance of impartiality than national courts can provide. A policy of stratified concurrent jurisdiction thus leads to anomalies of inversion in which crucial advantages flow to the leaders who are, by hypothesis, most responsible for the mass crimes, while the followers are subject to harsher treatment.[67]

Such anomalies of inversion became pronounced and problematic as the ICTR pursued its policy of stratified concurrent jurisdiction in relation to Rwandan national courts.[68] Many defendants who were not high-level leaders in the Rwandan genocide have been sentenced to death in Rwandan national courts, and some executed,[69] after summary trials, sometimes without defense counsel, while leaders of the genocide have received less severe sentences after trials with full due process at the ICTR.[70] Anomalous outcomes of this type will predictably

---

[66] *See supra* note 31.

[67] For a discussion of the advantages flowing to leaders because of "anomalies of inversion," *see* Morris, *supra* note 30, at 363–64, 371.

[68] *Id.*

[69] For example, on April 24, 1998, twenty-two individuals were executed pursuant to death penalties issued by Rwandan courts for genocide-related crimes. Among those executed were low-level functionaries including a Conseiller de Secteur (administrator of a political subdivision containing approximately 5,000–10,000 people) and a medical assistant at a government hospital, as well as two peasants who were ordinary members (that is, secteur- or cellule-level members) of political parties that were associated with the genocide (Coalition pour la Défense de la République and Mouvement Révolutionnaire Nationale pour le Développement, respectively). Interview with Faustin Ntezilyayo, Rwandan Minister of Justice Nov. 1996–Jan. 1999, in Durham, N.C. (Jan. 12, 1999).

[70] *See, e.g.*, The Prosecutor v. Jean-Paul Akayesu, Case No. ICTR–96–4–T (Trial Chamber, Sentence) (1998) (sentence of imprisonment for life); The Prosecutor v. Jean Kambanda, Case

occur where an international forum with primacy pursues a policy of stratified concurrent jurisdiction.

Stratified concurrent jurisdiction also tends to impede national plea bargaining arrangements. In order to facilitate investigations or to expedite prosecution of a large volume of cases, national justice systems may choose to grant defendants benefits (such as charge or sentence reductions) in return for guilty pleas or other cooperation. While plea bargaining may be an advantageous strategy, governments instituting such a system must avoid the appearance of leniency toward perpetrators. The leniency in sentencing that accompanies plea agreements can easily create a perception that impunity has prevailed unless at least the leaders are fully prosecuted and punished. Herein lies the second problem with stratified concurrent jurisdiction. If the international forum takes jurisdiction over the leaders, then the national forum will lack leaders to prosecute. Indeed, a national government seeking to institute a plea bargaining arrangement will have to acknowledge that, far from being "prosecuted to the full extent of the law," the leaders are away receiving substantial advantages in the international forum. With the leaders away receiving advantageous treatment and the followers getting "bargains" at home, a perception may be created, especially among the victim population, that the plea agreement program is in fact a program of impunity. National justice systems, consequently, may be impeded in their plea bargaining arrangements.

This problem is exemplified, once again, by the Rwandan experience. The Rwandan government implemented a specialized plea bargaining system to deal with the enormous volume of cases related to the Rwandan genocide of 1994.[71] The ICTR's repeatedly taking jurisdiction over the leadership-level suspects posed an obstacle to the political acceptability within Rwanda of the plea-bargaining system[72] and led to conflict and acrimony between the government of Rwanda and the ICTR.[73]

Stratified concurrent jurisdiction also may tend to undermine the authority of the national justice system in a principally affected state by depriving it of the opportunity to try those who were the leaders of the mass crimes that affected the country. This problem may be particularly significant in post-conflict situations where a new democratic regime is attempting to establish a strong and authoritative judiciary.

No. ICTR–97–23–S (Trial Chamber, Judgement and Sentence) 1998 (sentence of imprisonment for life).

[71] *See* Organic Law No. 08/96 of Aug. 30, 1996, on the Organization of Prosecutions for Offences Constituting the Crime of Genocide or Crimes Against Humanity Committed Since Oct. 1, 1990, arts. 4–18, *in Official Gazette of Rwanda*, Sept. 1, 1996.

[72] *See* Morris, *supra* note 30, at 363–64.

[73] *Id.*

c. *Principles for the Application of Complementarity in Contexts of Active Concurrent Jurisdiction*

Consistent with the principle of complementarity, the appropriate response of the ICC to divergences of interest arising in contexts of active concurrent jurisdiction will depend largely upon the motives for the state's justice efforts. Each of the four types of states' motives for exercising active concurrent jurisdiction requires a different analysis and a distinct course of action if the ICC is to balance appropriately the interests of principally affected states, victims, and majority states.

Where the first motive for a state's exercising concurrent jurisdiction applies (that is, a state exercises jurisdiction concurrently with the ICC because of an inability to obtain extradition or evidence abroad in particular cases), there should be little difficulty in avoiding anomalies of inversion, impediments to plea bargaining, or undermining of national judicial authority. The ICC, consistent with its role as a complement to national jurisdictions and thus acting only where states are unwilling or unable to act, would pursue only those cases that the state cannot because of a lack of intergovernmental cooperation. While in practice this may result in the ICC's disproportionately prosecuting leaders (because they are the individuals likely to have the resources to flee the country and the political connections to block intergovernmental cooperation), the leader-drain effect is likely to be far less pronounced than it would be under a deliberate policy of stratified concurrent jurisdiction. Therefore, the problems of anomalies of inversion, impediments to plea bargaining, and undermining of judicial authority will be reduced, if not eliminated.

A different analysis is warranted where the second state motive for active concurrent jurisdiction applies. Here, the state actively exercises jurisdiction concurrently with the ICC because, while the ICC considers the state unable to prosecute because of a collapsed justice system, the government's constituencies, including victim populations, view the number or array of prosecutions brought by the ICC as inadequate, and the state therefore considers it worthwhile to proceed with prosecutions notwithstanding the impaired condition of its justice system. In this context, it may be wise for the ICC prosecutor to negotiate with the national government to agree upon an ICC prosecutorial strategy, regarding the number and array of ICC cases, that would both satisfy the ICC's other goals *and* adequately fulfill the interests of the government and its constituencies, including victims, thus obviating the need for national trials. The existence and results of such a negotiation could be made public so that the relevant constituencies would be aware of the government's role in securing the desirable prosecutorial approach. Such negotiations would not constitute improper influence on the prosecutor or Court. While an overall approach as to the volume and array of cases would be agreed upon, the agreement need not involve commitments to prosecute particular defendants and, obviously, would not influence the outcome of the cases brought.

Where such negotiations are successful and the state foregoes national prosecutions, not only will anomalies of inversion and plea-bargaining problems be averted, but the potential injustices inherent in prosecutions by an impaired national justice system also will be avoided. Care will have to be taken in such cases that national judicial authority is not undermined by the decision to forego national trials. Rather, it should be emphasized that national judicial restraint demonstrates the commitment of the national government and justice system to due process as reflected in its declining to hold trials until such time as it can do so in an adequate manner. The net result may be actually to strengthen national judicial legitimacy.

Where negotiations are not successful in forestalling national prosecutions (and, given the political realities of such situations, this may frequently be the case), the ICC will have to shape its subsequent relations with the national jurisdiction according to the actual quality of the national justice efforts as they unfold. If national prosecutions are conducted with impartiality and something approaching due process, then the ICC should attempt to foster those proceedings. Such measures to foster national justice efforts should include the ICC prosecutor's taking into account potential anomalies of inversion, impediments to plea bargaining, and undermining of national judicial authority when designing criteria to govern the selection of defendants to be prosecuted before the ICC. This will often require the ICC prosecutor to pursue a prosecutorial policy other than stratified concurrent jurisdiction. If, on the other hand, national justice processes seriously lack impartiality or adequate due process, then the ICC may have to refuse to foster or cooperate with those national proceedings. In such cases, it may be appropriate for the ICC to proceed pursuant to the same or virtually the same principles and policies as would apply if the ICC were the sole active forum.

The situation is more complex where the third motive for active concurrent jurisdiction applies. Here, a state actively exercises jurisdiction concurrently with the ICC because it desires to consolidate the rule of law or reinforce national judicial authority and therefore, on balance, considers it worthwhile to proceed notwithstanding the impaired condition of its justice system. In this situation, the state seeks not only to assure a certain range of prosecutions, but also, specifically, to conduct some or all of those prosecutions in its national courts in order to reap national benefits. Here, the available range of ICC prosecutorial approaches is wide and the attendant political implications are widely divergent.

Where there is clearly no hope of any national prosecutions of acceptable quality occurring within an acceptable period, the ICC prosecutor would do well to attempt to convince the state to forego national trials. The prosecutor may note in this regard that the spectacle of gravely inadequate trials will do nothing to consolidate the rule of law or national judicial authority and will likely do just the reverse. Such attempts at persuasion may or may not convince a state to forego national prosecutions. If they do not, then, as in other cases where negotiations fail to forestall national prosecutions, the nature of the ICC's subsequent inter-actions with the national justice processes should depend upon the quality of those processes as they are implemented.

The completely collapsed justice system just discussed, however, represents the most extreme case. Not all countries with substantially collapsed justice systems will be completely incapable of conducting absolutely any satisfactory trials. Where a largely disabled justice system is capable of conducting one or two or a handful of adequate prosecutions (perhaps with substantial international assistance), and that state desires to pursue justice at the national level for rule of law-strengthening purposes, it may be possible to accommodate both national and international interests. Here, a useful strategy may be to reverse the traditionally-envisioned order of things and have the *national* courts conduct a very small number of high-profile prosecutions of prominent defendants while the international court conducts a somewhat larger number of other prosecutions. While this strategy is not suitable for all contexts, it may provide most fully for fulfillment of the interests of victims, principally affected states, and majority states under some circumstances.

A different strategy may be necessary where the fourth motive for active concurrent jurisdiction is operative. Where a state exercises jurisdiction concurrently with the ICC because state actors seek through national prosecutions to suppress, discredit, or wreak vengeance upon political adversaries, the ICC prosecutor may wish to negotiate with the national government regarding an ICC prosecutorial strategy that would fulfill legitimate state and victim interests sufficiently to obviate any real need for national trials. Obviously, however, where political suppression is the state's motive, it is less than likely (though not impossible, given the needs of states to maintain acceptable international appearances) that such an agreement could be reached.

ICC complementarity poses particularly complex issues when the ICC operates concurrently with active national fora. This concurrent operation may arise for reasons that are good, bad, or ambiguous. The ICC will have to employ a carefully constructed range of policy responses, some of which have been considered in the preceding pages, if it is to foster the interests of victims, principally affected states, and majority states both directly within the ICC and within the national fora with which it interacts.

D. THE LIMITS OF PROSECUTORIAL DISCRETION

The ICC Treaty's complementarity provisions are the product of political conflict and compromise. Like many such products, the provisions leave unaddressed issues that will be critical to their effective implementation.

In the absence of delineation of the necessary policies to govern the application of complementarity, fundamental decisions on the balancing and prioritization of the interests of victims, principally affected states, and majority states will fall by default to the ICC prosecutor. While an ICC prosecutor may appropriately be vested with some latitude in the exercise of prosecutorial discretion, the delineation of major policy principles that go to the fundamental purposes of the Court requires prior articulation by a deliberative and representative body. Particularly because some approaches that best serve the full range of majority state, principally affected state, and victim interests may be untraditional and perhaps counterintuitive, we cannot be sanguine that an ICC prosecutor, acting in the press of events, will pursue the most desirable prosecutorial approach. A failure of insight, an uncertainty about political acceptability, a concern with acting outside the prosecutor's proper authority, or a simple lack of time might prevent an ICC prosecutor, operating without clear policy guidance, from choosing the optimal course in a complex set of circumstances.

It is unreasonable to suppose that an ICC prosecutor, acting in the rush of politically charged international events, should undertake fundamental analysis and decision-making on broad policy issues. Moreover, even if one ICC prosecutor, operating without policy guidance, remarkably got the policy right, there is no reason to believe that the next prosecutor would do so or that there would be consistency or coherence in basic ICC policy on these matters over time. Even more fundamentally, the requirements of legitimate international law-making demand that the principal purposes and functions of a treaty-based body be decided by the States Parties themselves and not by an individual employed to execute one aspect of the treaty.

There is currently no procedure foreseen for the elaboration of the kind of ICC policy that I have argued is required. These policy issues are matters that could in theory be taken up by the Assembly of States Parties which is intended to provide oversight and guidance to the ICC.[74] However, given the politically sensitive nature of the issues and the absence, to date, of any indication of an intention to focus on these matters, it seems unlikely that the Assembly of States Parties will address these questions.

Failure to develop the needed policies to guide the work of the ICC could substantially undermine its likely value and effectiveness. In the absence of carefully developed and articulated policies to guide ICC practice on complementarity, there exists the very real risk that the ICC will create injustice rather than justice as it fails to serve the interests of states and victims and perhaps even impedes the fulfillment of those interests in state proceedings.

---

[74] *See* ICC Treaty, art. 112.

CHAPTER 16
THE UNITED STATES AND THE ICC

David Scheffer

Considerable attention has recently been given to the prospective reality of a permanent international criminal court. It is an important subject, but there are crimes from the past three decades that must not be ignored and must not be forgotten in the euphoria of a prospective permanent court. Much hard work remains from the 1970s with Cambodia, the 1980s with Iraq and elsewhere, and the 1990s with respect to too many areas to mention. There is thus a tremendous amount of accountability work to be done even before a permanent court is established, in order to deal with the crimes of the present generation. The work load is heavy and expanding every single day and with every atrocity.

There has been some confusion about the United States attitude towards a Permanent International Criminal Court and it is an understandable confusion. Journalists report on events in the starkest fashion possible and various presumptions follow from the reporting. Ultimately, it becomes "us" versus "them" as the theme of every article and every discussion on this subject, but that is an absolutely false presumption with which to approach discussion about the Permanent International Criminal Court. The United States has been deeply engaged, from the very beginning, in promoting the establishment of a Permanent International Criminal Court. The United States advanced the idea, was involved in all of the discussions, and sought ways to structure the ICC Statute so that it would have the support not only of the U.S. government but of other governments. President Clinton repeatedly committed himself to the establishment of a Permanent International Criminal Court by the end of this century. Secretary Albright repeatedly did so, both as Ambassador to the U.N. and as Secretary of state. There is no shortage of a public record concerning U.S. commitment to the establishment of a Permanent International Criminal Court. In fact, it has been the determined policy of the United States to have such a court.

In Rome, after so many years of hard work with so many governments— allies and other governments who would not be classified as allies but with whom the U.S. worked closely throughout the negotiations—the treaty text reflected a tremendous amount of input by the United States Government. In the give-and-take of negotiations the U.S. delegation fought provision by provision by provision to get the text correct, and in large part the results are right. There are major sections of the treaty in which the U.S. has tremendous interest and with which there is great satisfaction.

The principle of "complementarity" is well-embodied in the treaty and the U.S. is quite pleased with how complementarity evolved during the drafting, resulting in Articles 17 and 18 and 19 in the Statute. These are good articles. Obviously it is possible to argue that they could be better, but the U.S. was very pleased with the negotiations that resulted in those three articles of the Statute. John Holmes of Canada was actually responsible for melding together the different views of the delegations and keeping those Articles intact, showing rather masterful negotiating skills.

Part 9 of the treaty contains the set of Articles on cooperation and they resulted from intensive negotiations in Rome involving much discord and some confrontational discussions. It was important to weigh the interests of those delegations that simply wanted all states to have an obligation to comply immediately and without qualification with any order or direction by the Court, against the reality of the world system that states are not really going to act in that way. Each state must follow its national legal procedures—they can't simply throw out their constitutions—in order to be in a position to participate in and cooperate with an international court. The provisions had to be ironed out, clause by clause by clause. The results were successful and the U.S. is quite satisfied with Part 9.

Article 72 concerns how the Court can deal with sensitive information held by governments. It too required many rounds of negotiations to achieve satisfactory results from the U.S. perspective. The provision works for other key governments also and it will stand the test of time.

The U.S. took the lead with other governments in ensuring that crimes against humanity would be part of the jurisdiction of the ICC when committed, not only during international armed conflicts, but also during internal armed conflicts and internal disturbances that are not necessarily defined as armed conflicts. This constituted a very important statement of the U.S. view of current customary international law, but achieving it took a lot of work, because some governments disagree with the U.S. on the point.

The U.S. sought to establish a type of "reality check" for the International Criminal Court by requiring a significant number of crimes be committed in order for the situation to be properly within the jurisdiction of the court. The ICC should not deal with an isolated outbreak, with one criminal act by one individual, but it should concentrate instead on widespread commission of such crimes. Isolated incidents should be dealt with at the national court level. Those thresholds appear in the treaty and that is important in terms of how the United States and certain other countries can approach the treaty in a supportive fashion.

With respect to war crimes, there were long debates about the extent to which war crimes in internal armed conflicts should fall within the jurisdiction of this Court. Some countries wanted a long laundry list, while other countries wanted no list at all. After a lot of hard work, the Diplomatic Conference arrived at a pragmatic expression of customary international law as to the applicability of war crimes to internal armed conflicts. It can be generally accepted by governments, as it is now embodied in the Statute.

The U.S. placed a lot of emphasis on crimes against women. The Statute reflects this, containing the most explicit references to such crimes that have ever been incorporated in a treaty. The U.S. supports these provisions, because it views customary international law as having reached the stage where such crimes can be explicitly listed.

Defining the elements of crimes was another key issue. It is very important for a prosecutor, defense counsel or a judge to know what are the necessary elements to be established for any particular crime to be prosecuted or defended or judged in a courtroom. There were differences of opinion between common law and civil law representatives on these issues, but the conclusion produced a very satisfactory outcome. Article 9 of the treaty establishes that there will be a list of crimes and very good progress is being made on detailing the elements of crimes in the preparatory commission talks in New York. The U.S. paper is the lead paper in those discussions, although the U.S. government is working very closely with other key governments to modify the paper and arrive at language that can be broadly acceptable. In every case that comes up before the Yugoslav Tribunal or the Rwanda War Crimes Tribunal, the judges ask the prosecutor, "What are the elements of the crime?" In the ICC, the judges will not need to have that time-consuming question answered by the Prosecutor's Office. The elements will be before the Court and the judges can go straight to processing the case.

Those and many other aspects of the treaty are supported by the United States. Indeed, there is a tremendous portion of the Statute that is very satisfactory. The difficulty for the U.S., and the reason why it could not support adoption of the Statute in Rome, is a small part of the treaty, but it has a great deal of significance. Unfortunately, the controversy over the U.S. position shifts the focus from the perpetrators of atrocities who should be before the *ad hoc* tribunals, and ultimately the Permanent International Criminal Court.

Clearly, it is not the intention of other governments, or at least most of them, or of non-governmental organizations, to create an institution that targets the United States for investigation and prosecution. At the same time, the Statute must be drafted correctly in order for the United States to be able to participate, with all of its resources, all of its globally-deployed military, all of the clout that it can bring to such an institution. The issue that poses problems for the U.S. is an ironic one, being based on U.S. exposure as a non-party to the treaty, rather than on exposure as party. Many may suggest that the solution is simple: sign and ratify. But that is not going to happen, at least in the short term. The U.S. could sign tomorrow, but there is absolutely no assurance that the treaty will be ratified by the U.S. Senate. It must be assumed that it will take a certain number of years, and during that time the United States remains a non-party, even if the treaty comes into force and the Court begins functioning. The U.S. is concerned about exposure to the Court during the period of non-Party status. It is a relatively small issue, but it was a deal-breaker. The Law of the Sea Convention demonstrates the problem. The U.S. signed it in 1994 and the Executive Branch supports ratification, but there has been no action within the Senate. The U.S. remains a non-party to the Law of the Sea Convention and as a result it cannot have a judge on the Law of the Sea Tribunal.

The problem of non-party states is a very serious one, but it can be solved. Within the Preparatory Commission, work is progressing on the elements of crimes, on the rules of procedure and evidence, on other supplemental documents; and on how to resolve this problem for the United States. The U.S. does not have all the answers and is seeking suggestions from other governments and non-governmental organizations. The answer does not lie in merely signing the treaty to limit exposure. There are answers out there, requiring constructive and imaginative approaches.

In conclusion, there is a very interesting challenge in the Statute posed by the issue of aggression. It is mentioned in the Statute but it is not defined yet, which is a big problem. The Preparatory Commission has a difficult task ahead of it to address the issue of aggression. It must agree upon a definition which can be brought to a review conference seven years after the treaty enters into force, so that the treaty can be amended to include the actual count of aggression in the Statute of the Court.

That is the other major problem that must be resolved, so that the United States and other major powers that use their military for good reason do not come under unwarranted attack. The U.S. is constantly being asked to deploy its forces, particularly by those who want their rights protected. Aggression must be defined in a way that those who are prepared to use military force in defense of human rights, to prevent the spread of weapons of mass destruction, and to enforce international law are not subjected to spurious claims of violations of international law for having done so. If the definition of aggression is overbroad, it is likely to have dire consequences for the future of the Court. It is a huge challenge, but it can be solved through the work of governments and non-governmental organizations. It must be done right and done now, while there is an opportunity to move forward.

CHAPTER 17

THE ICC STATUTE:
PROTECTING THE SOVEREIGN
RIGHTS OF NON-PARTIES

Roger S. Clark

I had a writer's block preparing this contribution about the pros and cons of the Rome Statute. It started well. I organized several boxes of scattered files from the Preparatory Committee and the Diplomatic Conference on the creation of a Permanent International Criminal Court. I read a very clearly crafted speech that Ambassador David Scheffer gave in February 1999 to a distinguished gathering of military leaders.[1] Ambassador Scheffer's piece made me acutely aware of the dangers the Rome Treaty poses to those who choose not to become parties to it. I thought I should engage myself with these dangers, once again to conscript what my thirteen-year-old daughter calls "the good old SIS" (Satire, Irony, and Sarcasm). I drafted the heading, which she thought was an example of sarcasm rather than irony, and then found myself stalled for several hours in front of an otherwise blank screen, unable to deliver on the satire. Finally, quite late, I put it aside for another day, and listened to a new CD I had been given, a re-issue of Arlo Guthrie's 1968 recording "Alice's Restaurant." It is eighteen minutes and twenty seconds of irreverence, which someone later reminded me is exactly the same length of time as the mysterious gap in a famous Presidential tape recording. One might loosely describe Guthrie's topic and mine as both being the criminal law and the military.

I went off to sleep happy, but the ICC invaded my dreams. I was treated to long harangues from two motor-mouths who each sounded like a different incarnation of Guthrie. One of them was the Minister of Defense ("The Minister") from some small country called Erehwon. He was talking to a smart person called "The Innocent Bystander." Erehwon is a strange backwards place where the Ministry of Defense runs foreign policy, quite unlike the United States, for example, where the President and the state Department are in charge. The Innocent Bystander came from what was once called a non-governmental-organization, but is now known as "civil society." The conversation was so interesting that I tried

---

[1] David J. Scheffer, "Deterrence of War Crimes in the 21st Century," *Twelfth Annual U.S. Pacific Command, International Military Operations and Law Conference*, Honolulu, Hawaii, Feb. 23, 1999 (obtained from Coalition on the International Criminal Court Home Page).

desperately to capture it on the word processor when I woke early the next day. I am going to share my dream—nightmare, perhaps—as best I remembered it that morning.[2]

The time is early in the New Millennium. Erehwon has a small army that is used mainly for what might generically be referred to as the unsophisticated "peacekeeping operations." They actually fall into three relatively precise categories. Some of them are mounted formally under United Nations auspices, the Security Council having acted pursuant to Chapter VII of the United Nations Charter; the troops even have a stash of those famous blue helmets kept in a warehouse. Others are what The Minister describes as "Authorized Coalition Operations" (ACOs)—that is to say, the Security Council passes a vague resolution telling those states involved in an action to use whatever means are necessary to achieve whatever broadly stated purpose the Council has more or less agreed upon. A third class of "Unauthorized Coalition Operations" (UCOs) describes instances when action is necessary for the greater good of the international community but, because "the community" does not realize this (i.e., the votes are not forthcoming or some dastardly Permanent Member of the Security Council uses its veto power),[3] it is not possible to obtain formal authorization. Sometimes NATO will step in and offer its cloak of legitimacy to such endeavors. In engaging in any of these enterprises, the Erehwonians usually work closely with a friend who is one of the Permanent Members of the Security Council ("the P5").[4]

"How did Erehwon get into this line of work?" the Innocent Bystander asked innocently, apparently as an opening conversational gambit. The Minister explained that some of his ancestors were Hessians. They used to do enforcement work for the British, "even in New Jersey," he added, "dealing with those revolting colonials." Someone lurking in my dream must have known I'm from New Jersey. Anyway, he noted that it keeps the military employed and while they are off helping the World, they are too busy to plot coups. "Moreover," he added, adopting a high moral tone, "we like to make a contribution to peace and justice."

Erehwon was not represented at the Rome Conference. Resources were a little tight, and besides, the government had consulted its Friend on the Security

---

[2] Unlike Arlo and that fellow a couple of hundred years ago who composed the poem about Kubla Khan in his sleep, I can assure you that all I took was my blood pressure medication. Nobody even dared interrupt me as I wrote my dream down.

[3] Sometimes, but not always, the successor state to the entity once known as "The Evil Empire."

[4] Erehwon is a little perturbed that at least two of the P5 are delinquent in paying their dues to the U.N. This results in delaying the reimbursement for Erehwon's role in the operations mounted under U.N. auspices. In respect of the other operations, they are usually able to get fairly prompt aid payments from their larger P5 friend which offset the military costs.

Council and had been told that everything should turn out all right. The Friend had quite a large delegation in Rome.

What Erehwon thought made most sense for the ICC was something along the lines of Articles 35 and 36 of the Statute of the International Court of Justice. Members of the United Nations and the handful of other states that are parties to the ICJ Statute are in a great position. The Court is, as the Statute says,[5] "open" to them, but it is up to them to decide whether they use it or not.[6] Of course, if they are so inclined, they can run their candidates for election as judges, participate in shaping the budget (a pretty crucial way to keep it in line), and influence the drafting of the Rules. But unless they agree of their own free will, in particular or in general cases, they do not need to enter the quaint portals in The Hague. This is not like a real domestic court where appearance need not be voluntary if you are a defendant! The International Law Commission had made the point nicely in its Commentary on its Draft Statute for an International Criminal Court:

> [T]he Statute should distinguish, as the Statute of the International Court of Justice does, between participation and support for the structure and operation of the Court on the one hand and acceptance of substantive jurisdiction in a particular case on the other. The process of acceptance would be a separate one (as under Art. 36 of the Statute of the International Court of Justice).[7]

What a good way to have your cake and eat it!

Now The Minister knew that some of those self-righteous states calling themselves "Like-Minded" (at least it wasn't "Right-Minded" which would have been too much!) had objected to this. They wanted "inherent" jurisdiction over all the crimes within the subject-matter ken of the Court. The ILC had, in fact, conceded that there should be inherent jurisdiction for genocide. Erehwon could live with that, but one certainly did not want to contemplate the same regime for war crimes. Erehwon had committed its genocide during a prior century and that was safely behind it. There was no one left to repeat the deed on—they were all dead. On the other hand, the troops did get a bit out of control now and again, but the military can discipline itself; no need to be embarrassed at The Hague. Other less civilized places still seemed to think that genocide and the rest were acceptable in the twenty-first century. The new Court should be for straightening them out.

---

[5] Statute of the International Court of Justice, art. 35(1).

[6] *Id.*, art. 36(1) (jurisdiction over cases the parties refer to it, and matters provided for in treaties and conventions in force) and 36(2) (a state may declare that it accepts jurisdiction as "compulsory" in respect of another state accepting the same).

[7] ILC Draft Statute, *in* Report of the International Law Comission on the Work of its Forty-Sixth Session, May 2–July 22, 1994, 43 at 66, U.N. GAOR, 49th Sess., Supp. No. 10, U.N. Doc. A/49/10 (1994).

Aware that some of the Like-Minded folks even had the ill-manners to sneer at an Article 36 solution—coupled with the power of the Security Council to refer cases—as "permanent *ad hoc*-ery," the Minister looked to his Friend on the Security Council to protect just that, preferably by another name, such as "State Consent Regime" or some such Proper Noun. "No problem," he was told, "the Like-Minded will fall apart in Rome. The Canadians did their dash with that land-mines nonsense and won't take on the Americans again. The British may break with the other members of the P5, but they're ultimately soft on the issues and will water the whole thing down. The French will never make a separate peace." As it turned out, the Like-Minded became firmer, larger in number and ever more righteous as time went by in Rome. The British joined them, with a fair amount of enthusiasm, their Leader apparently having shown a penchant for leading. The French made a separate peace.[8] The result was inherent jurisdiction across the board.

Not only that, but the Statute includes an independent power of the Prosecutor to launch investigations. "How I would have loved to participate in that debate," said the Minister, who had studied Classics and Comparative Literature at an Old European University: "'*Ex officio*', '*sua sponte*' or '*proprio motu*'; I can hear them arguing about what to call it in a dead language. I thought for sure they would argue about Latin nomenclature as a smokescreen and then trash the whole concept. And then they go ahead and actually give the Prosecutor teeth! All those NGOs ('civil society' if you must) will be out there as they are at the U.N. in the human rights area—sending the Prosecutor material and trying to breathe life into the whole thing. It's mind-boggling. So much for permanent *ad hoc*. This is real."

The train of thought meandered a little. "I'm no feminist," The Minister added, "but I was pleased about getting the gender thing in there, with its truly awesome definition.[9] And pleased that the Holy See lost out in its efforts to muddy the abortion waters by talking about 'human beings.' Good that somebody got in something on the laws of war in non-international armed conflict. We don't have any non-international armed conflict either, so there's a cheap way to make political capital out of those who do. A good example of making rules that apply to other people, without messing with what we do! And I love that Preamble that

---

[8] The "Transitional Provision" allows a state to opt out of jurisdiction over war crimes "alleged to have been committed by its nationals or on its territory" for a period of seven years. Whether anyone will want to take the political heat of taking an action that might be characterized as "reserving the right to commit war crimes for seven years" is another matter. Note that a State Party exercising its opt-out rights is in a stronger position than a non-party whose nationals are alleged to have committed offenses elsewhere, i.e., the scenario discussed in the text.

[9] *See* Rome Statute, art. 7(3):

For the purpose of this Statute, it is understood that the term "gender" refers to the two sexes, male and female, within the context of society. The term "gender" does not indicate any meaning different from the above.

the Little states worked on, Andorra, Liechtenstein, Solomon Islands, Samoa and all. . . . It starts so eloquently with that image about the shattered mosaic which this Court will fix.[10] Of course, I liked even better the original Andorran one about the tapestry being rent asunder.[11] "Rent asunder"—Book of Ezekiel in the King James Version isn't it, all that calamity stuff?[12] Apparently it was culturally inapposite in some places, so it had to go. And they're going to stamp out impunity and deliver on deterrence. But I digress."

"Will Erehwon ratify soon?" asked The Innocent Bystander, seeing that the Minister had warmed to the Statute. "Oh no," said the Minister, "it is a flawed instrument which imposes too many obligations on non-parties. We must stand shoulder to shoulder and protect the other non-parties. Anyway, Erehwon is not big on ratifying multilateral treaties. Our Founding Mothers and Fathers were a bit like those fellows in Philadelphia in 1787, against foreign entanglements, weren't they? Still have some like that in the U.S. Senate. Ours too. You won't believe how long it took us to ratify the 1925 Geneva Protocol on Asphyxiating Gases, or the Genocide Convention, or those pesky human rights treaties everyone seems so keen about. Too destabilizing. Of course, we managed to put in some reservations to each of them. Shame we can't do that with the ICC Statute. We also rather liked the way they did that obfuscatory fix several years back to enable the Americans to become party to the Law of the Sea Convention. Couldn't have done better than that. I suppose that if the Americans ever take the deal they cut and come aboard we will too. What negotiating finesse, still ducking and weaving even after the Diplomatic Conference was long over!"

The Innocent Bystander was obviously missing something. It finally emerged. It seems that the military officials from Erehwon's Friend in the Security Council had presented him with some "talking points," his very own "scenario:" a Soldier from Erehwon gets captured during Operation against Evil Terrorist State ("ETS") carried out on ETS's soil. ETS is a party to the Statute of the ICC. Its agents quickly ship the soldier off to the Hague where he is incarcerated in the dungeons awaiting trial for war crimes. "No-one offered to nuke ETS or the Dutch in order to rescue him?" asked The Innocent Bystander, finally dripping a little sarcasm.[13]

---

[10] In his judgement in the *Pinochet* case, Lord Hutton quotes seven of the eleven paragraphs of the Preamble among the sources he uses to support his argument that "since the end of the Second World War there has been a clear recognition by the international community that certain crimes are so grave and so inhuman that they constitute crimes against international law and that the international community is under a duty to bring to justice a person who commits such crimes." R. v. Bartle and the Commissioner of Police for the Metropolis, *ex parte* Pinochet (H.L. 1999).

[11] U.N. Doc. A/CONF.183/C.1/L.32 (June 30, 1998).

[12] Book of Ezekiel, Chapter 30, verse 16: "Sin shall have great pain, and No shall be rent asunder, and Noph shall have disasters daily."

[13] Some may classify the comment as irony rather than sarcasm: The Innocent Bystander

"Don't be flip. We're talking principle here, not naked power. We have responsibilities and we can't have the likes of ETS interfering with them. Look at what the Statute does. It gives the ICC jurisdiction over a broad array of war crimes. Article 13 talks about the 'exercise of [that] jurisdiction.' It can be taken where a State Party refers a situation in which it appears that one or more crimes within the (subject-matter) jurisdiction have been committed. That dreadful ETS would be a 'State Party.' Then there is a further 'precondition' in Article 12 that the state where the events allegedly occurred or the state of nationality must concur, whether in general or in the specific case. There is that tricky OR in there. Again ETS is the territorial state. Its consent satisfies the precondition. We are the national state, but we don't count! Our boy is lost!"

"It was on their turf," said the Innocent Bystander testily. "You have all those people in jail for terrorist acts on your territory, some of them foreigners even. Anyway, I'm sure he'll get a fair trial, there are state of the art protections for the accused throughout the trial and appeal process. Unlike Nuremberg and Tokyo, there is no capital punishment, although my word that was an ugly issue at Rome! The Statute really takes care of the victims too, and that will be further spelled out in the Rules, but, I suppose that is not at the top of your mind. Still, there are worse places than Dutch jails. Boring though."

The Minister was contemplative. "Perhaps we should have gone to Rome and made sure that potential non-parties were adequately represented, as everybody else seems to have been. And those Germans and upstarts like their former colony Samoa going on about universal jurisdiction over war crimes. That's effectively what is happening here."

At this, The Innocent Bystander's mask of innocence dropped. "Funny, I thought that when you participate in a negotiation like this, you have in mind getting something you can live with at the end, not protecting yourself if you stay out. But let me walk you through the Statute. It's uncanny, but it's almost as if there was an Unseen Hand running interference for non-ratifiers, protecting their sovereign rights. There are so many ways in which your horrible hypothetical is unreal."

---

was referring to the fact that the ICC Statute makes it illegal *per se* to use dum-dum bullets and poison arrows, but not nuclear weapons, chemical, or biological ones, or land-mines. Think also about the power relationships involved. As between itself and Erehwon, ETS has a reasonable chance of exercising its territorial jurisdiction. The involvement of P5 changes the dynamics, as New Zealand discovered in the Rainbow Warrior affair. When agents of the French state sank a Greenpeace ship in Auckland Harbor, killing one of the crew, New Zealand prosecuted the two agents it captured. France responded by an effort to "nuke" part of the New Zealand economy. *See* Roger S. Clark, *state Terrorism: Some Lessons from the Sinking of the "Rainbow Warrior,"* 20 RUTGERS. L.J. 393 (1989). An effective, independent, International Criminal Court may be more secure in acting against the nationals of a powerful state than a small state would be. I regard that as desirable as a matter of policy. A different view of the policy of protecting small states from diplomatic pressure is offered by Madeline Morris, *infra* Chapter 18.

And here is the rest of what The Bystander, no longer Innocent, said:

Let's start with the universal jurisdiction point. I thought it was pretty clear under the Geneva Conventions that all states are supposed to search for those believed to be guilty of war crimes and try them or hand them over to some other state that will do so. In recent years, there has even been some exercise of this obligation. A number of European states have tried people on a universal jurisdiction basis for crimes occurring in the Balkans. At least, I have noted cases in the literature coming out of Switzerland, Germany, Denmark and the Netherlands.[14] If one state can exercise jurisdiction on its own in the name of the international community, why can't it pass that power on to a tribunal representing the whole international community? I thought something like that was the rationale for Nuremberg. I realize that the exact basis for the Nuremberg jurisdiction is debated. On one view, the Allies had power of what you would call the naked variety, as the functioning territorial state or state of nationality, by virtue of the surrender. On another view, they were acting on behalf of the community (or at least the winning team). I find the latter a loftier explanation and I think it's the politically correct one, exercising universal jurisdiction jointly that any one of them might have done alone.[15]

Be that as it may, the Nuremberg Tribunal made the point that what one state could do singly, it could do with a group. Isn't that what the ICC is about? And what if it's applied to non-parties? Sometimes the international community has to have the courage of its convictions. I don't recall that Iraq was asked for its consent to having Bagdad bombed, or that the Serbs were asked which city, if any,

---

[14] *See "Swiss Court Sentences a Rwandan [Niyonteze] to Life,"* PHILADELPHIA INQUIRER, May 2, 1999, at A 20; Swiss Military Tribunal Acquits Bosnian Serb Accused of Inflicting Injury and Degrading Treatment upon Civilians in Bosnian Pow Camps During Summer of 1992, 4 INT'L L. UPDATE 59 (1998) (failure of identification); Horst Fischer, *Some Aspects of German state Practice Concerning IHL,* 1 Y.B. INT'L HUMANITARIAN L. 380 (1998) (*Djajic* and *Jorgic* cases); Director of Public Prosecutions v. T. (Denmark, 1994), 1 Y.B. INT'L HUMANITARIAN L. 431 (conviction for crimes committed in Croatian POW camp); Supreme Court of Netherlands, 1997, Case of Darko Knesevic, 1 Y.B. INT'L HUMANITARIAN L. 600 (1998). When the International Criminal Tribunal for Rwanda relinquished its (concurrent but pre-emptive?) jurisdiction over an accused charged with killing ten Belgian peacekeeping soldiers in Rwanda, this paved the way for Belgium to seek to try them. One might have thought that the Belgian jurisdictional theory was passive personality, but a press release suggested that the theory was in fact one of universal jurisdiction. *See* The Prosecutor v. Bernard Ntuyahaga, ICTR Update, ICTR/UPD–013, Mar. 16, 1999. I appreciate that the Geneva Conventions *require* the exercise of jurisdiction on a universal basis only for grave breaches. What seems to be happening is that some states at least regard themselves as having a *permissive* jurisdiction in cases of "lesser" war crimes. On the distinction between obligatory and permissive jurisdiction, *see generally* Attorney-General of Israel v. Eichmann, 36 I.L.R. 5, 32–39 (Dist. Ct. Jerusalem, 1961) and 277, 289–304 (Sup. Ct. Israel, 1962).

[15] *See generally* William B. Simons, *The Jurisdictional Basis of the International Military Tribunal at Nuremberg, in* THE NUREMBERG TRIAL AND INTERNATIONAL LAW (George Ginsburgs and V.N. Kudriavstsev eds., 1990.).

they would like bombed. If we can bomb without consent, why can't we try without consent for international crimes? The rule of law and all that. It applies to Erehwon, ETS and the P5 alike. It is not as though we are talking some newfangled crimes here. We hit Former Yugoslavia and Rwanda with more sloppily drafted versions of the same offenses and the Statute, frankly, takes a pretty conservative view of what is banned by customary law. Substantive lowest common denominator, some procedural innovation. It seems even less controversial than Nuremberg and Tokyo to me. (The Bystander paused for air.)

You know what bothers me about your attitude? You seem to think it's all right to exercise jurisdiction unilaterally when it suits you; you even concede that right of others to act unilaterally. I didn't see you off making diplomatic protests to the Swiss, the Danes, the Germans and the Dutch about their unilateral efforts on alleged Bosnian criminals. Do you concede their right, a duty even? Is it the very concept of an international tribunal that bothers you? Others find the shift to an international body a very reasonable one. Put it another way: they see even greater legitimacy in an international effort than in a single state's effort. What perverted extreme view of sovereignty accepts unilateral universal jurisdiction (including yours over assorted terrorists) but balks at multilateral universal jurisdiction?[16] Is that your problem? (Getting really worked up, The Bystander was.)

But, it's my turn to digress, the Bystander commented. Let's cut to the chase in the scenario. It's a little difficult for a start to imagine the quick shipping off to the Hague part. The ICC doesn't work like a domestic court system. In domestic law, if a peace officer sees someone apparently committing an offence, she simply arrests the "accused" and then waits for the prosecutor to follow with the details. When ETS arrests your man (it looks as though at this point they have to do it for a breach of ETS law), they are in limbo for a while. They need to refer the "situation" to the Prosecutor in terms of Articles 13 and 14 of the Statute, so that the Prosecutor might determine whether one or more specific persons should be charged. On the face of it, the ICC has no power to hold anybody unless perhaps when they voluntarily surrender or until there is a warrant of arrest issued on a showing made pursuant to Article 58 of the Statute. Your Hypothetical Soldier is not about to go anywhere voluntarily, is he? Have to get an arrest warrant.

While the Prosecutor is trying to get the paperwork under control to apply for an arrest warrant, your Friend in the Security Council may swing into action. Article 16 provides that no investigation or prosecution may be commenced or proceeded with under the Statute for a period of 12 months after the Security Council in a resolution adopted under Chapter VII of the Charter has requested the Court to engage in such a delay. The risk you run, especially if this is an Unauthorized Enforcement Action, is that one of the P5 will veto and allow you

---

[16] Cf. Morris, *supra* note 12.

to stew in your own juice. Not to worry, though, there are plenty more hurdles before your person is in serious jeopardy, even if you stew a bit longer.

Article 18 is probably the next one chronologically, if the Security Council gambit fails. It talks about preliminary rulings regarding admissibility. (Can't say I ever understood exactly what admissibility means, but here it refers to an aspect of complementarity, another word of indeterminate meaning of which more anon. What we are talking about here is taking some jurisdiction away that the ICC might otherwise have.) When a situation has been referred by a State Party and the Prosecutor has determined that there would be a reasonable basis to commence an investigation, the Prosecutor is required to notify "all States Parties and those states which, taking into account the information available, would normally exercise jurisdiction over the crimes concerned." "Those states" obviously include non-parties, such as you in the hypothetical, who "would normally" exercise jurisdiction on the basis of territoriality or nationality, or if you like, because he's your guy. (You have a few Foreign Legion-type riffraff in your force who are not citizens, I suppose.) Now you have a month to inform the Court that you are investigating. Then you ask the Prosecutor to defer and that is effective for six months. I haven't quite figured out what happens to your person during the six months. The ICC has apparently no power to get him to the Hague, unless you can all work out something "voluntary." Perhaps he rots in ETS, perhaps someone leans on ETS. If you can get him back home, he should be safe, because as a non-party you do not have to cooperate in rendering people to the ICC. He'd be wise not to travel in such a case, though, because somebody else might lock him up, à la Pinochet. The deferral may be reviewed after six months. I think it probably ends there, and you win, although there is a complicated procedure involving the Pre-Trial Chamber (and appeals) if the Prosecutor wants to persist. Hurdles galore for the Prosecutor. You will want to investigate carefully won't you, and as a law-abiding state will allow the chips to fall where they may, utilizing your fine system of military justice.

Assuming this doesn't work and somehow the proceedings get to the next stage, you will need to make sure that a challenge to admissibility is mounted under Article 19. Your man and you both have standing to mount such a challenge.

This is perhaps the point to explain about "complementarity." I have to say that term was a new one to me when I first encountered it in the discussion of the ILC Draft and I couldn't find it in my Black's Law Dictionary. How I envied those diplomats who tossed it off their tongues as though they had been using it all their lives! Frauds most of them. What I think it means is that the ICC is a place of last resort. States have jurisdiction over all the offenses under the aegis of the ICC. The ICC's (concurrent) jurisdiction is secondary; theirs is primary. This is not a massive assault on sovereignty. Indeed, it's like human rights monitoring regimes. The whole point about them is to right the occasional wrong, but more important to try to keep states honest and have their own procedures in place. There won't be the resources to do many trials anyway, so there is little danger that the ICC will eat deeply into state criminal (and military) justice systems. It's a pity, though, it might have shaken things up a bit! Domestic legal systems prosecute few of their own war criminals and prosecutors seem pretty inept with the ones they do try. Take Canada in Somalia[17] and the U.S. in My Lai[18] as cases in point.

"Complementarity" got channeled into "admissibility" in the course of the negotiations. Article 17 describes admissibility in terms of its opposite, inadmissibility. A case is inadmissible where:

1. The case is being investigated by a state which has jurisdiction over it, unless the state is unwilling or unable genuinely to carry out the investigation or prosecution;
2. The case has been investigated by a state which has jurisdiction over it and the state has decided not to prosecute the person concerned, unless the decision resulted from the unwillingness or inability of the state genuinely to prosecute.

(Subparagraph c talks about situations of *ne bis in idem*, not relevant here. "*Ne bis*" or "*non bis*"—another truly illuminating debate that you would have loved, Minister! You really should have been there.)

"Unwilling" and "unable" are expanded upon, but you get the drift. It is very unlikely that you would be unable to get the case rendered inadmissible, to pile negative upon negative. Once again you will notice that the reference is to "a state" which includes non-party states. "Complementarity" does the trick. Your guy has little to fear. Do you feel better now?

There is one other provision in the Statute that is sheer inspiration, as part of a long-term strategy to protect the rights of non-parties,[19] although it doesn't seem possible to spring it in the particular situation in your scenario. It is Article 98(2) which reads:

2. The Court may not proceed with a request for surrender which would require the requested state to act inconsistently with its obligations under international agreements pursuant to which consent of a sending state is required to surrender a person of that state to the Court,

[17] *See, e.g.*, Katia Boustany, Brocklebank: *A Questionable Decision of the Court Martial Appeal Court of Canada*, 1 Y.B. INT'L HUMANITARIAN L. 371 (1998).

[18] *See* Roger S. Clark, *Medina: As Essay on Principles of Liability for Homicide*, 5 RUTGERS-CAMDEN L.J. 59 (1973) (inept prosecution in only case other than Lieutenant Calley). On the dearth of domestic prosecutions in general, *see* Axel Marschik, *The Politics of Prosecution: European National Approaches to War Crimes, in* THE LAW OF WAR CRIMES, NATIONAL AND INTERNATIONAL APPROACHES 65 (Timothy L.H. McCormack and Gerry J. Simpson eds., 1997).

[19] There may well be others that I did not find. Nobody is perfect.

unless the Court can first obtain the cooperation of the sending state for the giving of consent to the surrender.

I take it that in your strictly-U.N.-mounted efforts you have a pretty standard Status of Forces Agreement (SOFA) with the U.N. under which members of your force are subject to your exclusive national jurisdiction. That is to say, the SOFA cuts out any potential jurisdiction of a territorial state like ETS. If you have enough clout, you may be able to negotiate some further language in the future that, *ex abundante cautela*, denies the territorial state any power to hand over to the ICC. Only fair, since you are doing them a favor by being there. You can probably negotiate something like that (with the help of your Friend) whenever your presence is more or less voluntary on the part of the receiving state. It might be difficult, though, if you are invading them, or dropping bombs on them from the air. But then, you are just infantry, someone else drops the bombs. You might also be able to work something in advance along the lines of Article 98(2) in future extradition treaties too.[20] Very clever. I love to see professionals at work!

In short, Minister, the Unseen Hand was a genius. The rights of non-state parties are brilliantly protected.

---

[20] The Innocent Bystander's Innocent Intelligence Agency reports that one Large Power, the United States, has been endeavoring to negotiate both Extradition and Status of Forces Agreements with "Article 98(2) clauses."

CHAPTER 18

HIGH CRIMES AND MISCONCEPTIONS: THE ICC AND NON-PARTY STATES

Madeline Morris

A. INTRODUCTION

The Rome Treaty for an International Criminal Court (ICC)[1] provides for the establishment of an international court with jurisdiction over genocide, war crimes, and crimes against humanity.[2] Such crimes often are committed by or with the approval of governments. It is unlikely that a government sponsoring such crimes would consent to the prosecution of its national for his or her participation. Therein lies the problem with an international criminal court that may exercise jurisdiction only if the defendant's state of nationality consents. The very states that are most likely to be implicated in serious international crimes are the least likely to grant jurisdiction over their nationals to an international court.

The ICC Treaty avoids the dismal prospect of an international criminal court that cannot obtain jurisdiction over international criminals by providing that the ICC may exercise jurisdiction even over nationals of states that are not parties to the Treaty and have not otherwise consented to jurisdiction. Article 12 provides that, in addition to jurisdiction based on Security Council action under Chapter VII of the United Nations (U.N.) Charter and jurisdiction based on consent by the defendant's state of nationality, the ICC will have jurisdiction to prosecute the nationals of any state when crimes within the Court's subject-matter jurisdiction are committed on the territory of a state that is a party to the Treaty or that consents to ICC jurisdiction for that case. That territorial basis would empower the Court to exercise jurisdiction even in cases where the defendant's state of nationality is not a party to the Treaty and does not consent to the exercise of jurisdiction.[3]

---

[1] Rome Statute of the International Criminal Court, July 17, 1998, U.N. Doc. A/CONF. 183/9 [hereinafter ICC Treaty], *reprinted in* the Appendix to this volume.

[2] *See id.*, art. 5.

While the ICC Treaty also provides for jurisdiction over the crime of aggression, *see* ICC Treaty, art. 5(1)(d), it further provides that the ICC shall not exercise that part of its subject-matter jurisdiction until such time as the Treaty is amended to include provisions defining the crime of aggression and setting out the conditions under which the Court will exercise jurisdiction over that crime. *See id.*, art. 5(2).

[3] *See* ICC Treaty, art. 12.

The United States has objected to the ICC Treaty on the ground that, by purporting to confer upon the Court jurisdiction over the nationals of non-consenting non-party states, the Treaty would bind non-parties in contravention of the law
of treaties.[4] This objection has given rise to a heated controversy that has focused
on the particulars of the law of treaties and the law of jurisdiction. On close
inspection, however, we can detect a more basic issue struggling to make its way
to the surface.

The fundamental issue concerns the nature of the ICC as an international
institution. The jurisdictional structure of the ICC is based on a view of the ICC
as a criminal court, *tout court.* In this view, the job of the ICC is to adjudicate the
guilt or innocence of individuals accused of recognized international crimes. With
this model in mind, it makes sense to give the Court meaningful powers of compulsory jurisdiction, lest perpetrators of serious international crimes should
escape justice. From this perspective one might reason that, if the Court's subject-
matter jurisdiction is limited to established international crimes and the process
of the Court is fair, then no state—party or non-party—should have legitimate
objections to the Court's exercise of jurisdiction over its nationals.

The deficiency of this approach is that it reflects only one of the two types
of cases that the ICC will be called upon to decide. In addition to the cases that
are concerned solely with individual culpability, there will be ICC cases that focus
on the lawfulness of official acts of states. Even while individuals and not states
will be named in ICC indictments, there will be cases in which those individuals
are indicted for official acts taken pursuant to state policy and under state author-

---

Article 13(a) of the Treaty articulates a third condition permitting the exercise of ICC jurisdiction. Even in the absence of the nationality or territoriality pre-conditions articulated in
Article 12, the ICC may exercise jurisdiction if the case arises from a situation referred to the
ICC Prosecutor by the U.N. Security Council acting under Chapter VII of the U.N. Charter. *See
id.,* art. 13.

Where the defendant's state of nationality is a party to the ICC Treaty or specially consents
to ICC jurisdiction for the case in question, the ICC's jurisdiction is founded on the consent of
the state of nationality. Where ICC jurisdiction is based on Security Council action, the jurisdiction also arguably rests on the consent of the state of nationality (assuming that it is a U.N.
member state) through its membership in the U.N. which encompasses consent to cooperate with
Security Council actions taken under Chapter VII. *See* U.N. CHARTER art. 25. *But see* Brief for
the Appellant, Prosecutor v. Tadić, International Tribunal for the former Yugoslavia, Case No.
IT–94–1–AR72 (arguing that the Security Council is inherently incapable of legitimately establishing a judicial organ). The present article will focus not on these consent-based foundations
for ICC exercise of jurisdiction but, rather, on the territorially-based foundation which, by the
terms of the Treaty, allows the ICC to exercise jurisdiction over nationals of states that have not
consented to its jurisdiction.

4 *See* David Scheffer, U.S. Ambassador at Large for War Crimes Issues, "The International
Criminal Court: The Challenge of Jurisdiction," Address at the Annual Meeting of the American
Society of International Law (Mar. 26, 1999) (on file with author).

ity. These official-act cases may well include cases in which an official state act is characterized as criminal by the ICC prosecutor (acting, very possibly, on a referral from an aggrieved state), while the state whose national is being prosecuted maintains that the act was lawful. One can readily imagine ICC cases in which the act forming the basis for the indictment was a military intervention, deployment of a particular weapon, recourse to a certain method of warfare, or other official conduct that the responsible state maintains was lawful. Or the act forming the basis for the indictment might be an alleged official act that the concerned state maintains never occurred. In these sorts of ICC cases, notwithstanding the presence of individual defendants in the dock, the cases will represent *bona fide* legal disputes between states.

When the ICC is hearing cases in the official-acts category, its function will resemble less that of a municipal criminal court than that of an international court for the adjudication of interstate legal disputes. The shortcomings of the ICC jurisdictional structure and of the arguments that have been advanced in support of that structure stem from the fact that this second aspect of the ICC's character, that of a court for interstate dispute adjudication, is not adequately taken into account.

There is a range of mechanisms for the resolution of interstate disputes. Adjudication is among them, but is not always the approach best suited to a given dispute. Because in many circumstances states see diplomatic, non-adjudicatory dispute resolution as posing fewer risks and offering potentially more constructive resolutions than litigation would, states often are reluctant to submit their disputes to third-party adjudication. As we shall see, states are particularly unwilling to enter into broad commitments to adjudicate future disputes, the content and contours of which cannot be foreseen.

The interest of states in retaining discretion as to their methods of addressing interstate disputes is reflected in the jurisdictional structures of the International Court of Justice (ICJ) and of specialized international courts such as the Law of the Sea Tribunal and the World Trade Organization (WTO) dispute settlement system. The constituting instruments of those international courts reserve to states broad discretion over whether and when those courts will have decision-making authority.

The drafters of the ICC Treaty faced the dilemma of needing to fashion a jurisdictional scheme for the ICC that would be sufficiently aggressive to make the Court effective in the prosecution of criminals but also sufficiently consensual to make the Court a suitable institution for the adjudication of international disputes. A genuine quandary is posed by the need for a jurisdictional structure that will foster the ICC's effectiveness as a criminal court without engendering overreaching by the ICC into areas of interstate dispute settlement in which states have legitimate rights of discretion regarding methods and fora. The following discussion attempts to gain some purchase on the issue of the ICC's jurisdiction over non-party nationals by considering the Court's jurisdictional structure in the light of this dilemma.

The present chapter begins with a section examining the interests of states with respect to the jurisdiction of international courts and the consequent patterns in the jurisdictional structures of existing international courts. That section will conclude by evaluating the significant differences between the jurisdictional structure of the ICC and that of other international courts in light of the ICC's dual character as the adjudicator of individual culpability and of interstate legal disputes. Proceeding from that analytic basis, the subsequent sections will examine the strengths and the shortcomings of the theories supporting ICC jurisdiction over non-party nationals. The chapter will conclude that the ICC's jurisdictional structure and, more specifically, its provision for jurisdiction over non-party nationals, cannot be satisfactorily justified and that this is so, ultimately, because the ICC's role as an adjudicator of interstate disputes is not adequately accounted for in the Court's jurisdictional design.

B. THE JURISDICTION TO ADJUDICATE INTERSTATE DISPUTES

States are notoriously reluctant to submit their disputes to binding third-party adjudication. Despite a dramatic increase in the use of binding third-party adjudication at the international level in recent years, the use of such mechanisms to resolve international disputes remains minimal in comparison with the use of diplomatic means for addressing such disputes. The relative dearth of interstate disputes brought to the ICJ has given rise to extended consideration of why states make such limited use of the ICJ and how greater use might be encouraged.[5] The fact, quickly noted in discussions of the limited state use of the ICJ, is that states—perhaps more specifically, foreign ministry officials—are reluctant to relinquish control over their disputes to third parties, on either an *ad hoc* or a compulsory basis.[6] Such reluctance may be partly explained by states' concerns with a court's procedures or structure.[7] But even in the absence of such concerns,

---

[5] *See, e.g.*, JOHN G. MERRILLS, INTERNATIONAL DISPUTE SETTLEMENT 164–66, 285–311 (3d ed. 1998); Arthur Rovine, *The National Interest and the World Court, in* I THE FUTURE OF THE INTERNATIONAL COURT OF JUSTICE (Leo Gross ed., 1976); Gerald Fitzmaurice, *Enlargement of the Contentious Jurisdiction of the Court, in* II THE FUTURE OF THE INTERNATIONAL COURT OF JUSTICE 461–98 (Leo Gross ed., 1976); JUDICIAL SETTLEMENT OF INTERNATIONAL DISPUTES (H. Mosler & R. Bernhardt eds., 1974); L.V. Prott, *The Future of the International Court of Justice*, 33 Y.B. WORLD AFF. 284 (1979).

[6] *See* Rovine, *supra* note 5, at 317; Richard Bilder, *Some Limitations of Adjudication as an International Dispute Settlement Technique*, 23 VA. J. INT'L L. 1, 2–4 (1982); Richard Falk, *Realistic Horizons for International Adjudication*, 11 VA. J. INT'L L. 315, 321–22 (1971).

[7] *See* Leo Gross, *The International Court of Justice: Consideration of Requirements for Enhancing Its Role in the International Legal Order, in* I THE FUTURE OF THE INTERNATIONAL COURT OF JUSTICE 22–104 (Leo Gross ed., 1976); Edvard Hambro, *Will the Revised Rules of Court Lead to Greater Willingness on the Part of Prospective Clients?, in* I THE FUTURE OF THE

there is a more fundamental reluctance to submit to third-party adjudication that rests on the perceived advantages to states in some circumstances of retaining control over the resolution of their disputes.[8] As Arthur Rovine has put it, "It is one thing to show that resort to the ICJ is preferable to war or armed conflict; it is quite another matter to demonstrate that judicial processes are as valuable as ordinary out-of-court bargaining and discussion."[9]

Resolving interstate disputes through negotiation and other diplomatic means often is perceived by states as less risky and potentially more constructive than submitting the disputes for third-party adjudication. This is so for a number of reasons. Diplomatic approaches maintain the possibility of leaving the issue in abeyance should matters develop such that non-resolution appears preferable to immediate resolution.[10] Diplomatic methods are likely to result in less damage to the standing and prestige of the losing state, if there is in fact an identifiable loser. This consideration is heightened in cases where a loss would entail a finding that the losing state had been engaged in wrongdoing. In addition, diplomatically negotiated resolutions do not create legal precedents in the way that reasoned and published legal opinions inevitably do.[11] states may fear the creation of an authoritative (even if not binding) precedent contrary to their interests and, moreover, may object to the prospect of an international court, in effect, legislating international law where the litigated issue concerns an unsettled area of law.[12] Another influential factor is that, in a dispute between any two states, one party is likely to have a political advantage, a stronger bargaining position, that would be significant in the diplomatic arena but might be of little effect in an adjudicated settlement.[13] Moreover, diplomacy leaves room for compromise resolutions that adjudication generally does not.[14] Retaining control over a dispute allows states to respond in a nimble and nuanced way as a controversy and the options for its resolution unfold. All of this states are unwilling to give up wholesale.

INTERNATIONAL COURT OF JUSTICE 365–76 (Leo Gross ed., 1976); Leo Gross, *Review of the Role of the International Court of Justice*, 66 AM. J. INT'L L. 479 (1972).

[8] *See* Rovine, *supra* note 5; Fitzmaurice, *supra* note 5, at 462–73.

[9] Rovine, *supra* note 5, at 314.

[10] *See id.* at 317, 319.

[11] *See* Paul Szasz, *Enhancing the Advisory Competence of the World Court, in* II THE FUTURE OF THE INTERNATIONAL COURT OF JUSTICE 499–549 (Leo Gross ed., 1976) ("[T]he prospect that increased activity by the Court will help fill interstices in the international legal fabric or even expand its bounds, is likely to constitute, among diplomats, a negative rather than a positive argument for [enhancing the court's caseload].").

[12] *See* Rovine, *supra* note 5, at 315–16.

[13] *See id., supra* note 5, at 319–20.

[14] *See* Rovine, *supra* note 5, at 317; Bilder, *supra* note 6, at 2–4; Falk, *supra* note 6, at 321–22.

Generally, the more important and sensitive the subject of a dispute is to a state, the less willing the state is to submit the dispute for third-party adjudication.[15] Equally, the more uncertain the adjudicated outcome of a particular dispute would be, the less willing a state will be to seek binding third-party adjudication.[16] By extension, if states frequently are unwilling to submit for adjudication disputes that are important and whose adjudicated outcomes would be uncertain, states also will be unwilling to make broad grants of jurisdiction in advance that could later prove to include important disputes whose adjudicated outcomes would be uncertain.

As Professor Merrills has observed,

> Probably the most striking feature of adjudication is that it is dispositive. Because the decisions of courts and tribunals are treated as binding, litigation is a good way of disposing of a troublesome issue when the resolution of a dispute is considered to be more important than the result. Conversely, when the result is all-important, adjudication is unlikely to be used because it is simply too risky. These attitudes are reinforced by the fact that adjudication is not merely dispositive, but tends to produce a winner-takes-all type of solution. This can obviously render an unfavourable outcome a catastrophe and so encourages states to choose other procedures for disputes which they cannot afford to lose.
>
> Because adjudication is dispositive the attitude of states toward compulsory jurisdiction is conspicuously ambivalent. On the one hand, there is a good deal of support for the principle of the optional clause and similar arrangements [allowing states to consent in advance to the jurisdiction of an international court over future disputes, subject to such reservations as each state may make], since the idea of establishing a binding system to resolve international disputes is an attractive one. On the other hand, as soon as such arrangements are established, states become aware of the risks involved in a commitment to litigate disputes which cannot be foreseen and begin to have second thoughts. The result . . . is a reluctance to subscribe to the more general arrangements for compulsory jurisdiction and a preference for agreements concerned either with particular types of cases or individual disputes.[17]

Certainly, states sometimes do choose to submit their disputes for third-party adjudication. But, cognizant of both the advantages and the drawbacks of adjudication, states jealously guard their prerogative to select the circumstances under which they will do so. States' insistence on this prerogative has, in general, been

---

[15] *See* Rovine, *supra* note 5, at 319–20; Fitzmaurice, *supra* note 5, at 488; Falk, *supra* note 6, at 321.

[16] *See* Fitzmaurice, *supra* note 5, at 473; Szasz, *supra* note 11, at 511.

[17] MERRILLS, *supra* note 5, at 293–94.

viewed as legitimate (even while many have sought to expand consensual use of the ICJ[18]) and has been reflected in the treaties providing for third-party adjudicatory mechanisms.

All existing international courts have contentious jurisdiction[19] only over states that are parties to treaties providing for their jurisdiction.[20] Inspection of those treaties reveals that, in general, states have not seen fit to relinquish discretion over jurisdiction entirely, even by treaty. Rather, the treaties establishing international courts have been designed to afford states Parties significant continuing discretion over the powers that the respective courts will have relative to jurisdiction and, relatedly, to remedies. This is true of the ICJ, the Tribunal on the Law of the Sea, and the WTO dispute settlement system, which will serve as three principal examples, as well as of other international courts.[21]

---

[18] *See, e.g.*, sources cited *supra* note 5.

[19] The contentious jurisdiction of an international court is the court's jurisdiction to decide interstate disputes as distinct from its authority to render advisory opinions or to exercise other, incidental powers.

[20] *See* UNITED NATIONS, HANDBOOK ON THE PEACEFUL SETTLEMENT OF DISPUTES BETWEEN STATES 70 (1992) ("Settlement of international disputes by international courts is subject to the recognition by the states concerned of the jurisdiction of the courts over such disputes.").

[21] *See generally, id.*; MERRILLS, *supra* note 5 (providing a survey of the jurisdictional and other features of international dispute resolution mechanisms); INTERNATIONAL DISPUTES: THE LEGAL ASPECTS (C.M.H. Waldock ed., 1972) (same).

The European Court of Justice (ECJ) and the European Court of Human Rights (ECHR) provide contrasting examples insofar as each has automatic jurisdiction over States Parties to the treaties establishing the court. On examination, however, we see that neither of those courts in fact constitutes a counterexample to the proposition that states generally maintain significant continuing discretion over the powers that international courts will have relative to jurisdiction and, relatedly to remedies.

The ECJ must be distinguished from other international courts because it is the court of the European Communities. The European Communities, even while they are constituted by inter-state organizations, are part of a system of close regional economic integration. We would expect that the degree of authority that member states would be willing to vest in the European Communities' court would be greater than that which states would ordinarily be willing to vest in an international court that was not a constitutive part of an integrated regional economic system.

The ECHR, by contrast, is a creature of the Council of Europe. *See* FRANCIS JACOBS & ROBIN WHITE, THE EUROPEAN CONVENTION ON HUMAN RIGHTS 3–4 (1996). The ECHR has jurisdiction over "all matters concerning the interpretation and application of the [European] Convention [on Human Rights]," European Convention on Human Rights, art. 32 (1), including violations by States Parties of that convention and the human rights delineated therein. *See id.* arts. 33, 34. However, while the jurisdiction of the ECHR is compulsory, the provisions for remedies and for enforcement of ECHR decisions leave those matters to be decided largely through diplomatic and political processes within the Council of Europe. Where the court finds that a State Party has committed a violation, its judgment will so indicate and provide the reasons for its finding. It may also award compensation and costs. *See* LUKE CLEMENTS ET AL., EUROPEAN HUMAN RIGHTS: TAKING A CASE UNDER THE CONVENTION 103 (1999). It will not,

The contentious jurisdiction of the ICJ depends on the consent of the states that are parties to the dispute.[22] Consent to ICJ jurisdiction may be given in advance either through a compromissory clause in a treaty providing that some or all categories of disputes arising under that treaty will be submitted to the ICJ or through a declaration under the ICJ Statute's "optional clause."[23] By making a declaration under the optional clause, a state agrees to accept the ICJ's jurisdiction for some or all categories of future disputes.

A compromissory treaty clause giving jurisdiction to the ICJ tends to be more readily acceptable to states where the clause concerns a narrowly defined subject matter[24] than where the jurisdiction conferred is more open-ended.[25] States' practice in the use of the optional clause of the ICJ Statute shows similar tendencies for States to be conservative with regard to making grants of jurisdiction in advance. Less than a third of the members of the United Nations currently have in force declarations under the optional clause,[26] and many of

---

however, specify other measures, such as legal or structural reforms, that the offending State Party might need to take to remedy the violation (for example, where the violation is ongoing). *See id.* The Convention provides that "[t]he judgment of the Court shall be transmitted to the Committee of Ministers which shall supervise its execution." European Convention on Human Rights, Art. 46 (2). The Committee of Ministers is comprised of the foreign ministers of the member states of the Council of Europe. *See* CLEMENTS ET AL., *supra*, at 9–10. That Committee, in some cases, then negotiates with the offending State Party concerning what remedial measures will be taken. The Convention does not provide for sanctions for failure to implement an ECHR decision. Therefore, the actions that may be taken by the Committee of Ministers in negotiating the remedial measures for an ECHR decision and in ensuring its enforcement are limited to various forms of political pressure. *See* JACOBS & WHITE, *supra*, at 398. In sum, the power ceded to the ECHR in the court's jurisdictional structure is somewhat qualified by the remedial and enforcement structures.

[22] *See generally,* MERRILLS, *supra* note 5, at 121–45 (on the organization and procedures of the ICJ).

[23] *See* Statute of the International Court of Justice, June 26, 1945, art. 36(2), 59 Stat. 1055, 3 Bevans 1179 [hereinafter ICJ Statute].

[24] *See, e.g.,* Optional Protocol to the Vienna Convention on Diplomatic Relations Concerning the Compulsory Settlement of Disputes, Apr. 18, 1961, T.I.A.S. 7502, 500 U.N.T.S. 241, attached to the Vienna Convention on Diplomatic Relations, Apr. 18, 1961, T.I.A.S. 7502, 500 U.N.T.S. 95; Optional Protocol to the Vienna Convention on Consular Relations Concerning the Compulsory Settlement of Disputes, Apr. 24, 1963, T.I.A.S. 6820, 596 U.N.T.S. 487, attached to the Vienna Convention on Consular Relations, Apr. 24, 1963, T.I.A.S. 6820, 596 U.N.T.S. 261. The Optional Protocol and Convention of 1961 have 61 and 174 parties respectively. The Optional Protocol and Convention of 1963 have 44 and 153 parties respectively. *See* CHRISTIAN L. WIKTOR, MULTILATERAL TREATY CALENDAR 1648–1994, 726–27 (1998).

[25] *See, e.g.,* American Treaty on Pacific Settlement, Apr. 30, 1948, 30 U.N.T.S. 55 ("Pact of Bogata"); European Convention for the Peaceful Settlement of Disputes, Apr. 29, 1957, 320 U.N.T.S. 243, each of which has thirteen States Parties, many of whom have attached significant reservations. *See* WIKTOR, *supra* note 24, at 485, 657.

[26] *See* MERRILLS, *supra* note 5, at 123. *See also* John Merrills, *The Optional Clause Revisited,* 64 BRIT. Y.B. INT'L L. 197 (1993) (analyzing states' practice in use of the optional clause).

those states have made reservations substantially limiting the effect of their declarations.[27]

If consent to ICJ jurisdiction covering a given dispute has not been expressed in advance, the dispute may nevertheless be submitted for ICJ adjudication by special agreement of the parties.[28] In making such a special agreement, the parties may frame the legal issue in dispute and, to some extent, the basis on which the court should decide the issue.[29] Even in cases when the ICJ would have jurisdiction on another basis, the parties may choose for the ICJ to adjudicate pursuant to a special agreement.[30]

The jurisdiction of the ICJ, based as it is on a combination of compromissory clauses, optional-clause declarations, and special agreements, is quite thoroughly consent-based. Unsurprisingly, controversies have arisen regarding whether the interests of a non-consenting, third-party state would, in effect, be adjudicated in a case brought by other parties before the court. In the *Monetary Gold* case, four states that wished to submit a dispute for adjudication had all accepted ICJ jurisdiction. The ICJ nevertheless declined to adjudicate the case because Albania, whose property rights were the subject of the dispute, had not so consented.[31] The principle of the *Monetary Gold* decision has subsequently been further clarified. In the *Nicaragua* case, the ICJ held that the requirement for consent to jurisdiction by each party to the dispute applied only where the legal interests of the non-consenting state "would not only be affected by a decision, but would form the very subject matter of the decision."[32]

The ICC Treaty's jurisdictional provisions stand in stark contrast to those of the ICJ Statute. In ICC cases in which a state's national is prosecuted for an official act that the state maintains was lawful or that the state maintains did not occur, the lawfulness or the occurrence of that official state act—that is, the question whether the state had a right to take such action or whether it did so—would

---

[27] *See id. See generally*, Szasz, *supra* note 11, at 511 (observing that "[s]tates are reluctant to submit to international courts, particularly in broad terms and in advance. . . .").

[28] *See* ICJ Statute, art. 36(1); UNITED NATIONS, HANDBOOK ON THE PEACEFUL SETTLEMENT OF DISPUTES BETWEEN STATES, *supra* note 20, at 71–72 and cases cited therein.

[29] *See* MERRILLS, *supra* note 5, at 122–23.

[30] *See, e.g.*, Arbitral Award Made by the King of Spain on Dec. 23, 1906 (Hond. v. Nicar.), 1960 I.C.J. 192 (Judgment of Nov. 20) (exercising jurisdiction pursuant to a special agreement notwithstanding that the court also would have had jurisdiction on other bases).

[31] *See* Monetary Gold Removed from Rome in 1943 (Italy v. Fr., U.K., and U.S.), 1954 I.C.J. 19 (June 15).

[32] Concerning Military and Paramilitary Activities in and Against Nicaragua (Nicar. v. U.S.), 1984 I.C.J. 431(Jurisdiction and Admissibility Judgment of Nov. 26). *See also*, Certain Phosphate Lands in Nauru (Nauru v. Austl.), 1992 I.C.J. 240 (Preliminary Objections and Judgment of June 26) (following same rationale); Concerning East Timor (Port. v. Austl.), 1995 I.C.J. 90 (Judgment of June 30) (same).

"form the very subject matter of the dispute." Yet, by the terms of the ICC Treaty, the ICC would exercise jurisdiction in that case with or without the consent of the state whose official acts would form the subject of the adjudication.

Not only the ICJ with its open-ended subject-matter jurisdiction, but also international courts of limited subject-matter jurisdiction have jurisdictional structures providing significant discretion to states. Two principal examples of such courts are the Tribunal on the Law of the Sea[33] and the WTO dispute settlement mechanism.[34]

The United Nations Convention on the Law of the Sea (UNCLOS) provides that, if states are unable to settle their disputes relating to the convention through a prompt "exchange of views,"[35] then the convention's "Compulsory Procedures Entailing Binding Decisions" come into operation.[36] Those procedures afford to states an array of methods of binding dispute resolution from which they may select.

UNCLOS provides that each State Party make a declaration accepting the jurisdiction of at least one of four enumerated tribunals: the International Tribunal for the Law of the Sea, the ICJ, an arbitral tribunal, and a special arbitral tribunal. If both parties have accepted the same tribunal, then that tribunal (or another to which both parties agree) will be used. In the absence of such a match, the dispute may be referred to arbitration.

In addition to the considerable flexibility afforded by UNCLOS regarding methods of binding settlement, the Convention also exempts from the compulsory settlement system certain subject areas.[37] Article 297 exempts from compulsory settlement disputes relating to enumerated areas that involve the sovereign rights

---

[33]   United Nations Convention on the Law of the Sea, Dec. 10, 1982, Annex VI, Statute for the International Tribunal for the Law of the Sea, 21 I.L.M. 1345.

[34]   Agreement Establishing the World Trade Organization, Apr. 15, 1994, Annex 2, Understanding on Rules and Procedures Governing the Settlement of Disputes, 33 I.L.M. 1226 [hereinafter DSU].

For comprehensive treatments of the mechanisms for settlement of interstate disputes on specified subject areas, *see* UNITED NATIONS, HANDBOOK ON THE PEACEFUL SETTLEMENT OF DISPUTES BETWEEN STATES, *supra* note 20, 135–53; INTERNATIONAL DISPUTES: THE LEGAL ASPECTS, *supra* note 21, ch. 4.

[35]   United Nations Convention on the Law of the Sea, *opened for signature* Dec. 10, 1982, art. 283, 21 I.L.M. 1261 [hereinafter UNCLOS].

[36]   *See id.*, Part IV § 2.

The Convention also provides for a specialized Sea-Bed Dispute Chamber with jurisdiction specific to disputes regarding the Convention's arrangements regarding the deep sea-bed. *See* MERRILLS, *supra* note 5, at 187–90.

[37]   *See* UNCLOS, *supra* note 35, arts. 297–98.

of coastal states.[38] Article 298 permits exemption, at the option of each state party, of disputes relating to sea boundary delimitations and related matters, disputes being addressed by the U.N. Security Council and, most significantly for comparison with the ICC, disputes concerning military activities.[39] For disputes concerning these specified subject areas, the UNCLOS dispute settlement mechanisms otherwise applicable are available, but can be used only with the consent of all parties to the dispute.[40] The UNCLOS dispute resolution mechanisms thus retain considerable discretion for states regarding the forms of binding third-party settlement that they will accept and, equally significantly, allow states to exempt entirely from compulsory jurisdiction disputes concerning particularly sensitive areas, including military activities.

The WTO dispute settlement system is organized in rather a different way, still reserving to states significant flexibility relating to third-party adjudications, but providing that flexibility more in the remedy provisions than in the jurisdictional structure. The WTO Dispute Settlement Understanding (DSU)[41] provides that, when diplomatic means are unavailing in resolving a dispute arising under the covered trade agreements,[42] the dispute will be settled through the Dispute Settlement Body (DSB). In somewhat simplified form, the DSU provides that the DSB will create a panel which will assess the facts and law of the dispute and "make such other findings as will assist the DSB in making the recommendation or in giving the rulings provided for in the covered agreements."[43] The panel's final report must, within sixty days of its submission, be adopted by the DSB unless either there is a consensus within the DSB not to adopt or a party has given notice of appeal.[44] Appeals are limited to issues of law.[45] The appellate report is submitted to the DSB and must be unconditionally accepted by the parties unless the DSB decides by consensus not to adopt the report.[46]

The WTO dispute settlement system thus provides for little flexibility as to procedures and mechanisms. Perhaps as a consequence, substantial discretion is left to states elsewhere in the dispute settlement system. The remedy mechanism introduces considerable flexibility.

---

[38] *See id.*, art. 297.

[39] *See id.*, art. 298.

[40] *See id.*, art. 299.

[41] *See* DSU, *supra* note 34 .

[42] *See id.*, arts. 4–5.

[43] *Id.*, art. 11.

[44] *See* MERRILLS, *supra* note 5, at 205–08.

[45] *See* DSU, *supra* note 34 , art. 17(6).

[46] *See id.*, art. 17(14).

The possible remedies for violations of the covered trade agreements are several, ranging from the offending state's promptly bringing its practice into compliance, to that state's indicating that the practice will remain out of compliance "temporarily" (for an unspecified period) and then either paying compensation or doing nothing at all and standing subject to retorsion by the opposing state.[47] More specifically, when a panel report or, in case of appeal, the Appellate Body report holds that a state's trade measure is inconsistent with a covered agreement, the report must recommend that the measure be brought into compliance.[48] Within thirty days of adoption of that report, the state concerned must indicate its intentions relative to implementing that recommendation.[49] In the event that the compliance recommendation is not implemented within a reasonable period,[50] the offending state is obliged to negotiate with the complaining state "with a view to developing mutually acceptable compensation."[51] If no compensation arrangement has been agreed to within a reasonable period, then the complaining state may request the DSB to authorize countermeasures.[52] More precisely, the complaining state may request that the DSB authorize suspension of the complaining state's concessions or other obligations under the covered agreement in relation to the state in default.[53] By such a suspension of concessions and obligations, the complaining state is freed to take countermeasures. Should the level of countermeasures permitted be disputed by the offending state, then that level may be set by binding arbitration.[54]

The net result of such a suspension of concessions and obligations is, in a sense, to return the disputing parties to a regime of diplomatic, non-adjudicatory dispute resolution relative to the specific issue in dispute. Certainly, that diplomatic process would proceed very much in the light of the fact that the DSB had identified a violation and had authorized countermeasures. But the dispute would have been returned, in that posture, for diplomatic resolution by the parties. In that way, even while the WTO dispute settlement system provides for compulsory third-party decision making, the remedy mechanism is designed in such a way that, if an offending state chooses to neither bring its practice into compliance nor pay compensation, it may return the dispute to the realm of diplomatic interstate dispute resolution. The discretion regarding methods of dispute resolution that states give up in the jurisdictional aspects of the WTO dispute settlement system they thus partially recover in the remedy provisions.

---

[47] *See id.*, arts. 19–22.

[48] *See id.*, art. 19(1).

[49] *Id.*, art. 21.

[50] Regarding determination of reasonable time periods, *see id.*

[51] *Id.*, art. 22(2).

[52] *See id.*, art. 22.

[53] *See id.*

[54] *See id.*, art. 22(6).

We should note also, before leaving our discussion of the WTO dispute settlement system, the national security exception in the WTO system. Article XXI of the General Agreement on Tariffs and Trade, which forms a major part of the substantive law of the WTO, provides that,

> Nothing in this Agreement shall be construed
>
> a. to require any contracting party to furnish any information the disclosure of which it considers contrary to its essential security interests; or
>
> b. to prevent any contracting party from taking any action which it considers necessary for the protection of its essential security interests
>
> > i. relating to fissionable materials or the materials from which they are derived;
> >
> > ii. relating to traffic in arms, ammunition and implements of war and to such traffic in other goods and materials as is carried on directly or indirectly for the purpose of supplying a military establishment;
> >
> > iii. taken in time of war or other emergency in international relations; or
>
> c. to prevent any contracting party from taking any action in pursuance of its obligations under the United Nations Charter for the maintenance of international peace and security.[55]

Here we see, once again, that even when states are willing to grant some degree of authority over settlement of interstate disputes to a third-party decision maker, military and security-related matters are frequently exempted from that jurisdiction.

In looking at the relevant provisions of the ICJ Statute, UNCLOS, and the WTO's Dispute Settlement Understanding, we have seen that each treaty provides to states considerable discretion over the degree and type of authority that the respective courts will have over interstate disputes. The jurisdictional provisions of the ICC Treaty, by contrast, provide for no such discretion. Rather, the ICC Treaty provides that the ICC may exercise jurisdiction over the national of any state when crimes within the Court's subject-matter jurisdiction are committed on the territory of a state that has consented to the Court's jurisdiction.[56]

---

[55] General Agreement on Tariffs and Trade, Oct. 30, 1947, art. XXI, 61 Stat. A3, 55 U.N.T.S. 187.

[56] The ICC Treaty contains "admissibility" provisions that would deprive the ICC of the authority to exercise its jurisdiction under certain circumstances. A case is not admissible before the ICC if

On the surface, the very easy explanation for this difference in the nature of the ICC's jurisdiction from that of other international courts is that the other courts' purpose is to adjudicate disputes between states while the ICC's purpose is to adjudicate the criminal liability of individuals. If individuals have committed the crimes of genocide, war crimes, and crimes against humanity, which the community of states has already agreed are serious international crimes, then their prosecution can hardly be likened to a dispute between states. This difference between the missions of the ICC and other international courts might be thought entirely to justify the uniquely non-consensual basis of ICC jurisdiction.

To some extent, this explanation is cogent. For ICC cases concerned strictly with individual culpability, the ICC will have much in common with municipal criminal courts and relatively little in common with the other international courts such as the ICJ. A complexity arises, however, from the fact that, in addition to cases that are purely of the individual-culpability type, the ICC also will hear cases in which official acts—acts that the state in question maintains were lawful or whose very occurrence the state disputes—form the basis for an indictment.[57] In such cases, the lawfulness of the official acts of states will be adjudicated by the ICC. When the ICC is operating in this capacity, it will have less in common with municipal criminal courts and a great deal in common with other international courts such as the ICJ.

Since cases before the ICC will necessarily involve allegations of genocide, war crimes or crimes against humanity,[58] the subject matter of an ICC case of the interstate-dispute type will likely be considered important and sensitive by the

---

a. [t]he case is being investigated or prosecuted by a state which has jurisdiction over it, unless the state is unwilling or unable genuinely to carry out the investigation or prosecution;

b. [t]he case has been investigated by a state which has jurisdiction over it and the state has decided not to prosecute the person concerned, unless the decision resulted from the unwillingness or inability of the state genuinely to prosecute.

ICC Treaty, *supra* note 1, art. 17(a), (b). But those admissibility provisions do not address the fact that the state whose official acts are at issue may view those acts as lawful and, therefore, may see no basis for investigation or prosecution. In addition, the Treaty leaves undefined the type and extent of investigation required, the circumstances in which prosecution is required after investigation, and how much information about the investigation (including potentially sensitive data) may be required to satisfy the Court that the state has met its burden in demonstrating that it is neither unwilling nor unable to handle the matter properly at the national level. Therefore, while the admissibility provisions do ameliorate the problems of ICC jurisdiction, those provisions do not adequately respond to the concerns arising from the ultimate fact that the ICC's jurisdiction does not require that the defendant's state of nationality be a party to the Treaty or otherwise consent to ICC jurisdiction.

[57] The two different types of cases that will come before the ICC may not appear as pure types; any given case may have elements of each. For purposes of analysis, however, it will be useful to distinguish between cases of these two distinct characters.

[58] *See supra* note 2 and accompanying text.

involved states. The probable involvement of military activities would tend to heighten the sensitive nature of the cases. And, given the relatively undeveloped state of the law in this field,[59] the adjudicated outcome of such a dispute is likely to be uncertain. Such disputes, then, are of precisely the sort that states are most reluctant to submit for third-party adjudication.[60] While the prerogative of states to choose whether to adjudicate such disputes is protected in the ICJ Statute and other international court treaties, that prerogative has been overlooked in the drafting of the ICC Treaty.

This oversight may be attributable in part to the drafters of the ICC Treaty's having viewed the ICC primarily in its capacity as a criminal court determining individual guilt or innocence. Perhaps, in addition, some states wished to use ICC jurisdiction to effectuate a change in interstate power relations by moving an important category of interstate disputes out of the diplomatic realm and into that of compulsory adjudication. As Arthur Rovine has noted, "weaker states derive an obvious advantage from legal settlement in disputes with more powerful opponents. . . . Clearly, the strong give up much of their leverage in a contest of legal briefs and argumentation."[61] Or some participants in the ICC negotiations may have wished to expand the power of international institutions, including courts, without regard to the resultant redistribution of power among particular states.

Whatever were the motivating factors, the failure to protect states' prerogatives regarding jurisdiction over interstate disputes was bound to engender significant resistance to the ICC Treaty, some of which has already been manifested.[62] In addition to these political consequences, the failure to retain states' discretion regarding jurisdiction over interstate disputes also has legal implications that must be taken into account in any comprehensive analysis of the lawfulness of ICC jurisdiction over non-party nationals.

A number of theories have been advanced in support of the lawfulness of ICC jurisdiction over non-party nationals. While some of these theories have considerable initial appeal, none ultimately provides a satisfactory foundation for the form of jurisdiction claimed for the ICC. The shortcomings of these theories, as we shall see in the remaining sections of this chapter, are largely attributable to the fact that the jurisdictional provisions and the theories offered in their support focus on ICC cases of the individual-culpability type without attending to the legal implications of the fact that the ICC will also adjudicate cases of the interstate-dispute variety.

---

[59] *See infra* pp. 238–41.

[60] *See supra* pp. 222–25.

[61] Rovine, *supra* note 5, at 319.

[62] *See supra* p. 220, *infra* p. 279.

C. THEORIES OF DELEGATED JURISDICTION

As reflected in the Vienna Convention on the Law of Treaties,[63] treaties cannot "create . . . obligations" for non-parties.[64] The United States has claimed that the ICC Treaty, by providing for ICC jurisdiction over non-party nationals, violates this principle of the law of treaties.[65] The United States may have stated its complaint somewhat too simply. The ICC Treaty does not, *per se*, impose "obligations" (in the sense of duties or responsibilities) on non-parties by providing for jurisdiction over their nationals.[66]

The legal objection to ICC jurisdiction over non-party nationals is perhaps better articulated as a claim that the ICC Treaty, by conferring upon the ICC jurisdiction over non-party nationals, would abrogate the pre-existing rights of non-parties which, in turn, would violate the law of treaties. As the International Law Commission's official Commentaries on the Vienna Convention state, "International tribunals have been firm in laying down that in principle treaties, whether bilateral or multilateral, neither impose obligations on States which are not parties *nor modify in any way their legal rights* without their consent."[67] As Judge Huber stated rather succinctly in the *Island of Palmas* arbitration, "whatever may be the right construction of a treaty, it cannot be interpreted as disposing of the rights of independent third Powers."[68] ICC jurisdiction over non-party nationals would appear to be exorbitant jurisdiction under international law, as shall be discussed below. The right of a state to be free from the exercise of exorbitant jurisdiction over its nationals cannot be abrogated by a treaty to which it is not a party.

The legal basis for objection to ICC jurisdiction over non-party nationals turns, then, on the proposition that such jurisdiction would be exorbitant under the international law of jurisdiction. This proposition therefore requires careful scrutiny. The first critical question will be whether the traditional bases for states'

---

[63] *Opened for signature* May 23, 1969, arts. 34–38, 1155 U.N.T.S. 331, 8 I.L.M. 679.

[64] *See id.,* art. 34.

[65] *See supra* p. 220.

[66] *See* Philippe Kirsch, *The Rome Conference on the International Criminal Court: A Comment,* ASIL NEWSLETTER, 1 (Nov./Dec. 1998).

[67] Report of the International Law Commission on the Work of Its Eighteenth Session, "Draft Articles on the Law of Treaties with Commentaries, II Y.B. OF THE INT'L L. COMM'N 226 (1966) (Commentary to Draft Art. 30, "General Rule Regarding Third States") (emphasis added).

See also ARNOLD MCNAIR, THE LAW OF TREATIES 321 (1961) ("A State which learns that a treaty concluded between two other States has for its object or probable consequence the impairment of its rights, whether enjoyed under customary international law or under a treaty with one of the contracting parties, is entitled at once to lodge a diplomatic protest with those parties and to apply to the International Court of Justice . . . for a declaration and . . . for interim measures of protection.")

[68] Island of Palmas: U.N. Reports of International Arbitral Awards ii, 829, 842.

jurisdiction provide a legal foundation for ICC jurisdiction over non-party nationals. If, for example, the jurisdiction to be exercised by the ICC were the pre-existing jurisdiction of States Parties which they had delegated to the Court, then, arguably, the ICC Treaty, far from conferring exorbitant jurisdiction, would be merely an agreement among the States Parties regarding the manner in which they would exercise their lawful jurisdiction. Two plausible theories of ICC jurisdiction as delegated state jurisdiction will be examined here: delegated universal jurisdiction and delegated territorial jurisdiction. After concluding that neither of those theories, nor, indeed, any of the traditional bases for states' jurisdiction, provides a legal foundation for ICC jurisdiction over non-party nationals, we will then consider whether such jurisdiction would nevertheless be lawful as a new form of jurisdiction.

1. Delegated Universal Jurisdiction

Some proponents of the ICC Treaty have responded to objections to ICC jurisdiction over non-party nationals by arguing that ICC jurisdiction over the nationals of non-party states is based, fundamentally, upon the principles of universal jurisdiction pursuant to which the courts of any state may prosecute the nationals of any state for certain serious international crimes. Since any individual state could prosecute perpetrators regardless of their nationality, they reason, a group of states may create an international court empowered to do the same. Under this theory, each State Party, in effect, delegates to the international court its power to exercise universal jurisdiction.

This reliance on universal jurisdiction faces a number of difficulties. The first problem arises from the Treaty itself. The ICC Treaty does not vest the Court with universal jurisdiction but rather requires consent to jurisdiction (as expressed by ratifying or acceding to the Treaty or by special consent on a case by case basis) by the state of nationality or the state on whose territory the crimes allegedly were committed. The possibility of vesting the Court with universal jurisdiction was heavily debated in the negotiations leading up to adoption of the Treaty and was ultimately rejected in the Treaty as adopted.

Nevertheless, those Treaty provisions requiring consent by the territorial or national state might be viewed as simply reflecting a choice that the ICC will exercise only part of the full range of jurisdiction that it legally *could* under the customary law of universal jurisdiction.[69] Even if this saving interpretation is adopted, however, additional problems remain to be confronted.

---

[69] As Professor Scharf puts it, "[T]he drafters did not view the consent of the state of territoriality or nationality as necessary as a matter of international law to confer jurisdiction on the court. Rather, they adopted the consent regime as a limit to the exercise of the court's inherent jurisdiction as a politically expedient concession to the sovereignty of states in order to garner broad support for the Statute." Michael Scharf, *The ICC's Jurisdiction Over the Nationals of Non-Party States: A Critique of the U.S. Position*, 63 LAW & CONTEMP. PROBS. ____ (2000).

The theory of delegated universal jurisdiction as a basis for ICC jurisdiction fails to account for the ICC's jurisdiction over a number of crimes that the Treaty places within the subject-matter jurisdiction of the ICC but which are not subject to universal jurisdiction. Certain violations of Protocol I to the Geneva Conventions of 1949,[70] for instance, are not subject to universal jurisdiction under customary law.[71] For example, conscription of child soldiers, prohibited under Protocol I and elsewhere, is placed within the jurisdiction of the Court by the terms of the ICC Treaty,[72] but is not a crime customarily subject to universal jurisdiction.[73] A delegated universal jurisdiction theory of ICC jurisdiction over non-party nationals thus would not account for jurisdiction over some of the crimes within the jurisdiction of the Court under the Treaty.

Perhaps the inclusion of crimes not customarily subject to universal jurisdiction should be viewed as a "proposal," in effect, that customary law henceforth recognize those crimes as giving rise to universal jurisdiction.[74] If this proposed extension of universal jurisdiction meets with broad consent, then the law will change accordingly and this particular flaw in ICC jurisdiction will be eliminated. But even if all that comes to pass, a theory of delegated universal jurisdiction would nevertheless face a much more fundamental obstacle.

The fundamental problem with reliance on universal jurisdiction as a basis for ICC jurisdiction over non-party nationals turns on the question whether universal jurisdiction may be delegated to an international court. The proposition that

---

[70] Protocol Additional to the Geneva Conventions of Aug. 12, 1949, and Relating to the Protection of Victims of International Armed Conflicts (Protocol I), June 8, 1977, 1125 U.N.T.S. 3.

[71] *See* Ruth Wedgwood, *The International Criminal Court: An American View*, 10 EUR. J. INT'L L. 93, 102 (1999).

[72] *See* ICC Treaty, art. 8(xxvi).

[73] The prohibition on recruitment of children under fifteen years of age for service in armed forces, and the obligation to take measures that such children do not participate in hostilities, appear in the two 1977 Protocols to the Geneva Conventions as well as in the U.N. Convention on the Rights of the Child. *See* Protocol Additional to the Geneva Conventions of Aug. 12, 1949, and Relating to the Protection of Victims of International Armed Conflicts (Protocol I), *supra* note 24, art. 77(2); Protocol Additional to the Geneva Conventions of Aug. 12, 1949, and Relating to the Protection of Victims of Non-International Armed Conflicts (Protocol II), June 8, 1977, art. 4(3)(c) 1125 U.N.T.S. 609; Convention on the Rights of the Child, Nov. 20, 1989, art. 38, 28 I.L.M. 1457. In none of those treaties is there any suggestion that violations of the child soldier provisions constitute grave breaches or otherwise give rise to universal jurisdiction. Nor is there any other basis for a claim that utilization of child soldiers constitutes an international crime entailing universal jurisdiction. *See generally*, AMNESTY INTERNATIONAL, CHILD SOLDIERS: ONE OF THE WORST ABUSES OF CHILD LABOR (1999) (reviewing international legal prohibitions on utilization of child soldiers); ILENE COHN & GUY GOODWIN, CHILD SOLDIERS: THE ROLE OF CHILDREN IN ARMED CONFLICT 55–72 (1994).

[74] The status of the ICC Treaty as generating customary law will be considered below. *See infra* pp. 269–72.

the universal jurisdiction of states is delegable to an international entity warrants examination.

a. The Significance of Delegation

The delegation of states' universal jurisdiction to an international court would fundamentally alter the consequences of that jurisdiction, as will be demonstrated. The exercise of universal jurisdiction by an international court would have very different implications, involving a different set of state interests, than would the exercise of universal jurisdiction by a state. Because the consequences of universal jurisdiction would be fundamentally transformed by the delegation itself, consent to the universal jurisdiction of states should not be considered equivalent to consent to the delegation of universal jurisdiction to an international court.

Customary international law evolves as a reflection of the consent or acquiescence of states over time. Because consent to universal jurisdiction exercised by states is not equivalent to consent to delegated universal jurisdiction exercised by an international court, the customary law affirming the universal jurisdiction of states cannot be considered equivalent to customary law affirming the delegability of that jurisdiction to an international court.

There are sound reasons for which a state, even while acknowledging universal jurisdiction, might wish to reject the delegation of such jurisdiction for exercise by an international court. A state might reject compulsory third-party adjudication before the ICC in order to retain the discretion to address interstate-dispute type cases through bilateral relations, even while recognizing the possibility that those bilateral relations might in some cases entail the prosecution of that state's national in another state's courts under universal jurisdiction. The reasons for which states might prefer bilateral relations to third-party adjudication in interstate disputes involving international criminal law are essentially the same as the reasons, discussed earlier, for which states are generally reluctant to submit their interstate disputes to third-party adjudication.

States value the advantages that diplomatic methods of dispute settlement often afford. Particularly where an interstate dispute concerns an area of unsettled law, litigation may entail more risk than states can be expected to accept. If the subject matter is important and the law is unsettled, allowing a third party to, in effect, decide the binding law of the matter is a very perilous course of action. Cases involving highly contested facts also entail obvious risks. States may, therefore, perceive a number of drawbacks associated with compulsory adjudication before the ICC.

First, compromise outcomes of various sorts may be desirable in interstate-dispute type cases, especially in circumstances where the law is ambiguous. But compromise outcomes are unlikely to emerge from adjudicated rather than negotiated resolutions.

Second, states would have reason to be more concerned about the political impact of adjudications before an international court than before an individual states' courts. An even-remotely successful international court will have significant prestige and authority. The political repercussions of such a court's determining that a state's acts or policies were unlawful would be substantial indeed, and categorically different from the repercussion of the same verdict rendered by a national court. If a guilty verdict were passed by a national court in an official-acts case, the matter would remain a disagreement among equals, one state maintaining that an unlawful act had been committed, the other disputing its occurrence or defending its lawfulness. By contrast, were the ICC to pronounce an official act to constitute a crime, the decision would bear an authoritative weight and resulting political impact of a categorically different nature. The special political impact of ICC decisions will itself create heightened risks for states. It may also create situations in which states will be put to a choice of either revealing sensitive data as defense evidence or withholding that evidence and thereby risking severe political costs in case of a guilty verdict.

A third matter that may be of substantial concern to states is the role of an international criminal court in shaping the law. Because the decisions of an international court will tend to be more authoritative than would those of any individual state's courts, an international court would have the power to create law in a manner disproportionate to that of any state. This may be more law-making power than some states are comfortable granting to one international institution, especially in sensitive areas involving military activities and international security.

The law of genocide, war crimes, and crimes against humanity[75] is still very much in formation. Controversial and politically significant issues remain open, and major new questions continue to emerge. Reflecting the developing state of the law in this field, the appellate chamber of the International Criminal Tribunals for the former Yugoslavia and Rwanda (ICTY/R) has on more than one occasion reversed a trial chamber decision on a basic point of law.

Developments in the Tadić case illustrate the point. The grave breaches provisions of the Geneva Conventions of 1949 provide for universal jurisdiction over certain crimes when those crimes are committed in international armed conflicts.[76]

---

[75] I leave aside the crime of aggression which is not, for the time being, within the effective jurisdiction of the ICC. *See supra* note 2.

[76] *See* Geneva Convention I for the Amelioration of the Condition of the Wounded and Sick in Armed Forces in the Field, Aug. 12, 1949, arts. 2, 49, 50, 6 U.S.T. 3114, 75 U.N.T.S 31; Geneva Convention II for the Amelioration of the Condition of the Wounded, Sick and Shipwrecked Members of the Armed Forces at Sea, Aug. 12, 1949, arts. 2, 50, 51, 6 U.S.T. 3217, 75 U.N.T.S 85; Geneva Convention III Relative to the Treatment of Prisoners of War, Aug. 12, 1949, arts. 2, 129, 130, 75 U.N.T.S 135; Geneva Convention IV Relative to the Protection of Civilian Persons in Time of War, Aug. 12, 1949, arts. 2, 146, 147, 75 U.N.T.S 287.

Article 2 of the ICTY Statute provides that "The International Tribunal shall have the power to prosecute persons committing or ordering to be committed grave breaches of the Geneva Conventions of 12 August 1949, namely the following acts. . . ."[77] The ICTY trial chamber held in *Tadić* that, when acts defined as grave breaches in the Geneva Conventions are committed against persons or property categorized as protected under the Geneva Conventions, such conduct may be prosecuted before the ICTY regardless of whether the acts were committed in an international armed conflict. According to the trial chamber, Article 2 of the ICTY Statute,

> has been so drafted as to be self-contained rather than referential, save for the identification of the victims of enumerated acts; that identifica-tion and that alone involves going to the Conventions themselves for the definition of "persons or property protected. . . ."
>
> The requirement of international conflict does not appear on the face of Article 2. . . .
>
> [T]here is no ground for treating Article 2 as in effect importing into the Statute the whole of the terms of the Conventions, including the ref-erence in common Article 2 of the Geneva Convention[s] to international conflicts. . . .[78]

The ICTY appellate chamber rejected that holding, stating:

> With all due respect, the Trial Chamber's reasoning is based on a misconception of the grave breaches provisions and the extent of their incorporation into the Statute of the International Tribunal. . . . The inter-national armed conflict requirement was a necessary limitation on the grave breaches system in light of the intrusion on state sovereignty that such mandatory universal jurisdiction represents. State parties to the 1949 Geneva Conventions did not want to give other states jurisdiction over serious violations of international humanitarian law committed in their internal armed conflicts—at least not the mandatory universal juris-diction involved in the grave breaches system.
>
> [T]he Trial Chamber has misinterpreted the reference to the Geneva Conventions contained in the sentence of Article 2: "persons or property protected under the provisions of the relevant Geneva Conventions." . . . Clearly, these provisions of the Geneva Conventions apply to persons or

---

[77] Statute of the International Criminal Tribunal for the Prosecution of Persons Responsible for Serious Violations of International Humanitarian Law Committed in the Territory of the Former Yugoslavia Since 1991, *in* Report of the Secretary-General Pursuant to Paragraph 2 of Security Council Resolution 808, Annex, art. 2, U.N. Doc. S/25704 (1993).

[78] Prosecutor v. Dusko Tadić, Decision on the Defence Motion on Jurisdiction, Case No. IT–94–1–T, decision of Aug. 10, 1995, ¶¶ 49–51.

objects protected only to the extent that they are caught up in an international armed conflict. . . .

We find that our interpretation is the only one warranted. . . .[79]

The appellate chamber thus reversed the trial court on a very basic question of international criminal law. The trial chamber was prepared to treat the international-conflict requirement as merely incidental to the Geneva Conventions' definition of grave breaches. The appellate chamber ruled that the trial court's holding misconceived the limited nature of the consent to universal jurisdiction given by the States Parties to the Geneva Conventions. Such issues, of great significance going to the very basis of the legitimacy of international criminal law, are only now in the process of being decided, as the *Tadić* appeal demonstrates.

Appellate reversals of trial chamber decisions on major legal issues such as that in the *Tadić* case and in other cases before the ICTY/R[80] indicate that this is an area of law in formation and in which there will be disagreements among

---

[79] Prosecutor v. Dusko Tadić, Decision on the Defence Motion for Interlocutory Appeal on Jurisdiction, Case No. IT–94–1–AR72, decision of Oct. 2, 1995, ¶¶ 80–83 [hereinafter Tadić Appeal].

[80] Another example of the ICTY/R's addressing major and unsettled legal questions through the process of trial and appeal concerns a defendant's right to counsel. Jean-Paul Akayesu was an indigent defendant indicted for genocide and other crimes before the ICTR. *See* Prosecutor v. Jean-Paul Akayesu, Case No. ICTR–96–4–T, Trial Chamber decision of Sept. 2, 1998. After dismissing a number of lawyers assigned for his defense, *see* Prosecutor v. Jean-Paul Akayesu, Case No. ICTR–96–4–T, Appeals Chamber Decision Relating to the Assignment of Counsel, decision of July 27, 1999, 3, Akayesu decided that he wanted the Canadian lawyer, Jean Philpot, to represent him. *See id.* At Akayesu's request, Philpot was placed on the list of available counsel that is maintained by the ICTR Registrar, *see id.*, but the Registrar subsequently refused Akayesu's request to be represented by Philpot. *See id.* The Registrar's refusal was upheld by the ICTR trial chamber on the ground that too great a proportion of the counsel appointed by the ICTR were French or Canadian. *See* NYT, *At a Genocide Trial, French Is a Handicap*, N.Y. TIMES, Feb. 19, 1999, at A11. That trial chamber decision was reversed on appeal in a very narrow opinion tied closely to the facts of the case:

> [T]he practice of the Tribunal has been to provide a list of approved counsel from which an accused may choose. . . . Mr. Philpot was included in this list by the Registrar upon the insistence of the Appellant that he desired that Mr. Philpot be assigned to him. . . . [T]he Registrar thereby gave the Appellant a legitimate expectation that Mr. Philpot would be assigned to represent him before the Tribunal. Akeyesu Appeals Chamber Decision, *supra* at 3.

By basing its holding narrowly on Akayesu's legitimate expectations in the particular circumstances of the case, the appellate chamber chose not to address the broad issues that the case raised regarding the right to defense counsel and, in particular, the proper balancing of the defendant's interest in choice of counsel and the United Nations' interest in geographical representativeness of its personnel. These broader implications of the case were addressed in a number of petitions submitted to the Appellate Chamber. *See, e.g.*, Petition for the Intervention as Amicus Curiae of the International Criminal Defense Attorneys Association, filed on Apr. 28, 1999. The *Akayesu Defense Counsel* case thus represents another major question in international criminal law which has come before the ICTY/R, but in this case, the substance of the matter remains to be addressed.

experts about the content of the law. It is therefore likely that one state might take a different view of the legality of a particular act or policy than would another state or an international court. There are, of course, disagreements about the content of the law in domestic settings; and appellate courts reverse trial chambers' decisions in domestic judicial systems. This is precisely what makes the structure of the judiciary a crucial feature of states' constitutional designs. What is at issue in the ICC context is whether the judicial structure being proposed—which will then play an inevitably influential role in shaping the law—is acceptable to those who have been asked to join in constituting and accepting the jurisdiction of that judicial power.

The ICC will be a free-standing, international court. It will operate without benefit of a representative legislative branch that can both make law and, where appropriate, reject judge-made law through legislation effectively overturning judicial decisions.[81] States may have legitimate concerns about the compulsory jurisdiction of such a court; they may not see fit to have an international tribunal in effect legislate international law in areas where the law is relatively undeveloped. States might have sound reasons for preferring to retain more direct control, diffused among many states, over the shaping of international law in this critical field rather than to relegate a substantial proportion of that control to a single international entity operating in this posture.

States are keenly interested that the law in this field should develop in directions that are consistent with their views of international relations, with the extent and nature of their military engagements, as well as with their visions of what would provide the greatest justice and deterrence value. The development of international criminal law, like the development of other areas of international law, is a process of state consent, agreement, and acquiescence. Its development is, in that respect, a series of more or less directly negotiated outcomes in an incremental process. A state might be concerned about granting jurisdiction to an international court that inevitably would have great influence, disproportionate to that of any state, in the formation of that body of law.[82]

---

[81] The Assembly of States Parties, by the terms of the ICC Treaty, will provide only a rather minimal form of oversight of the Court's operations. *See* ICC Treaty, art. 112 (establishing an Assembly of States Parties with oversight functions relative to the ICC).

[82] States may reasonably have significant concerns about ICC jurisdiction not only with regard to official-acts cases but also in relation to cases of the individual-culpability type. In individual-culpability cases, the concerns will relate primarily to diplomatic protection. If a state finds it necessary to provide diplomatic protection to ensure just treatment of a national who is facing prosecution, that state may confront significant disadvantages in interacting with the ICC rather than with another state. In a sense, the need to provide diplomatic protection to ensure just treatment of a national in an individual-culpability case transforms that case, or at least the aspect of it involving the diplomatic-protection issue, into a dispute between the state of the defendant's nationality and the prosecuting authority. Where that dispute is with a state, bilateral diplomatic methods may be employed. Where that authority is an international court,

In the ways just described, the consequences and implications of ICC juris-diction are materially different from those of national jurisdiction. These differ-ences are sufficiently significant so that the customary international law of universal jurisdiction should not be quickly presumed to entail the delegability of that jurisdiction from states to an international court. Because different states' interests are affected by the two forms of jurisdiction, consent to or acquiescence in one is not equivalent to consent to or acquiescence in the other.

The arguments, frequently offered as a response to concerns about ICC juris-diction, that the ICC would address only very grave crimes, that the ICC prose-cutor would be a person of distinction and fine judgment, and that the ICC is not intended to interfere in the affairs of basically law abiding states, do not ade-quately respond to the fundamental concerns that states may have. Reactions to the NATO intervention in Kosovo illustrate that the arguments offered are some-what beside the point.

Some NATO military actions during the armed conflict in Kosovo were char-acterized by a number of distinguished international lawyers and political actors as war crimes.[83] South African Minister of Education (formerly Minister of Water Affairs and Forestry) Kader Asmal stated in July 1999 that NATO's "bombing of water resources in [the Kosovo campaign] is a war crime."[84] On May 10, 1999, international law professor Ian Brownlie argued on behalf of the Federal Republic of Yugoslavia (FRY) before the ICJ that the NATO action was in violation of international law for reasons including "the unlawful modalities of the aerial bom-bardment."[85] On the same day, lawyers from several countries filed a complaint with the ICTY Prosecutor against NATO officials and leaders of NATO member states for alleged war crimes committed in NATO's armed intervention in Yugoslavia.[86] ICTY Prosecutor Louise Arbour subsequently indicated that she would investigate those charges.[87] On May 28, 1999, law professor Michael Byers stated on BBC Radio that NATO's use of depleted uranium, cluster bombs, and carpet bombing might constitute war crimes within the jurisdiction of the ICTY

---

the nature of the dispute resolution process would be entirely different. Indeed, no process for the resolution of such disputes with the ICC has been articulated.

[83] I leave aside here the legality of the NATO military intervention itself because the crime of aggression is not currently within effective ICC jurisdiction as framed by the ICC Treaty. *See supra* note 2.

[84] *See* Alex Kirby, *Kosovo Waterways Bombing a "War Crime"* <http://news2.thls.bbc.co.uk/hi/english/ world/newsid_394000/394326.stm> (visited Mar. 22, 2000) .

[85] Ian Brownlie, Co-Agent for the Federal Republic of Yugoslavia, Remarks before the ICJ in the Case Concerning Legality of the Use of Force (May 10, 1999) (on file with author).

[86] *See* Bruce Zagaris, *Complaint Before War Crimes Tribunal Charges NATO Leaders with War Crimes*, 15 INT'L L. ENFORCEMENT REP. 249 (1999).

[87] *See Burden of Proof* (CNN television broadcast, June, 1, 1999) (statement of Professor Michael Scharf).

and suggested that prosecution for such crimes be duly considered by the ICTY prosecutor.[88] All of these statements were made by persons of judgment and distinction. Each was a person who would be a credible candidate for office within the ICC. One need not assume that the ICC would act unreasonably or abusively to envision that any state's action, viewed by that state as lawful, could someday become the subject of an ICC prosecution.

One aspect of Professor Byers' remarks bears particular notice in this respect. Professor Byers suggested that, if indeed war crimes had been committed in the NATO action, it would be particularly important to prosecute those crimes in order to demonstrate the even-handedness of the ICTY.[89] Such an approach would be consistent with prior ICTY prosecutorial strategy in which, for example, one stated purpose for indictment of a number of Croats at the particular time that they were indicted was to dispel Serbian suspicions that the ICTY was anti-Serb.[90] If this view regarding the place of "even-handedness" in international prosecutorial strategy is applied by the ICC, then it could become even more likely that the actions of non-"rogue" states would become the subject of ICC prosecutions.

Thus, even if the ICC will prosecute only grave crimes, will have a distinguished prosecutor with fine judgment, and will not interfere in the affairs of basically law abiding states, this does not mean that the actions of any given state could never realistically become the subject of ICC prosecutions. Therefore, the question whether ICC jurisdiction is acceptable to a given state must be evaluated on the assumption that ICC jurisdiction may actually be applied.

b. The Content of Custom

As we have seen, there are comprehensible and sometimes even good reasons for which a state might object to the delegation of states' universal jurisdiction to the ICC. We turn now to a closer examination of the legal status of such objections.

We have seen that the consequences of universal jurisdiction exercised by a state are significantly different from the consequences of delegated universal jurisdiction exercised by an international court. For that reason, consent to states' exercise of universal jurisdiction is not equivalent to consent to the delegation of universal jurisdiction to an international court. By extension, customary law supporting the exercise of universal jurisdiction by states is not equivalent to customary law supporting the delegation of states' universal jurisdiction to an international court. Therefore, we may not simply assume that states' universal

---

[88] *See The World Tonight* (BBC Radio 4 radio broadcast, May 28, 1999) (interview with Michael Byers, Fellow of Jesus College, Oxford University).

[89] *Id.*

[90] Conversation of author with Richard Goldstone, then-Prosecutor, ICTY/R, in Brussels, Belgium (July 20, 1996).

jurisdiction may be delegated to an international court as a matter of customary international law. Rather, the question whether states' universal jurisdiction may lawfully be delegated to an international court requires analysis.

Universal jurisdiction arises as a matter of customary international law.[91] If, by custom, universal jurisdiction were delegable to an international court, then states would be obliged to accept such delegation and, by extension, to accept ICC jurisdiction over non-party nationals. If, however, delegation of universal jurisdiction to an international court would constitute an innovation beyond the customary meaning of universal jurisdiction, then the legal status of jurisdiction based on such delegation would remain to be determined. The initial question, then, is whether the customary international law of universal jurisdiction, as it has developed through the state practice and *opinio juris*, entails the possibility of delegation to an international court.

State practice relating to the exercise of criminal jurisdiction by an international court has been limited. The International Criminal Tribunals for the former Yugoslavia and Rwanda (ICTY/R) are believed by some to found their jurisdiction on the delegated universal jurisdiction of states.[92] However, as the ICTY/R are products of U.N. Security Council action under Chapter VII of the U.N. Charter,[93] the tribunals' jurisdiction is more properly viewed as arising from the powers of the Security Council to take such steps as are required to restore or maintain international peace and security. In responding to jurisdictional challenges going to the legitimacy of the establishment of the ICTY and ICTR, each tribunal has responded by affirming the power of the Security Council, acting under Chapter VII, to establish a judicial tribunal as an instrument for the maintenance of international peace and security and has cited that Security Council power as forming the jurisdictional foundation of the tribunal.[94] Neither tribunal

---

[91] *Cf. infra* pp. 273–78 (regarding the notion of universal jurisdiction created by treaty).

[92] *See, e.g.*, REVISED REPORT OF THE WORKING GROUP ON THE DRAFT STATUTE FOR AN INTERNATIONAL CRIMINAL COURT, ¶¶ 72–73, U.N Doc. A/CN.4/L.490 and Add.1 (1993); Yoram Dinstein, *The Universality Principle and War Crimes, in* THE LAW OF ARMED CONFLICT: INTO THE NEXT MILLENIUM 17–37 (Michael Schmitt & Leslie Green eds., 1998).

[93] *See* U.N. S.C. Res. 827, U.N. Doc. S/Res. 827 (1993) and U.N. S.C. Res. 955, U.N. SCOR, 3453d mtg. (1994) (specifying that, in establishing the ICTY and ICTR, respectively, the Security Council was acting under Chapter VII).

[94] *See* Tadić Appeal, *supra* note 79, at 5–24; Prosecutor v. Joseph Kanyabashi, ICTR, Decision on the Defence Motion on Jurisdiction, Case No. ICTR–96–15–T, June 18, 1997, ¶¶ 7–29.

In April 1999, the Federal Republic of Yugoslavia (FRY) brought suit before the ICJ accusing ten NATO countries of violating international obligations to refrain from the use of force against another state. *See* ICJ, Press Communiqué 99/39, July 2, 1999, <http://www.icj–cij.org> (visited Mar. 22, 2000). Several of those NATO respondents, including the United States, in response challenged the FRY's right to bring suit under the ICJ's optional-clause jurisdiction on the basis that the FRY was not a member of the United Nations. *See, e.g.*, Legality of Use of

has invoked delegated universal jurisdiction or any other form of universal jurisdiction as the basis of its jurisdiction.[95]

The other international criminal tribunals that some view as precedents for
the collective exercise of universal jurisdiction are the International Military
Tribunal ("Nuremberg tribunal") and the International Military Tribunal for the
Far East ("Tokyo tribunal") established in the aftermath of World War II
(WWII).[96] But, in fact, neither the Nuremberg nor the Tokyo tribunal based its
competence on collective exercise of universal jurisdiction. Rather, the Nuremberg

---

Force (Yugo v. Can.), Request for the Indication of Provisional Measures, 1999 I.C.J. Public
Sitting CR99/16 at para. 10 (statement of Philippe Kirsch, Agent of Canada) <http://www.
icj–cij.org/icj/idocket/iyall/iyall_iyca_icr9916_19990510.htlm> (visited Mar. 22, 2000). To support the claim that the FRY was not a U.N. member, the respondents made reference to U.N.
Security Council Resolution 777 of 1992 and U.N. General Assembly Resolution 47/1 of 1992.
See id. at para. 11. The FRY argued, in response, that those resolutions excluded the FRY only
from occupying its seat in the General Assembly but not from other participation in the U.N.
system. The ICJ declined the FRY's request for provisional measures in the case, but did so on
other grounds without addressing the U.N.-membership issue. *See* ICJ, Press Communiqué,
supra.

These circumstances raise the question of what authority the ICTY has in the FRY in light
of the fact that the ICTY's jurisdiction and other authority arises from U.N. Security Council
action. If the FRY is not a U.N. member (and already was not a member as of 1992 when the
two relevant U.N. resolutions were adopted), then, one could argue, the ICTY (which was established in 1993) has no powers in the FRY and no jurisdiction over FRY nationals.

There are a number of appropriate responses to this set of circumstances. First, we must recognize that the status of the FRY is not settled. If the FRY's own position on this matter prevails,
then the FRY is indeed a U.N. member and, perforce, bound by the Security Council action
establishing the ICTY (notwithstanding the FRY's own protests, on other grounds, to ICTY
jurisdiction). *See* Letter from the Charge d'affaires, a.i., of the Permanent Mission of Yugoslavia
to the United Nations Addressed to the the Secretary-General of the United Nations (May 19,
1993) (U.N. Doc. A/48/170–S/25801 (1993)). Given that the FRY's mission to the U.N. has continued to exist and to receive official U.N. communications, that the FRY flag has continued to
fly outside U.N. headquarters, and other indicia of U.N. membership, it is not entirely farfetched
that the FRY would be found to hold membership.

If on the other hand, the FRY were found to be a non-member of the U.N., then the question
whether the U.N. Charter is binding on non-parties would be directly posed. Regarding this
debate, *see infra* pp. 263–69. If the Charter were found to be binding in a robust way on non-
parties, then the ICTY would maintain its powers in the FRY. If, however, the Charter were
found not to be binding on non-members in the relevant respects, then this would have far-reaching and profound consequences, quite possibly among them the loss of the ICTY's powers
within the FRY and jurisdiction over FRY nationals.

[95]   By contrast, the ICTY has made reference to the principles underlying universal jurisdiction in justifying the primacy of the ICTY over national courts (the concept of primacy is not
adopted by the ICC Treaty) and in justifying prosecution of defendants before the international
forum rather than before their "natural" (national) fora. *See* Tadić Appeal, *supra* note 79, at
32–33 (primacy), 34 ("natural forum"). The ICTY has not, however, stated or in any way
implied that universal jurisdiction formed the basis for its jurisdiction.

[96]   *See, e.g.,* Christopher Greenwood, *The Prosecution of War Crimes in the Former
Yugoslavia,* 26 BRACTON L.J. 13, 16 (1994).

and Tokyo tribunals each, in different ways, based their jurisdiction on the consent of the state of nationality of the defendants.

This is not to say that those WWII tribunals were right to have based their jurisdiction on the consent of the defendants' states of nationality. Strong arguments have been made that the claimed jurisdictional basis was flawed by the coerced nature of the consent.[97] But, even if the jurisdiction of those tribunals were flawed by the coerced nature of the consent, that would mean nothing more than that the jurisdiction was flawed. It would not imply that the tribunals' jurisdiction had rested on some other basis, such as collective exercise of universal jurisdiction.

In the case of the Tokyo tribunal, the Japanese government (which, at least formally, retained sovereign power in Japan after the war) acceded, in the Instrument of Surrender,[98] to prosecution of Japanese nationals before the International Military Tribunal for the Far East. The Instrument of Surrender states that the Japanese government accepts the provisions set forth in the Potsdam Declaration of July 26, 1945,[99] and undertakes to "take whatever action may be required by the Supreme Commander for the Allied Powers or by any other designated representative of the Allied Powers for the purpose of giving effect to that declaration."[100] The Potsdam Declaration, in turn, provides that "stern justice shall be meted out to all war criminals."[101] The Potsdam Declaration further states that the terms of the Cairo Declaration shall be carried out.[102] The Cairo Declaration included the statement that "The . . . allies are fighting this war to restrain and punish the aggression of Japan."[103] The primacy of the Instrument of Surrender, read together with the two Declarations, in constituting Japan's consent and, thereby, forming the jurisdictional basis for the Tokyo tribunal, is affirmed both in the Tokyo tribunal's charter and in its judgment.[104]

---

[97] *See, e.g.,* R. JOHN PRITCHARD, AN OVERVIEW OF THE HISTORICAL IMPORTANCE OF THE TOKYO WAR TRIAL 8–10 (1987) [hereinafter PRITCHARD, AN OVERVIEW] (regarding Tokyo); *cf.* Hans Kelsen, *The Legal Status of Germany According to the Declaration of Berlin*, 39 AM. J. INT'L L. 518, 523 (1945)(noting that the Allies did not afford German citizens political rights and representation).

[98] Sept. 2, 1945, 3 Bevans 1251.

[99] 3 Bevans 1204. *See* Instrument of Surrender, *supra* note 98, at 1251.

[100] Instrument of Surrender, *supra* note 98, at 1252.

[101] Potsdam Declaration, *supra* note 99, at 1205, ¶ 10.

[102] *See id.,* ¶ 8.

[103] Communiqué, First Cairo Conference, Dec. 1, 1943, 3 Bevans 858. *See also* PRITCHARD, AN OVERVIEW, *supra* note 97, at 9; R. JOHN PRITCHARD, *The International Military Tribunal for the Far East and Its Contemporary Resonances*, 149 MIL. L. REV. 25, 27–28 (1995) [hereinafter, Pritchard, *The International Tribunal*].

[104] *See* PRITCHARD, AN OVERVIEW, *supra* note 97, at 9 n.16 (citing Proceedings, Vol. 20; Judgment, T.48415–19, and Annex A–1—A–5). *See also* John Pritchard, *The International*

With regard to the Nuremberg tribunal, the story is more complex. The four Allied states that established the Nuremberg tribunal had taken on supreme authority in Germany. As stated in the Berlin Declaration of June 5, 1945,

> The Governments of the United States of America, The Union of Soviet Socialist Republics and the United Kingdom, and the Provisional Government of the French Republic, hereby assume supreme authority with respect to Germany, including all the powers possessed by the German Government, the High Command and any state, municipal, or local government or authority.[105]

In that position, the Allies exercised judicial and all other powers of sovereignty in Germany. At a minimum, the Allies, acting in their capacity as the effective German sovereign, consented to the prosecution of German nationals at the Nuremberg tribunal. A maximalist reading would be that the Nuremberg prosecutions were actually an exercise of national jurisdiction by the effective German sovereign, the Allies. In either case, the effective German sovereign consented to the prosecutions.

One may debate whether the Allies were the German sovereign in 1945 or merely stood *in loco sovereigntis*. Clearly, the Allies stood in a position essentially different from that of mere occupiers.[106] There has been no disagreement as to

---

Military Tribunal for the Far East and its Contemporary Resonances: A General Preface to the Collection, in THE TOKYO MAJOR WAR CRIMES TRIAL xxxi (J. Pritchard ed., 1998); *In re* Yamashita, 327 U.S. 4, 13 (1945) ("Japan, by her acceptance of the Potsdam Declaration and her surrender, has acquiesced in the trials of those guilty of violations of the law of war.").

[105] Berlin Declaration, June 5, 1945, 60 Stat. 1649, 1650. *See also* Agreement Between the Governments of the United States of America and the Union of Soviet Socialist Republics and the United Kingdom and the Provisional Government of the French Republic on Certain Additional Requirements to be Imposed on Germany, Sept. 20, 1945, 3 Bevans 1254 (further delineating the powers to be exercised by the Allies including prosecutions for war crimes).

[106] As Fritz Mann reasoned at that time,

[T]o place the City of Koenigsberg and the territories east of the Oder-Neisse line under Soviet and Polish administration respectively far exceed the limits within which a mere belligerent occupant could act, no belligerent occupant could withdraw diplomatic missions or require 'German authorities and all persons in Germany' to hand over all gold, silver and platinum, or acquire the right to have placed 'at the unrestricted disposal of the Allied Representatives' the entire German shipping and the whole of the German inland transport system. And if one looks at the legislation of the Control Council, one finds Law No. 4 about the reorganisation of the German judicial system. . . .

The Allies' failure to exercise the qualified rights of a belligerent occupant seems to be undeniable. . . . The material question is why the Allies have an internationally recognisable right to behave otherwise than as belligerent occupants. . . .

Although neither the end of hostilities nor the unconditional surrender nor the disappearance of a central government could, in themselves, have entitled the Allied Governments to adopt an attitude other than that of a belligerent occupant, it is, in the peculiar situation of Germany in 1945, the co-existence of these three facts which provides

whether the Allies' position in post-war Germany exceeded the traditional bounds of occupation.[107] Rather, debate focused on whether the Allies were actually the sovereign(s) in post-war Germany or only stood in the place of the sovereign. Fritz Mann took the position that the Allies, while not having assumed territorial sovereignty, nevertheless assumed governmental sovereignty and, thus, occupied the status of the Government of Germany. As he wrote,

> From the point of view of international law, Germany is a dependent state. . . . The position of the Allied Governments probably is that they exercise what certain publicists have described as co-imperium. While in the case of a condominium a community of states has sovereignty over a territory belonging to them jointly, a co-imperium exists, if several states jointly exercise jurisdiction or governmental functions and powers in territory belonging to another state. . . .[108]

Georg Schwarzenberger argued that the Allies were co-sovereigns of Germany and that they conducted the Nuremberg tribunal in that capacity. In his words,

> [B]y *deballatio*, [the Allies] became the joint sovereigns of Germany. Little importance need, therefore, be attached to the circumstance that the joint sovereigns exercised their jurisdiction as the fountain of law and justice in Germany by an international treaty; for this mode of co-ordinating their sovereign wills is not so much determined by the object of their joint deliberations as by the character of the joint sovereigns as four distinct subjects of international law. As the Tribunal stated in its judgment, there would have been little doubt regarding the municipal char-

---

an internationally recognisable justification for Allied action. The rules relating to belligerent occupation seek to establish a compromise between military necessities and the interests of the inhabitants. . . . They expect, from both sides, a standard of conduct which becomes impracticable when every single activity of the occupied state expresses a doctrine the eradication of which is the very aim of the war. . . . No German Government could have been formed to co-operate with a mere belligerent occupant. If the Allies had assumed only the role of belligerent occupants, they and the United Nations in whose interests they act, could not achieve their war aims, which go far beyond military victory; indeed, they would have failed to fulfil their duty and historic mission. It is the unique character of the circumstances which required and sanctioned a unique solution, a new departure.

Fritz A. Mann, *The Present Legal Status of Germany*, 1 INT'L L.Q. 314, 321–23 (1947).

[107] For this reason, the argument made by some defendants in post-war prosecutions in Germany, that the occupiers' military commissions did not have the right to try offenders for crimes committed prior to the occupation, was misplaced. For such an argument, *see, e.g., Trial of Afons Klein, Adolf Wahlmann, Heinrich Ruoff, Karl Willig, Adolf Merkle, Irmgard Huber, and Philipp Blum (The Hadamar Trial)*, 1 LAW REPORTS OF TRIALS OF WAR CRIMINALS (1949).

[108] Mann, *The Present Legal Status of Germany*, *supra* note 106, at 330, 334–35.

acter of the Tribunal if one state alone had overrun Germany and established such a tribunal, instead of four victorious Powers combining their efforts towards the same end: "The Signatory Power created this Tribunal, defined the law it was to administer, and made regulations for the proper conduct of the Trial. In doing so, they have done together what any of them might have done singly." [Citing the Nuremberg Judgment, *infra* note 111.] . . . Furthermore, in accordance with Article 29 of the Tribunal's Charter, the right of pardon rests with the Control Council for Germany. In substance, therefore, the Tribunal is a municipal tribunal of extraordinary jurisdiction which the four Contracting Powers share in common.[109]

Hans Kelsen also took the view that the Allies had the right to conduct the Nuremberg tribunal based on their position as German sovereign. As he said,

the criminal prosecution of Germans for illegal acts of their state could have been based on national law, enacted for this purpose by the competent authorities. These competent authorities were the four occupant powers exercising their joint sovereignty in a condominium over the territory and the population of subjugated Germany through the Control Council as the legitimate successor of the last German Government.[110]

We may conclude, at a minimum, that the Nuremberg tribunal, having acted with the consent of the Allies, acted with the consent of the effective sovereign of the defendants' state of nationality. It may also be that, beyond merely consenting to the Nuremberg tribunal prosecutions, the Allies actually created the tribunal and conducted those prosecutions in their capacity as effective sovereign. Indeed, this is the view reflected in the Judgment of the Nuremberg tribunal, which states:

[T]he making of the Charter [establishing the Nuremberg tribunal] was the exercise of the sovereign legislative power by the countries to which the German Reich unconditionally surrendered; and the undoubted right

---

[109] Georg Schwarzenberger, *The Problem of an International Criminal Law*, 3 CURRENT LEGAL PROBS., 263, 290–91 (1950). *See also* Georg Schwarzenberger, *The Judgment of Nuremberg*, 21 TUL. L. REV. 329, 334–35 (1947).

[110] Hans Kelsen, *Will the Judgment in the Nuremberg Trial Constitute a Precedent in International Law?*, 1 INT'L L.Q. 153, 167 (1947).

Kelsen, however, went on to reason (in a manner of particular interest for our question of ICC jurisdiction over non-party nationals) that if, as he believed was the case, the Allies did not exercise jurisdiction based on their sovereignty in Germany but rather attempted to represent the Nuremberg tribunal as an international tribunal, then its jurisdiction was illegitimate precisely because it lacked the consent of non-parties to the London Agreement, the treaty that formed the basis of the Nuremberg tribunal's jurisdiction. *See id.* at 168.

of these countries to legislate for the occupied territories has been recognized by the civilized world.[111]

The jurisdictional basis of the Nuremberg tribunal was not delineated with greater precision than that in the tribunal's Charter or Judgment. While the language quoted above is strong evidence that the Nuremberg tribunal based its jurisdiction on the consent of the Allies as effective German sovereign, an alternative theory, that the Nuremberg tribunal based its jurisdiction on universal jurisdiction, has attained some currency over the years. The passage from the U.N. Secretary-General's 1949 Report on the Nuremberg tribunal from which this theory may have garnered some of its force begins by quoting the same sentence from the Nuremberg Judgment quoted immediately above. It then goes on to say:

> In this statement the Court refers to the particular legal situation arising out of the unconditional surrender of Germany in May 1945, and the declaration issued in Berlin on 5 June 1945, by the four Allied states, signatories of the London Agreement. By this declaration the said countries assumed supreme authority with respect to Germany, including all the powers possessed by the German Government, the High Command and any state, municipal or local government or authority. The Court apparently held that in virtue of these acts the sovereignty of Germany had passed into the hands of the four states and that these countries thereby were authorized under international law to establish the Tribunal and invest it with the power to try and punish the major German war criminals.
>
> The Court, however, also indicated another basis for its jurisdiction, a basis of more general scope. "The Signatory Powers" [the Tribunal said], "created this Tribunal, defined the law it was to administer, and made regulations for the proper conduct of the trial. In doing so, they have done together what any one of them might have done singly; for it is not to be doubted that any nation has the right thus to set up special courts to administer law." The statement is far from clear, but, with some hesitation, the following alternative interpretations may be offered. It is possible that the Court meant that the several signatory Powers had jurisdiction over the crimes defined in the Charter because these crimes threatened the security of each of them. The Court may, in other words, have intended to assimilate the said crimes, in regard to jurisdiction, to such offences as the counterfeiting of currency. On the other hand, it is also possible and perhaps more probable, that the Court considered the crimes under the Charter to be, as international crimes, subject to the jurisdiction of every state. The case of piracy would then be the appropriate parallel. This interpretation seems to be supported by the fact that the Court affirmed that the signatory Powers in creating the Tribunal had

---

[111] Judgment of the International Military Tribunal, Sept. 30, 1946, *reprinted in* RICHARD A. FALK ET AL., CRIMES OF WAR 96 (1971).

made use of a right belonging to any nation. But it must be conceded, at the same time, that the phrase "right thus to set up special courts to administer law" is too vague to admit of definite conclusions.[112]

The Secretary-General was right to be wary of drawing, from that passage in the Nuremberg Judgment, the conclusion that the Nuremberg tribunal's jurisdiction was based on either the protective principle (the reference to counterfeiting) or the universality principle (the reference to piracy). Rather, the assertion in the Nuremberg Judgment that, in establishing the Nuremberg tribunal, the Allies had "done together what any one of them might have done singly"[113] is equally applicable to a sovereign-consent theory as to a universal-jurisdiction theory of that tribunal's jurisdiction. Indeed, read together with the passage of the Judgment which states that "the making of the Charter was the exercise of the sovereign legislative power by the countries to which the German Reich unconditionally surrendered,"[114] the meaning seems more consistent with the view that the jurisdiction of the Nuremberg tribunal rested on the effective sovereign powers of the Allies to prosecute or consent to the prosecution of German nationals.

These considerations have not precluded the occasional assertion that the Nuremberg tribunal rested its competence on the collective exercise of universal jurisdiction. For example, the U.N. Commission of Experts on the former Yugoslavia made the claim that,

> States may choose to combine their jurisdictions under the universality principle and vest this combined jurisdiction in an international tribunal. The Nuremberg International Military Tribunal may be said to have derived its jurisdiction from such a combination of the national jurisdiction of the States Parties to the London Agreement setting up that Tribunal.[115]

For this assertion, the Commission provided no support whatsoever. In light of the evidence that the Nuremberg tribunal rested its jurisdiction on the exercise of effective sovereignty by the Allies or, at a minimum, on the consent of that effective sovereign, quite substantial evidence, which does not appear to exist, would be required to uphold the Commission's claim.

---

[112] SECRETARY-GENERAL OF THE UNITED NATIONS, THE CHARTER AND JUDGMENT OF THE NUREMBERG TRIBUNAL: HISTORY AND ANALYSIS at 80, U.N. Doc. A/CN.4/5, U.N. Sales No. 1949V.7 (1949).

[113] 22 TRIAL OF THE MAJOR WAR CRIMINALS BEFORE THE INTERNATIONAL MILITARY TRIBUNAL 461 (S. Paul A. Joosten ed., 1948).

[114] Judgment of the International Military Tribunal, *supra* note 111, at 96.

[115] Interim Report of the Independent Commission of Experts Established Pursuant to Security Council Resolution 780, 1992, ¶ 73, U.N. Doc. S/25274 (1993).

The warranted conclusion appears to be that the jurisdictional basis of the Nuremberg and Tokyo tribunals was not the exercise of universal jurisdiction but, rather, the consent of the defendants' states of nationality. With regard to Tokyo, this conclusion is uncontroversial. Regarding Nuremberg, what must be said, at a minimum, is that the tribunal rested its jurisdiction largely on the fact that the Allies as effective sovereign in post-war Germany consented to the trial of German nationals.[116]

Based on the evidence regarding the jurisdictional bases of the Nuremberg and Tokyo tribunals, those tribunals cannot be relied upon as state practice providing precedent for the delegation of universal jurisdiction to an international court. Nor, as we have seen, do the ICTY/R represent such precedents. Thus, none of the four international criminal tribunals that have been established to date provides evidence that the customary international law of universal jurisdiction encompasses the option of delegation to an international criminal court. Nor are there alternative sources of law to be relied on to that effect.[117]

---

[116] One may certainly question whether the Allies should have acted *in loco sovereigntis* in post-war Germany. Concerns could be raised as to whether the Allies were sufficiently interested in the welfare of the German population to act as the German sovereign. In this regard, *see* Kelsen, *supra* note 97, at 523 ("the occupant state . . . will not confer upon the former citizens of the occupied state political rights with respect to its own legislative or executive organs. . . ."). Conducting or consenting to war-crimes prosecutions at the Nuremberg Tribunal could be among the points of concern. But the questions of the wisdom and legitimacy of Allied government in post-war Germany need not be resolved in order to acknowledge that precisely such a government did exist. In the position of sovereign or acting sovereign, the Allies fulfilled the role of the government of Germany and, in that capacity, conducted or consented to the prosecution of German nationals by the Nuremberg tribunal.

[117] It has occasionally been suggested that the Genocide Convention or the Apartheid Convention provide support for the collective exercise of universal jurisdiction over non-party nationals. Neither convention, however, provides such support.

The Genocide Convention provides for jurisdiction by the territorial state "or by such international penal tribunal as may have jurisdiction *with respect to those Contracting Parties as shall have accepted its jurisdiction.*" Convention on the Prevention and Punishment of the Crime of Genocide, Dec. 9, 1948, art. VI, 78 U.N.T.S. 277 (emphasis added). It thus does not envision that the court would have jurisdiction with respect to non-contracting parties. The international tribunal provision was included in the Genocide Convention essentially for the purpose of avoiding the necessity of amending the Convention's jurisdictional provisions in the future should an international tribunal with competence over genocide be established. *See* U.N. GAOR 6th Comm., 3d Sess., 97th mtg. at 369, U.N. Doc. A/C.6/SR 61–140 (1948) (Mr. Demesmin, Haiti); U.N. GAOR 6th Comm., 3d Sess., 130 mtg. at 675, U.N. Doc. A/C.6/SR 61–140 (1948) (Mr. DeBeus, Netherlands); U.S. SENATE COMM. ON FOREIGN REL., REPORT ON INT'L CONVENTION ON THE PREVENTION AND PUNISHMENT OF GENOCIDE, 28 I.L.M. 754, 765 (1989). The specifics of creation of such a court and its competence were left open by the Convention. This meant that even States Parties to the Genocide Convention did not, by becoming parties, grant jurisdiction to or in any other way alter their status or the status of their nationals relative to any international court that might in the future be created. *See* U.N. GAOR 6th Comm., 3d Sess., 130th mtg. at 684, 676 U.N. Doc. A/C.6/SR 61–140 (1948) (remarks of Mr. Fitzmaurice, U.K.) (stating that the U.K. "could not commit itself to support a court which did not yet exist and the

The delegated universal jurisdiction theory of ICC jurisdiction over non-party nationals, in sum, faces a number of difficulties. The theory may be inconsistent with the ICC Treaty's reliance on nationality and territoriality as conditions for the exercise of jurisdiction. The delegated universal jurisdiction theory also does not account for a number of crimes within the subject-matter jurisdiction of the ICC that are not subject to universal jurisdiction. More importantly, because universal jurisdiction delegated to an international court would have materially different implications for states than would the exercise of universal jurisdiction by individual states, consent to the latter is not equivalent to consent to the former. For that reason, customary development of one should not be presumed to entail customary development of the other.

Rather, the question whether the delegation of universal jurisdiction is lawful requires a distinct analysis. In pursuing that analysis, we have found no precedent in state practice for the delegation of universal jurisdiction to an international court. This absence of precedent precludes the possibility that delegability has been affirmatively entailed within the customary law of universal jurisdiction as it has developed through state practice and *opinio juris*. It remains to be considered whether delegation of universal jurisdiction to an international court, even if not affirmatively entailed within the customary international law of universal jurisdiction, may nevertheless be lawful. That question will be examined shortly. First, however, we will consider an alternative theory supporting ICC jurisdiction over non-party nationals based on the delegated jurisdiction of states.

2. Delegated Territorial Jurisdiction

The jurisdictional provisions of the ICC Treaty suggest an alternative to the delegated universal jurisdiction theory of ICC jurisdiction over non-party nationals. This alternative approach would rest on a theory of delegated territorial juris-

---

scope of which was not known," and accepting Article VI only on the ground that it "put the court on a hypothetical, facultative basis and did not compel the parties to accept its jurisdiction"); NEREMIAH ROBINSON, THE GENOCIDE CONVENTION: A COMMENTARY 80 (1960); LAWRENCE J. LEBLANC, THE UNITED STATES AND THE GENOCIDE CONVENTION 165–67 (1991); Matthew Lippman, *The Convention on the Prevention and Punishment of the Crime of Genocide: Fifty Years Later*, 15 ARIZ. J. INT'L & COMP. L. 415, 461 (1998).

Neither does the Apartheid Convention constitute a precedent for jurisdiction of an international tribunal over nationals of non-party states. The Apartheid Convention's provisions regarding an international penal tribunal echo those of the Genocide Convention, stating that persons charged with the crime of apartheid may be tried in the national courts of States Parties or "by an international penal tribunal having jurisdiction *with respect to those States Parties having accepted its jurisdiction.*" International Convention on the Suppression and Punishment of the Crime of Apartheid, Nov. 30, 1973, art. V, 1015 U.N.T.S. 243 (emphasis added). Moreover, even with that safeguard, the jurisdictional provisions of the Apartheid Convention proved extremely controversial and were cited by many states as among their reasons for rejecting the convention. *See* 27 Y.B. OF THE U.N. 100 (1973) (remarks of Finland [speaking also on behalf of Denmark, Iceland, Norway, and Sweden], Turkey, United States, Portugal, Spain, United Kingdom, Australia, Costa Rica, Equador, and France).

diction. The notion here is that, when a non-party national is prosecuted before the ICC for crimes committed on the territory of a state that consents to ICC jurisdiction, the ICC exercises territorial jurisdiction that is delegated to the Court by the territorial state. Under Article 12 of the ICC Treaty, the ICC may exercise jurisdiction if the territorial state is a State Party or provides *ad hoc* consent. If the territorial state, which would ordinarily have jurisdiction, may delegate that territorial jurisdiction to a court outside its own national judicial system, including an international court, then arguably the ICC may legitimately exercise that delegated jurisdiction.

Here, the question arises whether, as a matter of customary international law, territorial jurisdiction may be delegated to an international court without the consent of the defendant's state of nationality. As we shall see, the consequences of delegated territorial jurisdiction are quite different from those of territorial jurisdiction exercised by the territorial state, particularly for interstate-dispute type cases. As was true in the case of universal jurisdiction, because the implications of state-exercised jurisdiction and jurisdiction exercised by an international court are not equivalent, states' consent to one is not equivalent to states' consent to the other. We may not simply assume, therefore, that states' territorial jurisdiction may be delegated to an international criminal court as a matter of customary law.

It will be useful to consider first whether a state's territorial jurisdiction may be delegated to another state and then to ask whether it may be delegated to an international court. It appears that a state may, under some circumstances, delegate its territorial jurisdiction over a given case to another state.[118] Delegation or "vicarious jurisdiction" is unproblematic when the defendant's state of nationality consents. Such vicarious exercise of jurisdiction with consent by the state of nationality occurs, for example, among parties to the European Convention on the Transfer of Proceedings in Criminal Matters.[119]

It is less clear that a state may delegate its territorial jurisdiction to another state in the absence of consent by the defendant's state of nationality. There seems to be no precedent for such exercise of jurisdiction, including under the European Convention on Transfer of Proceedings in Criminal Matters.[120] The possibility of transfer of jurisdiction where the defendant is a national of a third-party state is not precluded by the terms of that convention, which provide that:

1. For the purposes of applying this Convention, any Contracting state shall have competence to prosecute under its own criminal law any

---

[118] *See* Ethan A. Nadelman, *The Role of the United States in the International Enforcement of Criminal Law,* 31 HARV. INT'L L.J. 37, 69–70 (1990) (discussing vicarious jurisdiction).

[119] The European Convention on the Transfer of Proceedings in Criminal Matters, Mar. 30, 1978, Europ. T.S. No. 73.

[120] *Id.*

offence to which the law of another Contracting state is applicable.[121]

It appears that in practice, however, there has been no case of a transfer of criminal proceedings under the Convention in which the defendant was a national of a non-party to the Convention and the state of nationality did not consent to the transfer.[122] If such a transfer of proceedings were attempted, involving a delegation of territorial jurisdiction without the consent of the defendant's state of nationality, that state of nationality might well protest the prosecution as an invalid exercise of jurisdiction. It would remain to be seen what the result would be of such a challenge.[123]

If it is dubious that territorial jurisdiction may be delegated from one state to another without consent by the state of nationality, it is even less clear that territorial jurisdiction may be delegated, without that consent, to an international court. There has been no previous instance of delegation of territorial jurisdiction to an international court. Of the four international courts in recent history, the ICTY/R and the Nuremberg and Tokyo tribunals, none has based its jurisdiction on delegated territorial jurisdiction. As discussed earlier, the ICTY/R base their jurisdiction on the Security Council's Chapter VII powers, and the Nuremberg and Tokyo tribunals each founded its jurisdiction on the consent of the state of nationality.[124] (Indeed, far from basing jurisdiction on delegated territoriality, the Charter of the Nuremberg tribunal specifically indicated that the tribunal was to prosecute war criminals "whose offenses have no particular geographical location."[125])

Beyond the absence of precedent in state practice, there are legally significant reasons that states might object to the delegation of jurisdiction to an international court. These reasons, elaborated earlier in the context of universal jurisdiction, arise from the fact that the consequences for states of the compul-

---

[121] *Id.*, art. 2.

[122] *See* Communication from M. Cunha, *Responsable de l'application des conventions pénales du Conseil de l'Europe*, (conveyed via Marc Henzelin, University of Geneva Faculty of Law) (on file with author).

[123] In 1988, a Select Committee of Experts on Extraterritorial Jurisdiction, convened by the Council of Europe's Committee on Crime Problems, rendered an analysis of the exercise of extraterritorial jurisdiction in Europe including jurisdiction exercised pursuant to the European Convention on Transfer of Proceedings in Criminal Matters. *See* COUNCIL OF EUROPE, SELECT COMMITTEE OF EXPERTS ON EXTRATERRITORIAL JURISDICTION, EXTRATERRITORIAL CRIMINAL JURISDICTION (1990). The Committee did not, in the course of its deliberations or in its published study, examine the question of the applicability of the Convention to cases where defendants were non-party nationals. *See* Telephone Interview with Maurice Harari, Scientific Expert, Council of Europe's Select Committee of Experts on Extraterritorial Jurisdiction, in Geneva, Switz. (May 10, 1999).

[124] *See supra* pp. 244–52.

[125] Agreement for the Prosecution and Punishment of the Major War Criminals of the European Axis and the Charter of the International Military Tribunal annexed thereto, Aug. 8, 1945, art.1, 82 U.N.T.S. 279.

sory jurisdiction of an international court are fundamentally different from the consequences of the jurisdiction of national courts. As was discussed at length above, the delegation of jurisdiction to an international court may raise concerns for states regarding the diminished availability of compromise outcomes in inter-state disputes, the heightened political impact of verdicts, the role of an international court in shaping the law, and the possible impediments to diplomatic protection of nationals.[126] Transforming territorial jurisdiction into ICC jurisdiction through delegation would thus produce jurisdictional features entirely distinct from those envisioned in the customary law of territorial jurisdiction. For this reason, coupled with the absence of precedent for the delegation of territorial jurisdiction to an international court, it does not appear that the customary international law of territorial jurisdiction, as that law has evolved through state practice and *opinio juris*, has entailed the option of delegation of territorial jurisdiction to an international court.

Not only does the delegation of territorial jurisdiction to an international court lack grounding in customary international law, but the delegation of states' territorial jurisdiction may also be subject to abuse. The primary basis for the unquestioned place of territorial jurisdiction among internationally recognized bases for jurisdiction is the fact that the state where the crime occurred is presumed to have a legitimate interest in seeing that the crime is punished. That crucial linkage between territorial jurisdiction and the legitimate prosecutorial interests of the territorial state would be broken if territorial jurisdiction were delegated to a state on whose territory the crime did not occur. With that linkage broken, the door may be opened to the exercise of jurisdiction for illegitimate or abusive purposes.

To illustrate the problem, it may be helpful to consider an example involving a state-to-state delegation of jurisdiction. Imagine that France is holding for trial a United States national who has committed a crime on French territory. The United States has no basis to object to the exercise by France of its territorial jurisdiction over the United States national. Now let us imagine that France proposes to delegate its territorial jurisdiction to Libya and to transfer the defendant to Libya for prosecution. (Just to flesh out the tale, let us say that Libya is holding a French national for trial and is willing to transfer that case to France in exchange for the case of the United States national.) The United States would be correct in arguing that Libya does not have territorial (or any other internationally recognized basis for) jurisdiction and that France cannot confer, by delegation or otherwise, territorial jurisdiction upon a state on whose territory the conduct did not occur. While France has a recognized and legitimate interest in the punishment of the crime committed on French territory, Libya lacks that nexus with the crime that forms the basis for territorial jurisdiction. Libya might be motivated to make the jurisdictional trade for reasons that were illegitimate or

---

[126] *Supra* pp. 222–31.

abusive, for instance, to strengthen its hand in its political dealings with the United States. In any case, the traded jurisdiction would not conform with the principles (in particular, the recognition of the legitimate prosecutorial interests of the territorial state) on which territorial jurisdiction is founded.

The potential for abuse arising from delegation of territorial jurisdiction between individual states presumably is reduced where the jurisdiction is transferred not to an individual state but, rather, to an international court. Where that international court is controlled by a large number of states, the various States Parties may provide checks and balances against abuses being perpetrated in the interests of one state or a small group of states. The ICC Treaty provides that the Treaty will come into force only when there are a minimum of sixty States Parties. Since most of those sixty or more states presumably would be disinclined to permit the Court to be used for the corrupt purposes of one or a few states, corrupt motives would be unlikely to prevail.

Nevertheless, while the potential for abuse may be thus reduced, it is not eliminated. At the beginning of the twenty-first century, the world is not divided into opposing camps, as it was during the decades of the cold war. In the current political context, sixty states would represent an assortment of cross-cutting interests, which would make it difficult for one state or faction to turn the Court to the service of its own purposes. But the re-emergence of a bipolar (or even tripolar) world, along any number of foreseeable or unforeseeable fault lines, is not difficult to imagine. In a polarized world, sixty states could represent one faction or at least be amenable to strong influence by one or a few states. In such circumstances, the potential for the abusive delegation of territorial jurisdiction would not be negated by the requirement that the ICC Treaty have at least sixty States Parties to come into force. Rather, in those circumstances, permitting territorial jurisdiction to be treated as a form of negotiable instrument, to be used or conveyed, could have unintended and destructive consequences.

In this section, we have seen that there is an absence of precedent in state practice for the delegation of territorial jurisdiction to an international court. We also have seen that such delegation would have implications and consequences that are significantly different from those envisioned in the customary international law of territorial jurisdiction. These factors, in combination, suggest strongly that delegability to an international court is not entailed in the existing customary law of territorial jurisdiction.

D. THE LEGAL ACCEPTABILITY OF DELEGATED UNIVERSAL JURISDICTION OR DELEGATED TERRITORIAL JURISDICTION AS A LEGAL INNOVATION

Even if the option of delegating universal or territorial jurisdiction to an international court is not affirmatively encompassed within the existing customary law of universal or territorial jurisdiction, such a delegation of jurisdiction might nevertheless be lawful. In the *Lotus Case*,[127] the Permanent Court of International Justice (PCIJ) stated in dictum that, where a prosecuting state's jurisdiction is challenged, the burden rests with the challenging state to show what rule of international law the exercise of jurisdiction violates, and does not rest with the prosecuting state to show what principle of international law supports the jurisdiction. If *Lotus* were to be read in its strongest possible sense, then virtually all innovative bases for jurisdiction, including delegation of states' universal or territorial jurisdiction to the ICC, would be permissible since, being new, there would be, as yet, no rule against them.[128]

But that strong reading of *Lotus*, even if it were good law when *Lotus* was decided (which is itself doubtful[129]), is not an accurate description of the law now.[130] Rather than being strictly based on a permissive view that all jurisdiction is lawful unless the challenging state can point to a rule that it violates, the customary international law of criminal jurisdiction is based on a perceptible, if somewhat ill-defined, set of principles regarding the legitimate prosecutorial interests of states. In most criminal cases, those underlying principles are not relied upon explicitly, because the customary law of criminal jurisdiction recognizes an identifiable set of valid bases for jurisdiction. When jurisdiction can be justified by reference to one of those recognized bases, as is usually the case, reiteration of the underlying principles regarding the legitimate prosecutorial interests of states is not necessary.

The usual list of recognized bases of jurisdiction includes: territoriality, nationality, protective principle, universality, and passive personality (the last being the least robustly accepted). Some influential authorities maintain that this list is exclusive.[131] Since the list of recognized bases for jurisdiction is not arbi-

---

[127] *S.S. Lotus* (Fr. v. Turk.), 1927 P.C.I.J. (ser. A) No. 10.

[128] For an application of this approach to ICC jurisdiction over non-party nationals, *see* Scharf, *supra* note 69.

[129] The *Lotus* decision was controversial. The decision was rendered by an evenly divided court, with the president of the court breaking the tie with a casting vote. At the time of *Lotus'* publication, the academic literature was replete with vociferous objections to the court's reasoning. *See* FRITZ A. MANN, STUDIES IN INTERNATIONAL LAW 26 n.3 (1973) (and sources cited therein); IAN BROWNLIE, PRINCIPLES OF PUBLIC INTERNATIONAL LAW 302 n.24 (4th ed. 1990) (and sources cited therein).

[130] *See* MANN, STUDIES IN INTERNATIONAL LAW, *supra* note 129, at 26–27; BROWNLIE, PRINCIPLES OF PUBLIC INTERNATIONAL LAW, *supra* note 129, at 302–303; Prosper Weil, *International Law Limitations on state Jurisdiction, in* EXTRATERRITORIAL APPLICATION OF LAWS AND RESPONSES THERETO (Cecil Olmstead ed., 1983).

[131] *See, e.g.,* OSCAR SCHACHTER, INTERNATIONAL LAW IN THEORY AND PRACTICE 254–55, 257 (1991) ("any one of the [list of five] bases of jurisdiction just mentioned may meet the minimum international law requirements for jurisdiction to prescribe. If none is present, the application of domestic law in the particular case would be 'exorbitant,' that is, impermissible."); RESEARCH IN INTERNATIONAL LAW OF THE HARVARD LAW SCHOOL, II JURISDICTION WITH RESPECT TO CRIME, DRAFT CONVENTION WITH COMMENT, Supplement to 29 AM. J. INT'L L. 435, 445, 446 (1935).

trary but has developed to reflect an evolving delineation of the legitimate pros-ecutorial interests of states, it is unlikely that the list is actually closed. Rather, what appears to be true is that jurisdictional bases that are already recognized are uncontroversially acceptable, while the legitimacy of claimed new bases must be determined.

Michael Akehurst has noted that,

What *is* significant is the fact that writers almost always list specific heads of jurisdiction, thereby implying that all other types of jurisdiction are illegal, instead of simply stating the general presumption that all types of jurisdiction are legal and then listing specific heads of jurisdiction which are proved to be illegal.[132]

Akehurst is correct in observing that the practice of enumerating specific heads of jurisdiction that are lawful, rather than listing heads of jurisdiction that are pro-hibited, is both pervasive and significant. Any number of articles and briefs have been written that, after briefly citing *Lotus*, proceed to devote lengthy arguments to demonstrating that the jurisdiction being argued for fits into one or more of the five recognized bases for jurisdiction. *Lotus* itself is a specimen of this sort. After articulating the broad "*Lotus* principle" that "restrictions on the independence of states cannot . . . be presumed,"[133] the court then proceeded to base its decision upholding a challenged exercise of jurisdiction largely on an argument that the jurisdiction asserted was a form of territorial jurisdiction. The court interpreted territorial jurisdiction to encompass the territorial effects theory—which the court was then at pains to demonstrate had been previously internationally accepted as a valid basis for jurisdiction![134]

Were the lesson of *Lotus* very simply that jurisdiction is legitimate unless it violates an identifiable rule, then it would be hard to explain why the *Lotus* court went to great effort to show that the jurisdiction that it was upholding fell within a previously approved category of jurisdiction. Whatever the *Lotus* court's dicta, its opinion *in toto* reflects the subtler reality that determining the acceptability of a claimed form of jurisdiction requires either the short-cut of demonstrating that the jurisdiction falls within a previously accepted category, or the more complex task of determining whether the form of jurisdiction claimed comports with the underlying principles governing the international law of jurisdiction.

In addition to the writings of courts and commentators, state practice too reflects the fact that there is an identifiable universe of recognized bases for juris-diction under international law and an identifiable set of principles underlying those bases. When one state challenges another's exercise of jurisdiction, the chal-

---

[132] MICHAEL AKEHURST, JURISDICTION IN INTERNATIONAL LAW 167 (1974).

[133] *S.S. Lotus* (Fr. v. Turk.), 1927 P.C.I.J. (Ser. A) No. 10, at 18.

[134] *See id.*

lenged state routinely responds by reference to one or more of the internationally recognized bases for jurisdiction and, where warranted, to the rationales underlying those bases.[135] This approach stands to reason. It cannot be that any new basis for jurisdiction, however extravagant or nonsensical, is legitimate simply because it has not been previously claimed and has, therefore, not been previously rejected.

The point here is not to question the very general precept of *Lotus* that international law leaves to states "a wide measure of discretion which is only limited in certain cases by prohibitive rules."[136] Rather, the point is that the general precept articulated in *Lotus* must be read together with the other principles underlying and defining the customary law of jurisdiction. In short, the legitimacy of claimed new forms of jurisdiction must be determined, not assumed. The *Lotus* case places the burden of proof for this determination on the challenging state. But *Lotus* does not eliminate the necessity of making the determination of whether a claimed new form of jurisdiction is legitimate.

When a new basis for jurisdiction is claimed or proposed, its validity is evaluated by consideration of its appropriateness, measured in terms of the underlying principles and rationales governing jurisdiction under customary international law. Typically, this evaluation of appropriateness has meant a form of nexus analysis. The central question has been whether the conduct to be regulated is sufficiently linked to the legitimate interests of the state claiming jurisdiction to warrant recognition of jurisdiction. As Professor Mann puts it, "in essence criminal jurisdiction is determined not by such external, mechanical and inflexible tests as territoriality or nationality, but by the closeness of a state's connection with, or the intimacy and legitimacy of its interests in, the facts in issue."[137]

But this sort of nexus analysis would be inapposite in determining the appropriateness of ICC jurisdiction over non-party nationals. The ICC is not a state and has no "interests" of its own apart from those delegated to it by the States Parties to the Treaty. This is where nexus analysis fails us: the legitimacy of the original jurisdiction (universal or territorial) of those States Parties, based on their legitimate state interests, is unquestioned. What is at issue, rather, is the validity of the delegation of that jurisdiction, an issue with respect to which nexus analysis is unhelpful.

In evaluating the appropriateness of the delegation of universal or territorial jurisdiction, it may be useful to begin by articulating the basic principle, perhaps

---

[135] *See generally* VAUGHN LOWE, EXTRATERRITORIAL JURISDICTION: AN ANNOTATED COLLECTION OF LEGAL MATERIALS (1983) (reviewing a multitude of challenges by one state of another's asserted jurisdiction); *cf.* Attorney General of Israel v. Eichmann , 36 I.L.R. 283–87 (1962) (citing *Lotus* to support jurisdiction but then relying extensively on other, positive bases).

[136] *Lotus*, 1927 P.C.I.J. at 18.

[137] MANN, STUDIES IN INTERNATIONAL LAW, *supra* note 129, at 80.

rising to the level of a general principle of law, that legal relations that are based on mutual consent (or acquiescence) may not be altered by one party to the detriment of the other. In treaty law and contract law, this principle is reflected in the axiom *"pacta sunt servanda."*[138] In the context of customary international law, the principle prohibiting unilateral alteration of legal relations that are based on consent or acquiescence is reflected in the requirement that customary law develop through pervasive state practice and *opinio juris.*

Universal and territorial jurisdiction exist within and are defined by customary international law. Customary international law, in turn, comes into being through the consent or acquiescence of states over time. In this way, the definition and parameters of universal and territorial jurisdiction have come into being through the consent and acquiescence of states. In that sense, the rights and obligations of states relative to universal and territorial jurisdiction constitute a set of legal relations based on mutual consent and acquiescence over time.

In the debate about ICC jurisdiction over non-party nationals, there is no controversy about the principle that legal relations based on mutual consent or acquiescence may not unilaterally be materially altered.[139] Nor is there any controversy over the proposition that the law of universal and territorial jurisdiction is customary law which, in turn, is founded on the consent or acquiescence of states. Rather, the debate concerns whether incorporating the option of delegating universal or territorial jurisdiction to an international court should be considered to constitute a material alteration of the law of universal and territorial jurisdiction.

In addressing this question, we may benefit from an examination of the treatment of an analogous question in another area of law. The law of assignments addresses the question of whether and when the delegation or, more properly, the "assignment" of a right[140] should be considered a material alteration to a legal relationship. The law of assignments outlines an approach to this question that is suggestive for the present problem regarding the delegation of jurisdiction.

In the assignments context, the question is whether a party holding a contractual right may assign that right to a third party. The basic principle of the law of assignments, which is pervasively applied in municipal law[141] and private inter-

---

[138] Translated as: "Agreements (and stipulations) of the parties (to a contract) must be observed." BLACK'S LAW DICTIONARY 998 (5th ed. 1979).

[139] *Cf. infra* pp. 269–72 regarding whether the ICC Treaty has already altered customary law.

[140] In the context of the ICC debate, the word "delegation" has been used to refer to the transfer of a right (to prosecute). This language is different from that used in the law of assignments, in which "assignment" would refer to the transfer of a right while "delegation" would refer to transfer of an obligation.

[141] *See* MANN, STUDIES IN INTERNATIONAL LAW, *supra* note 129, at 363.

national law,[142] is that rights may be assigned only when the assignment does not prejudice the obligor's position.[143] As described in the *Restatement of Contracts 2d*, "A contractual right may be assigned unless [] the substitution of a right of the assignee for the right of the assignor would materially change the duty of the obligor, or materially increase the burden or risk imposed on him. . . ."[144] While assignment is not generally a feature of public international law,[145] proposals to incorporate the concept of assignment into the law of treaties consistently treat as foundational the principle of non-prejudice to the interests of the obligor.[146] The non-prejudice rule provides a method for upholding, in cases in which assignment of a right is contemplated, the principle that legal relations that are based on mutual consent or acquiescence may not be materially altered by one party to the detriment of the other.

As was argued earlier, the delegation of states' universal or territorial jurisdiction to an international court would materially increase the risk or burden imposed on a state whose national may be subject to prosecution for an international crime. This increased risk or burden arises, primarily in interstate-dispute type cases,[147] from the elimination of states' discretion regarding methods of interstate dispute resolution, and from the potential practical, political, and precedential disadvantages that this loss of discretion implies. Applying the non-prejudice principle to the question whether states may delegate (or "assign") jurisdiction to the ICC would lead to the conclusion that the delegation of jurisdiction from a state to the ICC is not permissible without the consent of what might be called the obligor state (the defendant's state of nationality) because it would materially increase the burden or risk imposed on that state.

The point here is not to suggest that the law of assignments has legal force in the very different field of the customary international law of jurisdiction. The relevance of the law of assignments is that it is a body of law concerned centrally with the question of when the delegation of a right is permissible, and that it offers a cogent framework for approaching that issue. The law of assignments is therefore suggestive of how we might usefully evaluate whether and when the delegation of jurisdiction should be considered permissible.

---

[142] *See, e.g.,* U.N. COMM'N ON INT'L TRADE L., DRAFT CONVENTION ON ASSIGNMENT OF RECEIVABLES FINANCING: TEXT WITH REMARKS AND SUGGESTIONS, U.N. Doc. A/CN.9/WG.II/WP.104 (July 16, 1999).

[143] *See* MANN, STUDIES IN INTERNATIONAL LAW, *supra* note 129, at 363.

[144] RESTATEMENT (SECOND) OF CONTRACTS § 317(2) (1981).

[145] *See* BROWNLIE, PRINCIPLES OF PUBLIC INTERNATIONAL LAW, *supra* note 129, at 678.

[146] *See, e.g.,* MANN, STUDIES IN INTERNATIONAL LAW, *supra* note 129, at 363 ("the paramount rule being that [the obligor's] position is not to be prejudiced as a result of the assignment"); CHRISTINE CHINKIN, THIRD PARTIES IN INTERNATIONAL LAW 58 (1992).

[147] There may also be increased burdens and risks in individual-culpability cases if a state wishes to provide diplomatic protection. *See supra* note 82.

Analysis of the delegated universal jurisdiction theory and the delegated territorial jurisdictional theory has resulted in the conclusion that delegability to an international court is not a feature of universal or territorial jurisdiction under existing customary international law. Using the non-prejudice principle to analyze the appropriateness of delegated universal or territorial jurisdiction as an innovative form of jurisdiction suggests that delegation of universal or territorial jurisdiction to an international court would not constitute an appropriate innovation. In sum, analyzing ICC jurisdiction over non-party nationals as the delegated jurisdiction of states has not provided an adequate legal foundation for the jurisdiction claimed.

E. JURISDICTION WITHOUT DELEGATION

The theories that conceptualize ICC jurisdiction over non-party nationals as the delegated jurisdiction of states rest on the premise that such delegation is permissible under customary international law. That premise is deeply problematic, as we have seen. Eliminating the delegated jurisdiction theories, as appears to be warranted, leaves the ICC Treaty itself, without support from the pre-existing jurisdiction of states, as the sole foundation of ICC jurisdiction over non-party nationals. We will therefore consider whether there is a legal basis for the ICC Treaty's creating ICC jurisdiction over non-party nationals as a strictly new base of jurisdiction. Such a legal basis might rest upon a theory of global treaties, or a theory of the ICC Treaty as generating new customary law, or on an analogy between the ICC Treaty and the anti-terrorism treaties.

1. Global Treaties

It has been suggested that there exists a genre of treaties that are globally binding because they foster the common interests of humanity.[148] The ICC Treaty might be thought to fall within that genre. If the ICC Treaty were globally binding, then all states would be bound to accept the Treaty's jurisdictional provisions even if those provisions departed from the customary international law of jurisdiction.

A threshold problem with the theory of global treaties is that there will inevitably be disagreement about what in fact will serve the common interests of humanity. An equally formidable problem confronting the theory of global treaties is that, even if that which would serve the common interests of humanity could be dispositively identified, that alone would not bind states who would find unacceptable a particular distribution of the burdens involved in serving those interests. For both of these reasons, the mere invocation of common interests does not resolve the matter.

---

[148] *See* GENNADY M. DANILENKO, LAW-MAKING IN THE INTERNATIONAL COMMUNITY 64–68 (1993).

An effort was made by some states to treat the U.N. Convention on the Law of the Sea as globally binding by virtue of its perceived importance for the common interests of humanity.[149] Just as one might expect, notwithstanding declarations by some states that the deep sea-bed mining regime of the Law of the Sea Convention was binding on non-parties, non-party states rejected that view and proceeded with legislation and agreements regarding reciprocal recognition of mining sites that were prohibited by the treaty.[150] The point here is not that states flout treaties. Rather, the point is that invocation of the interests of humanity does not resolve political debate, and it has not proved successful in binding non-parties to treaty obligations.

In the ICC context, the United States has argued, in effect, that humanity is best served by the U.S. remaining free in its peacekeeping and humanitarian activities from such inhibitions as implementation of the current ICC Treaty would pose.[151] As Ambassador Scheffer has stated,

> the consequence imposed by Article 12, particularly for non-parties to the treaty, will be to limit severely those lawful, but highly controversial and inherently risky, interventions that the advocates of human rights and world peace so desperately seek from the United States and other military powers. There will be significant new legal and political risks in such interventions. . . .[152]

Proponents of the ICC Treaty take the view that the benefits to humanity offered by implementation of the Treaty would outweigh whatever might be lost by way of inhibition of U.S. humanitarian action. Regardless of the merits of that debate, invocation of the interests of humanity clearly does not resolve the issue and only raises again the question of who has the right to decide. Claiming that a particular treaty serves the common interests of humanity does nothing fundamentally to alter the debate.

Before leaving this debate, however, we must examine what some might view as the best example of a treaty entailing global application by virtue of its claim to global benefits. This is the United Nations Charter and, particularly, Article 2 of the Charter, which enunciates the Charter's fundamental principles. Article 2 (6) of the Charter states: "The organization shall ensure that states which are not members of the United Nations act in accordance with these principles so far as that may be necessary for the maintenance of international peace and security."

---

[149] *See id.*, at 66.

[150] *See id.*

[151] *See supra* text accompanying note 205.

[152] David J. Scheffer, *The United States and the International Criminal Court*, 93 AM. J. INT'L L. 12, 19 (1999) [hereinafter Scheffer, *The United States and the International Criminal Court*].

Some authorities interpret that article as reflecting that the Charter imposes obligations on non-members of the U.N.[153] But that view is controversial.[154] An alternative interpretation is that,

> Article 2(6) is addressed to the United Nations and its members. While members of the organization may be under a charter obligation to ensure that all states act in accordance with the Charter, as a treaty provision this rule still remains *inter alios acta* for the third states which are under no legal duty to comply with it. Indeed, the practice of non-member states shows that they do not consider themselves as legally bound by the Charter of the United Nations."[155]

Certainly, non-members of the United Nations, including Switzerland, take the view that they are not bound by the Charter.[156]

Whatever may be the current status of U.N. Charter Article 2 (6) with regard to binding third parties, the only relevant issue in drawing an analogy with the current status of the ICC Treaty is the status of third parties relative to the Charter at the time of its adoption. Even if we were to assume that customary law has developed in the years since the Charter's adoption, such that the principles referred to in Article 2(6) are now binding on non-parties, this would imply nothing for the ICC Treaty except that, in future years, customary law might develop such that aspects of the ICC Treaty would pass into customary law and thereby become binding on non-parties to the Treaty.[157] What is relevant for present purposes is not whether the U.N. Charter has come to bind non-parties as a matter of subsequent custom but whether it bound non-parties upon its adoption by virtue of its humanitarian aims and global purposes.

---

[153] *See, e.g.*, RICHARD FALK, THE STATUS OF LAW IN INTERNATIONAL SOCIETY 185 (1970); BROWNLIE, PRINCIPLES OF PUBLIC INTERNATIONAL LAW, *supra* note 129, at 694.

[154] *See generally* BRUNO SIMMA ET AL., THE CHARTER OF THE UNITED NATIONS: A COMMENTARY 131–39 (1994) (discussing art. 2(6) of the U.N. Charter and the controversy regarding the legal effects of the Charter on non-members of the U.N.).

[155] DANILENKO, *supra* note 148, at 60. *See also* RICHARD A. FALK, THE AUTHORITY OF THE UNITED NATIONS TO CONTROL NON-MEMBERS 73–74 (1965). *But see* Kunz, *Revolutionary Creation of Norms of International Law*, 41 AM. J. INT'L L. 119,124 (1947) (taking the view that this analysis evades the core issue of the legal authority of the United Nations to exercise power over non-members); OPPENHEIM-LAUTERPACHT, INTERNATIONAL LAW 928 (8th ed. 1955) (same).

[156] *See* 26 SJIR 84–88 (1970) (official statement of Swiss position); 39 SJIR 264–67 (1983) (same).

[157] The prospect of the ICC Treaty passing into customary law will be considered *infra* pp. 269–72.

As to the question whether customary law developments prompted by the Charter itself have given rise to a new customary regime of global treaties, *see infra* pp. 268–69.

The present analysis of whether Article 2(6) was regarded as binding on non-parties at the time of the U.N. Charter's adoption will be limited to analysis of the U.N. Charter as a multilateral treaty. There are those who argue that Article 2(6) has bound non-members since the Charter's adoption by virtue of the Charter's being a "world constitution"[158] or other unique instrument.[159] Whatever the merits of those claims, they are, by their very nature, inapplicable to the ICC Treaty. Viewing the Charter as a treaty (and therefore analogous in at least some ways to the ICC Treaty), we must conclude that the Charter did not, upon adoption, bind third parties to obligations not previously existing under customary law.

Bentwich and Martin's 1950 Commentary on the Charter of the United Nations states:

> [T]he Charter does not purport to impose legal obligations on non-members. It does, however, impose upon the Organization itself an obligation to ensure—by persuasion, if possible, but by the application of force, if necessary—the compliance of non-members with the Principles of the United Nations. The former will have to obey not as a matter of law, but as the result of the realities of power.[160]

Numerous such commentaries, reflecting the view that the U.N. Charter did not legally bind non-parties, were written in the early years of the U.N.'s existence. Those early commentators on the U.N. Charter who viewed the Charter as a treaty virtually uniformly took this position.[161]

There is also reflected in the writing of that time, however, an increasing anticipation that the advent of the U.N. system itself and its Charter provisions might lead to an erosion in some contexts of the principle that treaties cannot bind third parties. The treatment of this issue in successive editions of the Oppenheim-Lauterpacht treatise on international law is illustrative. Lauterpacht wrote in the seventh edition in 1948 that "Non-members are not bound by [Article 2(6)] and

---

[158] FALK, THE AUTHORITY OF THE UNITED NATIONS TO CONTROL NON-MEMBERS, *supra* note 155, at 51. *See, e.g.*, ROSS, CONSTITUTION OF THE UNITED NATIONS 32 (1950); Bardo Fassbender, *The United Nations Charter as Constitution of the International Community*, 36 COLUM. J. TRANSNAT'L L. 529 (1998).

[159] *See* FALK, THE AUTHORITY OF THE UNITED NATIONS TO CONTROL NON-MEMBERS, *supra* note 155, at 66–67, 70, 101.

[160] NORMAN BENTWICH & ANDREW MARTIN, A COMMENTARY ON THE CHARTER OF THE UNITED NATIONS 14 (1950).

[161] *See, e.g.*, Kunz, *supra* note 155, 156, at 119–26; LELAND M. GOODRICH & EDVARD I. HAMBRO, THE CHARTER OF THE UNITED NATIONS: COMMENTARY AND DOCUMENTS 108–10 (1st ed. 1946); BENTWICH & MARTIN, *supra* note 160, at 14; 1 GUGGENHEIM, LEHRBUCH DES VOLKERRECHTS 92 (1948); Kunz, *General International Law and the Law of International Organizations*, 48 AM. J. INT'L L. 456, 457 (1953); I OPPENHEIM-LAUTERPACHT, INTERNATIONAL LAW 928–29 (7th ed. 1948); *cf.* PHILIP C. JESSUP, A MODERN LAW OF NATIONS 168 (1948).

they may choose to react accordingly."[162] By the eighth edition, published in 1955, Lauterpacht wrote,

> International Law does not as yet recognize anything in the nature of a legislative process by which rules of law are imposed upon a dissenting minority of states. However, in proportion as international society is transformed into an integrated community, a departure from the accepted principle becomes unavoidable, in particular in the sphere of preservation of international peace and security. . . . Both the Covenant . . . and the Charter . . . must therefore be regarded as having set a limit, determined by the general interest of the international community, to the rule that a treaty cannot impose obligations upon states which are not parties to it.[163]

There is a similar progression in the treatment of Article 2(6) in successive editions of Goodrich and Hambro's commentaries on the U.N. Charter. The first edition, published in 1946 states that,

> The Charter does not of course create any legal obligation for states not Members of the Organization. They are therefore not obligated in a legal sense to act according to the Principles of the Charter for any purpose whatsoever. The Charter system therefore provides for the imposition, by force if necessary, of the prescribed conduct without any legal basis in contractual agreement.[164]

By 1949, Goodrich and Hambro had softened their language, stating,

> It is doubtful whether an international instrument can impose legal obligations on states which are not parties to it. The traditional theory, which is not unanimously held [here, the authors cite Kelsen], is that treaties cannot obligate third parties.[165]

Hans Kelsen has indeed been prominently, but somewhat erroneously, associated with the view that Article 2(6) bound non-members to new obligations from the time of the Charter's adoption. He stated in his 1950 book that

> non-Member states are obliged by the Charter just as Members are, to settle their disputes by peaceful means, to refrain in the relation to other

---

[162] I OPPENHEIM-LAUTERPACHT, INTERNATIONAL LAW, *supra* note 161.

[163] I OPPENHEIM-LAUTERPACHT, INTERNATIONAL LAW 652 (8th ed. 1955).

[164] LELAND M. GOODRICH & EDVARD I. HAMBRO, THE CHARTER OF THE UNITED NATIONS: COMMENTARY AND DOCUMENTS 71 (1st ed. 1946).

[165] LELAND M. GOODRICH & EDVARD I. HAMBRO, THE CHARTER OF THE UNITED NATIONS: COMMENTARY AND DOCUMENTS 108–09 (2d ed. 1949).

states from the threat or use of force, to give the United Nations every assistance in any action it takes in accordance with the Charter, and to refrain from giving assistance to any state against which the United Nations is taking preventive or enforcement action.[166]

But Kelsen seems to have meant not that this interpretation of Article 2(6) was law in 1950 but, rather, that such an interpretation of Article 2(6) could or should be law, the final ascertainment of which, however, would have to await the development of custom. As Kelsen wrote, continuing the passage quoted above,

> From the point of view of existing international law, the attempt of the Charter to apply to states which are not contracting parties to it must be characterized as revolutionary. Whether it will be considered as a violation of the old, or as the beginning of a new international law, remains to be seen.[167]

Thus, the prevailing view at the time of the U.N. Charter's adoption was that it was not binding on non-parties. There was some thought in the years following its adoption that the emergence of the U.N. system and the very fact of the Charter's adoption, including Article 2(6), might effect a movement away from the strict application of the *pacta tertiis* principle. In retrospect, we may fairly conclude that such an expectation was not fulfilled. Rather, the scope of coverage of Article 2(6) remains somewhat controversial,[168] and the authorities that do view the Charter provisions as binding on non-parties generally maintain that this is so as a consequence of the development of customary law concerning the Charter, not by virtue of an exception to the *pacta tertiis* principle.[169] Significantly, the U.N. Charter has not proven to be the herald of a new era of international law featuring global treaties that bind parties and non-parties alike.

The U.N. Charter thus does not provide a precedential foundation for the ICC Treaty's binding non-parties. It would be bootstrapping to suggest that a theory of global treaties can be supported by reference to the U.N. Charter, which itself was not regarded as "global" when adopted and which, even now, can claim universal applicability, if at all, only by virtue of the usual processes of customary law development.

In the end, the global treaty theory as a basis for ICC jurisdiction over non-parties is untenable not only as a matter of customary law but also as a practical

---

[166] HANS KELSEN, THE LAW OF THE UNITED NATIONS: A CRITICAL ANALYSIS OF ITS FUNDAMENTAL PROBLEMS 107 (1950).

[167] *Id.* at 109–10. *See also* Verdross, *Le Nazioni Unite e i Terzi state*, 2 LA COMUNITA INTERNAZIONALE 455 (1947) (taking a similar view).

[168] *See* SIMMA ET AL., *supra* note 154.

[169] *See id.* at 137–38.

matter. The practical problem is that the theory of global treaties merely reframes the question whether a treaty may bind non-parties as the question whether a treaty may bind non-parties if it purports to pronounce what is best for humanity—without providing any means for resolving the inevitable disagreements about what is best for humanity and about distributing the burdens of achieving humanitarian goals.

The existence of *jus cogens* norms and *erga omnes* obligations does not help to resolve these issues. *Jus cogens* norms and *erga omnes* obligations include obligations on states to prevent and, in some circumstances, to prosecute and punish genocide, war crimes and crimes against humanity—the crimes that form the subject-matter jurisdiction of the ICC.[170] But those *jus cogens* norms and *erga omnes* obligations do not include a requirement that prevention and punishment occur through the mechanism of an international criminal court. Even while customary *jus cogens* and *erga omnes* norms have evolved in certain areas of substantive law, customary law has not developed, as we have seen, to require enforcement of that substantive law through an international court. In fact, as has been discussed, there are reasons for which alternatives to international adjudication may sometimes be preferable in cases that involve interstate legal disputes. Reference to the universally binding nature of the substantive norms of international criminal law cannot be relied on to do double duty to form the basis also for an argument that use of the ICC mechanism is also obligatory or that the ICC Treaty is a global treaty, with jurisdictional obligations binding on all states.

2. The ICC Treaty as Generating Customary Law

Even if a treaty cannot be said to bind non-parties simply by virtue of its claim to serve humanity, there remains the possibility that the content of a treaty may become part of customary law and thereby bind non-parties. Viewing the ICC solely in its posture as adjudicator of individual culpability, one might conclude that ICC jurisdiction over non-party nationals would constitute only an incremental step in the development of customary law from the existing customary law of universal or territorial jurisdiction. When the ICC's role as an adjudicator of interstate disputes is also taken into account, however, the difference between states' universal or territorial jurisdiction and ICC jurisdiction is revealed to be very significant, as we have seen. When this second aspect of the ICC's character is considered, it becomes clear that establishing customary law supporting ICC jurisdiction over non-party nationals would involve not a minor or an incremental step but a distinct new departure in the law of jurisdiction.

---

[170] *See generally* ANDRÉ DE HOOGH, OBLIGATIONS ERGA OMNES AND INTERNATIONAL CRIMES (1996) (on development of the *erga omnes* and *jus cogens* doctrines as applicable to international crime); *cf.* Prosper Weil, *Towards Relative Normativity in International Law*, 77 AM. J. INT'L L. 413 (1983) (questioning the wisdom of development of the *jus cogens* and *erga omnes* doctrines).

Considering the process by which the content of a treaty may become part of customary law, the International Court of Justice (ICJ) in the Continental Shelf case stated that:

> With respect to the other elements usually regarded as necessary before a conventional rule can be considered to have become a general rule of international law, it might be that, even without the passage of any considerable period of time, a very widespread and representative participation in the convention might suffice of itself, provided it included that of states whose interests were specially affected. . . .
>
> Although the passage of only a short period of time is not necessarily, or of itself, a bar to the formation of a new rule of customary international law on the basis of what was originally a purely conventional rule, an indispensable requirement would be that within the period in question, short though it might be, state practice, including that of states whose interests are specially affected, should have been both extensive and virtually uniform in the sense of the provision invoked;— and should moreover have occurred in such a way as to show a general recognition that a rule of law or legal obligation is involved.[171]

It would be difficult to argue that the ICC Treaty has generated customary law supporting ICC jurisdiction over non-party nationals. There has been no period of time in which "extensive and virtually uniform" state practice has supported the form of jurisdiction in question. This is true even if we take the adoption of the ICC Treaty by 120 states at the Rome conference as a form of state practice.[172] Even in a situation in which a treaty faced less opposition than did the ICC Treaty (seven states voted against adoption, twenty-one states abstained),[173] reliance on adoption of a treaty at a diplomatic conference alone would be a precarious basis for a claim to creation of customary law. In the case of the ICC Treaty, with only four States Parties and eighty-four signatories at present,[174] the ICC Treaty cannot be said to enjoy participation that is "very widespread and representative" much less "virtually uniform." As the ICJ stated in the Continental

---

[171]   North Sea Continental Shelf, 1969 I.C.J. 3, at 41–42.

[172]   On the debate regarding the treatment of treaty participation as a form of state practice for purposes of customary law development, *see* Oscar Schachter, *Entangled Treaty and Custom, in* INTERNATIONAL LAW AT A TIME OF PERPLEXITY 724–26 (Yoram Dinstein ed., 1989); Arthur Weisburd, *Customary International Law: The Problem of Treaties*, 21 VAND. J. TRANSNAT'L L. 1 (1988); ANTHONY A. D'AMATO, THE CONCEPT OF CUSTOM IN INTERNATIONAL LAW 3–4, 89–90, 103–65 (1971).

[173]   U.N. Conference of Plenipotentiaries on the Establishment of an International Criminal Court, *U.N. Diplomatic Conference Concludes in Rome with Decision to Establish Permanent International Court*, Press Release L/ROM/22, July 17, 1998 <http://www.un.org/icc/> (visited Mar. 22, 2000) .

[174]   United Nations, *Rome Statute of International Criminal Court: Ratification Status* <http://www.un.org/law/icc/statute/status/htm> (last modified Mar. 9, 2000).

Shelf case, "the number of ratifications and accessions so far secured is . . . hardly sufficient. That non-ratification may sometimes be due to factors other than active disapproval of the convention concerned can hardly constitute a basis on which positive acceptance of its principles can be implied."[175] Nor does such participation as there is in the ICC Treaty actually include "that of states whose interests are specially affected." The United States, which is disproportionately involved in military activities throughout the world, has vocally rejected aspects of the treaty, most particularly including its jurisdictional provisions.

Perhaps the most illuminating point regarding whether participation in the ICC Treaty can currently be said to constitute state practice sufficient to have generated customary law is simply that the Treaty, by its own terms, requires sixty ratifications or accessions before it can come into force. The Treaty's drafters recognized that this was the minimum degree of support that would be required before the ICC could become a credible international court. Since the Treaty does not yet have the degree of adherence that the Court's supporters recognized was required to make the Court a credible international institution, and since the jurisdictional issue was among the most controversial aspects in the Treaty negotiations,[176] it is difficult to see how the Treaty can be said already to have sufficient adherence, particularly on the issue of jurisdiction, to constitute the necessary state practice to generate customary law on ICC jurisdiction.

A number of scholars of customary international law have argued that state practice is not a separate element required for the generation of customary law but is relevant only as evidence of *opinio juris*.[177] Based on that view, some have argued for the possibility of instant custom.[178] All, however, ultimately rest their arguments for instant custom on the existence of consensus or virtual consensus regarding the subject at issue—a consensus which is obviously lacking in the case of the ICC Treaty.

Bin Cheng's theory of "instant customary law" begins with the premise that the fundamental substance of customary international law is *opinio juris*. Practice, he reasons, is not a constitutive element of custom but, rather, provides evidence of the existence and content of the requisite *opinio juris*. As he puts it,

> If states consider themselves bound by a given rule of international law,
> it is difficult to see why it should not be treated as such in so far as these

---

[175] Continental Shelf, 169 I.C.J. at 42.

[176] *See* Philippe Kirsch and John T. Holmes, *The Rome Conference on an International Criminal Court: The Negotiating Process*, 93 AM. J. INT'L L. 2, 7–9 (1999).

[177] *See, e.g.*, Bin Cheng, *United Nations Resolutions on Outer Space: "Instant" International Customary Law?*, 5 INDIAN J. OF INT'L L. 23 (1965).

[178] *See, e.g., id.*

states are concerned, especially when the rule does not infringe the right of third states not sharing the same *opinio juris*. . . .

From this point of view, there is no reason why an *opinio juris communis* may not grow up in a very short period of time among all or simply some Members of the United Nations with the result that a new rule of international customary law comes into being among them. . . .

There is no reason why a new *opinio juris* may not grow overnight between states so that a new rule of international customary law (or unwritten international law) comes into existence instantly.[179]

In Cheng's theory of "instant custom," then, we find simply the unexceptionable proposition that those who agree to be bound now may be bound now but may not bind others.

Anthony D'Amato has made a similar point, though he places greater emphasis on the need for consensus if all, rather than only some, states are to be bound:

[t]o the extent that a widely adopted multilateral convention represents the consensus of states on the precepts contained therein those precepts are part of international law by that fact alone. In this sense, multilateral treaties are and historically have been more important than bilateral ones. But this effect is not due to anything connected with the concept of custom; it involves a separate phenomenon—"consensus"—which deserves separate study as to its nature, identification and provability.[180]

The theory of instant customary law and D'Amato's closely related theory of consensus can be eliminated as plausible bases for ICC jurisdiction over non-party nationals. Those theories rest, as they must, on the observation that if consent is so pervasive as to be consensus then, all agreeing to be bound, all are bound. Such a consensus, or even pervasive acquiescence including specially interested states, is conspicuously absent in the case of the ICC Treaty. The Treaty thus cannot currently be said to have created custom, instant or otherwise, with regard to ICC jurisdiction over non-party nationals.[181]

---

[179] *Id.* at 37, 46.

[180] D'AMATO, *supra* note 172, at 165.

[181] Even if the ICC Treaty has not as yet generated customary law supporting ICC jurisdiction over non-party nationals, such custom could conceivably emerge in the future. If and when such a development should take place, the United States presumably would be in a position to claim persistent objector status with regard to ICC jurisdiction over its nationals, having clearly articulated its objections to the purported jurisdiction immediately and consistently from the time it was proposed. For analyses of the preconditions for and consequences of persistent objector status, *see* Jonathan Charney, *Universal International Law*, 87 AM. J. INT'L L. 529 (1993); David Colson, *How Persistent Must the Persistent Objector Be?*, 61 WASH. L. REV. 957 (1986).

3. The Terrorism Treaties

A number of treaties, primarily concerned with terrorism, concluded in the 1970s and 1980s[182] have been understood by some to "create" universal jurisdiction over the crimes that are the subject matter of those treaties.[183] It has been suggested that the terrorism treaties reflect a power of states to create, by treaty, extraterritorial jurisdiction having no other legal basis, and then to exercise that jurisdiction over the nationals of non-party states. If the terrorism treaties can thus create jurisdiction that can be exercised over non-party nationals, the argument proceeds, then the ICC Treaty must be able to do the same. As will be demonstrated in the following pages, the terrorism treaties, if they "create" universal jurisdiction at all, do so through contributing to the development of customary law, not through some exceptional form of fiat by treaty. The terrorism treaties thus cannot be relied upon as precedents validating ICC jurisdiction over non-party nationals.

Treaties on hijacking[184] and other crimes on aircraft,[185] crimes against the safety of maritime navigation,[186] hostage-taking,[187] attacks on internationally protected persons,[188] and U.N. personnel,[189] terrorist bombings,[190] and torture,[191] each contain provisions permitting a State Party to prosecute individuals believed to have committed the enumerated crimes when such individuals are found within

---

[182] *See infra* notes 184–191 and accompanying text.

[183] *See, e.g.,* Scharf, *supra* note 69.

[184] *See* Convention for the Suppression of Unlawful Seizure of Aircraft, Dec. 16, 1970, 22 U.S.T. 1641, 860 U.N.T.S. 105.

[185] *See* Montreal Convention for the Suppression of Unlawful Acts Against the Safety of Civil Aviation, Sept. 23, 1971, 24 U.S.T. 564, 974 U.N.T.S. 177; Protocol for the Suppression of Unlawful Acts of Violence at Airports Serving International Civil Aviation, supplementary to the Convention of Sept. 23, 1971, Feb. 24, 1988, S. Treaty Doc. No. 100–19.

[186] *See* Convention and Protocol on the Suppression of Unlawful Acts Against the Safety of Maritime Navigation, Mar. 10, 1988, 27 I.L.M. 668.

[187] *See* International Convention Against the Taking of Hostages, Dec. 17, 1979, TIAS No. 11,081, 1316 U.N.T.S. 205.

[188] *See* Convention on the Prevention and Punishment of Crimes Against Internationally Protected Persons, Including Diplomatic Agents, Dec. 14, 1973, 28 U.S.T. 1975, 1035 U.N.T.S. 167.

[189] *See* Convention on the Safety of United Nations and Associated Personnel, Dec. 15, 1995, U.N. GAOR 49th Sess., Supp. No. 49, Vol. 1, at 299, U.N. Doc. A/49/49 (1994), 34 I.L.M. 482 (1995).

[190] *See* International Convention for the Suppression of Terrorist Bombings, 37 I.L.M. 249 (1998).

[191] *See* Convention Against Torture and Other Cruel, Inhuman or Degrading Treatment or Punishment, opened for signature Dec. 10, 1984, 23 I.L.M. 1027, 1465 U.N.T.S. 85. Torture is not a terrorism offense, but the Torture Convention's jurisdictional provisions fit within the mold of the provisions found in the terrorism conventions.

its territory. As no link other than presence of the suspect is required, jurisdiction would not be based on territoriality, nationality, protective principle nor passive personality but, rather, upon universality of jurisdiction. Since the crimes covered by the treaties in question arguably were not previously recognized as entailing universal jurisdiction, and yet the treaties provide that universal jurisdiction may be exercised over those crimes, the treaties, it is argued, must have created universal jurisdiction over those crimes.

But that conclusion must be incorrect. States are not obliged simply to accept purported new subjects of universal jurisdiction. In the absence of customary law recognizing universal jurisdiction over a given crime, each state may acquiesce in or protest against a proposed new subject of universal jurisdiction. In the event of a protest, the ensuing debate would invoke the usual criteria for determining the legitimacy of a new form of jurisdiction.[192] Customary law governing the matter would then emerge accordingly. The terrorism treaties that some believe create universal jurisdiction represent agreements by the States Parties not to object when others (or, at least, other States Parties) exercise jurisdiction as delineated by the treaties. But the treaties cannot bind non-parties similarly to accept the treaties' terms.

How, then, are we to understand the import of the treaties that do appear on their face to purport to create universal jurisdiction? Are they simply void, having exceeded the bounds of the customary international law of universal jurisdiction? Some have taken that view.[193] An alternative theory, however, would view the treaties as "proposing" the development of customary law.

The terrorism treaties that are cited as creating universal jurisdiction all concern crimes that were, at the time of the treaties' conclusion, already prime candidates for universal jurisdiction. Some of the crimes were already considered by some to entail universal jurisdiction.[194] And even those that arguably did not yet entail universal jurisdiction shared the principal indicia of crimes over which universal jurisdiction is suitable. They were crimes of substantial seriousness, of concern to all states, and which are difficult to control without substantial international cooperation.[195] What the treaties did was, in effect, to propose—to

---

[192] *See supra* pp. 257–63.

[193] *See, e.g.*, Jordan Paust, *Extradition of the Achille-Lauro Hostage-Takers: Navigating the Hazards*, 20 VAND. J. TRANSNAT'L L. 235, 254 (1987) ("universal jurisdiction under the Hostages Convention . . . is highly suspect with regard to defendants who are not nationals of a signatory to the Hostages Convention").

[194] *See, e.g.*, Kenneth C. Randall, *Universal Jurisdiction Under International Law*, 66 TEX. L. REV. 785, 834–38 (1988); RESTATEMENT (THIRD) OF THE FOREIGN RELATIONS LAW OF THE UNITED STATES § 404 (1987).

[195] Michael Akehurst has made a similar observation:

Hijacking is probably not covered by the definition of piracy in international law, but there is doctrinal authority for the view that it is subject to universal jurisdiction nevertheless;

articulate[196] in a clear form—the suggestion that the crimes become recognized as entailing universal jurisdiction. States were then free to respond to that proposal, by active acceptance (in becoming States Parties to the treaties) or active rejection (by objecting to the treaties or to prosecutions brought pursuant to them) or passive acquiescence (by accepting, or refraining from objecting to, the treaties or prosecutions pursuant thereto). As D'Amato has put it,

> The articulation of a rule of international law—whether it be a new rule or a departure from and modification of an existing rule—in advance of or concurrently with a positive act (or omission) of a state gives a state notice that its action or decision will have legal implications. In other words, given such notice, statesmen will be able freely to decide whether or not to pursue various policies, knowing that their acts may create or modify international law.[197]

It appears that, as one might have predicted, the response to the jurisdictional provisions of the terrorism treaties has been acceptance and acquiescence. There have been a number of prosecutions under the terrorism treaties of individuals who were not nationals of States Parties to those treaties, and yet there appears to be thus far no case in which the defendant's state of nationality has objected to that exercise of jurisdiction.

In the *Yunis* case,[198] for example, the United States prosecuted a Lebanese national under the United States' implementing legislation for the Convention for the Suppression of Unlawful Seizure of Aircraft[199] and the International Convention Against the Taking of Hostages.[200] Lebanon was a party to the former but not the latter convention. Nevertheless, Lebanon raised no objection to the prosecution of Yunis for hostage taking.

It is significant to note as well that the United States, in *Yunis*, did not take the position that the terrorism treaties themselves created universal jurisdiction. Rather the United States in its appellate brief argued that,

---

Japan in fact claimed universal jurisdiction even before the Hague Convention. Hijacking threatens international communications to the same extent as piracy; it is an attack on international order and injures the international community as a whole, which means that all states have a legitimate interest in repressing it. The policy reasons which justify universal jurisdiction over piracy justify it equally in the case of hijacking.

Michael Akehurst, *Jurisdiction in International Law*, 1973 BRIT. Y.B. INT'L L. 145, 161–62.

[196] On the role of articulation in the development of customary international law, *see* D'AMATO, *supra* note 172, 74–87.

[197] *Id.* at 75.

[198] United States v. Yunis, 681 F. Supp. 896 (D.D.C. 1988); United States v. Yunis, 924 F.2d 1086 (D.C. Cir. 1991).

[199] *Supra* note 184.

[200] *Supra* note 187.

the universal and passive personality theories of extraterritorial jurisdiction "together provide ample ground [ ] to assert jurisdiction over Yunis", [quoting the trial court's opinion in *Yunis*].

As that [trial court] decision explains, the universal theory recognizes that certain offenses are so heinous and widely condemned that "any state if it captures the offender may prosecute and punish that person on behalf of the world community regardless of the nationality of the offender or victim or where the crime was committed."

Both the offenses of aircraft hijacking and hostage taking fall squarely within this principle. Air piracy has been condemned by the 143 nations that are signatories of the Hague Convention, a treaty that, as explained previously, expressly authorizes prosecution on the basis of the universal principle. Hostage taking has been condemned by the international community in the International Convention Against the Taking of Hostages, which, likewise, recognizes the assertion of extraterritorial jurisdiction under the universal theory. Congress was, therefore, well within its authority to create extraterritorial criminal jursidiction over such universally condemned crimes.

The offense of hostage taking is also cognizable under the "passive personality" theory of jurisdiction which authorizes a state to assert jurisdiction over offenses commited against their citizens abroad.[201]

U.S. v. Rezaq[202] is the other case sometimes cited to demonstrate that the United States prosecutes nationals of states not parties to the terrorism treaties under legislation implementing those treaties. But Rezaq, a Palestinian, was not a national of a state whose treaty participation the United States would have recognized or whose diplomatic objection the United States would have recognized even if, contrary to the facts as they actually unfolded, an attempt had been made to lodge a protest against the exercise of jurisdiction over Rezaq.[203] Because of those features of the *Rezaq* case, the fact that no state objected to the prosecution of Rezaq does little to clarify one way or the other the status of the terrorism treaties relative to the customary law of universal jurisdiction.

---

[201] Brief for the United States at 32–34, U.S. v. Yunis, 924 F.2d 1086 (D.C. Cir. 1991) (No. 89–3208).

[202] United States v. Rezaq, 899 F. Supp. 697 (D.D.C. 1995); United States v. Rezaq, 134 F.3d 1121 (D.C. Cir. 1998).

[203] *See* Telephone Interview with Scott Glick, prosecuting attorney in *U.S. v. Rezaq*, U.S. Department of Justice, Terrorism Division, in Washington, D.C., on Sept. 15, 1999.

A claim, by Rezaq, to Jordanian nationality would not have been helpful to his case. Jordan was a party to the hijacking convention pursuant to which Rezaq was prosecuted. *See id.*

A similar circumstance arose in the case of *Public Prosecutor v. S.H.T.*, prosecuted in the Netherlands pursuant to the Convention for the Suppression of Unlawful Seizure of Aircraft, *supra* note 184, and the Convention for the Suppression of Unlawful Acts against the Safety of Civil Aviation, *supra* note 187, in which the defendant "had been born in Jerusalem and was a resident of East Jerusalem." Public Prosecutor v. S.H.T., 74 INT'L L. REP. 162, 163 (1987).

As of the time of this writing, there have been, to the author's knowledge, no diplomatic protests against the exercise of universal jurisdiction over the crimes that form the subject matter of the terrorism treaties. There is therefore reason to believe that universal jurisdiction over these crimes has or will pass into customary law.

Through the process of a treaty proposing a new application of universal jurisdiction, the usual processes of customary law development may be accelerated. This occurs not through any deviation from the usual principles governing the development of custom, but simply through an increased rate of occurrence of those actions (acceptance, acquiescence, expressions of *opinio juris*, and the like) through which customary law develops.[204] The treaty itself does not "create" universal jurisdiction, and it could not do so insofar as that would involve the alteration of customary international law without the necessary processes of state practice and *opinio juris*. Rather, each of the treaties floats a clear proposal for response. If a non-party state *were* to object to the jurisdiction proposed or to its exercise (as has occurred in the case of the ICC Treaty), the validity of the jurisdiction would have to be evaluated in the usual way. A determination would have to be made as to whether the claimed new basis of jurisdiction comported with the principles underlying and defining the customary international law of jurisdiction.

The merits of this theory of the terrorism treaties as proposing the development of custom may be clarified by a contrasting example. Imagine that, rather

---

[204] This approach to the meaning of the jurisdictional provisions of the terrorism treaties is reflected in Professor Schachter's reasoning. As he has written:

several multinational conventions dealing with crimes of international significance such as hijacking and sabotage of aircraft, hostage-taking, [and] injury to internationally protected persons . . . oblige the parties to extradite or alternatively try and punish individuals accused of the crime covered by the convention. A significant feature is that the treaty obligation applies to all offenders apprehended by the state in question, whether the crime was committed in or outside of the state and whether or not it involved injury to nationals. An inference has been drawn from the fact that these conventions have been adopted and ratified by a large number of states that 'universal jurisdiction' applies to the crimes in question. . . . The reasoning here is that if a large number of states have agreed to the obligation to try and punish such offences, the states must, as a matter of logic, have the *right* to exercise such jurisdiction under general (i.e., customary) international law. It follows that the right under customary law extends to all states, parties and non-parties. . . .

To reach the conclusion that customary law allows for universal jurisdiction in regard to the crimes covered by the treaties, one has to rely on three conditions:
1. The adoption of the conventions by overwhelmingly large majorities of states;
2. The implication drawn from these conventions that international law permits states to exercise jurisdiction on a universal basis in regard to the crimes in question;
3. The widespread ratification of the Conventions considered as relevant state practice that conforms to the implicit customary law principle stated in (2) above.

Oscar Schachter, *Entangled Treaty and Custom, supra* note 172, at 725–26.

than providing for universal jurisdiction over hijacking, hostage taking, and the like, the treaties had provided for universal jurisdiction over larceny. The larceny treaty or prosecutions brought pursuant thereto presumably would have been objected to promptly by states preferring to retain exclusive jurisdiction over larceny committed on their own territory when that larceny has no special link with other states. It is hard to imagine how the larceny treaty's universal jurisdiction provisions could be defended. Non-party states would readily prevail by showing that there is no support in customary law principles for the claimed jurisdiction and that treaties to which they are not parties cannot "create" otherwise baseless jurisdiction over crimes committed on their territories.

The difference between the hypothetical larceny treaty and the terrorism treaties is that the various forms of terrorism, if and to the extent that they were not already subject to universal jurisdiction at the time of the treaties' promulgation, were likely candidates for universal jurisdiction (meaning that such jurisdiction was likely to be accepted and become customary) while larceny is not. The crimes covered by the terrorism treaties are crimes of concern to all states regardless of where the offense is committed, and are crimes of the sort that would be difficult to control without substantial international cooperation. Ordinary larceny, by contrast, shares neither of those characteristics. For that reason, states would be unlikely to accept the universal jurisdiction proposed in the hypothetical larceny treaty even while states appear, thus far, to be willing to accept the universal jurisdiction proposed in the terrorism treaties.

To the extent that the terrorism treaties are viewed as proposing a new feature of customary law, subject to acceptance or rejection by non-parties, they are a potentially constructive contribution to international legal development. Viewed as an attempt simply to impose otherwise non-existent jurisdiction over the nationals of non-party states without those states' consent, the treaties would simply be void.

The terrorism treaties do not represent any exceptional power to create universal jurisdiction by treaty or in any other exceptional way to alter the customary international law of jurisdiction. Rather, the terrorism treaties, properly viewed, are an example of the development of customary international law through the catalyst of treaty making. All that treaties can do, relative to the incorporation of new bases of jurisdiction into the customary law of jurisdiction, is to propose the desired innovation. Where the proposal is widely accepted, the jurisdictional innovation will pass into custom. The terrorism treaties appear to exemplify this process. The hypothetical treaty providing for universal jurisdiction over larceny is meant as an example of a proposal that would be rejected and, consequently, would not generate custom. The ICC Treaty, and in particular its jurisdictional provisions, can do no more than to propose a jurisdictional innovation to be accepted or rejected by states.

F. CONCLUSION

The ICC is intended to do an overwhelmingly important job. An international criminal court will, in many instances, be the only meaningful forum in which to pursue justice for crimes of the greatest enormity. The dilemma underlying the debate about ICC jurisdiction over non-party nationals stems primarily from the conflicting needs for the ICC both to have sufficiently aggressive jurisdictional powers to bring to justice perpetrators of genocide, war crimes, and crimes against humanity and, simultaneously, to allow to states appropriate discretion regarding methods of dispute settlement when the lawfulness of their official acts is in dispute.

Given the terms of the ICC Treaty, the ICC would very likely engage in the compulsory adjudication of interstate disputes through the mechanism of criminal prosecutions, a prospect that many states will, and perhaps should, reject. Fundamental principles of international law reserve to states the right to resolve their disputes by such mechanisms as they find most suitable, limited by such obligations as they have agreed to by treaty or become bound to by custom. The resolution of interstate disputes by the ICC through the mechanism of criminal prosecutions is not a method that non-parties to the ICC Treaty have agreed to or become bound to by custom. Thus, the very Treaty that would establish a new court to enforce international law may itself breach certain important international law principles. Until this basic issue is confronted and satisfactorily resolved,[205] the ICC and, in turn, the critical human interests that the Court is intended to serve, will likely suffer from a truly unfortunate lack of participation.

---

[205] The United States proposed, in the course of the ICC Treaty negotiations, a mechanism that would permit ICC jurisdiction over non-party nationals but would allow states to exempt from that jurisdiction cases arising from actions that the state identified as its official acts. *See* U.N. Doc. A/CONF.183/C.1/L.90 (1998). *See also* Theodore Meron, *The Court We Want*, WASH. POST, Oct. 13, 1998, at A15. Ambassador Scheffer argued that such an arrangement "would require a nonparty state to acknowledge responsibility for an atrocity in order to be exempted, an unlikely occurrence for those who usually commit genocide or other heinous crimes. In contrast, the United States would not hesitate to acknowledge that the humanitarian interventions, peacekeeping actions, or defensive actions to eliminate weapons of mass destruction are 'official state actions'." Scheffer, *The United States and the International Criminal Court, supra* note 152, at 20.

The U.S. proposal was an undeveloped one. It did not delineate what it would mean to acknowledge an official act. Would a state seeking to exempt its official conduct from ICC jurisdiction be required to stipulate to the facts exactly as alleged by the prosecutor? If so, then the proposal would provide rather slim protection to states. Or could a state successfully exempt official conduct from ICC jurisdiction by saying "We disagree with your view of the facts. Not 100,000 people but 10 people were killed, and they were killed not by our troops but by our opponents' troops. In any event, any actions that we took in relation to that incident were constituted entirely by official acts"? If such a statement would suffice, then the proposal would create a jurisdictional loophole so broad as to defeat in large part the purposes that the ICC is intended to fulfill. It may be that the U.S. proposal, with further development, could contribute to a resolution of the dilemma of ICC jurisdiction over non-party nationals. Or it may well be that the problems with such an approach would prove intractable.

ROME STATUTE OF THE INTERNATIONAL CRIMINAL COURT

(as corrected by the *procés-verbaux* of November 10, 1998, and July 12, 1999)

PREAMBLE

The States Parties to this Statute,

Conscious that all peoples are united by common bonds, their cultures pieced together in a shared heritage, and concerned that this delicate mosaic may be shattered at any time,

Mindful that during this century millions of children, women and men have been victims of unimaginable atrocities that deeply shock the conscience of humanity,

Recognizing that such grave crimes threaten the peace, security and well-being of the world,

Affirming that the most serious crimes of concern to the international community as a whole must not go unpunished and that their effective prosecution must be ensured by taking measures at the national level and by enhancing international cooperation,

Determined to put an end to impunity for the perpetrators of these crimes and thus to contribute to the prevention of such crimes,

Recalling that it is the duty of every state to exercise its criminal jurisdiction over those responsible for international crimes,

Reaffirming the Purposes and Principles of the Charter of the United Nations, and in particular that all states shall refrain from the threat or use of force against the territorial integrity or political independence of any state, or in any other manner inconsistent with the Purposes of the United Nations,

Emphasizing in this connection that nothing in this Statute shall be taken as authorizing any State Party to intervene in an armed conflict or in the internal affairs of any state,

Determined to these ends and for the sake of present and future generations, to establish an independent permanent International Criminal Court in relationship with the United Nations system, with jurisdiction over the most serious crimes of concern to the international community as a whole,

Emphasizing that the International Criminal Court established under this Statute shall be complementary to national criminal jurisdictions,

Resolved to guarantee lasting respect for and the enforcement of international justice,

Have agreed as follows:

PART 1. ESTABLISHMENT OF THE COURT

Article 1
The Court

An International Criminal Court ("the Court") is hereby established. It shall be a permanent institution and shall have the power to exercise its jurisdiction over persons for the most serious crimes of international concern, as referred to in this Statute, and shall be complementary to national criminal jurisdictions. The jurisdiction and functioning of the Court shall be governed by the provisions of this Statute.

Article 2
Relationship of the Court with the United Nations

The Court shall be brought into relationship with the United Nations through an agreement to be approved by the Assembly of States Parties to this Statute and thereafter concluded by the President of the Court on its behalf.

Article 3
Seat of the Court

1.   The seat of the Court shall be established at The Hague in the Netherlands ("the host state").

2.   The Court shall enter into a headquarters agreement with the host state, to be approved by the Assembly of States Parties and thereafter concluded by the President of the Court on its behalf.

3.   The Court may sit elsewhere, whenever it considers it desirable, as provided in this Statute.

Article 4
Legal status and powers of the Court

1.   The Court shall have international legal personality. It shall also have such legal capacity as may be necessary for the exercise of its functions and the fulfilment of its purposes.

2.   The Court may exercise its functions and powers, as provided in this Statute, on the territory of any State Party and, by special agreement, on the territory of any other state.

PART 2. JURISDICTION, ADMISSIBILITY AND APPLICABLE LAW

Article 5
Crimes within the jurisdiction of the Court

1.   The jurisdiction of the Court shall be limited to the most serious crimes of concern to the international community as a whole. The Court has jurisdiction in accordance with this Statute with respect to the following crimes:

    (a)   The crime of genocide;
    (b)   Crimes against humanity;

    (c)   War crimes;

    (d)   The crime of aggression.

2.   The Court shall exercise jurisdiction over the crime of aggression once a provision is adopted in accordance with Articles 121 and 123 defining the crime and setting out the conditions under which the Court shall exercise jurisdiction with respect to this crime. Such a provision shall be consistent with the relevant provisions of the Charter of the United Nations.

Article 6
Genocide

For the purpose of this Statute, "genocide" means any of the following acts committed with intent to destroy, in whole or in part, a national, ethnical, racial or religious group, as such:

    (a)   Killing members of the group;

    (b)   Causing serious bodily or mental harm to members of the group;

    (c)   Deliberately inflicting on the group conditions of life calculated to bring about its physical destruction in whole or in part;

    (d)   Imposing measures intended to prevent births within the group;

    (e)   Forcibly transferring children of the group to another group.

Article 7
Crimes against humanity

1.   For the purpose of this Statute, "crime against humanity" means any of the following acts when committed as part of a widespread or systematic attack directed against any civilian population, with knowledge of the attack:

    (a)   Murder;

    (b)   Extermination;

    (c)   Enslavement;

    (d)   Deportation or forcible transfer of population;

    (e)   Imprisonment or other severe deprivation of physical liberty in violation of fundamental rules of international law;

    (f)   Torture;

    (g)   Rape, sexual slavery, enforced prostitution, forced pregnancy, enforced sterilization, or any other form of sexual violence of comparable gravity;

    (h)   Persecution against any identifiable group or collectivity on political, racial, national, ethnic, cultural, religious, gender as defined in paragraph 3, or other grounds that are universally recognized as impermissible under international law, in connection with any act referred to in this paragraph or any crime within the jurisdiction of the Court;

    (i)   Enforced disappearance of persons;

    (j)   The crime of apartheid;

    (k)   Other inhumane acts of a similar character intentionally causing great suffering, or serious injury to body or to mental or physical health.

2.   For the purpose of paragraph 1:

    (a)   "Attack directed against any civilian population" means a course of conduct involving the multiple commission of acts referred to in paragraph 1 against any civilian population, pursuant to or in furtherance of a state or organizational policy to commit such attack;

(b) "Extermination" includes the intentional infliction of conditions of life, *inter alia* the deprivation of access to food and medicine, calculated to bring about the destruction of part of a population;

(c) "Enslavement" means the exercise of any or all of the powers attaching to the right of ownership over a person and includes the exercise of such power in the course of trafficking in persons, in particular women and children;

(d) "Deportation or forcible transfer of population" means forced displacement of the persons concerned by expulsion or other coercive acts from the area in which they are lawfully present, without grounds permitted under international law;

(e) "Torture" means the intentional infliction of severe pain or suffering, whether physical or mental, upon a person in the custody or under the control of the accused; except that torture shall not include pain or suffering arising only from, inherent in or incidental to, lawful sanctions;

(f) "Forced pregnancy" means the unlawful confinement of a woman forcibly made pregnant, with the intent of affecting the ethnic composition of any population or carrying out other grave violations of international law. This definition shall not in any way be interpreted as affecting national laws relating to pregnancy;

(g) "Persecution" means the intentional and severe deprivation of fundamental rights contrary to international law by reason of the identity of the group or collectivity;

(h) "The crime of apartheid" means inhumane acts of a character similar to those referred to in paragraph 1, committed in the context of an institutionalized regime of systematic oppression and domination by one racial group over any other racial group or groups and committed with the intention of maintaining that regime;

(i) "Enforced disappearance of persons" means the arrest, detention or abduction of persons by, or with the authorization, support or acquiescence of, a state or a political organization, followed by a refusal to acknowledge that deprivation of freedom or to give information on the fate or whereabouts of those persons, with the intention of removing them from the protection of the law for a prolonged period of time.

3.   For the purpose of this Statute, it is understood that the term "gender" refers to the two sexes, male and female, within the context of society. The term "gender" does not indicate any meaning different from the above.

Article 8
War crimes

1.   The Court shall have jurisdiction in respect of war crimes in particular when committed as part of a plan or policy or as part of a large-scale commission of such crimes.

2.   For the purpose of this Statute, "war crimes" means:

(a)   Grave breaches of the Geneva Conventions of 12 August 1949, namely, any of the following acts against persons or property protected under the provisions of the relevant Geneva Convention:

(i)   Wilful killing;

(ii)   Torture or inhuman treatment, including biological experiments;

(iii)   Wilfully causing great suffering, or serious injury to body or health;

(iv)   Extensive destruction and appropriation of property, not justified by military necessity and carried out unlawfully and wantonly;

(v)   Compelling a prisoner of war or other protected person to serve in the forces of a hostile Power;

(vi)   Wilfully depriving a prisoner of war or other protected person of the rights of fair and regular trial;

(vii)   Unlawful deportation or transfer or unlawful confinement;

(viii)   Taking of hostages.

(b)   Other serious violations of the laws and customs applicable in international armed conflict, within the established framework of international law, namely, any of the following acts:

(i)   Intentionally directing attacks against the civilian population as such or against individual civilians not taking direct part in hostilities;

(ii)   Intentionally directing attacks against civilian objects, that is, objects which are not military objectives;

(iii)   Intentionally directing attacks against personnel, installations, material, units or vehicles involved in a humanitarian assistance or peacekeeping mission in accordance with the Charter of the United Nations, as long as they are entitled to the protection given to civilians or civilian objects under the international law of armed conflict;

(iv)   Intentionally launching an attack in the knowledge that such attack will cause incidental loss of life or injury to civilians or damage to civilian objects or widespread, long-term and severe damage to the natural environment which would be clearly excessive in relation to the concrete and direct overall military advantage anticipated;

(v)   Attacking or bombarding, by whatever means, towns, villages, dwellings or buildings which are undefended and which are not military objectives;

(vi)   Killing or wounding a combatant who, having laid down his arms or having no longer means of defence, has surrendered at discretion;

(vii)   Making improper use of a flag of truce, of the flag or of the military insignia and uniform of the enemy or of the United Nations, as well as of the distinctive emblems of the Geneva Conventions, resulting in death or serious personal injury;

(viii)   The transfer, directly or indirectly, by the Occupying Power of parts of its own civilian population into the territory it occupies, or the deportation or transfer of all or parts of the population of the occupied territory within or outside this territory;

(ix)   Intentionally directing attacks against buildings dedicated to religion, education, art, science or charitable purposes, historic monuments, hospitals and places where the sick and wounded are collected, provided they are not military objectives;

(x)   Subjecting persons who are in the power of an adverse party to physical mutilation or to medical or scientific experiments of any kind which are neither justified by the medical, dental or hospital treatment of the person concerned nor carried out in his or her interest, and which cause death to or seriously endanger the health of such person or persons;

(xi)   Killing or wounding treacherously individuals belonging to the hostile nation or army;

(xii)   Declaring that no quarter will be given;

(xiii)   Destroying or seizing the enemy's property unless such destruction or seizure be imperatively demanded by the necessities of war;

(xiv)   Declaring abolished, suspended or inadmissible in a court of law the rights and actions of the nationals of the hostile party;

(xv)   Compelling the nationals of the hostile party to take part in the operations of war directed against their own country, even if they were in the belligerent's service before the commencement of the war;

(xvi)   Pillaging a town or place, even when taken by assault;

(xvii)   Employing poison or poisoned weapons;

(xviii) Employing asphyxiating, poisonous or other gases, and all analogous liquids, materials or devices;

(xix) Employing bullets which expand or flatten easily in the human body, such as bullets with a hard envelope which does not entirely cover the core or is pierced with incisions;

(xx) Employing weapons, projectiles and material and methods of warfare which are of a nature to cause superfluous injury or unnecessary suffering or which are inherently indiscriminate in violation of the international law of armed conflict, provided that such weapons, projectiles and material and methods of warfare are the subject of a comprehensive prohibition and are included in an annex to this Statute, by an amendment in accordance with the relevant provisions set forth in Articles 121 and 123;

(xxi) Committing outrages upon personal dignity, in particular humiliating and degrading treatment;

(xxii) Committing rape, sexual slavery, enforced prostitution, forced pregnancy, as defined in Article 7, paragraph 2 (f), enforced sterilization, or any other form of sexual violence also constituting a grave breach of the Geneva Conventions;

(xxiii) Utilizing the presence of a civilian or other protected person to render certain points, areas or military forces immune from military operations;

(xxiv) Intentionally directing attacks against buildings, material, medical units and transport, and personnel using the distinctive emblems of the Geneva Conventions in conformity with international law;

(xxv) Intentionally using starvation of civilians as a method of warfare by depriving them of objects indispensable to their survival, including wilfully impeding relief supplies as provided for under the Geneva Conventions;

(xxvi) Conscripting or enlisting children under the age of fifteen years into the national armed forces or using them to participate actively in hostilities.

(c) In the case of an armed conflict not of an international character, serious violations of Article 3 common to the four Geneva Conventions of 12 August 1949, namely, any of the following acts committed against persons taking no active part in the hostilities, including members of armed forces who have laid down their arms and those placed *hors de combat* by sickness, wounds, detention or any other cause:

(i) Violence to life and person, in particular murder of all kinds, mutilation, cruel treatment and torture;

(ii) Committing outrages upon personal dignity, in particular humiliating and degrading treatment;

(iii) Taking of hostages;

(iv) The passing of sentences and the carrying out of executions without previous judgement pronounced by a regularly constituted court, affording all judicial guarantees which are generally recognized as indispensable.

(d) Paragraph 2 (c) applies to armed conflicts not of an international character and thus does not apply to situations of internal disturbances and tensions, such as riots, isolated and sporadic acts of violence or other acts of a similar nature.

(e) Other serious violations of the laws and customs applicable in armed conflicts not of an international character, within the established framework of international law, namely, any of the following acts:

(i) Intentionally directing attacks against the civilian population as such or against individual civilians not taking direct part in hostilities;

(ii) Intentionally directing attacks against buildings, material, medical units and transport, and personnel using the distinctive emblems of the Geneva Conventions in conformity with international law;

(iii)   Intentionally directing attacks against personnel, installations, material, units or vehicles involved in a humanitarian assistance or peacekeeping mission in accordance with the Charter of the United Nations, as long as they are entitled to the protection given to civilians or civilian objects under the international law of armed conflict;

(iv)   Intentionally directing attacks against buildings dedicated to religion, education, art, science or charitable purposes, historic monuments, hospitals and places where the sick and wounded are collected, provided they are not military objectives;

(v)   Pillaging a town or place, even when taken by assault;

(vi)   Committing rape, sexual slavery, enforced prostitution, forced pregnancy, as defined in Article 7, paragraph 2 (f), enforced sterilization, and any other form of sexual violence also constituting a serious violation of Article 3 common to the four Geneva Conventions;

(vii)   Conscripting or enlisting children under the age of fifteen years into armed forces or groups or using them to participate actively in hostilities;

(viii)   Ordering the displacement of the civilian population for reasons related to the conflict, unless the security of the civilians involved or imperative military reasons so demand;

(ix)   Killing or wounding treacherously a combatant adversary;

(x)   Declaring that no quarter will be given;

(xi)   Subjecting persons who are in the power of another party to the conflict to physical mutilation or to medical or scientific experiments of any kind which are neither justified by the medical, dental or hospital treatment of the person concerned nor carried out in his or her interest, and which cause death to or seriously endanger the health of such person or persons;

(xii)   Destroying or seizing the property of an adversary unless such destruction or seizure be imperatively demanded by the necessities of the conflict;

(f)   Paragraph 2 (e) applies to armed conflicts not of an international character and thus does not apply to situations of internal disturbances and tensions, such as riots, isolated and sporadic acts of violence or other acts of a similar nature. It applies to armed conflicts that take place in the territory of a state when there is protracted armed conflict between governmental authorities and organized armed groups or between such groups.

3.   Nothing in paragraph 2 (c) and (e) shall affect the responsibility of a Government to maintain or re-establish law and order in the state or to defend the unity and territorial integrity of the state, by all legitimate means.

Article 9
Elements of Crimes

1.   Elements of Crimes shall assist the Court in the interpretation and application of Articles 6, 7 and 8. They shall be adopted by a two-thirds majority of the members of the Assembly of States Parties.

2.   Amendments to the Elements of Crimes may be proposed by:
   (a)   Any State Party;
   (b)   The judges acting by an absolute majority;
   (c)   The Prosecutor.
Such amendments shall be adopted by a two-thirds majority of the members of the Assembly of States Parties.

3.   The Elements of Crimes and amendments thereto shall be consistent with this Statute.

Article 10

Nothing in this Part shall be interpreted as limiting or prejudicing in any way existing or developing rules of international law for purposes other than this Statute.

Article 11
Jurisdiction ratione temporis

1.   The Court has jurisdiction only with respect to crimes committed after the entry into force of this Statute.

2.   If a state becomes a Party to this Statute after its entry into force, the Court may exercise its jurisdiction only with respect to crimes committed after the entry into force of this Statute for that state, unless that state has made a declaration under Article 12, paragraph 3.

Article 12
Preconditions to the exercise of jurisdiction

1.   A state which becomes a Party to this Statute thereby accepts the jurisdiction of the Court with respect to the crimes referred to in Article 5.

2.   In the case of Article 13, paragraph (a) or (c), the Court may exercise its jurisdiction if one or more of the following states are Parties to this Statute or have accepted the jurisdiction of the Court in accordance with paragraph 3:
   (a)   The state on the territory of which the conduct in question occurred or, if the crime was committed on board a vessel or aircraft, the state of registration of that vessel or aircraft;
   (b)   The state of which the person accused of the crime is a national.

3.   If the acceptance of a state which is not a Party to this Statute is required under paragraph 2, that state may, by declaration lodged with the Registrar, accept the exercise of jurisdiction by the Court with respect to the crime in question. The accepting state shall cooperate with the Court without any delay or exception in accordance with Part 9.

Article 13
Exercise of jurisdiction

The Court may exercise its jurisdiction with respect to a crime referred to in Article 5 in accordance with the provisions of this Statute if:
   (a)   A situation in which one or more of such crimes appears to have been committed is referred to the Prosecutor by a State Party in accordance with Article 14;
   (b)   A situation in which one or more of such crimes appears to have been committed is referred to the Prosecutor by the Security Council acting under Chapter VII of the Charter of the United Nations; or
   (c)   The Prosecutor has initiated an investigation in respect of such a crime in accordance with Article 15.

Article 14
Referral of a situation by a State Party

1.   A State Party may refer to the Prosecutor a situation in which one or more crimes within the jurisdiction of the Court appear to have been committed requesting the

Prosecutor to investigate the situation for the purpose of determining whether one or more specific persons should be charged with the commission of such crimes.

2. As far as possible, a referral shall specify the relevant circumstances and be accompanied by such supporting documentation as is available to the state referring the situation.

Article 15
Prosecutor

1. The Prosecutor may initiate investigations *proprio motu* on the basis of information on crimes within the jurisdiction of the Court.

2. The Prosecutor shall analyse the seriousness of the information received. For this purpose, he or she may seek additional information from states, organs of the United Nations, intergovernmental or non-governmental organizations, or other reliable sources that he or she deems appropriate, and may receive written or oral testimony at the seat of the Court.

3. If the Prosecutor concludes that there is a reasonable basis to proceed with an investigation, he or she shall submit to the Pre-Trial Chamber a request for authorization of an investigation, together with any supporting material collected. Victims may make representations to the Pre-Trial Chamber, in accordance with the Rules of Procedure and Evidence.

4. If the Pre-Trial Chamber, upon examination of the request and the supporting material, considers that there is a reasonable basis to proceed with an investigation, and that the case appears to fall within the jurisdiction of the Court, it shall authorize the commencement of the investigation, without prejudice to subsequent determinations by the Court with regard to the jurisdiction and admissibility of a case.

5. The refusal of the Pre-Trial Chamber to authorize the investigation shall not preclude the presentation of a subsequent request by the Prosecutor based on new facts or evidence regarding the same situation.

6. If, after the preliminary examination referred to in paragraphs 1 and 2, the Prosecutor concludes that the information provided does not constitute a reasonable basis for an investigation, he or she shall inform those who provided the information. This shall not preclude the Prosecutor from considering further information submitted to him or her regarding the same situation in the light of new facts or evidence.

Article 16
Deferral of investigation or prosecution

No investigation or prosecution may be commenced or proceeded with under this Statute for a period of 12 months after the Security Council, in a resolution adopted under Chapter VII of the Charter of the United Nations, has requested the Court to that effect; that request may be renewed by the Council under the same conditions.

Article 17
Issues of admissibility

1. Having regard to paragraph 10 of the Preamble and Article 1, the Court shall determine that a case is inadmissible where:

(a) The case is being investigated or prosecuted by a state which has jurisdiction over it, unless the state is unwilling or unable genuinely to carry out the investigation or prosecution;

(b) The case has been investigated by a state which has jurisdiction over it and the state has decided not to prosecute the person concerned, unless the decision resulted from the unwillingness or inability of the state genuinely to prosecute;

(c) The person concerned has already been tried for conduct which is the subject of the complaint, and a trial by the Court is not permitted under Article 20, paragraph 3;

(d) The case is not of sufficient gravity to justify further action by the Court.

2. In order to determine unwillingness in a particular case, the Court shall consider, having regard to the principles of due process recognized by international law, whether one or more of the following exist, as applicable:

(a) The proceedings were or are being undertaken or the national decision was made for the purpose of shielding the person concerned from criminal responsibility for crimes within the jurisdiction of the Court referred to in Article 5;

(b) There has been an unjustified delay in the proceedings which in the circumstances is inconsistent with an intent to bring the person concerned to justice;

(c) The proceedings were not or are not being conducted independently or impartially, and they were or are being conducted in a manner which, in the circumstances, is inconsistent with an intent to bring the person concerned to justice.

3. In order to determine inability in a particular case, the Court shall consider whether, due to a total or substantial collapse or unavailability of its national judicial system, the state is unable to obtain the accused or the necessary evidence and testimony or otherwise unable to carry out its proceedings.

Article 18
Preliminary rulings regarding admissibility

1. When a situation has been referred to the Court pursuant to Article 13 (a) and the Prosecutor has determined that there would be a reasonable basis to commence an investigation, or the Prosecutor initiates an investigation pursuant to Articles 13 (c) and 15, the Prosecutor shall notify all States Parties and those states which, taking into account the information available, would normally exercise jurisdiction over the crimes concerned. The Prosecutor may notify such states on a confidential basis and, where the Prosecutor believes it necessary to protect persons, prevent destruction of evidence or prevent the absconding of persons, may limit the scope of the information provided to states.

2. Within one month of receipt of that notification, a state may inform the Court that it is investigating or has investigated its nationals or others within its jurisdiction with respect to criminal acts which may constitute crimes referred to in Article 5 and which relate to the information provided in the notification to states. At the request of that state, the Prosecutor shall defer to the state's investigation of those persons unless the Pre-Trial Chamber, on the application of the Prosecutor, decides to authorize the investigation.

3. The Prosecutor's deferral to a state's investigation shall be open to review by the Prosecutor six months after the date of deferral or at any time when there has been a significant change of circumstances based on the state's unwillingness or inability genuinely to carry out the investigation.

4.   The state concerned or the Prosecutor may appeal to the Appeals Chamber against a ruling of the Pre-Trial Chamber, in accordance with Article 82. The appeal may be heard on an expedited basis.

5.   When the Prosecutor has deferred an investigation in accordance with paragraph 2, the Prosecutor may request that the state concerned periodically inform the Prosecutor of the progress of its investigations and any subsequent prosecutions. States Parties shall respond to such requests without undue delay.

6.   Pending a ruling by the Pre-Trial Chamber, or at any time when the Prosecutor has deferred an investigation under this article, the Prosecutor may, on an exceptional basis, seek authority from the Pre-Trial Chamber to pursue necessary investigative steps for the purpose of preserving evidence where there is a unique opportunity to obtain important evidence or there is a significant risk that such evidence may not be subsequently available.

7.   A state which has challenged a ruling of the Pre-Trial Chamber under this article may challenge the admissibility of a case under Article 19 on the grounds of additional significant facts or significant change of circumstances.

Article 19
Challenges to the jurisdiction of the Court or the admissibility of a case

1.   The Court shall satisfy itself that it has jurisdiction in any case brought before it. The Court may, on its own motion, determine the admissibility of a case in accordance with Article 17.

2.   Challenges to the admissibility of a case on the grounds referred to in Article 17 or challenges to the jurisdiction of the Court may be made by:
    (a)   An accused or a person for whom a warrant of arrest or a summons to appear has been issued under Article 58;
    (b)   A state which has jurisdiction over a case, on the ground that it is investigating or prosecuting the case or has investigated or prosecuted; or
    (c)   A state from which acceptance of jurisdiction is required under Article 12.

3.   The Prosecutor may seek a ruling from the Court regarding a question of jurisdiction or admissibility. In proceedings with respect to jurisdiction or admissibility, those who have referred the situation under Article 13, as well as victims, may also submit observations to the Court.

4.   The admissibility of a case or the jurisdiction of the Court may be challenged only once by any person or state referred to in paragraph 2. The challenge shall take place prior to or at the commencement of the trial. In exceptional circumstances, the Court may grant leave for a challenge to be brought more than once or at a time later than the commencement of the trial. Challenges to the admissibility of a case, at the commencement of a trial, or subsequently with the leave of the Court, may be based only on Article 17, paragraph 1 (c).

5.   A state referred to in paragraph 2 (b) and (c) shall make a challenge at the earliest opportunity.

6.   Prior to the confirmation of the charges, challenges to the admissibility of a case or challenges to the jurisdiction of the Court shall be referred to the Pre-Trial Chamber. After

confirmation of the charges, they shall be referred to the Trial Chamber. Decisions with respect to jurisdiction or admissibility may be appealed to the Appeals Chamber in accordance with Article 82.

7.   If a challenge is made by a state referred to in paragraph 2 (b) or (c), the Prosecutor shall suspend the investigation until such time as the Court makes a determination in accordance with Article 17.

8.   Pending a ruling by the Court, the Prosecutor may seek authority from the Court:

(a)   To pursue necessary investigative steps of the kind referred to in Article 18, paragraph 6;

(b)   To take a statement or testimony from a witness or complete the collection and examination of evidence which had begun prior to the making of the challenge; and

(c)   In cooperation with the relevant states, to prevent the absconding of persons in respect of whom the Prosecutor has already requested a warrant of arrest under Article 58.

9.   The making of a challenge shall not affect the validity of any act performed by the Prosecutor or any order or warrant issued by the Court prior to the making of the challenge.

10.   If the Court has decided that a case is inadmissible under Article 17, the Prosecutor may submit a request for a review of the decision when he or she is fully satisfied that new facts have arisen which negate the basis on which the case had previously been found inadmissible under Article 17.

11.   If the Prosecutor, having regard to the matters referred to in Article 17, defers an investigation, the Prosecutor may request that the relevant state make available to the Prosecutor information on the proceedings. That information shall, at the request of the state concerned, be confidential. If the Prosecutor thereafter decides to proceed with an investigation, he or she shall notify the state to which deferral of the proceedings has taken place.

Article 20
Ne bis in idem

1.   Except as provided in this Statute, no person shall be tried before the Court with respect to conduct which formed the basis of crimes for which the person has been convicted or acquitted by the Court.

2.   No person shall be tried by another court for a crime referred to in Article 5 for which that person has already been convicted or acquitted by the Court.

3.   No person who has been tried by another court for conduct also proscribed under Article 6, 7 or 8 shall be tried by the Court with respect to the same conduct unless the proceedings in the other court:

(a)   Were for the purpose of shielding the person concerned from criminal responsibility for crimes within the jurisdiction of the Court; or

(b)   Otherwise were not conducted independently or impartially in accordance with the norms of due process recognized by international law and were conducted in a manner which, in the circumstances, was inconsistent with an intent to bring the person concerned to justice.

Article 21
Applicable law

1.   The Court shall apply:
     (a)   In the first place, this Statute, Elements of Crimes and its Rules of Procedure and Evidence;
     (b)   In the second place, where appropriate, applicable treaties and the principles and rules of international law, including the established principles of the international law of armed conflict;
     (c)   Failing that, general principles of law derived by the Court from national laws of legal systems of the world including, as appropriate, the national laws of states that would normally exercise jurisdiction over the crime, provided that those principles are not inconsistent with this Statute and with international law and internationally recognized norms and standards.

2.   The Court may apply principles and rules of law as interpreted in its previous decisions.

3.   The application and interpretation of law pursuant to this article must be consistent with internationally recognized human rights, and be without any adverse distinction founded on grounds such as gender as defined in Article 7, paragraph 3, age, race, colour, language, religion or belief, political or other opinion, national, ethnic or social origin, wealth, birth or other status.

PART 3.   GENERAL PRINCIPLES OF CRIMINAL LAW
Article 22
Nullum crimen sine lege

1.   A person shall not be criminally responsible under this Statute unless the conduct in question constitutes, at the time it takes place, a crime within the jurisdiction of the Court.

2.   The definition of a crime shall be strictly construed and shall not be extended by analogy. In case of ambiguity, the definition shall be interpreted in favour of the person being investigated, prosecuted or convicted.

3.   This article shall not affect the characterization of any conduct as criminal under international law independently of this Statute.

Article 23
Nulla poena sine lege

A person convicted by the Court may be punished only in accordance with this Statute.

Article 24
Non-retroactivity *ratione personae*

1.   No person shall be criminally responsible under this Statute for conduct prior to the entry into force of the Statute.

2.   In the event of a change in the law applicable to a given case prior to a final judgement, the law more favourable to the person being investigated, prosecuted or convicted shall apply.

Article 25
Individual criminal responsibility

1. The Court shall have jurisdiction over natural persons pursuant to this Statute.

2. A person who commits a crime within the jurisdiction of the Court shall be individually responsible and liable for punishment in accordance with this Statute.

3. In accordance with this Statute, a person shall be criminally responsible and liable for punishment for a crime within the jurisdiction of the Court if that person:

   (a) Commits such a crime, whether as an individual, jointly with another or through another person, regardless of whether that other person is criminally responsible;

   (b) Orders, solicits or induces the commission of such a crime which in fact occurs or is attempted;

   (c) For the purpose of facilitating the commission of such a crime, aids, abets or otherwise assists in its commission or its attempted commission, including providing the means for its commission;

   (d) In any other way contributes to the commission or attempted commission of such a crime by a group of persons acting with a common purpose. Such contribution shall be intentional and shall either:

      (i)   Be made with the aim of furthering the criminal activity or criminal purpose of the group, where such activity or purpose involves the commission of a crime within the jurisdiction of the Court; or

      (ii) Be made in the knowledge of the intention of the group to commit the crime;

   (e) In respect of the crime of genocide, directly and publicly incites others to commit genocide;

   (f) Attempts to commit such a crime by taking action that commences its execution by means of a substantial step, but the crime does not occur because of circumstances independent of the person's intentions. However, a person who abandons the effort to commit the crime or otherwise prevents the completion of the crime shall not be liable for punishment under this Statute for the attempt to commit that crime if that person completely and voluntarily gave up the criminal purpose.

4. No provision in this Statute relating to individual criminal responsibility shall affect the responsibility of states under international law.

Article 26
Exclusion of jurisdiction over persons under eighteen

The Court shall have no jurisdiction over any person who was under the age of 18 at the time of the alleged commission of a crime.

Article 27
Irrelevance of official capacity

1. This Statute shall apply equally to all persons without any distinction based on official capacity. In particular, official capacity as a Head of state or Government, a member of a Government or parliament, an elected representative or a government official shall in no case exempt a person from criminal responsibility under this Statute, nor shall it, in and of itself, constitute a ground for reduction of sentence.

2. Immunities or special procedural rules which may attach to the official capacity of a person, whether under national or international law, shall not bar the Court from exercising its jurisdiction over such a person.

Article 28
Responsibility of commanders and other superiors

In addition to other grounds of criminal responsibility under this Statute for crimes within the jurisdiction of the Court:

(a) A military commander or person effectively acting as a military commander shall be criminally responsible for crimes within the jurisdiction of the Court committed by forces under his or her effective command and control, or effective authority and control as the case may be, as a result of his or her failure to exercise control properly over such forces, where:

(i)   That military commander or person either knew or, owing to the circumstances at the time, should have known that the forces were committing or about to commit such crimes; and

(ii)   That military commander or person failed to take all necessary and reasonable measures within his or her power to prevent or repress their commission or to submit the matter to the competent authorities for investigation and prosecution.

(b) With respect to superior and subordinate relationships not described in paragraph (a), a superior shall be criminally responsible for crimes within the jurisdiction of the Court committed by subordinates under his or her effective authority and control, as a result of his or her failure to exercise control properly over such subordinates, where:

(i)   The superior either knew, or consciously disregarded information which clearly indicated, that the subordinates were committing or about to commit such crimes;

(ii)   The crimes concerned activities that were within the effective responsibility and control of the superior; and

(iii)   The superior failed to take all necessary and reasonable measures within his or her power to prevent or repress their commission or to submit the matter to the competent authorities for investigation and prosecution.

Article 29
Non-applicability of statute of limitations

The crimes within the jurisdiction of the Court shall not be subject to any statute of limitations.

Article 30
Mental element

1. Unless otherwise provided, a person shall be criminally responsible and liable for punishment for a crime within the jurisdiction of the Court only if the material elements are committed with intent and knowledge.

2. For the purposes of this article, a person has intent where:

(a) In relation to conduct, that person means to engage in the conduct;

(b) In relation to a consequence, that person means to cause that consequence or is aware that it will occur in the ordinary course of events.

3.   For the purposes of this Article, "knowledge" means awareness that a circumstance exists or a consequence will occur in the ordinary course of events. "Know" and "knowingly" shall be construed accordingly.

Article 31
Grounds for excluding criminal responsibility

1.   In addition to other grounds for excluding criminal responsibility provided for in this Statute, a person shall not be criminally responsible if, at the time of that person's conduct:

(a)   The person suffers from a mental disease or defect that destroys that person's capacity to appreciate the unlawfulness or nature of his or her conduct, or capacity to control his or her conduct to conform to the requirements of law;

(b)   The person is in a state of intoxication that destroys that person's capacity to appreciate the unlawfulness or nature of his or her conduct, or capacity to control his or her conduct to conform to the requirements of law, unless the person has become voluntarily intoxicated under such circumstances that the person knew, or disregarded the risk, that, as a result of the intoxication, he or she was likely to engage in conduct constituting a crime within the jurisdiction of the Court;

(c)   The person acts reasonably to defend himself or herself or another person or, in the case of war crimes, property which is essential for the survival of the person or another person or property which is essential for accomplishing a military mission, against an imminent and unlawful use of force in a manner proportionate to the degree of danger to the person or the other person or property protected. The fact that the person was involved in a defensive operation conducted by forces shall not in itself constitute a ground for excluding criminal responsibility under this subparagraph;

(d)   The conduct which is alleged to constitute a crime within the jurisdiction of the Court has been caused by duress resulting from a threat of imminent death or of continuing or imminent serious bodily harm against that person or another person, and the person acts necessarily and reasonably to avoid this threat, provided that the person does not intend to cause a greater harm than the one sought to be avoided. Such a threat may either be:

(i)   Made by other persons; or

(ii)   Constituted by other circumstances beyond that person's control.

2.   The Court shall determine the applicability of the grounds for excluding criminal responsibility provided for in this Statute to the case before it.

3.   At trial, the Court may consider a ground for excluding criminal responsibility other than those referred to in paragraph 1 where such a ground is derived from applicable law as set forth in Article 21. The procedures relating to the consideration of such a ground shall be provided for in the Rules of Procedure and Evidence.

Article 32
Mistake of fact or mistake of law

1.   A mistake of fact shall be a ground for excluding criminal responsibility only if it negates the mental element required by the crime.

2.   A mistake of law as to whether a particular type of conduct is a crime within the jurisdiction of the Court shall not be a ground for excluding criminal responsibility. A mistake

of law may, however, be a ground for excluding criminal responsibility if it negates the mental element required by such a crime, or as provided for in Article 33.

Article 33
Superior orders and prescription of law

1. The fact that a crime within the jurisdiction of the Court has been committed by a person pursuant to an order of a Government or of a superior, whether military or civilian, shall not relieve that person of criminal responsibility unless:

    (a) The person was under a legal obligation to obey orders of the Government or the superior in question;

    (b) The person did not know that the order was unlawful; and

    (c) The order was not manifestly unlawful.

2. For the purposes of this Article, orders to commit genocide or crimes against humanity are manifestly unlawful.

PART 4. COMPOSITION AND ADMINISTRATION OF THE COURT

Article 34
Organs of the Court

The Court shall be composed of the following organs:

(a) The Presidency;

(b) An Appeals Division, a Trial Division and a Pre-Trial Division;

(c) The Office of the Prosecutor;

(d) The Registry.

Article 35
Service of judges

1. All judges shall be elected as full-time members of the Court and shall be available to serve on that basis from the commencement of their terms of office.

2. The judges composing the Presidency shall serve on a full-time basis as soon as they are elected.

3. The Presidency may, on the basis of the workload of the Court and in consultation with its members, decide from time to time to what extent the remaining judges shall be required to serve on a full-time basis. Any such arrangement shall be without prejudice to the provisions of Article 40.

4. The financial arrangements for judges not required to serve on a full-time basis shall be made in accordance with Article 49.

Article 36
Qualifications, nomination and election of judges

1. Subject to the provisions of paragraph 2, there shall be 18 judges of the Court.

2. (a) The Presidency, acting on behalf of the Court, may propose an increase in the number of judges specified in paragraph 1, indicating the reasons why this is considered

necessary and appropriate. The Registrar shall promptly circulate any such proposal to all States Parties.

(b) Any such proposal shall then be considered at a meeting of the Assembly of States Parties to be convened in accordance with Article 112. The proposal shall be considered adopted if approved at the meeting by a vote of two thirds of the members of the Assembly of States Parties and shall enter into force at such time as decided by the Assembly of States Parties.

(c) (i)   Once a proposal for an increase in the number of judges has been adopted under subparagraph (b), the election of the additional judges shall take place at the next session of the Assembly of States Parties in accordance with paragraphs 3 to 8, and Article 37, paragraph 2;

(ii)   Once a proposal for an increase in the number of judges has been adopted and brought into effect under subparagraphs (b) and (c) (i), it shall be open to the Presidency at any time thereafter, if the workload of the Court justifies it, to propose a reduction in the number of judges, provided that the number of judges shall not be reduced below that specified in paragraph 1. The proposal shall be dealt with in accordance with the procedure laid down in subparagraphs (a) and (b). In the event that the proposal is adopted, the number of judges shall be progressively decreased as the terms of office of serving judges expire, until the necessary number has been reached.

3.   (a) The judges shall be chosen from among persons of high moral character, impartiality and integrity who possess the qualifications required in their respective states for appointment to the highest judicial offices.

(b) Every candidate for election to the Court shall:

(i)   Have established competence in criminal law and procedure, and the necessary relevant experience, whether as judge, prosecutor, advocate or in other similar capacity, in criminal proceedings; or

(ii)   Have established competence in relevant areas of international law such as international humanitarian law and the law of human rights, and extensive experience in a professional legal capacity which is of relevance to the judicial work of the Court;

(c) Every candidate for election to the Court shall have an excellent knowledge of and be fluent in at least one of the working languages of the Court.

4.   (a) Nominations of candidates for election to the Court may be made by any State Party to this Statute, and shall be made either:

(i)   By the procedure for the nomination of candidates for appointment to the highest judicial offices in the state in question; or

(ii)   By the procedure provided for the nomination of candidates for the International Court of Justice in the Statute of that Court. Nominations shall be accompanied by a statement in the necessary detail specifying how the candidate fulfils the requirements of paragraph 3.

(b) Each State Party may put forward one candidate for any given election who need not necessarily be a national of that State Party but shall in any case be a national of a State Party.

(c) The Assembly of States Parties may decide to establish, if appropriate, an Advisory Committee on nominations. In that event, the Committee's composition and mandate shall be established by the Assembly of States Parties.

5.   For the purposes of the election, there shall be two lists of candidates:

List A containing the names of candidates with the qualifications specified in paragraph 3 (b) (i); and List B containing the names of candidates with the qualifications specified in paragraph 3 (b) (ii).

A candidate with sufficient qualifications for both lists may choose on which list to appear. At the first election to the Court, at least nine judges shall be elected from list A and at least five judges from list B. Subsequent elections shall be so organized as to maintain the equivalent proportion on the Court of judges qualified on the two lists.

6. (a) The judges shall be elected by secret ballot at a meeting of the Assembly of States Parties convened for that purpose under Article 112. Subject to paragraph 7, the persons elected to the Court shall be the 18 candidates who obtain the highest number of votes and a two-thirds majority of the States Parties present and voting.

(b) In the event that a sufficient number of judges is not elected on the first ballot, successive ballots shall be held in accordance with the procedures laid down in subparagraph (a) until the remaining places have been filled.

7. No two judges may be nationals of the same state. A person who, for the purposes of membership of the Court, could be regarded as a national of more than one state shall be deemed to be a national of the state in which that person ordinarily exercises civil and political rights.

8. (a) The States Parties shall, in the selection of judges, take into account the need, within the membership of the Court, for:

      (i)   The representation of the principal legal systems of the world;

      (ii)   Equitable geographical representation; and

      (iii)   A fair representation of female and male judges.

(b) States Parties shall also take into account the need to include judges with legal expertise on specific issues, including, but not limited to, violence against women or children.

9. (a) Subject to subparagraph (b), judges shall hold office for a term of nine years and, subject to subparagraph (c) and to Article 37, paragraph 2, shall not be eligible for re-election.

(b) At the first election, one third of the judges elected shall be selected by lot to serve for a term of three years; one third of the judges elected shall be selected by lot to serve for a term of six years; and the remainder shall serve for a term of nine years.

(c) A judge who is selected to serve for a term of three years under subparagraph (b) shall be eligible for re-election for a full term.

10. Notwithstanding paragraph 9, a judge assigned to a Trial or Appeals Chamber in accordance with Article 39 shall continue in office to complete any trial or appeal the hearing of which has already commenced before that Chamber.

Article 37
Judicial vacancies

1. In the event of a vacancy, an election shall be held in accordance with Article 36 to fill the vacancy.

2. A judge elected to fill a vacancy shall serve for the remainder of the predecessor's term and, if that period is three years or less, shall be eligible for re-election for a full term under Article 36.

Article 38
The Presidency

1.   The President and the First and Second Vice-Presidents shall be elected by an absolute majority of the judges. They shall each serve for a term of three years or until the end of their respective terms of office as judges, whichever expires earlier. They shall be eligible for re-election once.

2.   The First Vice-President shall act in place of the President in the event that the President is unavailable or disqualified. The Second Vice-President shall act in place of the President in the event that both the President and the First Vice-President are unavailable or disqualified.

3.   The President, together with the First and Second Vice-Presidents, shall constitute the Presidency, which shall be responsible for:

  (a) The proper administration of the Court, with the exception of the Office of the Prosecutor; and

  (b) The other functions conferred upon it in accordance with this Statute.

4.   In discharging its responsibility under paragraph 3 (a), the Presidency shall coordinate with and seek the concurrence of the Prosecutor on all matters of mutual concern.

Article 39
Chambers

1.   As soon as possible after the election of the judges, the Court shall organize itself into the divisions specified in Article 34, paragraph (b). The Appeals Division shall be composed of the President and four other judges, the Trial Division of not less than six judges and the Pre-Trial Division of not less than six judges. The assignment of judges to divisions shall be based on the nature of the functions to be performed by each division and the qualifications and experience of the judges elected to the Court, in such a way that each division shall contain an appropriate combination of expertise in criminal law and procedure and in international law. The Trial and Pre-Trial Divisions shall be composed predominantly of judges with criminal trial experience.

2.   (a) The judicial functions of the Court shall be carried out in each division by Chambers.

  (b) (i)   The Appeals Chamber shall be composed of all the judges of the Appeals Division;

      (ii)   The functions of the Trial Chamber shall be carried out by three judges of the Trial Division;

      (iii)   The functions of the Pre-Trial Chamber shall be carried out either by three judges of the Pre-Trial Division or by a single judge of that division in accordance with this Statute and the Rules of Procedure and Evidence;

  (c) Nothing in this paragraph shall preclude the simultaneous constitution of more than one Trial Chamber or Pre-Trial Chamber when the efficient management of the Court's workload so requires.

3.   (a) Judges assigned to the Trial and Pre-Trial Divisions shall serve in those divisions for a period of three years, and thereafter until the completion of any case the hearing of which has already commenced in the division concerned.

(b) Judges assigned to the Appeals Division shall serve in that division for their entire term of office.

4. Judges assigned to the Appeals Division shall serve only in that division. Nothing in this Article shall, however, preclude the temporary attachment of judges from the Trial Division to the Pre-Trial Division or vice versa, if the Presidency considers that the efficient management of the Court's workload so requires, provided that under no circumstances shall a judge who has participated in the pre-trial phase of a case be eligible to sit on the Trial Chamber hearing that case.

Article 40
Independence of the judges

1. The judges shall be independent in the performance of their functions.

2. Judges shall not engage in any activity which is likely to interfere with their judicial functions or to affect confidence in their independence.

3. Judges required to serve on a full-time basis at the seat of the Court shall not engage in any other occupation of a professional nature.

4. Any question regarding the application of paragraphs 2 and 3 shall be decided by an absolute majority of the judges. Where any such question concerns an individual judge, that judge shall not take part in the decision.

Article 41
Excusing and disqualification of judges

1. The Presidency may, at the request of a judge, excuse that judge from the exercise of a function under this Statute, in accordance with the Rules of Procedure and Evidence.

2. (a) A judge shall not participate in any case in which his or her impartiality might reasonably be doubted on any ground. A judge shall be disqualified from a case in accordance with this paragraph if, *inter alia*, that judge has previously been involved in any capacity in that case before the Court or in a related criminal case at the national level involving the person being investigated or prosecuted. A judge shall also be disqualified on such other grounds as may be provided for in the Rules of Procedure and Evidence.

(b) The Prosecutor or the person being investigated or prosecuted may request the disqualification of a judge under this paragraph.

(c) Any question as to the disqualification of a judge shall be decided by an absolute majority of the judges. The challenged judge shall be entitled to present his or her comments on the matter, but shall not take part in the decision.

Article 42
The Office of the Prosecutor

1. The Office of the Prosecutor shall act independently as a separate organ of the Court. It shall be responsible for receiving referrals and any substantiated information on crimes within the jurisdiction of the Court, for examining them and for conducting investigations and prosecutions before the Court. A member of the Office shall not seek or act on instructions from any external source.

2.   The Office shall be headed by the Prosecutor. The Prosecutor shall have full authority over the management and administration of the Office, including the staff, facilities and other resources thereof. The Prosecutor shall be assisted by one or more Deputy Prosecutors, who shall be entitled to carry out any of the acts required of the Prosecutor under this Statute. The Prosecutor and the Deputy Prosecutors shall be of different nationalities. They shall serve on a full-time basis.

3.   The Prosecutor and the Deputy Prosecutors shall be persons of high moral character, be highly competent in and have extensive practical experience in the prosecution or trial of criminal cases. They shall have an excellent knowledge of and be fluent in at least one of the working languages of the Court.

4.   The Prosecutor shall be elected by secret ballot by an absolute majority of the members of the Assembly of States Parties. The Deputy Prosecutors shall be elected in the same way from a list of candidates provided by the Prosecutor. The Prosecutor shall nominate three candidates for each position of Deputy Prosecutor to be filled. Unless a shorter term is decided upon at the time of their election, the Prosecutor and the Deputy Prosecutors shall hold office for a term of nine years and shall not be eligible for re-election.

5.   Neither the Prosecutor nor a Deputy Prosecutor shall engage in any activity which is likely to interfere with his or her prosecutorial functions or to affect confidence in his or her independence. They shall not engage in any other occupation of a professional nature.

6.   The Presidency may excuse the Prosecutor or a Deputy Prosecutor, at his or her request, from acting in a particular case.

7.   Neither the Prosecutor nor a Deputy Prosecutor shall participate in any matter in which their impartiality might reasonably be doubted on any ground. They shall be disqualified from a case in accordance with this paragraph if, *inter alia*, they have previously been involved in any capacity in that case before the Court or in a related criminal case at the national level involving the person being investigated or prosecuted.

8.   Any question as to the disqualification of the Prosecutor or a Deputy Prosecutor shall be decided by the Appeals Chamber.

   (a)   The person being investigated or prosecuted may at any time request the disqualification of the Prosecutor or a Deputy Prosecutor on the grounds set out in this article;

   (b)   The Prosecutor or the Deputy Prosecutor, as appropriate, shall be entitled to present his or her comments on the matter;

9.   The Prosecutor shall appoint advisers with legal expertise on specific issues, including, but not limited to, sexual and gender violence and violence against children.

Article 43
The Registry

1.   The Registry shall be responsible for the non-judicial aspects of the administration and servicing of the Court, without prejudice to the functions and powers of the Prosecutor in accordance with Article 42.

2.   The Registry shall be headed by the Registrar, who shall be the principal administrative officer of the Court. The Registrar shall exercise his or her functions under the authority of the President of the Court.

3.   The Registrar and the Deputy Registrar shall be persons of high moral character, be highly competent and have an excellent knowledge of and be fluent in at least one of the working languages of the Court.

4.   The judges shall elect the Registrar by an absolute majority by secret ballot, taking into account any recommendation by the Assembly of States Parties. If the need arises and upon the recommendation of the Registrar, the judges shall elect, in the same manner, a Deputy Registrar.

5.   The Registrar shall hold office for a term of five years, shall be eligible for re-election once and shall serve on a full-time basis. The Deputy Registrar shall hold office for a term of five years or such shorter term as may be decided upon by an absolute majority of the judges, and may be elected on the basis that the Deputy Registrar shall be called upon to serve as required.

6.   The Registrar shall set up a Victims and Witnesses Unit within the Registry. This Unit shall provide, in consultation with the Office of the Prosecutor, protective measures and security arrangements, counselling and other appropriate assistance for witnesses, victims who appear before the Court, and others who are at risk on account of testimony given by such witnesses. The Unit shall include staff with expertise in trauma, including trauma related to crimes of sexual violence.

Article 44
Staff

1.   The Prosecutor and the Registrar shall appoint such qualified staff as may be required to their respective offices. In the case of the Prosecutor, this shall include the appointment of investigators.

2.   In the employment of staff, the Prosecutor and the Registrar shall ensure the highest standards of efficiency, competency and integrity, and shall have regard, *mutatis mutandis*, to the criteria set forth in Article 36, paragraph 8.

3.   The Registrar, with the agreement of the Presidency and the Prosecutor, shall propose Staff Regulations which include the terms and conditions upon which the staff of the Court shall be appointed, remunerated and dismissed. The Staff Regulations shall be approved by the Assembly of States Parties.

4.   The Court may, in exceptional circumstances, employ the expertise of gratis personnel offered by States Parties, intergovernmental organizations or non-governmental organizations to assist with the work of any of the organs of the Court. The Prosecutor may accept any such offer on behalf of the Office of the Prosecutor. Such gratis personnel shall be employed in accordance with guidelines to be established by the Assembly of States Parties.

Article 45
Solemn undertaking

Before taking up their respective duties under this Statute, the judges, the Prosecutor, the Deputy Prosecutors, the Registrar and the Deputy Registrar shall each make a solemn undertaking in open court to exercise his or her respective functions impartially and conscientiously.

Article 46
Removal from office

1.   A judge, the Prosecutor, a Deputy Prosecutor, the Registrar or the Deputy Registrar shall be removed from office if a decision to this effect is made in accordance with paragraph 2, in cases where that person:

(a)   Is found to have committed serious misconduct or a serious breach of his or her duties under this Statute, as provided for in the Rules of Procedure and Evidence; or

(b)   Is unable to exercise the functions required by this Statute.

2.   A decision as to the removal from office of a judge, the Prosecutor or a Deputy Prosecutor under paragraph 1 shall be made by the Assembly of States Parties, by secret ballot:

(a)   In the case of a judge, by a two-thirds majority of the States Parties upon a recommendation adopted by a two-thirds majority of the other judges;

(b)   In the case of the Prosecutor, by an absolute majority of the States Parties;

(c)   In the case of a Deputy Prosecutor, by an absolute majority of the States Parties upon the recommendation of the Prosecutor.

3.   A decision as to the removal from office of the Registrar or Deputy Registrar shall be made by an absolute majority of the judges.

4.   A Judge, Prosecutor, Deputy Prosecutor, Registrar or Deputy Registrar whose conduct or ability to exercise the functions of the office as required by this Statute is challenged under this article shall have full opportunity to present and receive evidence and to make submissions in accordance with the Rules of Procedure and Evidence. The person in question shall not otherwise participate in the consideration of the matter.

Article 47
Disciplinary measures

A judge, Prosecutor, Deputy Prosecutor, Registrar or Deputy Registrar who has committed misconduct of a less serious nature than that set out in Article 46, paragraph 1, shall be subject to disciplinary measures, in accordance with the Rules of Procedure and Evidence.

Article 48
Privileges and immunities

1.   The Court shall enjoy in the territory of each State Party such privileges and immunities as are necessary for the fulfilment of its purposes.

2.   The judges, the Prosecutor, the Deputy Prosecutors and the Registrar shall, when engaged on or with respect to the business of the Court, enjoy the same privileges and immunities as are accorded to heads of diplomatic missions and shall, after the expiry of their terms of office, continue to be accorded immunity from legal process of every kind in respect of words spoken or written and acts performed by them in their official capacity.

3.   The Deputy Registrar, the staff of the Office of the Prosecutor and the staff of the Registry shall enjoy the privileges and immunities and facilities necessary for the performance of their functions, in accordance with the agreement on the privileges and immunities of the Court.

4.   Counsel, experts, witnesses or any other person required to be present at the seat of the Court shall be accorded such treatment as is necessary for the proper functioning of the Court, in accordance with the agreement on the privileges and immunities of the Court.

5.   The privileges and immunities of:
    (a)   A judge or the Prosecutor may be waived by an absolute majority of the judges;
    (b)   The Registrar may be waived by the Presidency;
    (c)   The Deputy Prosecutors and staff of the Office of the Prosecutor may be waived by the Prosecutor;
    (d)   The Deputy Registrar and staff of the Registry may be waived by the Registrar.

Article 49
Salaries, allowances and expenses

The Judges, the Prosecutor, the Deputy Prosecutors, the Registrar and the Deputy Registrar shall receive such salaries, allowances and expenses as may be decided upon by the Assembly of States Parties. These salaries and allowances shall not be reduced during their terms of office.

Article 50
Official and working languages

1.   The official languages of the Court shall be Arabic, Chinese, English, French, Russian and Spanish. The judgements of the Court, as well as other decisions resolving fundamental issues before the Court, shall be published in the official languages. The Presidency shall, in accordance with the criteria established by the Rules of Procedure and Evidence, determine which decisions may be considered as resolving fundamental issues for the purposes of this paragraph.

2.   The working languages of the Court shall be English and French. The Rules of Procedure and Evidence shall determine the cases in which other official languages may be used as working languages.

3.   At the request of any party to a proceeding or a state allowed to intervene in a proceeding, the Court shall authorize a language other than English or French to be used by such a party or state, provided that the Court considers such authorization to be adequately justified.

Article 51
Rules of Procedure and Evidence

1.   The Rules of Procedure and Evidence shall enter into force upon adoption by a two-thirds majority of the members of the Assembly of States Parties.

2.   Amendments to the Rules of Procedure and Evidence may be proposed by:
    (a)   Any State Party;
    (b)   The judges acting by an absolute majority; or
    (c)   The Prosecutor.
Such amendments shall enter into force upon adoption by a two-thirds majority of the members of the Assembly of States Parties.

3.   After the adoption of the Rules of Procedure and Evidence, in urgent cases where the Rules do not provide for a specific situation before the Court, the judges may, by a two-

thirds majority, draw up provisional Rules to be applied until adopted, amended or rejected at the next ordinary or special session of the Assembly of States Parties.

4.   The Rules of Procedure and Evidence, amendments thereto and any provisional Rule shall be consistent with this Statute. Amendments to the Rules of Procedure and Evidence as well as provisional Rules shall not be applied retroactively to the detriment of the person who is being investigated or prosecuted or who has been convicted.

5.   In the event of conflict between the Statute and the Rules of Procedure and Evidence, the Statute shall prevail.

Article 52
Regulations of the Court

1.   The judges shall, in accordance with this Statute and the Rules of Procedure and Evidence, adopt, by an absolute majority, the Regulations of the Court necessary for its routine functioning.

2.   The Prosecutor and the Registrar shall be consulted in the elaboration of the Regulations and any amendments thereto.

3.   The Regulations and any amendments thereto shall take effect upon adoption unless otherwise decided by the judges. Immediately upon adoption, they shall be circulated to States Parties for comments. If within six months there are no objections from a majority of States Parties, they shall remain in force.

PART 5. INVESTIGATION AND PROSECUTION

Article 53
Initiation of an investigation

1.   The Prosecutor shall, having evaluated the information made available to him or her, initiate an investigation unless he or she determines that there is no reasonable basis to proceed under this Statute. In deciding whether to initiate an investigation, the Prosecutor shall consider whether:

  (a)   The information available to the Prosecutor provides a reasonable basis to believe that a crime within the jurisdiction of the Court has been or is being committed;

  (b)   The case is or would be admissible under Article 17; and

  (c)   Taking into account the gravity of the crime and the interests of victims, there are nonetheless substantial reasons to believe that an investigation would not serve the interests of justice.

  If the Prosecutor determines that there is no reasonable basis to proceed and his or her determination is based solely on subparagraph (c) above, he or she shall inform the Pre-Trial Chamber.

2.   If, upon investigation, the Prosecutor concludes that there is not a sufficient basis for a prosecution because:

  (a)   There is not a sufficient legal or factual basis to seek a warrant or summons under Article 58;

  (b)   The case is inadmissible under Article 17; or

  (c)   A prosecution is not in the interests of justice, taking into account all the circumstances, including the gravity of the crime, the interests of victims and the age or infirmity of the alleged perpetrator, and his or her role in the alleged crime;the Prosecutor shall inform the Pre-Trial Chamber and the state making a referral under Article 14 or the Security Council in a case under Article 13, paragraph (b), of his or her conclusion and the reasons for the conclusion.

3.   (a)   At the request of the state making a referral under Article 14 or the Security Council under Article 13, paragraph (b), the Pre-Trial Chamber may review a decision of the Prosecutor under paragraph 1 or 2 not to proceed and may request the Prosecutor to reconsider that decision.

(b)   In addition, the Pre-Trial Chamber may, on its own initiative, review a decision of the Prosecutor not to proceed if it is based solely on paragraph 1 (c) or 2 (c). In such a case, the decision of the Prosecutor shall be effective only if confirmed by the Pre-Trial Chamber.

4.   The Prosecutor may, at any time, reconsider a decision whether to initiate an investigation or prosecution based on new facts or information.

Article 54
Duties and powers of the Prosecutor with respect to investigations

1.   The Prosecutor shall:

(a)   In order to establish the truth, extend the investigation to cover all facts and evidence relevant to an assessment of whether there is criminal responsibility under this Statute, and, in doing so, investigate incriminating and exonerating circumstances equally;

(b)   Take appropriate measures to ensure the effective investigation and prosecution of crimes within the jurisdiction of the Court, and in doing so, respect the interests and personal circumstances of victims and witnesses, including age, gender as defined in Article 7, paragraph 3, and health, and take into account the nature of the crime, in particular where it involves sexual violence, gender violence or violence against children; and

(c)   Fully respect the rights of persons arising under this Statute.

2.   The Prosecutor may conduct investigations on the territory of a state:

(a)   In accordance with the provisions of Part 9; or

(b)   As authorized by the Pre-Trial Chamber under Article 57, paragraph 3 (d).

3.   The Prosecutor may:

(a)   Collect and examine evidence;

(b)   Request the presence of and question persons being investigated, victims and witnesses;

(c)   Seek the cooperation of any state or intergovernmental organization or arrangement in accordance with its respective competence and/or mandate;

(d)   Enter into such arrangements or agreements, not inconsistent with this Statute, as may be necessary to facilitate the cooperation of a state, intergovernmental organization or person;

(e)   Agree not to disclose, at any stage of the proceedings, documents or information that the Prosecutor obtains on the condition of confidentiality and solely for the purpose of generating new evidence, unless the provider of the information consents; and

(f)   Take necessary measures, or request that necessary measures be taken, to ensure the confidentiality of information, the protection of any person or the preservation of evidence.

Article 55
Rights of persons during an investigation

1.   In respect of an investigation under this Statute, a person:

(a)   Shall not be compelled to incriminate himself or herself or to confess guilt;

(b)   Shall not be subjected to any form of coercion, duress or threat, to torture or to any other form of cruel, inhuman or degrading treatment or punishment;

(c)   Shall, if questioned in a language other than a language the person fully understands and speaks, have, free of any cost, the assistance of a competent interpreter and such translations as are necessary to meet the requirements of fairness; and

(d)   Shall not be subjected to arbitrary arrest or detention, and shall not be deprived of his or her liberty except on such grounds and in accordance with such procedures as are established in this Statute.

2.   Where there are grounds to believe that a person has committed a crime within the jurisdiction of the Court and that person is about to be questioned either by the Prosecutor, or by national authorities pursuant to a request made under Part 9, that person shall also have the following rights of which he or she shall be informed prior to being questioned:

(a)   To be informed, prior to being questioned, that there are grounds to believe that he or she has committed a crime within the jurisdiction of the Court;

(b)   To remain silent, without such silence being a consideration in the determination of guilt or innocence;

(c)   To have legal assistance of the person's choosing, or, if the person does not have legal assistance, to have legal assistance assigned to him or her, in any case where the interests of justice so require, and without payment by the person in any such case if the person does not have sufficient means to pay for it; and

(d)   To be questioned in the presence of counsel unless the person has voluntarily waived his or her right to counsel.

Article 56
Role of the Pre-Trial Chamber in relation
to a unique investigative opportunity

1.   (a)   Where the Prosecutor considers an investigation to present a unique opportunity to take testimony or a statement from a witness or to examine, collect or test evidence, which may not be available subsequently for the purposes of a trial, the Prosecutor shall so inform the Pre-Trial Chamber.

(b)   In that case, the Pre-Trial Chamber may, upon request of the Prosecutor, take such measures as may be necessary to ensure the efficiency and integrity of the proceedings and, in particular, to protect the rights of the defence.

(c)   Unless the Pre-Trial Chamber orders otherwise, the Prosecutor shall provide the relevant information to the person who has been arrested or appeared in response to a summons in connection with the investigation referred to in subparagraph (a), in order that he or she may be heard on the matter.

2.   The measures referred to in paragraph 1 (b) may include:

(a)   Making recommendations or orders regarding procedures to be followed;

(b)   Directing that a record be made of the proceedings;

(c)   Appointing an expert to assist;

(d)   Authorizing counsel for a person who has been arrested, or appeared before the Court in response to a summons, to participate, or where there has not yet been such an arrest or appearance or counsel has not been designated, appointing another counsel to attend and represent the interests of the defence;

(e)   Naming one of its members or, if necessary, another available judge of the Pre-Trial or Trial Division to observe and make recommendations or orders regarding the collection and preservation of evidence and the questioning of persons;

(f)   Taking such other action as may be necessary to collect or preserve evidence.

3.   (a)   Where the Prosecutor has not sought measures pursuant to this Article but the Pre-Trial Chamber considers that such measures are required to preserve evidence that it deems would be essential for the defence at trial, it shall consult with the Prosecutor as to whether there is good reason for the Prosecutor's failure to request the measures. If upon consultation, the Pre-Trial Chamber concludes that the Prosecutor's failure to request such measures is unjustified, the Pre-Trial Chamber may take such measures on its own initiative.

(b)   A decision of the Pre-Trial Chamber to act on its own initiative under this paragraph may be appealed by the Prosecutor. The appeal shall be heard on an expedited basis.

4.   The admissibility of evidence preserved or collected for trial pursuant to this article, or the record thereof, shall be governed at trial by Article 69, and given such weight as determined by the Trial Chamber.

Article 57
Functions and powers of the Pre-Trial Chamber

1.   Unless otherwise provided in this Statute, the Pre-Trial Chamber shall exercise its functions in accordance with the provisions of this article.

2.   (a)   Orders or rulings of the Pre-Trial Chamber issued under Articles 15, 18, 19, 54, paragraph 2, 61, paragraph 7, and 72 must be concurred in by a majority of its judges.

(b)   In all other cases, a single judge of the Pre-Trial Chamber may exercise the functions provided for in this Statute, unless otherwise provided for in the Rules of Procedure and Evidence or by a majority of the Pre-Trial Chamber.

3.   In addition to its other functions under this Statute, the Pre-Trial Chamber may:

(a)   At the request of the Prosecutor, issue such orders and warrants as may be required for the purposes of an investigation;

(b)   Upon the request of a person who has been arrested or has appeared pursuant to a summons under Article 58, issue such orders, including measures such as those described in Article 56, or seek such cooperation pursuant to Part 9 as may be necessary to assist the person in the preparation of his or her defence;

(c)   Where necessary, provide for the protection and privacy of victims and witnesses, the preservation of evidence, the protection of persons who have been arrested or appeared in response to a summons, and the protection of national security information;

(d)   Authorize the Prosecutor to take specific investigative steps within the territory of a State Party without having secured the cooperation of that state under Part 9 if, whenever possible having regard to the views of the state concerned, the Pre-Trial Chamber has determined in that case that the state is clearly unable to execute a request for cooperation due to the unavailability of any authority or any component of its judicial system competent to execute the request for cooperation under Part 9.

(e)   Where a warrant of arrest or a summons has been issued under Article 58, and having due regard to the strength of the evidence and the rights of the parties concerned, as provided for in this Statute and the Rules of Procedure and Evidence, seek the cooperation of states pursuant to Article 93, paragraph 1 (k), to take protective measures for the purpose of forfeiture, in particular for the ultimate benefit of victims.

Article 58
Issuance by the Pre-Trial Chamber of a warrant of arrest or a summons to appear

1.   At any time after the initiation of an investigation, the Pre-Trial Chamber shall, on the application of the Prosecutor, issue a warrant of arrest of a person if, having examined the application and the evidence or other information submitted by the Prosecutor, it is satisfied that:

(a)   There are reasonable grounds to believe that the person has committed a crime within the jurisdiction of the Court; and

(b)   The arrest of the person appears necessary:

(i)   To ensure the person's appearance at trial,

(ii)   To ensure that the person does not obstruct or endanger the investigation or the court proceedings, or

(iii)   Where applicable, to prevent the person from continuing with the commission of that crime or a related crime which is within the jurisdiction of the Court and which arises out of the same circumstances.

2.   The application of the Prosecutor shall contain:

(a)   The name of the person and any other relevant identifying information;

(b)   A specific reference to the crimes within the jurisdiction of the Court which the person is alleged to have committed;

(c)   A concise statement of the facts which are alleged to constitute those crimes;

(d)   A summary of the evidence and any other information which establish reasonable grounds to believe that the person committed those crimes; and

(e)   The reason why the Prosecutor believes that the arrest of the person is necessary.

3.   The warrant of arrest shall contain:

(a)   The name of the person and any other relevant identifying information;

(b)   A specific reference to the crimes within the jurisdiction of the Court for which the person's arrest is sought; and

(c)   A concise statement of the facts which are alleged to constitute those crimes.

4.   The warrant of arrest shall remain in effect until otherwise ordered by the Court.

5.   On the basis of the warrant of arrest, the Court may request the provisional arrest or the arrest and surrender of the person under Part 9.

6.   The Prosecutor may request the Pre-Trial Chamber to amend the warrant of arrest by modifying or adding to the crimes specified therein. The Pre-Trial Chamber shall so amend the warrant if it is satisfied that there are reasonable grounds to believe that the person committed the modified or additional crimes.

7.   As an alternative to seeking a warrant of arrest, the Prosecutor may submit an application requesting that the Pre-Trial Chamber issue a summons for the person to appear. If the Pre-Trial Chamber is satisfied that there are reasonable grounds to believe that the person committed the crime alleged and that a summons is sufficient to ensure the person's

appearance, it shall issue the summons, with or without conditions restricting liberty (other than detention) if provided for by national law, for the person to appear. The summons shall contain:

    (a)   The name of the person and any other relevant identifying information;

    (b)   The specified date on which the person is to appear;

    (c)   A specific reference to the crimes within the jurisdiction of the Court which the person is alleged to have committed; and

    (d)   A concise statement of the facts which are alleged to constitute the crime. The summons shall be served on the person.

Article 59
Arrest proceedings in the custodial state

1.   A State Party which has received a request for provisional arrest or for arrest and surrender shall immediately take steps to arrest the person in question in accordance with its laws and the provisions of Part 9.

2.   A person arrested shall be brought promptly before the competent judicial authority in the custodial state which shall determine, in accordance with the law of that state, that:

    (a)   The warrant applies to that person;

    (b)   The person has been arrested in accordance with the proper process; and

    (c)   The person's rights have been respected.

3.   The person arrested shall have the right to apply to the competent authority in the custodial state for interim release pending surrender.

4.   In reaching a decision on any such application, the competent authority in the custodial state shall consider whether, given the gravity of the alleged crimes, there are urgent and exceptional circumstances to justify interim release and whether necessary safeguards exist to ensure that the custodial state can fulfil its duty to surrender the person to the Court. It shall not be open to the competent authority of the custodial state to consider whether the warrant of arrest was properly issued in accordance with Article 58, paragraph 1 (a) and (b).

5.   The Pre-Trial Chamber shall be notified of any request for interim release and shall make recommendations to the competent authority in the custodial state. The competent authority in the custodial state shall give full consideration to such recommendations, including any recommendations on measures to prevent the escape of the person, before rendering its decision.

6.   If the person is granted interim release, the Pre-Trial Chamber may request periodic reports on the status of the interim release.

7.   Once ordered to be surrendered by the custodial state, the person shall be delivered to the Court as soon as possible.

Article 60
Initial proceedings before the Court

1.   Upon the surrender of the person to the Court, or the person's appearance before the Court voluntarily or pursuant to a summons, the Pre-Trial Chamber shall satisfy itself that the person has been informed of the crimes which he or she is alleged to have committed,

and of his or her rights under this Statute, including the right to apply for interim release pending trial.

2. A person subject to a warrant of arrest may apply for interim release pending trial. If the Pre-Trial Chamber is satisfied that the conditions set forth in Article 58, paragraph 1, are met, the person shall continue to be detained. If it is not so satisfied, the Pre-Trial Chamber shall release the person, with or without conditions.

3. The Pre-Trial Chamber shall periodically review its ruling on the release or detention of the person, and may do so at any time on the request of the Prosecutor or the person. Upon such review, it may modify its ruling as to detention, release or conditions of release, if it is satisfied that changed circumstances so require.

4. The Pre-Trial Chamber shall ensure that a person is not detained for an unreasonable period prior to trial due to inexcusable delay by the Prosecutor. If such delay occurs, the Court shall consider releasing the person, with or without conditions.

5. If necessary, the Pre-Trial Chamber may issue a warrant of arrest to secure the presence of a person who has been released.

Article 61
Confirmation of the charges before trial

1. Subject to the provisions of paragraph 2, within a reasonable time after the person's surrender or voluntary appearance before the Court, the Pre-Trial Chamber shall hold a hearing to confirm the charges on which the Prosecutor intends to seek trial. The hearing shall be held in the presence of the Prosecutor and the person charged, as well as his or her counsel.

2. The Pre-Trial Chamber may, upon request of the Prosecutor or on its own motion, hold a hearing in the absence of the person charged to confirm the charges on which the Prosecutor intends to seek trial when the person has:
   (a) Waived his or her right to be present; or
   (b) Fled or cannot be found and all reasonable steps have been taken to secure his or her appearance before the Court and to inform the person of the charges and that a hearing to confirm those charges will be held. In that case, the person shall be represented by counsel where the Pre-Trial Chamber determines that it is in the interests of justice.

3. Within a reasonable time before the hearing, the person shall:
   (a) Be provided with a copy of the document containing the charges on which the Prosecutor intends to bring the person to trial; and
   (b) Be informed of the evidence on which the Prosecutor intends to rely at the hearing.
   The Pre-Trial Chamber may issue orders regarding the disclosure of information for the purposes of the hearing.

4. Before the hearing, the Prosecutor may continue the investigation and may amend or withdraw any charges. The person shall be given reasonable notice before the hearing of any amendment to or withdrawal of charges. In case of a withdrawal of charges, the Prosecutor shall notify the Pre-Trial Chamber of the reasons for the withdrawal.

5. At the hearing, the Prosecutor shall support each charge with sufficient evidence to establish substantial grounds to believe that the person committed the crime charged. The

Prosecutor may rely on documentary or summary evidence and need not call the witnesses expected to testify at the trial.

6.   At the hearing, the person may:
(a)   Object to the charges;
(b)   Challenge the evidence presented by the Prosecutor; and
(c)   Present evidence.

7.   The Pre-Trial Chamber shall, on the basis of the hearing, determine whether there is sufficient evidence to establish substantial grounds to believe that the person committed each of the crimes charged. Based on its determination, the Pre-Trial Chamber shall:

(a)   Confirm those charges in relation to which it has determined that there is sufficient evidence, and commit the person to a Trial Chamber for trial on the charges as confirmed;

(b)   Decline to confirm those charges in relation to which it has determined that there is insufficient evidence;

(c)   Adjourn the hearing and request the Prosecutor to consider:

(i)   Providing further evidence or conducting further investigation with respect to a particular charge; or

(ii)   Amending a charge because the evidence submitted appears to establish a different crime within the jurisdiction of the Court.

8.   Where the Pre-Trial Chamber declines to confirm a charge, the Prosecutor shall not be precluded from subsequently requesting its confirmation if the request is supported by additional evidence.

9.   After the charges are confirmed and before the trial has begun, the Prosecutor may, with the permission of the Pre-Trial Chamber and after notice to the accused, amend the charges. If the Prosecutor seeks to add additional charges or to substitute more serious charges, a hearing under this article to confirm those charges must be held. After commencement of the trial, the Prosecutor may, with the permission of the Trial Chamber, withdraw the charges.

10.   Any warrant previously issued shall cease to have effect with respect to any charges which have not been confirmed by the Pre-Trial Chamber or which have been withdrawn by the Prosecutor.

11.   Once the charges have been confirmed in accordance with this article, the Presidency shall constitute a Trial Chamber which, subject to paragraph 9 and to Article 64, paragraph 4, shall be responsible for the conduct of subsequent proceedings and may exercise any function of the Pre-Trial Chamber that is relevant and capable of application in those proceedings.

PART 6. THE TRIAL

Article 62
Place of trial

Unless otherwise decided, the place of the trial shall be the seat of the Court.

Article 63
Trial in the presence of the accused

1.   The accused shall be present during the trial.

2.   If the accused, being present before the Court, continues to disrupt the trial, the Trial Chamber may remove the accused and shall make provision for him or her to observe the trial and instruct counsel from outside the courtroom, through the use of communications technology, if required. Such measures shall be taken only in exceptional circumstances after other reasonable alternatives have proved inadequate, and only for such duration as is strictly required.

Article 64
Functions and powers of the Trial Chamber

1.   The functions and powers of the Trial Chamber set out in this article shall be exercised in accordance with this Statute and the Rules of Procedure and Evidence.

2.   The Trial Chamber shall ensure that a trial is fair and expeditious and is conducted with full respect for the rights of the accused and due regard for the protection of victims and witnesses.

3.   Upon assignment of a case for trial in accordance with this Statute, the Trial Chamber assigned to deal with the case shall:

    (a)   Confer with the parties and adopt such procedures as are necessary to facilitate the fair and expeditious conduct of the proceedings;

    (b)   Determine the language or languages to be used at trial; and

    (c)   Subject to any other relevant provisions of this Statute, provide for disclosure of documents or information not previously disclosed, sufficiently in advance of the commencement of the trial to enable adequate preparation for trial.

4.   The Trial Chamber may, if necessary for its effective and fair functioning, refer preliminary issues to the Pre-Trial Chamber or, if necessary, to another available judge of the Pre-Trial Division.

5.   Upon notice to the parties, the Trial Chamber may, as appropriate, direct that there be joinder or severance in respect of charges against more than one accused.

6.   In performing its functions prior to trial or during the course of a trial, the Trial Chamber may, as necessary:

    (a)   Exercise any functions of the Pre-Trial Chamber referred to in Article 61, paragraph 11;

    (b)   Require the attendance and testimony of witnesses and production of documents and other evidence by obtaining, if necessary, the assistance of states as provided in this Statute;

    (c)   Provide for the protection of confidential information;

(d) Order the production of evidence in addition to that already collected prior to the trial or presented during the trial by the parties;

(e) Provide for the protection of the accused, witnesses and victims; and

(f) Rule on any other relevant matters.

7. The trial shall be held in public. The Trial Chamber may, however, determine that special circumstances require that certain proceedings be in closed session for the purposes set forth in Article 68, or to protect confidential or sensitive information to be given in evidence.

8. (a) At the commencement of the trial, the Trial Chamber shall have read to the accused the charges previously confirmed by the Pre-Trial Chamber. The Trial Chamber shall satisfy itself that the accused understands the nature of the charges. It shall afford him or her the opportunity to make an admission of guilt in accordance with Article 65 or to plead not guilty.

(b) At the trial, the presiding judge may give directions for the conduct of proceedings, including to ensure that they are conducted in a fair and impartial manner. Subject to any directions of the presiding judge, the parties may submit evidence in accordance with the provisions of this Statute.

9. The Trial Chamber shall have, *inter alia*, the power on application of a party or on its own motion to:

(a) Rule on the admissibility or relevance of evidence; and

(b) Take all necessary steps to maintain order in the course of a hearing.

10. The Trial Chamber shall ensure that a complete record of the trial, which accurately reflects the proceedings, is made and that it is maintained and preserved by the Registrar.

Article 65
Proceedings on an admission of guilt

1. Where the accused makes an admission of guilt pursuant to Article 64, paragraph 8 (a), the Trial Chamber shall determine whether:

(a) The accused understands the nature and consequences of the admission of guilt;

(b) The admission is voluntarily made by the accused after sufficient consultation with defence counsel; and

(c) The admission of guilt is supported by the facts of the case that are contained in:

(i) The charges brought by the Prosecutor and admitted by the accused;

(ii) Any materials presented by the Prosecutor which supplement the charges and which the accused accepts; and

(iii) Any other evidence, such as the testimony of witnesses, presented by the Prosecutor or the accused.

2. Where the Trial Chamber is satisfied that the matters referred to in paragraph 1 are established, it shall consider the admission of guilt, together with any additional evidence presented, as establishing all the essential facts that are required to prove the crime to which the admission of guilt relates, and may convict the accused of that crime.

3. Where the Trial Chamber is not satisfied that the matters referred to in paragraph 1 are established, it shall consider the admission of guilt as not having been made, in which case it shall order that the trial be continued under the ordinary trial procedures provided by this Statute and may remit the case to another Trial Chamber.

4.   Where the Trial Chamber is of the opinion that a more complete presentation of the facts of the case is required in the interests of justice, in particular the interests of the victims, the Trial Chamber may:

(a)   Request the Prosecutor to present additional evidence, including the testimony of witnesses; or

(b)   Order that the trial be continued under the ordinary trial procedures provided by this Statute, in which case it shall consider the admission of guilt as not having been made and may remit the case to another Trial Chamber.

5.   Any discussions between the Prosecutor and the defence regarding modification of the charges, the admission of guilt or the penalty to be imposed shall not be binding on the Court.

Article 66
Presumption of innocence

1.   Everyone shall be presumed innocent until proved guilty before the Court in accordance with the applicable law.

2.   The onus is on the Prosecutor to prove the guilt of the accused.

3.   In order to convict the accused, the Court must be convinced of the guilt of the accused beyond reasonable doubt.

Article 67
Rights of the accused

1.   In the determination of any charge, the accused shall be entitled to a public hearing, having regard to the provisions of this Statute, to a fair hearing conducted impartially, and to the following minimum guarantees, in full equality:

(a)   To be informed promptly and in detail of the nature, cause and content of the charge, in a language which the accused fully understands and speaks;

(b)   To have adequate time and facilities for the preparation of the defence and to communicate freely with counsel of the accused's choosing in confidence;

(c)   To be tried without undue delay;

(d)   Subject to Article 63, paragraph 2, to be present at the trial, to conduct the defence in person or through legal assistance of the accused's choosing, to be informed, if the accused does not have legal assistance, of this right and to have legal assistance assigned by the Court in any case where the interests of justice so require, and without payment if the accused lacks sufficient means to pay for it;

(e)   To examine, or have examined, the witnesses against him or her and to obtain the attendance and examination of witnesses on his or her behalf under the same conditions as witnesses against him or her. The accused shall also be entitled to raise defences and to present other evidence admissible under this Statute;

(f)   To have, free of any cost, the assistance of a competent interpreter and such translations as are necessary to meet the requirements of fairness, if any of the proceedings of or documents presented to the Court are not in a language which the accused fully understands and speaks;

(g)   Not to be compelled to testify or to confess guilt and to remain silent, without such silence being a consideration in the determination of guilt or innocence;

(h)   To make an unsworn oral or written statement in his or her defence; and

(i)   Not to have imposed on him or her any reversal of the burden of proof or any onus of rebuttal.

2.   In addition to any other disclosure provided for in this Statute, the Prosecutor shall, as soon as practicable, disclose to the defence evidence in the Prosecutor's possession or control which he or she believes shows or tends to show the innocence of the accused, or to mitigate the guilt of the accused, or which may affect the credibility of prosecution evidence. In case of doubt as to the application of this paragraph, the Court shall decide.

Article 68
Protection of the victims and witnesses and their participation in the proceedings

1.   The Court shall take appropriate measures to protect the safety, physical and psychological well-being, dignity and privacy of victims and witnesses. In so doing, the Court shall have regard to all relevant factors, including age, gender as defined in Article 7, paragraph 3, and health, and the nature of the crime, in particular, but not limited to, where the crime involves sexual or gender violence or violence against children. The Prosecutor shall take such measures particularly during the investigation and prosecution of such crimes. These measures shall not be prejudicial to or inconsistent with the rights of the accused and a fair and impartial trial.

2.   As an exception to the principle of public hearings provided for in Article 67, the Chambers of the Court may, to protect victims and witnesses or an accused, conduct any part of the proceedings *in camera* or allow the presentation of evidence by electronic or other special means. In particular, such measures shall be implemented in the case of a victim of sexual violence or a child who is a victim or a witness, unless otherwise ordered by the Court, having regard to all the circumstances, particularly the views of the victim or witness.

3.   Where the personal interests of the victims are affected, the Court shall permit their views and concerns to be presented and considered at stages of the proceedings determined to be appropriate by the Court and in a manner which is not prejudicial to or inconsistent with the rights of the accused and a fair and impartial trial. Such views and concerns may be presented by the legal representatives of the victims where the Court considers it appropriate, in accordance with the Rules of Procedure and Evidence.

4.   The Victims and Witnesses Unit may advise the Prosecutor and the Court on appropriate protective measures, security arrangements, counselling and assistance as referred to in Article 43, paragraph 6.

5.   Where the disclosure of evidence or information pursuant to this Statute may lead to the grave endangerment of the security of a witness or his or her family, the Prosecutor may, for the purposes of any proceedings conducted prior to the commencement of the trial, withhold such evidence or information and instead submit a summary thereof. Such measures shall be exercised in a manner which is not prejudicial to or inconsistent with the rights of the accused and a fair and impartial trial.

6.   A state may make an application for necessary measures to be taken in respect of the protection of its servants or agents and the protection of confidential or sensitive information.

Article 69
Evidence

1.   Before testifying, each witness shall, in accordance with the Rules of Procedure and Evidence, give an undertaking as to the truthfulness of the evidence to be given by that witness.

2.   The testimony of a witness at trial shall be given in person, except to the extent provided by the measures set forth in Article 68 or in the Rules of Procedure and Evidence. The Court may also permit the giving of *viva voce* (oral) or recorded testimony of a witness by means of video or audio technology, as well as the introduction of documents or written transcripts, subject to this Statute and in accordance with the Rules of Procedure and Evidence. These measures shall not be prejudicial to or inconsistent with the rights of the accused.

3.   The parties may submit evidence relevant to the case, in accordance with Article 64. The Court shall have the authority to request the submission of all evidence that it considers necessary for the determination of the truth.

4.   The Court may rule on the relevance or admissibility of any evidence, taking into account, *inter alia*, the probative value of the evidence and any prejudice that such evidence may cause to a fair trial or to a fair evaluation of the testimony of a witness, in accordance with the Rules of Procedure and Evidence.

5.   The Court shall respect and observe privileges on confidentiality as provided for in the Rules of Procedure and Evidence.

6.   The Court shall not require proof of facts of common knowledge but may take judicial notice of them.

7.   Evidence obtained by means of a violation of this Statute or internationally recognized human rights shall not be admissible if:
    (a)   The violation casts substantial doubt on the reliability of the evidence; or
    (b)   The admission of the evidence would be antithetical to and would seriously damage the integrity of the proceedings.

8.   When deciding on the relevance or admissibility of evidence collected by a state, the Court shall not rule on the application of the state's national law.

Article 70
Offences against the administration of justice

1.   The Court shall have jurisdiction over the following offences against its administration of justice when committed intentionally:
    (a)   Giving false testimony when under an obligation pursuant to Article 69, paragraph 1, to tell the truth;
    (b)   Presenting evidence that the party knows is false or forged;
    (c)   Corruptly influencing a witness, obstructing or interfering with the attendance or testimony of a witness, retaliating against a witness for giving testimony or destroying, tampering with or interfering with the collection of evidence;
    (d)   Impeding, intimidating or corruptly influencing an official of the Court for the purpose of forcing or persuading the official not to perform, or to perform improperly, his or her duties;

(e) Retaliating against an official of the Court on account of duties performed by that or another official;

(f) Soliciting or accepting a bribe as an official of the Court in connection with his or her official duties.

2. The principles and procedures governing the Court's exercise of jurisdiction over offences under this Article shall be those provided for in the Rules of Procedure and Evidence. The conditions for providing international cooperation to the Court with respect to its proceedings under this article shall be governed by the domestic laws of the requested state.

3. In the event of conviction, the Court may impose a term of imprisonment not exceeding five years, or a fine in accordance with the Rules of Procedure and Evidence, or both.

4. (a) Each State Party shall extend its criminal laws penalizing offences against the integrity of its own investigative or judicial process to offences against the administration of justice referred to in this article, committed on its territory, or by one of its nationals;

(b) Upon request by the Court, whenever it deems it proper, the State Party shall submit the case to its competent authorities for the purpose of prosecution. Those authorities shall treat such cases with diligence and devote sufficient resources to enable them to be conducted effectively.

Article 71
Sanctions for misconduct before the Court

1. The Court may sanction persons present before it who commit misconduct, including disruption of its proceedings or deliberate refusal to comply with its directions, by administrative measures other than imprisonment, such as temporary or permanent removal from the courtroom, a fine or other similar measures provided for in the Rules of Procedure and Evidence.

2. The procedures governing the imposition of the measures set forth in paragraph 1 shall be those provided for in the Rules of Procedure and Evidence.

Article 72
Protection of national security information

1. This article applies in any case where the disclosure of the information or documents of a state would, in the opinion of that state, prejudice its national security interests. Such cases include those falling within the scope of Article 56, paragraphs 2 and 3, Article 61, paragraph 3, Article 64, paragraph 3, Article 67, paragraph 2, Article 68, paragraph 6, Article 87, paragraph 6 and Article 93, as well as cases arising at any other stage of the proceedings where such disclosure may be at issue.

2. This Article shall also apply when a person who has been requested to give information or evidence has refused to do so or has referred the matter to the state on the ground that disclosure would prejudice the national security interests of a state and the state concerned confirms that it is of the opinion that disclosure would prejudice its national security interests.

3. Nothing in this article shall prejudice the requirements of confidentiality applicable under Article 54, paragraph 3 (e) and (f), or the application of Article 73.

4.   If a state learns that information or documents of the state are being, or are likely to be, disclosed at any stage of the proceedings, and it is of the opinion that disclosure would prejudice its national security interests, that state shall have the right to intervene in order to obtain resolution of the issue in accordance with this article.

5.   If, in the opinion of a state, disclosure of information would prejudice its national security interests, all reasonable steps will be taken by the state, acting in conjunction with the Prosecutor, the defence or the Pre-Trial Chamber or Trial Chamber, as the case may be, to seek to resolve the matter by cooperative means. Such steps may include:

(a)   Modification or clarification of the request;

(b)   A determination by the Court regarding the relevance of the information or evidence sought, or a determination as to whether the evidence, though relevant, could be or has been obtained from a source other than the requested state;

(c)   Obtaining the information or evidence from a different source or in a different form; or

(d)   Agreement on conditions under which the assistance could be provided including, among other things, providing summaries or redactions, limitations on disclosure, use of *in camera* or *ex parte* proceedings, or other protective measures permissible under the Statute and the Rules of Procedure and Evidence.

6.   Once all reasonable steps have been taken to resolve the matter through cooperative means, and if the state considers that there are no means or conditions under which the information or documents could be provided or disclosed without prejudice to its national security interests, it shall so notify the Prosecutor or the Court of the specific reasons for its decision, unless a specific description of the reasons would itself necessarily result in such prejudice to the state's national security interests.

7.   Thereafter, if the Court determines that the evidence is relevant and necessary for the establishment of the guilt or innocence of the accused, the Court may undertake the following actions:

(a)   Where disclosure of the information or document is sought pursuant to a request for cooperation under Part 9 or the circumstances described in paragraph 2, and the state has invoked the ground for refusal referred to in Article 93, paragraph 4:

(i)   The Court may, before making any conclusion referred to in subparagraph 7 (a) (ii), request further consultations for the purpose of considering the state's representations, which may include, as appropriate, hearings *in camera* and *ex parte*;

(ii)   If the Court concludes that, by invoking the ground for refusal under Article 93, paragraph 4, in the circumstances of the case, the requested state is not acting in accordance with its obligations under this Statute, the Court may refer the matter in accordance with Article 87, paragraph 7, specifying the reasons for its conclusion; and

(iii)   The Court may make such inference in the trial of the accused as to the existence or non-existence of a fact, as may be appropriate in the circumstances; or

(b)   In all other circumstances:

(i)   Order disclosure; or

(ii)   To the extent it does not order disclosure, make such inference in the trial of the accused as to the existence or non-existence of a fact, as may be appropriate in the circumstances.

Article 73
Third-party information or documents

If a State Party is requested by the Court to provide a document or information in its custody, possession or control, which was disclosed to it in confidence by a state, inter-governmental organization or international organization, it shall seek the consent of the originator to disclose that document or information. If the originator is a State Party, it shall either consent to disclosure of the information or document or undertake to resolve the issue of disclosure with the Court, subject to the provisions of Article 72. If the origina-tor is not a State Party and refuses to consent to disclosure, the requested state shall inform the Court that it is unable to provide the document or information because of a pre-exist-ing obligation of confidentiality to the originator.

Article 74
Requirements for the decision

1. All the judges of the Trial Chamber shall be present at each stage of the trial and throughout their deliberations. The Presidency may, on a case-by-case basis, designate, as available, one or more alternate judges to be present at each stage of the trial and to replace a member of the Trial Chamber if that member is unable to continue attending.

2. The Trial Chamber's decision shall be based on its evaluation of the evidence and the entire proceedings. The decision shall not exceed the facts and circumstances described in the charges and any amendments to the charges. The Court may base its decision only on evidence submitted and discussed before it at the trial.

3. The judges shall attempt to achieve unanimity in their decision, failing which the decision shall be taken by a majority of the judges.

4. The deliberations of the Trial Chamber shall remain secret.

5. The decision shall be in writing and shall contain a full and reasoned statement of the Trial Chamber's findings on the evidence and conclusions. The Trial Chamber shall issue one decision. When there is no unanimity, the Trial Chamber's decision shall contain the views of the majority and the minority. The decision or a summary thereof shall be deliv-ered in open court.

Article 75
Reparations to victims

1. The Court shall establish principles relating to reparations to, or in respect of, victims, including restitution, compensation and rehabilitation. On this basis, in its decision the Court may, either upon request or on its own motion in exceptional circumstances, deter-mine the scope and extent of any damage, loss and injury to, or in respect of, victims and will state the principles on which it is acting.

2. The Court may make an order directly against a convicted person specifying appro-priate reparations to, or in respect of, victims, including restitution, compensation and rehabilitation.

Where appropriate, the Court may order that the award for reparations be made through the Trust Fund provided for in Article 79.

3.   Before making an order under this article, the Court may invite and shall take account of representations from or on behalf of the convicted person, victims, other interested persons or interested states.

4.   In exercising its power under this article, the Court may, after a person is convicted of a crime within the jurisdiction of the Court, determine whether, in order to give effect to an order which it may make under this article, it is necessary to seek measures under Article 93, paragraph 1.

5.   A State Party shall give effect to a decision under this article as if the provisions of Article 109 were applicable to this article.

6.   Nothing in this Article shall be interpreted as prejudicing the rights of victims under national or international law.

Article 76
Sentencing

1.   In the event of a conviction, the Trial Chamber shall consider the appropriate sentence to be imposed and shall take into account the evidence presented and submissions made during the trial that are relevant to the sentence.

2.   Except where Article 65 applies and before the completion of the trial, the Trial Chamber may on its own motion and shall, at the request of the Prosecutor or the accused, hold a further hearing to hear any additional evidence or submissions relevant to the sentence, in accordance with the Rules of Procedure and Evidence.

3.   Where paragraph 2 applies, any representations under Article 75 shall be heard during the further hearing referred to in paragraph 2 and, if necessary, during any additional hearing.

4.   The sentence shall be pronounced in public and, wherever possible, in the presence of the accused.

PART 7. PENALTIES

Article 77
Applicable penalties

1.   Subject to Article 110, the Court may impose one of the following penalties on a person convicted of a crime referred to in Article 5 of this Statute:

   (a)   Imprisonment for a specified number of years, which may not exceed a maximum of 30 years; or

   (b)   A term of life imprisonment when justified by the extreme gravity of the crime and the individual circumstances of the convicted person.

2.   In addition to imprisonment, the Court may order:

   (a)   A fine under the criteria provided for in the Rules of Procedure and Evidence;

   (b)   A forfeiture of proceeds, property and assets derived directly or indirectly from that crime, without prejudice to the rights of bona fide third parties.

Article 78
Determination of the sentence

1. In determining the sentence, the Court shall, in accordance with the Rules of Procedure and Evidence, take into account such factors as the gravity of the crime and the individual circumstances of the convicted person.

2. In imposing a sentence of imprisonment, the Court shall deduct the time, if any, previously spent in detention in accordance with an order of the Court. The Court may deduct any time otherwise spent in detention in connection with conduct underlying the crime.

3. When a person has been convicted of more than one crime, the Court shall pronounce a sentence for each crime and a joint sentence specifying the total period of imprisonment. This period shall be no less than the highest individual sentence pronounced and shall not exceed 30 years imprisonment or a sentence of life imprisonment in conformity with Article 77, paragraph 1 (b).

Article 79
Trust Fund

1. A Trust Fund shall be established by decision of the Assembly of States Parties for the benefit of victims of crimes within the jurisdiction of the Court, and of the families of such victims.

2. The Court may order money and other property collected through fines or forfeiture to be transferred, by order of the Court, to the Trust Fund.

3. The Trust Fund shall be managed according to criteria to be determined by the Assembly of States Parties.

Article 80
Non-prejudice to national application of penalties and national laws

Nothing in this Part affects the application by states of penalties prescribed by their national law, nor the law of States which do not provide for penalties prescribed in this Part.

PART 8. APPEAL AND REVISION

Article 81
Appeal against decision of acquittal or conviction
or against sentence

1. A decision under Article 74 may be appealed in accordance with the Rules of Procedure and Evidence as follows:
    (a) The Prosecutor may make an appeal on any of the following grounds:
        (i)   Procedural error,
        (ii) Error of fact, or
        (iii) Error of law;
    (b) The convicted person, or the Prosecutor on that person's behalf, may make an appeal on any of the following grounds:
        (i)   Procedural error,
        (ii) Error of fact,

  (iii) Error of law, or
  (iv) Any other ground that affects the fairness or reliability of the proceedings or decision.

2. (a) A sentence may be appealed, in accordance with the Rules of Procedure and Evidence, by the Prosecutor or the convicted person on the ground of disproportion between the crime and the sentence;
  (b) If on an appeal against sentence the Court considers that there are grounds on which the conviction might be set aside, wholly or in part, it may invite the Prosecutor and the convicted person to submit grounds under Article 81, paragraph 1 (a) or (b), and may render a decision on conviction in accordance with Article 83;
  (c) The same procedure applies when the Court, on an appeal against conviction only, considers that there are grounds to reduce the sentence under paragraph 2 (a).

3. (a) Unless the Trial Chamber orders otherwise, a convicted person shall remain in custody pending an appeal;
  (b) When a convicted person's time in custody exceeds the sentence of imprisonment imposed, that person shall be released, except that if the Prosecutor is also appealing, the release may be subject to the conditions under subparagraph (c) below;
  (c) In case of an acquittal, the accused shall be released immediately, subject to the following:
    (i) Under exceptional circumstances, and having regard, *inter alia*, to the concrete risk of flight, the seriousness of the offence charged and the probability of success on appeal, the Trial Chamber, at the request of the Prosecutor, may maintain the detention of the person pending appeal;
    (ii) A decision by the Trial Chamber under subparagraph (c) (i) may be appealed in accordance with the Rules of Procedure and Evidence.

4. Subject to the provisions of paragraph 3 (a) and (b), execution of the decision or sentence shall be suspended during the period allowed for appeal and for the duration of the appeal proceedings.

Article 82
Appeal against other decisions

1. Either party may appeal any of the following decisions in accordance with the Rules of Procedure and Evidence:
  (a) A decision with respect to jurisdiction or admissibility;
  (b) A decision granting or denying release of the person being investigated or prosecuted;
  (c) A decision of the Pre-Trial Chamber to act on its own initiative under Article 56, paragraph 3;
  (d) A decision that involves an issue that would significantly affect the fair and expeditious conduct of the proceedings or the outcome of the trial, and for which, in the opinion of the Pre-Trial or Trial Chamber, an immediate resolution by the Appeals Chamber may materially advance the proceedings.

2. A decision of the Pre-Trial Chamber under Article 57, paragraph 3 (d), may be appealed against by the state concerned or by the Prosecutor, with the leave of the Pre-Trial Chamber. The appeal shall be heard on an expedited basis.

3.   An appeal shall not of itself have suspensive effect unless the Appeals Chamber so orders, upon request, in accordance with the Rules of Procedure and Evidence.

4.   A legal representative of the victims, the convicted person or a bona fide owner of property adversely affected by an order under Article 75 may appeal against the order for reparations, as provided in the Rules of Procedure and Evidence.

Article 83
Proceedings on appeal

1.   For the purposes of proceedings under Article 81 and this Article, the Appeals Chamber shall have all the powers of the Trial Chamber.

2.   If the Appeals Chamber finds that the proceedings appealed from were unfair in a way that affected the reliability of the decision or sentence, or that the decision or sentence appealed from was materially affected by error of fact or law or procedural error, it may:

    (a)   Reverse or amend the decision or sentence; or

    (b)   Order a new trial before a different Trial Chamber.

For these purposes, the Appeals Chamber may remand a factual issue to the original Trial Chamber for it to determine the issue and to report back accordingly, or may itself call evidence to determine the issue. When the decision or sentence has been appealed only by the person convicted, or the Prosecutor on that person's behalf, it cannot be amended to his or her detriment.

3.   If in an appeal against sentence the Appeals Chamber finds that the sentence is disproportionate to the crime, it may vary the sentence in accordance with Part 7.

4.   The judgement of the Appeals Chamber shall be taken by a majority of the judges and shall be delivered in open court. The judgement shall state the reasons on which it is based. When there is no unanimity, the judgement of the Appeals Chamber shall contain the views of the majority and the minority, but a judge may deliver a separate or dissenting opinion on a question of law.

5.   The Appeals Chamber may deliver its judgement in the absence of the person acquitted or convicted.

Article 84
Revision of conviction or sentence

1.   The convicted person or, after death, spouses, children, parents or one person alive at the time of the accused's death who has been given express written instructions from the accused to bring such a claim, or the Prosecutor on the person's behalf, may apply to the Appeals Chamber to revise the final judgement of conviction or sentence on the grounds that:

    (a)   New evidence has been discovered that:

        (i)   Was not available at the time of trial, and such unavailability was not wholly or partially attributable to the party making application; and

        (ii)   Is sufficiently important that had it been proved at trial it would have been likely to have resulted in a different verdict;

    (b)   It has been newly discovered that decisive evidence, taken into account at trial and upon which the conviction depends, was false, forged or falsified;

(c)   One or more of the judges who participated in conviction or confirmation of the charges has committed, in that case, an act of serious misconduct or serious breach of duty of sufficient gravity to justify the removal of that judge or those judges from office under Article 46.

2.   The Appeals Chamber shall reject the application if it considers it to be unfounded. If it determines that the application is meritorious, it may, as appropriate:

(a)   Reconvene the original Trial Chamber;

(b)   Constitute a new Trial Chamber; or

(c)   Retain jurisdiction over the matter, with a view to, after hearing the parties in the manner set forth in the Rules of Procedure and Evidence, arriving at a determination on whether the judgement should be revised.

Article 85
Compensation to an arrested or convicted person

1.   Anyone who has been the victim of unlawful arrest or detention shall have an enforceable right to compensation.

2.   When a person has by a final decision been convicted of a criminal offence, and when subsequently his or her conviction has been reversed on the ground that a new or newly discovered fact shows conclusively that there has been a miscarriage of justice, the person who has suffered punishment as a result of such conviction shall be compensated according to law, unless it is proved that the non-disclosure of the unknown fact in time is wholly or partly attributable to him or her.

3.   In exceptional circumstances, where the Court finds conclusive facts showing that there has been a grave and manifest miscarriage of justice, it may in its discretion award compensation, according to the criteria provided in the Rules of Procedure and Evidence, to a person who has been released from detention following a final decision of acquittal or a termination of the proceedings for that reason.

PART 9. INTERNATIONAL COOPERATION AND JUDICIAL ASSISTANCE

Article 86
General obligation to cooperate

States Parties shall, in accordance with the provisions of this Statute, cooperate fully with the Court in its investigation and prosecution of crimes within the jurisdiction of the Court.

Article 87
Requests for cooperation: general provisions

1.   (a)   The Court shall have the authority to make requests to States Parties for cooperation. The requests shall be transmitted through the diplomatic channel or any other appropriate channel as may be designated by each State Party upon ratification, acceptance, approval or accession. Subsequent changes to the designation shall be made by each State Party in accordance with the Rules of Procedure and Evidence.

(b)   When appropriate, without prejudice to the provisions of subparagraph (a), requests may also be transmitted through the International Criminal Police Organization or any appropriate regional organization.

2.   Requests for cooperation and any documents supporting the request shall either be in or be accompanied by a translation into an official language of the requested state or one of the working languages of the Court, in accordance with the choice made by that state upon ratification, acceptance, approval or accession. Subsequent changes to this choice shall be made in accordance with the Rules of Procedure and Evidence.

3.   The requested state shall keep confidential a request for cooperation and any documents supporting the request, except to the extent that the disclosure is necessary for execution of the request.

4.   In relation to any request for assistance presented under this Part, the Court may take such measures, including measures related to the protection of information, as may be necessary to ensure the safety or physical or psychological well-being of any victims, potential witnesses and their families. The Court may request that any information that is made available under this Part shall be provided and handled in a manner that protects the safety and physical or psychological well-being of any victims, potential witnesses and their families.

5.   (a)   The Court may invite any state not party to this Statute to provide assistance under this Part on the basis of an ad hoc arrangement, an agreement with such state or any other appropriate basis.
        (b)   Where a state not party to this Statute, which has entered into an ad hoc arrangement or an agreement with the Court, fails to cooperate with requests pursuant to any such arrangement or agreement, the Court may so inform the Assembly of States Parties or, where the Security Council referred the matter to the Court, the Security Council.

6.   The Court may ask any intergovernmental organization to provide information or documents. The Court may also ask for other forms of cooperation and assistance which may be agreed upon with such an organization and which are in accordance with its competence or mandate.

7.   Where a State Party fails to comply with a request to cooperate by the Court contrary to the provisions of this Statute, thereby preventing the Court from exercising its functions and powers under this Statute, the Court may make a finding to that effect and refer the matter to the Assembly of States Parties or, where the Security Council referred the matter to the Court, to the Security Council.

Article 88
Availability of procedures under national law

States Parties shall ensure that there are procedures available under their national law for all of the forms of cooperation which are specified under this Part.

Article 89
Surrender of persons to the Court

1.   The Court may transmit a request for the arrest and surrender of a person, together with the material supporting the request outlined in Article 91, to any state on the territory of which that person may be found and shall request the cooperation of that state in the arrest and surrender of such a person. States Parties shall, in accordance with the provisions of this Part and the procedure under their national law, comply with requests for arrest and surrender.

2.   Where the person sought for surrender brings a challenge before a national court on the basis of the principle of *ne bis in idem* as provided in Article 20, the requested state

shall immediately consult with the Court to determine if there has been a relevant ruling on admissibility. If the case is admissible, the requested state shall proceed with the execution of the request. If an admissibility ruling is pending, the requested state may postpone the execution of the request for surrender of the person until the Court makes a determination on admissibility.

3.　(a)　A State Party shall authorize, in accordance with its national procedural law, transportation through its territory of a person being surrendered to the Court by another state, except where transit through that state would impede or delay the surrender.

　　(b)　A request by the Court for transit shall be transmitted in accordance with Article 87. The request for transit shall contain:

　　　　(i)　A description of the person being transported;

　　　　(ii)　A brief statement of the facts of the case and their legal characterization; and

　　　　(iii)　The warrant for arrest and surrender;

　　(c)　A person being transported shall be detained in custody during the period of transit;

　　(d)　No authorization is required if the person is transported by air and no landing is scheduled on the territory of the transit state;

　　(e)　If an unscheduled landing occurs on the territory of the transit state, that state may require a request for transit from the Court as provided for in subparagraph (b). The transit state shall detain the person being transported until the request for transit is received and the transit is effected, provided that detention for purposes of this subparagraph may not be extended beyond 96 hours from the unscheduled landing unless the request is received within that time.

4.　If the person sought is being proceeded against or is serving a sentence in the requested state for a crime different from that for which surrender to the Court is sought, the requested state, after making its decision to grant the request, shall consult with the Court.

Article 90
Competing requests

1.　A State Party which receives a request from the Court for the surrender of a person under Article 89 shall, if it also receives a request from any other state for the extradition of the same person for the same conduct which forms the basis of the crime for which the Court seeks the person's surrender, notify the Court and the requesting state of that fact.

2.　Where the requesting state is a State Party, the requested state shall give priority to the request from the Court if:

　　(a)　The Court has, pursuant to Article 18 or 19, made a determination that the case in respect of which surrender is sought is admissible and that determination takes into account the investigation or prosecution conducted by the requesting state in respect of its request for extradition; or

　　(b)　The Court makes the determination described in subparagraph (a) pursuant to the requested state's notification under paragraph 1.

3.　Where a determination under paragraph 2 (a) has not been made, the requested state may, at its discretion, pending the determination of the Court under paragraph 2 (b), proceed to deal with the request for extradition from the requesting state but shall not extradite the person until the Court has determined that the case is inadmissible. The Court's determination shall be made on an expedited basis.

4.　If the requesting state is a state not Party to this Statute the requested state, if it is not under an international obligation to extradite the person to the requesting state, shall give priority to the request for surrender from the Court, if the Court has determined that the case is admissible.

5.　Where a case under paragraph 4 has not been determined to be admissible by the Court, the requested state may, at its discretion, proceed to deal with the request for extradition from the requesting state.

6.　In cases where paragraph 4 applies except that the requested state is under an existing international obligation to extradite the person to the requesting state not Party to this Statute, the requested state shall determine whether to surrender the person to the Court or extradite the person to the requesting state. In making its decision, the requested state shall consider all the relevant factors, including but not limited to:

　　(a)　The respective dates of the requests;

　　(b)　The interests of the requesting state including, where relevant, whether the crime was committed in its territory and the nationality of the victims and of the person sought; and

　　(c)　The possibility of subsequent surrender between the Court and the requesting state.

7.　Where a State Party which receives a request from the Court for the surrender of a person also receives a request from any state for the extradition of the same person for conduct other than that which constitutes the crime for which the Court seeks the person's surrender:

　　(a)　The requested state shall, if it is not under an existing international obligation to extradite the person to the requesting state, give priority to the request from the Court;

　　(b)　The requested state shall, if it is under an existing international obligation to extradite the person to the requesting state, determine whether to surrender the person to the Court or to extradite the person to the requesting state. In making its decision, the requested state shall consider all the relevant factors, including but not limited to those set out in paragraph 6, but shall give special consideration to the relative nature and gravity of the conduct in question.

8.　Where pursuant to a notification under this article, the Court has determined a case to be inadmissible, and subsequently extradition to the requesting state is refused, the requested state shall notify the Court of this decision.

Article 91
Contents of request for arrest and surrender

1.　A request for arrest and surrender shall be made in writing. In urgent cases, a request may be made by any medium capable of delivering a written record, provided that the request shall be confirmed through the channel provided for in Article 87, paragraph 1 (a).

2.　In the case of a request for the arrest and surrender of a person for whom a warrant of arrest has been issued by the Pre-Trial Chamber under Article 58, the request shall contain or be supported by:

　　(a)　Information describing the person sought, sufficient to identify the person, and information as to that person's probable location;

(b)   A copy of the warrant of arrest; and

(c)   Such documents, statements or information as may be necessary to meet the requirements for the surrender process in the requested state, except that those requirements should not be more burdensome than those applicable to requests for extradition pursuant to treaties or arrangements between the requested state and other states and should, if possible, be less burdensome, taking into account the distinct nature of the Court.

3.   In the case of a request for the arrest and surrender of a person already convicted, the request shall contain or be supported by:

(a)   A copy of any warrant of arrest for that person;

(b)   A copy of the judgement of conviction;

(c)   Information to demonstrate that the person sought is the one referred to in the judgement of conviction; and

(d)   If the person sought has been sentenced, a copy of the sentence imposed and, in the case of a sentence for imprisonment, a statement of any time already served and the time remaining to be served.

4.   Upon the request of the Court, a State Party shall consult with the Court, either generally or with respect to a specific matter, regarding any requirements under its national law that may apply under paragraph 2 (c). During the consultations, the State Party shall advise the Court of the specific requirements of its national law.

Article 92
Provisional arrest

1.   In urgent cases, the Court may request the provisional arrest of the person sought, pending presentation of the request for surrender and the documents supporting the request as specified in Article 91.

2.   The request for provisional arrest shall be made by any medium capable of delivering a written record and shall contain:

(a)   Information describing the person sought, sufficient to identify the person, and information as to that person's probable location;

(b)   A concise statement of the crimes for which the person's arrest is sought and of the facts which are alleged to constitute those crimes, including, where possible, the date and location of the crime;

(c)   A statement of the existence of a warrant of arrest or a judgement of conviction against the person sought; and

(d)   A statement that a request for surrender of the person sought will follow.

3.   A person who is provisionally arrested may be released from custody if the requested state has not received the request for surrender and the documents supporting the request as specified in Article 91 within the time limits specified in the Rules of Procedure and Evidence. However, the person may consent to surrender before the expiration of this period if permitted by the law of the requested state. In such a case, the requested state shall proceed to surrender the person to the Court as soon as possible.

4.   The fact that the person sought has been released from custody pursuant to paragraph 3 shall not prejudice the subsequent arrest and surrender of that person if the request for surrender and the documents supporting the request are delivered at a later date.

Article 93
Other forms of cooperation

1.   States Parties shall, in accordance with the provisions of this Part and under procedures of national law, comply with requests by the Court to provide the following assistance in relation to investigations or prosecutions:

(a)   The identification and whereabouts of persons or the location of items;

(b)   The taking of evidence, including testimony under oath, and the production of evidence, including expert opinions and reports necessary to the Court;

(c)   The questioning of any person being investigated or prosecuted;

(d)   The service of documents, including judicial documents;

(e)   Facilitating the voluntary appearance of persons as witnesses or experts before the Court;

(f)   The temporary transfer of persons as provided in paragraph 7;

(g)   The examination of places or sites, including the exhumation and examination of grave sites;

(h)   The execution of searches and seizures;

(i)   The provision of records and documents, including official records and documents;

(j)   The protection of victims and witnesses and the preservation of evidence;

(k)   The identification, tracing and freezing or seizure of proceeds, property and assets and instrumentalities of crimes for the purpose of eventual forfeiture, without prejudice to the rights of bona fide third parties; and

(l)   Any other type of assistance which is not prohibited by the law of the requested state, with a view to facilitating the investigation and prosecution of crimes within the jurisdiction of the Court.

2.   The Court shall have the authority to provide an assurance to a witness or an expert appearing before the Court that he or she will not be prosecuted, detained or subjected to any restriction of personal freedom by the Court in respect of any act or omission that preceded the departure of that person from the requested state.

3.   Where execution of a particular measure of assistance detailed in a request presented under paragraph 1, is prohibited in the requested state on the basis of an existing fundamental legal principle of general application, the requested state shall promptly consult with the Court to try to resolve the matter. In the consultations, consideration should be given to whether the assistance can be rendered in another manner or subject to conditions. If after consultations the matter cannot be resolved, the Court shall modify the request as necessary.

4.   In accordance with Article 72, a State Party may deny a request for assistance, in whole or in part, only if the request concerns the production of any documents or disclosure of evidence which relates to its national security.

5.   Before denying a request for assistance under paragraph 1 (l), the requested state shall consider whether the assistance can be provided subject to specified conditions, or whether the assistance can be provided at a later date or in an alternative manner, provided that if the Court or the Prosecutor accepts the assistance subject to conditions, the Court or the Prosecutor shall abide by them.

6.   If a request for assistance is denied, the requested State Party shall promptly inform the Court or the Prosecutor of the reasons for such denial.

7. (a) The Court may request the temporary transfer of a person in custody for purposes of identification or for obtaining testimony or other assistance. The person may be transferred if the following conditions are fulfilled:

(i) The person freely gives his or her informed consent to the transfer; and

(ii) The requested state agrees to the transfer, subject to such conditions as that state and the Court may agree.

(b) The person being transferred shall remain in custody. When the purposes of the transfer have been fulfilled, the Court shall return the person without delay to the requested state.

8. (a) The Court shall ensure the confidentiality of documents and information, except as required for the investigation and proceedings described in the request.

(b) The requested state may, when necessary, transmit documents or information to the Prosecutor on a confidential basis. The Prosecutor may then use them solely for the purpose of generating new evidence.

(c) The requested state may, on its own motion or at the request of the Prosecutor, subsequently consent to the disclosure of such documents or information. They may then be used as evidence pursuant to the provisions of Parts 5 and 6 and in accordance with the Rules of Procedure and Evidence.

9. (a) (i) In the event that a State Party receives competing requests, other than for surrender or extradition, from the Court and from another state pursuant to an international obligation, the State Party shall endeavour, in consultation with the Court and the other state, to meet both requests, if necessary by postponing or attaching conditions to one or the other request.

(ii) Failing that, competing requests shall be resolved in accordance with the principles established in Article 90.

(b) Where, however, the request from the Court concerns information, property or persons which are subject to the control of a third state or an international organization by virtue of an international agreement, the requested states shall so inform the Court and the Court shall direct its request to the third state or international organization.

10. (a) The Court may, upon request, cooperate with and provide assistance to a State Party conducting an investigation into or trial in respect of conduct which constitutes a crime within the jurisdiction of the Court or which constitutes a serious crime under the national law of the requesting state.

(b) (i) The assistance provided under subparagraph (a) shall include, *inter alia:*

a. The transmission of statements, documents or other types of evidence obtained in the course of an investigation or a trial conducted by the Court; and

b. The questioning of any person detained by order of the Court;

(ii) In the case of assistance under subparagraph (b) (i) a:

a. If the documents or other types of evidence have been obtained with the assistance of a state, such transmission shall require the consent of that state;

b. If the statements, documents or other types of evidence have been provided by a witness or expert, such transmission shall be subject to the provisions of Article 68.

(c) The Court may, under the conditions set out in this paragraph, grant a request for assistance under this paragraph from a state which is not a Party to this Statute.

Article 94
Postponement of execution of a request in respect
of ongoing investigation or prosecution

1.   If the immediate execution of a request would interfere with an ongoing investigation or prosecution of a case different from that to which the request relates, the requested state may postpone the execution of the request for a period of time agreed upon with the Court. However, the postponement shall be no longer than is necessary to complete the relevant investigation or prosecution in the requested state. Before making a decision to postpone, the requested state should consider whether the assistance may be immediately provided subject to certain conditions.

2.   If a decision to postpone is taken pursuant to paragraph 1, the Prosecutor may, however, seek measures to preserve evidence, pursuant to Article 93, paragraph 1 (j).

Article 95
Postponement of execution of a request in
respect of an admissibility challenge

Where there is an admissibility challenge under consideration by the Court pursuant to Article 18 or 19, the requested state may postpone the execution of a request under this Part pending a determination by the Court, unless the Court has specifically ordered that the Prosecutor may pursue the collection of such evidence pursuant to Article 18 or 19.

Article 96
Contents of request for other forms of assistance under Article 93

1.   A request for other forms of assistance referred to in Article 93 shall be made in writing. In urgent cases, a request may be made by any medium capable of delivering a written record, provided that the request shall be confirmed through the channel provided for in Article 87, paragraph 1 (a).

2.   The request shall, as applicable, contain or be supported by the following:

(a)   A concise statement of the purpose of the request and the assistance sought, including the legal basis and the grounds for the request;

(b)   As much detailed information as possible about the location or identification of any person or place that must be found or identified in order for the assistance sought to be provided;

(c)   A concise statement of the essential facts underlying the request;

(d)   The reasons for and details of any procedure or requirement to be followed;

(e)   Such information as may be required under the law of the requested state in order to execute the request; and

(f)   Any other information relevant in order for the assistance sought to be provided.

3.   Upon the request of the Court, a State Party shall consult with the Court, either generally or with respect to a specific matter, regarding any requirements under its national law that may apply under paragraph 2 (e). During the consultations, the State Party shall advise the Court of the specific requirements of its national law.

4.   The provisions of this Article shall, where applicable, also apply in respect of a request for assistance made to the Court.

Article 97
Consultations

Where a State Party receives a request under this Part in relation to which it identifies problems which may impede or prevent the execution of the request, that state shall consult with the Court without delay in order to resolve the matter. Such problems may include, *inter alia:*

(a) Insufficient information to execute the request;

(b) In the case of a request for surrender, the fact that despite best efforts, the person sought cannot be located or that the investigation conducted has determined that the person in the requested state is clearly not the person named in the warrant; or

(c) The fact that execution of the request in its current form would require the requested state to breach a pre-existing treaty obligation undertaken with respect to another state.

Article 98
Cooperation with respect to waiver of immunity
and consent to surrender

1. The Court may not proceed with a request for surrender or assistance which would require the requested state to act inconsistently with its obligations under international law with respect to the state or diplomatic immunity of a person or property of a third state, unless the Court can first obtain the cooperation of that third state for the waiver of the immunity.

2. The Court may not proceed with a request for surrender which would require the requested state to act inconsistently with its obligations under international agreements pursuant to which the consent of a sending state is required to surrender a person of that state to the Court, unless the Court can first obtain the cooperation of the sending state for the giving of consent for the surrender.

Article 99
Execution of requests under Articles 93 and 96

1. Requests for assistance shall be executed in accordance with the relevant procedure under the law of the requested state and, unless prohibited by such law, in the manner specified in the request, including following any procedure outlined therein or permitting persons specified in the request to be present at and assist in the execution process.

2. In the case of an urgent request, the documents or evidence produced in response shall, at the request of the Court, be sent urgently.

3. Replies from the requested state shall be transmitted in their original language and form.

4. Without prejudice to other articles in this Part, where it is necessary for the successful execution of a request which can be executed without any compulsory measures, including specifically the interview of or taking evidence from a person on a voluntary basis, including doing so without the presence of the authorities of the requested State Party if it is essential for the request to be executed, and the examination without modification of a public site or other public place, the Prosecutor may execute such request directly on the territory of a state as follows:

(a) When the State Party requested is a state on the territory of which the crime is alleged to have been committed, and there has been a determination of admissibility pursuant to Article 18 or 19, the Prosecutor may directly execute such request following all possible consultations with the requested State Party;

(b) In other cases, the Prosecutor may execute such request following consultations with the requested State Party and subject to any reasonable conditions or concerns raised by that State Party. Where the requested State Party identifies problems with the execution of a request pursuant to this subparagraph it shall, without delay, consult with the Court to resolve the matter.

5. Provisions allowing a person heard or examined by the Court under Article 72 to invoke restrictions designed to prevent disclosure of confidential information connected with national security shall also apply to the execution of requests for assistance under this article.

Article 100
Costs

1. The ordinary costs for execution of requests in the territory of the requested state shall be borne by that state, except for the following, which shall be borne by the Court:

(a) Costs associated with the travel and security of witnesses and experts or the transfer under Article 93 of persons in custody;

(b) Costs of translation, interpretation and transcription;

(c) Travel and subsistence costs of the judges, the Prosecutor, the Deputy Prosecutors, the Registrar, the Deputy Registrar and staff of any organ of the Court;

(d) Costs of any expert opinion or report requested by the Court;

(e) Costs associated with the transport of a person being surrendered to the Court by a custodial state; and

(f) Following consultations, any extraordinary costs that may result from the execution of a request.

2. The provisions of paragraph 1 shall, as appropriate, apply to requests from States Parties to the Court. In that case, the Court shall bear the ordinary costs of execution.

Article 101
Rule of speciality

1. A person surrendered to the Court under this Statute shall not be proceeded against, punished or detained for any conduct committed prior to surrender, other than the conduct or course of conduct which forms the basis of the crimes for which that person has been surrendered.

2. The Court may request a waiver of the requirements of paragraph 1 from the state which surrendered the person to the Court and, if necessary, the Court shall provide additional information in accordance with Article 91. States Parties shall have the authority to provide a waiver to the Court and should endeavour to do so.

Article 102
Use of terms

For the purposes of this Statute:

(a) "surrender" means the delivering up of a person by a state to the Court, pursuant to this Statute.

(b) "extradition" means the delivering up of a person by one state to another as provided by treaty, convention or national legislation.

PART 10. ENFORCEMENT

Article 103
Role of states in enforcement of sentences of imprisonment

1. (a) A sentence of imprisonment shall be served in a state designated by the Court from a list of states which have indicated to the Court their willingness to accept sentenced persons.

(b) At the time of declaring its willingness to accept sentenced persons, a state may attach conditions to its acceptance as agreed by the Court and in accordance with this Part.

(c) A state designated in a particular case shall promptly inform the Court whether it accepts the Court's designation.

2. (a) The state of enforcement shall notify the Court of any circumstances, including the exercise of any conditions agreed under paragraph 1, which could materially affect the terms or extent of the imprisonment. The Court shall be given at least 45 days' notice of any such known or foreseeable circumstances. During this period, the state of enforcement shall take no action that might prejudice its obligations under Article 110.

(b) Where the Court cannot agree to the circumstances referred to in subparagraph (a), it shall notify the state of enforcement and proceed in accordance with Article 104, paragraph 1.

3. In exercising its discretion to make a designation under paragraph 1, the Court shall take into account the following:

(a) The principle that States Parties should share the responsibility for enforcing sentences of imprisonment, in accordance with principles of equitable distribution, as provided in the Rules of Procedure and Evidence;

(b) The application of widely accepted international treaty standards governing the treatment of prisoners;

(c) The views of the sentenced person;

(d) The nationality of the sentenced person;

(e) Such other factors regarding the circumstances of the crime or the person sentenced, or the effective enforcement of the sentence, as may be appropriate in designating the state of enforcement.

4. If no state is designated under paragraph 1, the sentence of imprisonment shall be served in a prison facility made available by the host state, in accordance with the conditions set out in the headquarters agreement referred to in Article 3, paragraph 2. In such a case, the costs arising out of the enforcement of a sentence of imprisonment shall be borne by the Court.

Article 104
Change in designation of state of enforcement

1. The Court may, at any time, decide to transfer a sentenced person to a prison of another state.

2.   A sentenced person may, at any time, apply to the Court to be transferred from the state of enforcement.

Article 105
Enforcement of the sentence

1.   Subject to conditions which a state may have specified in accordance with Article 103, paragraph 1 (b), the sentence of imprisonment shall be binding on the States Parties, which shall in no case modify it.

2.   The Court alone shall have the right to decide any application for appeal and revision. The state of enforcement shall not impede the making of any such application by a sentenced person.

Article 106
Supervision of enforcement of sentences and conditions of imprisonment

1.   The enforcement of a sentence of imprisonment shall be subject to the supervision of the Court and shall be consistent with widely accepted international treaty standards governing treatment of prisoners.

2.   The conditions of imprisonment shall be governed by the law of the state of enforcement and shall be consistent with widely accepted international treaty standards governing treatment of prisoners; in no case shall such conditions be more or less favourable than those available to prisoners convicted of similar offences in the state of enforcement.

3.   Communications between a sentenced person and the Court shall be unimpeded and confidential.

Article 107
Transfer of the person upon completion of sentence

1.   Following completion of the sentence, a person who is not a national of the state of enforcement may, in accordance with the law of the state of enforcement, be transferred to a state which is obliged to receive him or her, or to another state which agrees to receive him or her, taking into account any wishes of the person to be transferred to that state, unless the state of enforcement authorizes the person to remain in its territory.

2.   If no state bears the costs arising out of transferring the person to another state pursuant to paragraph 1, such costs shall be borne by the Court.

3.   Subject to the provisions of Article 108, the state of enforcement may also, in accordance with its national law, extradite or otherwise surrender the person to a state which has requested the extradition or surrender of the person for purposes of trial or enforcement of a sentence.

Article 108
Limitation on the prosecution or punishment of other offences

1.   A sentenced person in the custody of the state of enforcement shall not be subject to prosecution or punishment or to extradition to a third state for any conduct engaged in prior

to that person's delivery to the state of enforcement, unless such prosecution, punishment or extradition has been approved by the Court at the request of the state of enforcement.

2.   The Court shall decide the matter after having heard the views of the sentenced person.

3.   Paragraph 1 shall cease to apply if the sentenced person remains voluntarily for more than 30 days in the territory of the state of enforcement after having served the full sentence imposed by the Court, or returns to the territory of that state after having left it.

Article 109
Enforcement of fines and forfeiture measures

1.   States Parties shall give effect to fines or forfeitures ordered by the Court under Part 7, without prejudice to the rights of bona fide third parties, and in accordance with the procedure of their national law.

2.   If a State Party is unable to give effect to an order for forfeiture, it shall take measures to recover the value of the proceeds, property or assets ordered by the Court to be forfeited, without prejudice to the rights of bona fide third parties.

3.   Property, or the proceeds of the sale of real property or, where appropriate, the sale of other property, which is obtained by a State Party as a result of its enforcement of a judgement of the Court shall be transferred to the Court.

Article 110
Review by the Court concerning reduction of sentence

1.   The state of enforcement shall not release the person before expiry of the sentence pronounced by the Court.

2.   The Court alone shall have the right to decide any reduction of sentence, and shall rule on the matter after having heard the person.

3.   When the person has served two thirds of the sentence, or 25 years in the case of life imprisonment, the Court shall review the sentence to determine whether it should be reduced. Such a review shall not be conducted before that time.

4.   In its review under paragraph 3, the Court may reduce the sentence if it finds that one or more of the following factors are present:
   (a)   The early and continuing willingness of the person to cooperate with the Court in its investigations and prosecutions;
   (b)   The voluntary assistance of the person in enabling the enforcement of the judgements and orders of the Court in other cases, and in particular providing assistance in locating assets subject to orders of fine, forfeiture or reparation which may be used for the benefit of victims; or
   (c)   Other factors establishing a clear and significant change of circumstances sufficient to justify the reduction of sentence, as provided in the Rules of Procedure and Evidence.

5.   If the Court determines in its initial review under paragraph 3 that it is not appropriate to reduce the sentence, it shall thereafter review the question of reduction of sentence at such intervals and applying such criteria as provided for in the Rules of Procedure and Evidence.

Article 111
Escape

If a convicted person escapes from custody and flees the state of enforcement, that state may, after consultation with the Court, request the person's surrender from the state in which the person is located pursuant to existing bilateral or multilateral arrangements, or may request that the Court seek the person's surrender, in accordance with Part 9. It may direct that the person be delivered to the state in which he or she was serving the sentence or to another state designated by the Court.

PART 11. ASSEMBLY OF STATES PARTIES

Article 112
Assembly of States Parties

1.   An Assembly of States Parties to this Statute is hereby established. Each State Party shall have one representative in the Assembly who may be accompanied by alternates and advisers. Other states which have signed this Statute or the Final Act may be observers in the Assembly.

2.   The Assembly shall:

(a) Consider and adopt, as appropriate, recommendations of the Preparatory Commission;

(b) Provide management oversight to the Presidency, the Prosecutor and the Registrar regarding the administration of the Court;

(c) Consider the reports and activities of the Bureau established under paragraph 3 and take appropriate action in regard thereto;

(d) Consider and decide the budget for the Court;

(e) Decide whether to alter, in accordance with Article 36, the number of judges;

(f) Consider pursuant to Article 87, paragraphs 5 and 7, any question relating to non-cooperation;

(g) Perform any other function consistent with this Statute or the Rules of Procedure and Evidence.

3.   (a) The Assembly shall have a Bureau consisting of a President, two Vice-Presidents and 18 members elected by the Assembly for three-year terms.

(b) The Bureau shall have a representative character, taking into account, in particular, equitable geographical distribution and the adequate representation of the principal legal systems of the world.

(c) The Bureau shall meet as often as necessary, but at least once a year. It shall assist the Assembly in the discharge of its responsibilities.

4.   The Assembly may establish such subsidiary bodies as may be necessary, including an independent oversight mechanism for inspection, evaluation and investigation of the Court, in order to enhance its efficiency and economy.

5.   The President of the Court, the Prosecutor and the Registrar or their representatives may participate, as appropriate, in meetings of the Assembly and of the Bureau.

6.   The Assembly shall meet at the seat of the Court or at the Headquarters of the United Nations once a year and, when circumstances so require, hold special sessions. Except as

otherwise specified in this Statute, special sessions shall be convened by the Bureau on its own initiative or at the request of one third of the States Parties.

7.   Each State Party shall have one vote. Every effort shall be made to reach decisions by consensus in the Assembly and in the Bureau. If consensus cannot be reached, except as otherwise provided in the Statute:

(a)   Decisions on matters of substance must be approved by a two-thirds majority of those present and voting provided that an absolute majority of States Parties constitutes the quorum for voting;

(b)   Decisions on matters of procedure shall be taken by a simple majority of States Parties present and voting.

8.   A State Party which is in arrears in the payment of its financial contributions towards the costs of the Court shall have no vote in the Assembly and in the Bureau if the amount of its arrears equals or exceeds the amount of the contributions due from it for the preceding two full years. The Assembly may, nevertheless, permit such a State Party to vote in the Assembly and in the Bureau if it is satisfied that the failure to pay is due to conditions beyond the control of the State Party.

9.   The Assembly shall adopt its own rules of procedure.

10.   The official and working languages of the Assembly shall be those of the General Assembly of the United Nations.

PART 12. FINANCING

Article 113
Financial Regulations

Except as otherwise specifically provided, all financial matters related to the Court and the meetings of the Assembly of States Parties, including its Bureau and subsidiary bodies, shall be governed by this Statute and the Financial Regulations and Rules adopted by the Assembly of States Parties.

Article 114
Payment of expenses

Expenses of the Court and the Assembly of States Parties, including its Bureau and subsidiary bodies, shall be paid from the funds of the Court.

Article 115
Funds of the Court and of the Assembly of States Parties

The expenses of the Court and the Assembly of States Parties, including its Bureau and subsidiary bodies, as provided for in the budget decided by the Assembly of States Parties, shall be provided by the following sources:

(a)   Assessed contributions made by States Parties;

(b)   Funds provided by the United Nations, subject to the approval of the General Assembly, in particular in relation to the expenses incurred due to referrals by the Security Council.

Article 116
Voluntary contributions

Without prejudice to Article 115, the Court may receive and utilize, as additional funds, voluntary contributions from Governments, international organizations, individuals, corporations and other entities, in accordance with relevant criteria adopted by the Assembly of States Parties.

Article 117
Assessment of contributions

The contributions of States Parties shall be assessed in accordance with an agreed scale of assessment, based on the scale adopted by the United Nations for its regular budget and adjusted in accordance with the principles on which that scale is based.

Article 118
Annual audit

The records, books and accounts of the Court, including its annual financial statements, shall be audited annually by an independent auditor.

PART 13. FINAL CLAUSES

Article 119
Settlement of disputes

1. Any dispute concerning the judicial functions of the Court shall be settled by the decision of the Court.

2. Any other dispute between two or more States Parties relating to the interpretation or application of this Statute which is not settled through negotiations within three months of their commencement shall be referred to the Assembly of States Parties. The Assembly may itself seek to settle the dispute or may make recommendations on further means of settlement of the dispute, including referral to the International Court of Justice in conformity with the Statute of that Court.

Article 120
Reservations

No reservations may be made to this Statute.

Article 121
Amendments

1. After the expiry of seven years from the entry into force of this Statute, any State Party may propose amendments thereto. The text of any proposed amendment shall be submitted to the Secretary-General of the United Nations, who shall promptly circulate it to all States Parties.

2. No sooner than three months from the date of notification, the Assembly of States Parties, at its next meeting, shall, by a majority of those present and voting, decide whether to take up the proposal. The Assembly may deal with the proposal directly or convene a Review Conference if the issue involved so warrants.

3.   The adoption of an amendment at a meeting of the Assembly of States Parties or at a Review Conference on which consensus cannot be reached shall require a two-thirds majority of States Parties.

4.   Except as provided in paragraph 5, an amendment shall enter into force for all States Parties one year after instruments of ratification or acceptance have been deposited with the Secretary-General of the United Nations by seven-eighths of them.

5.   Any amendment to Articles 5, 6, 7 and 8 of this Statute shall enter into force for those States Parties which have accepted the amendment one year after the deposit of their instruments of ratification or acceptance. In respect of a State Party which has not accepted the amendment, the Court shall not exercise its jurisdiction regarding a crime covered by the amendment when committed by that State Party's nationals or on its territory.

6.   If an amendment has been accepted by seven-eighths of States Parties in accordance with paragraph 4, any State Party which has not accepted the amendment may withdraw from this Statute with immediate effect, notwithstanding Article 127, paragraph 1, but subject to Article 127, paragraph 2, by giving notice no later than one year after the entry into force of such amendment.

7.   The Secretary-General of the United Nations shall circulate to all States Parties any amendment adopted at a meeting of the Assembly of States Parties or at a Review Conference.

Article 122
Amendments to provisions of an institutional nature

1.   Amendments to provisions of this Statute which are of an exclusively institutional nature, namely, Article 35, Article 36, paragraphs 8 and 9, Article 37, Article 38, Article 39, paragraphs 1 (first two sentences), 2 and 4, Article 42, paragraphs 4 to 9, Article 43, paragraphs 2 and 3, and Articles 44, 46, 47 and 49, may be proposed at any time, notwithstanding Article 121, paragraph 1, by any State Party. The text of any proposed amendment shall be submitted to the Secretary-General of the United Nations or such other person designated by the Assembly of States Parties who shall promptly circulate it to all States Parties and to others participating in the Assembly.

2.   Amendments under this article on which consensus cannot be reached shall be adopted by the Assembly of States Parties or by a Review Conference, by a two-thirds majority of States Parties. Such amendments shall enter into force for all States Parties six months after their adoption by the Assembly or, as the case may be, by the Conference.

Article 123
Review of the Statute

1.   Seven years after the entry into force of this Statute the Secretary-General of the United Nations shall convene a Review Conference to consider any amendments to this Statute. Such review may include, but is not limited to, the list of crimes contained in Article 5. The Conference shall be open to those participating in the Assembly of States Parties and on the same conditions.

2.   At any time thereafter, at the request of a State Party and for the purposes set out in paragraph 1, the Secretary-General of the United Nations shall, upon approval by a majority of States Parties, convene a Review Conference.

3.   The provisions of Article 121, paragraphs 3 to 7, shall apply to the adoption and entry into force of any amendment to the Statute considered at a Review Conference.

Article 124
Transitional Provision

Notwithstanding Article 12, paragraphs 1 and 2, a state, on becoming a party to this Statute, may declare that, for a period of seven years after the entry into force of this Statute for the state concerned, it does not accept the jurisdiction of the Court with respect to the category of crimes referred to in Article 8 when a crime is alleged to have been committed by its nationals or on its territory. A declaration under this article may be withdrawn at any time. The provisions of this article shall be reviewed at the Review Conference convened in accordance with Article 123, paragraph 1.

Article 125
Signature, ratification, acceptance, approval or accession

1.   This Statute shall be open for signature by all states in Rome, at the headquarters of the Food and Agriculture Organization of the United Nations, on 17 July 1998. Thereafter, it shall remain open for signature in Rome at the Ministry of Foreign Affairs of Italy until 17 October 1998. After that date, the Statute shall remain open for signature in New York, at United Nations Headquarters, until 31 December 2000.

2.   This Statute is subject to ratification, acceptance or approval by signatory states. Instruments of ratification, acceptance or approval shall be deposited with the Secretary-General of the United Nations.

3.   This Statute shall be open to accession by all states. Instruments of accession shall be deposited with the Secretary-General of the United Nations.

Article 126
Entry into force

1.   This Statute shall enter into force on the first day of the month after the 60th day following the date of the deposit of the 60th instrument of ratification, acceptance, approval or accession with the Secretary-General of the United Nations.

2.   For each state ratifying, accepting, approving or acceding to this Statute after the deposit of the 60th instrument of ratification, acceptance, approval or accession, the Statute shall enter into force on the first day of the month after the 60th day following the deposit by such state of its instrument of ratification, acceptance, approval or accession.

Article 127
Withdrawal

1.   A State Party may, by written notification addressed to the Secretary-General of the United Nations, withdraw from this Statute. The withdrawal shall take effect one year after the date of receipt of the notification, unless the notification specifies a later date.

2.   A state shall not be discharged, by reason of its withdrawal, from the obligations arising from this Statute while it was a Party to the Statute, including any financial obligations which may have accrued. Its withdrawal shall not affect any cooperation with the Court in connection with criminal investigations and proceedings in relation to which the with-

drawing state had a duty to cooperate and which were commenced prior to the date on which the withdrawal became effective, nor shall it prejudice in any way the continued consideration of any matter which was already under consideration by the Court prior to the date on which the withdrawal became effective.

Article 128
Authentic texts

The original of this Statute, of which the Arabic, Chinese, English, French, Russian and Spanish texts are equally authentic, shall be deposited with the Secretary-General of the United Nations, who shall send certified copies thereof to all states.

IN WITNESS WHEREOF, the undersigned, being duly authorized thereto by their respective Governments, have signed this Statute.

DONE at Rome, this 17th day of July 1998.

INDEX